Universal Jurisdiction in International Criminal Law

With the sensational arrest of former Chilean dictator Augusto Pinochet in 1998, the rise to prominence of universal jurisdiction over crimes against international law seemed to be assured. The arrest of Pinochet and the ensuing proceedings before the UK courts brought universal jurisdiction into the foreground of the 'fight against impunity' and the principle was read as an important complementary mechanism for international justice – one that could offer justice to victims denied an avenue by the limited jurisdiction of international criminal tribunals. Yet by the time of the International Court of Justice's Arrest Warrant judgment four years later, the picture looked much bleaker and the principle was being read as a potential tool for politically motivated trials.

This book explores the debate over universal jurisdiction in international criminal law, aiming to unpack a practice in which international lawyers continue to disagree over the concept of universal jurisdiction. Using Martti Koskenniemi's work as a foil, this book exposes the argumentative techniques in operation in national and international adjudication since the 1990s. Drawing on overarching patterns within the debate, Aisling O'Sullivan argues that it is bounded by a tension between contrasting political preferences or positions, labelled as moralist ('ending impunity') and formalist ('avoiding abuse') and she reads the debate as a movement of hegemonic and counter-hegemonic positions that struggle for hegemonic control. However, she draws out how these positions (moralist/formalist) merge into one another and this produces a tendency towards a 'middle' position that continues to prefer a particular preference (moralist or formalist). Aisling O'Sullivan then traces the transformation towards this tendency that reflects an internal split among international lawyers between building a utopia ('court of humanity') and recognizing its impossibility of being realized.

Aisling O'Sullivan is a Lecturer in Law at the University of Sussex, UK.

Routledge Research in International Law

Available:

The Right to Democracy in International Law
Between Procedure, Substance and the Philosophy of John Rawls
Khalifa A. Alfadhel

The Rule of Law in the United Nations Security Council Decision-Making Process
Turning the Focus Inwards
Sherif Elgebeily

Forthcoming titles in this series include:

Technology and the Law on the Use of Force
New Security Challenges in the Twenty First Century
Jackson Maogoto

International Law and the Rights of those Displaced by Armed Conflict
Elena Katselli Proukaki

International Criminal Law and Sexual Violence against Women
The Interpretation of Gender in the Contemporary International Criminal Trial
Daniela Nadj

Fighting and Victimhood in International Criminal Law
Joanna Nicholson

Human Security Discourse and International Law
A Principled Approach
Shireen Daft

Queering International Law
Possibilities, Alliances, Complicities, Risks
Dianne Otto

Universal Jurisdiction in International Criminal Law

The Debate and the Battle for Hegemony

Aisling O'Sullivan

Routledge
Taylor & Francis Group
LONDON AND NEW YORK

First published 2017
by Routledge

2 Park Square, Milton Park, Abingdon, Oxfordshire OX14 4RN
52 Vanderbilt Avenue, New York, NY 10017

Routledge is an imprint of the Taylor & Francis Group, an informa business

First issued in paperback 2018

British Library Cataloguing in Publication Data
A catalogue record for this book is available from the British Library

Library of Congress Cataloging in Publication Data
Names: O'Sullivan, Aisling, (Law teacher)
Title: Universal jurisdiction in international criminal law : the debate and the battle for hegemony / Aisling O'Sullivan.
Description: New York : Routledge, 2017. | Series: Routledge research in international law | Includes bibliographical references and index.
Identifiers: LCCN 2016047464| ISBN 9781138123946 (hbk) | ISBN 9781315648507 (ebk)
Subjects: LCSH: Jurisdiction (International law). | International criminal law. | International criminal courts.
Classification: LCC KZ7375 .O8 2017 | DDC 345/.0122—dc23
LC record available at https://lccn.loc.gov/2016047464

ISBN: 978-1-138-12394-6 (hbk)
ISBN: 978-0-367-07555-2 (pbk)

Typeset in ITC Galliard Std
by Swales & Willis Ltd, Exeter, Devon, UK

Table of contents

List of cases

Acknowledgements

I am sincerely grateful to my PhD supervisor Dr Kathleen Cavanaugh for patiently guiding and supporting me and for her endless encouragement – all of which made this book possible. I also sincerely thank my examiners Professor Martti Koskenniemi and Dr Ekaterina Yahyaoui who took the time to read my thesis, were challenging and insightful in my viva and provided me with very valuable feedback. In particular, I am very grateful to Martti Koskenniemi for his invaluable guidance and encouragement as I prepared this book for submission. Special thanks also to all the staff in the Irish Centre for Human Rights, NUI Galway, in particular Professor William Schabas, Professor Ray Murphy, Dr Shane Darcy and Professor Vinodh Jaichand for their advice and support during my doctoral studies.

I also extend special thanks to the two anonymous reviewers whose insights were very helpful for preparing this book and to many friends who have shared their wisdom and support during my doctoral studies and in the preparation of this book, in particular Vicky Germanakou, Rachel Martin, Dr Susan Leahy, Dr Roja Fazaeli, Dr Verona Ní Dhrisceoil, Dr Eugene O'Brien, Dr Michelle Farrell, Anna Keely, Sinead Hutchison, Dr Wynette Redington, Margaret Carey, Sarah Deegan, Tanja Florath, Margaret Deegan, Dr Alexis Bushnell, Dr Tarik Kochi, Dr Stephanie Berry, Dr Edward Guntrip, Dr Maria Varaki, Kate O'Flynn, Dr Nicholas Strapatsas, Dr Andrea Breslin, Dr Edel Hughes, Dr Peter Fitzmaurice, Dr Anthony Cullen and Dr Eadaoin O'Brien. I would like to express my gratitude to Olivia Manley at Routledge who guided and supported me through the authoring process. I am also very grateful to the Irish Centre for Human Rights, the Australian Endeavour Scholarship Programme and National University of Ireland Galway for funding various stages of my doctoral research. Finally, I would like to thank Liam, Ann, Caoimhe and Cian for their love, support, generosity and encouragement and to dedicate this work to them.

Foreword

Historians of international law are beginning to perceive the extraordinary significance of the 1990s for the development of the field. That it was a decade of unprecedented institutional growth has been long evident – growth of human rights law and environmental law, the establishment of the World Trade Organization, the newly found consensus among the members of the UN Security Council. And to cap it all, the rallying of like-minded actors and institutions under the banner of the 'international community' behind the effort to eradicate war crimes and crimes against humanity. The project to draft a code of international crimes and to provide for the criminal responsibility of high military and political leaders had been under way in the UN since the end of the Second World War. Finally in the 1990s, the Statute of an International Criminal Court was adopted (1998) and proceedings began in many domestic courts against foreign leaders accused of grave violations during their time in office. From the perspective of activities and expectations of the long years of the Cold War, these developments – that belong together in a kind of liberal revolution – were indeed remarkable.

But equally astonishing has been the backlash in the second decade of the 2000s against many, if not most, of these developments. The illegal war in Iraq, with all its repercussions in the West and, of course, in the Middle East, the failure of the Arab Spring, Russian occupation of Crimea, the so-called 'refugee crisis' and the economic downturn since 2008 either crushed the liberal consensus, or at least demonstrated the extreme fragility of what had been achieved. Historians' interest in the 1990s is not, therefore, just about what made 1990s seem so 'progressive' in the eyes of most, but how such a sense of progress was so easily dispelled. Of course, to some extent, the backlash was caused by forces that had never joined the consensus. But there must have been something in the institutional and legal projects themselves that contributed to the present malaise and stagnation. What did we fail to see then? There is a great need to place the period 1989–2016 under close analysis, in part so that we who are contemporaries of the events would understand, but also for those who in the future will try to advance the objectives of peace and justice through international institutions. Nothing has undermined the value of those objectives – human rights, a clean environment, peace, economic and social progress, democracy. But something about the projects of the 1990s made them appear much more complex than many of us believed at that time. What was it?

In this book, Aisling O'Sullivan begins the works of rethinking the legacy of the 1990s with reference to the developments within the 'fight against impunity'. What happened to the effort to bring those accused of having committed grave violations to face justice in domestic courts under the principle of 'universal jurisdiction'? Why did the effort to recognize all States' authority to adjudicate heinous crimes irrespective of where they were committed collapse? Between the prosecution of the former Chilean dictator Augusto Pinochet in Britain and the repeal of the law on universal jurisdiction in Belgium in 2003, a huge change took place in international attitudes towards bringing foreign political or military leaders to trial in foreign states – or actually *European* States as it was mostly thought of. The issue of (neo-) imperialism and Western hegemony was of course raised by the fact that most of those accused, or suspected as potential targets for procedures, were from the developing world. Universal jurisdiction was seen in the Third World as one more effort to impose Western interests under the smoke-screen of humanitarian values. That may of course have been the case, at least to some extent. Behind diplomatic hypocrisy, however, there was also some genuine effort to outlaw tyranny on a global scale and to create deterrence. Nor was the critique itself by no means free of hypocrisy.

The collapse of universal jurisdiction provides an excellent foil to examine the fate of the liberal hubris, the disappointments in practice, and the gradual rise of an altogether changed intellectual landscape. The great contribution of Aisling O'Sullivan is that she avoids both 'idealist' lamentation of the bad faith and egoism of diplomats and domestic leaders as well as 'realist' celebrations of supposedly eternal laws of power as the relevant explanatory grids. Instead, she questions the conceptual apparatus that was put to play by both supporters and detractors of universal jurisdiction. All sides, it appears, were equally ignorant of the fragility and manipulable character of the 'fight against impunity'. Where humanitarians erred, she lets us realize, was in believing that the 1990s had created a situation where moral principles could be implemented directly, without the mediation of 'political' institutions and preferences. But critics were equally wrong in believing that formalist reliance on state power and diplomacy would protect from 'moralist' excess and bad faith. 'Realism' is in itself a covert morality. This problem of course vastly exceeds the scope of international criminal law. The suggestion that international efforts could be based on the unmediated values or objectives that are, as it were, somehow authentically part of 'world history' or the structure of the (international) world has often accompanied internationalisms. How disturbing are moral complexity and diplomatic bargaining in a fluid conceptual world!

Aisling O'Sullivan produces here an illuminating 'deconstruction' of the conceptual oppositions ostensibly governing debates on universal jurisdiction: idealism and realism, moral principles and formalist axioms, international community and statehood, and so on – familiar pairs of concepts that supposedly point to and undergird specific international policies and priorities. Even as the 'linguistic turn' took place in social sciences decades ago, its penetration in international law has been slow. Here, however, such analysis is employed with great force that extends from criminal law to many other international legal projects. When apparently contradictory principles actually turn out to presuppose each other, and then lose their directive force, focus will inevitably turn to the interpretative moves and background assumptions that give both 'moral principles' and 'formalism' the sense that enables adversaries to apply them against each other. This highlights the irreducible 'politics' of a project such as making tyrants criminally accountable. Who is a 'criminal' and what does 'accountability' mean? If certain actors are blamed, which actors are then excused? Who is entitled to throw the first stone? Humanitarian activists often believe that their adversaries are motivated by evil intentions (just as they often believe that 'human rights' stands for 'good' outcomes). But everyone who participates in these debates feels themselves motivated both by good faith and suspicion of bad faith in others, a suspicion often grounded in experience. Words can stand for many kinds of policies, and the meaning of such policies is not independent from the position from which individual actors speak: we may believe it is obvious as to who is 'judge' and who is 'criminal' because we are so accustomed to thinking of ourselves in the former role. After all, we international lawyers are regarded as the masters of that (linguistic) competence that enables us to make such determinations. But as the history from the 1990s to the present should teach us, and as Aisling O'Sullivan's work demonstrates in detail, none of these positions are obvious or non-political. As long as liberal humanitarians have not learned this lesson, they will continue to be disappointed. And that is surely a reason of concern for everyone.

Martti Koskenniemi, FBA
Academy Professor (University of Helsinki)

Introduction

With the sensational arrest of former Chilean dictator Augusto Pinochet in 1998, the rise to prominence of universal jurisdiction over crimes against international law seemed to be assured.[1] The arrest of Pinochet and the ensuing proceedings before the UK courts brought universal jurisdiction into the foreground in the 'fight against impunity'. Universal jurisdiction was read as an important complementary mechanism for international justice in that it could supplement the jurisdiction of international criminal tribunals and ensure the broadest jurisdictional reach for crimes against international law.[2] Of course, the *Pinochet* proceedings highlighted how limitations on the scope of universal jurisdiction must be considered, not least questions raised by the immunity of state officials.[3] Even so, against the context of the Rome Statute of the International Criminal Court and continuing practice of the Former Yugoslav and Rwandan tribunals, the future seemed bright.[4]

Nevertheless, by the time of the International Court of Justice's *Arrest Warrant* judgment, the picture looked much bleaker and the principle was being read as a potential tool for politically motivated trials.[5] The *Arrest Warrant* judgment seemed to trigger a rapid retreat from what was read as an exceptionally expansive jurisdiction of domestic courts over crimes that 'shock the conscience of mankind'.[6] As Cassese questioned at the time, was 'the bell . . . tolling' for universal jurisdiction?[7] Since the *Arrest Warrant*, international lawyers continue to disagree over justification and content of the principle and when one examines the UN General Assembly's Sixth Committee debates on scope of the principle, these competing positions are marked. Notwithstanding, international lawyers

1 See generally N Roht-Arriaza *The Pinochet Effect: Transitional Justice in the Age of Human Rights* (University of Pennsylvania Press Philadelphia 2006).

2 UN Secretary General Ban Ki-Moon, Report of 'The scope and application of the principle of Universal Jurisdiction' (29 July 2010) UN Doc A/65/181 para 9.

3 *R v. Bow St. Metropolitan Stipendiary Magistrate, ex parte Pinochet Ugarte (No.3)* (1999) 2 All ER 97.

4 Roht-Arriaza (n 1).

5 Report of the UN Secretary General (n 2) para 9.

6 *AG v Eichmann* (1968) 36 ILR 5, 24.

7 A Cassese 'Is the Bell Tolling for Universality? A Plea for a Sensible Notion of Universal Jurisdiction' (2003) 1 *Journal of International Criminal Justice* 589.

continue to draw attention to a concept of universal jurisdiction in the debate surrounding the 'fight against impunity'.[8]

This book's main concern is to disentangle the seemingly endless oppositions within the debate surrounding universal jurisdiction in international criminal law in order to make sense of what appears to be chaotic international legal practice. Drawing on the debate's overarching themes, this book argues that it is bounded by the tension between contrasting political preferences or positions, labelled as moralist ('ending impunity') and formalist ('avoiding abuse'). A moralist approach challenges what it reads as the injustice of impunity, privileging the moral value of criminal accountability for mass atrocities and stressing state consent to individual criminal liability and universal accountability. A formalist approach challenges what it reads as the injustice of politically motivated or 'show' trials, privileging the moral value of maintaining order among states and stressing state consent to jurisdiction and non-interference. What this book draws out is that these contrasting political sensibilities or approaches operate simultaneously in every position within the debate, that is, the moralist and formalist approaches merge into one another.[9] Due to the resulting incoherence, the debate overall tends to move towards the 'middle' because the contrasting preferences are forced to recognize that the ancillary concern (and the counter-principle) is also 'valid'.

In this sense, this book approaches international law from the perspective of literary style that reads international law as a language domain of lawyers, who engage in a practice underpinned by liberal ideas as the chosen political sensibility.[10] Therefore, this book's approach recognizes international law's linguistic indeterminacy and its institutional bias.[11] Using Martti Koskenniemi's work as a foil, it draws out the descending (more normative, less concrete) and ascending (more concrete, less normative) patterns of argument within national and international adjudication.[12] These techniques reflect the two projects Koskenniemi identifies as characterizing international law, either transforming 'sovereign egoism into world unity' or transforming 'oppressive uniformity of global domination into self-determination and identity'.[13] As the dimensions of 'humanity' and the 'state' are present in every position, the resulting incoherence permits any position to be put forward and counter-argued by an opposing position. Each of the legal outcomes involve a political choice between competing,

8 For example, M Tran 'CIA Torture Report sparks renewed calls to prosecute senior US officials', *The Guardian* (12 December 2014) URL: http://www.theguardian.com/us-news/2014/dec/12/cia-torture-report-prosecute-senior-us-officials and DG for External Policies, European Parliament 'The Application of universal jurisdiction in the fight against impunity' (L Reydams, March 2016).

9 M Koskenniemi 'What Is International Law for?' in M Evans *International Law* 4th edn (Oxford University Press Oxford 2014).

10 M Koskenniemi *From Apology to Utopia: The Structure of the International Legal Argument* (Cambridge University Press Cambridge 2005) 570.

11 ibid.

12 ibid 61–4.

13 M Koskenniemi 'International Law and Hegemony: A Reconfiguration' (2004) 17 *Cambridge Review of International Affairs* 197, 200.

structurally incoherent, arguments where one argument accords with the structural bias of the institution and therefore, is more persuasive in the moment than its counter-point.[14] This is the operation of the language as a battleground or a site of politics in which participants struggle for hegemony over their opponents.[15] Here, the language 'offers a defence for hegemonic and non-hegemonic practices equally'.[16]

It follows then that the debate over the principle of universal jurisdiction is best read as a movement of hegemonic and counter-hegemonic positions in which contrasting positions of ending impunity and avoiding abuse struggle for hegemonic control, with the inevitable move towards a 'middle' position. Yet this middle position continues to prefer one political preference or sensibility over another (the hegemonic choice) that remains open to challenge from its counter-position, which is brought in initially to support the main point. In other words, this book shows the debate as a series of moves and counter-moves from what appear to be the margins of competing positions to a middle position that conceals a particular hegemonic choice. This demonstrates how the debate over universal jurisdiction brings into focus one of the 'dark sides' of the international criminal law regime because it highlights the boundaries of what we are willing to believe is possible in realizing the fight against impunity.[17] In this sense, the book echoes other critiques of the field's missionary zeal[18] as the field's practice reveals how our acceptance of and commitment to individual criminal responsibility has not produced its logical corollary: a 'court of humanity' that will never adjourn.[19] Instead, the construction of this utopia ('court of humanity') in the legal imagination of international lawyers is immediately recognized as being incapable of being realized and this paradox means international lawyers swing back and forth endlessly between moralist and formalist preferences.

This book then draws out the structural properties of each position within the debate and portrays the transformation of hegemonic claims situated in the wider disciplinary context. This is 'a lawyer's view' of the legal discourse,[20] addressing the debate surrounding universal jurisdiction from the 'inside' (or the politics of universal jurisdiction). Therefore, it adopts a 'language and technique' suited to the academic context, which is 'defined by [such] kinds of cultural

14 M Koskenniemi *The Politics of International Law* (Hart Publishing Oxford 2011).

15 E Jouannet 'Koskenniemi: A Critical Introduction' in M Koskenniemi *The Politics of International Law* (Hart Publishing Oxford 2011) 7.

16 Koskenniemi (n 10) 241.

17 D Kennedy *The Dark Sides of Virtue: Reassessing International Humanitarianism* (Princeton University Press Princeton 2005).

18 M Koskenniemi and P Leino 'Fragmentation of International Law? Postmodern Anxieties' (2002) 15 *Leiden Journal of International Law* 553, 579. See also S Kendall 'Critical Orientations: a Critique of International Criminal Court Practice' and C Schwoebel 'The Market and Marketing Culture of International Criminal Law' in C Schwoebel (ed) *Critical Approaches to International Criminal Law: An Introduction* (Routledge London 2014), 264.

19 *The Einsatzgruppen Trial: Trial of Otto Ohlendorf and Others* (1948) IV Trials of War Criminals before the Nuremberg Military Tribunals Green Series (1946–49) 499.

20 G Simpson *Law, War and Crime* (Polity Press Cambridge 2007), 2.

conventions',[21] rather than a style of professional practice that analyses the principle's status in law (Reydams,[22] Henzelin[23] and Macedo[24]) or its institutional history (Reydams,[25] Roht-Arriaza,[26] Davies,[27] Lutz and Reiger,[28] Bassiouni[29] and Kaleck[30]). Its adopted style challenges other conceptual frames on the debate that do not problematize the underlying liberal assumptions of international law. Rather than a debate of polar opposites (Goran and Sluiter[31] and Seyedin-Noor[32]) or as polar opposites and a third middle position (Becker[33]), this book exposes the refined nuances of the debate (shades of grey) as the dimensions of 'humanity' and 'state' are in every position. In this sense, the debate is not simply a conflict between two fixed points or, for that matter, 'resolved' by a middle position.

Accordingly, this book reads the debate in terms of a set of limited rhetorical positions that have been repeated over time, transforming what appear to be competing positions and illustrating the continuities and discontinuities within the legal discourse. Nonetheless, it differs from other ways of reading debates and practice within the field (Baars[34]) through its illustration of a tendency towards the middle that reflects a tendency in legal discourse in general.[35] It pulls upon the set of dilemmas or relationships identified as forming the field's structural properties (Simpson[36]). However, it captures the debate in a sense of overarching binaries that, in turn, reflect the concerns of those sets of relationships as reflected

21 M Koskenniemi, 'Letter to the Editors of the Symposium', (1999) 93 *American Journal of International Law* 351, 357.
22 L Reydams *Universal Jurisdiction: International and Municipal Perspectives* (Oxford University Press Oxford 2003).
23 M Henzelin *Le Principe de l'universalité en droit penal international* (Helbing & Lichtenhahn Bruylant 2000).
24 S Macedo (ed) *Universal Jurisdiction: National Courts and the Prosecution of Serious Crimes under International Law* (Princeton University Press Princeton 2004).
25 Reydams (n 22).
26 Roht-Arriaza (n 1).
27 M Davis (ed) *The Pinochet Case: Origins, Progress and Implications* (Institute of Latin American Studies London 2003).
28 EL Lutz and C Reiger (ed) *Prosecuting Heads of State* (Cambridge University Press Cambridge 2009).
29 MC Bassiouni 'Universal Jurisdiction for International Crimes: Historical Perspectives and Contemporary Practice' (2001–02) 42 *Virginia Journal of International Law* 81.
30 W Kaleck 'From Pinochet to Rumsfeld: Universal Jurisdiction in Europe 1998–2008' (2008–09) 30 *Michigan Journal of International Law* 927.
31 A Zahar and G Sluiter *International Criminal Law* (Oxford University Press Oxford 2008).
32 S Seyedin-Noor 'The Spanish Prisoner: Understanding the Prosecution of Senator Augusto Pinochet Ugarte' (2000) 6 *University of California Davis Journal of International Law and Policy* 41, 76 (absolutists and proceduralists).
33 S Becker 'Universal Jurisdiction: How Universal is it?' (2003) 12 *Palestine Yearbook of International Law* 49.
34 G Baars 'Making ICL History: On the Need to Move Beyond Pre-fab Critiques of ICL' in C Schwöbel (ed) *Critical Approaches to International Criminal Law: An Introduction* (Routledge London 2014) 196.
35 Koskenniemi (n 10).
36 Simpson (n 20).

in the ending impunity/avoiding show trials rhetoric (Koskenniemi[37]). This book also tries to account for moves in wider disciplinary style and structural context that inform the structural biases of institutions. In this sense, it agrees that critical accounts helpfully demonstrate how each position is internally incoherent and a politics of international law takes place (Robinson[38]). However, it disagrees with the implication that a discussion over how to choose would in some measure reconstruct legal discourse.[39] Rather all styles/positions engage in the play of argumentation and each outcome is different every time. As Kennedy explains, there is 'an irreducible element of the absurd and the free in people's choices to fit themselves into these patterns'.[40]

In terms of structure, the book divides into two parts. The first part (Chapters 1–3) describes the type and operation of the binary oppositions within public international law in the current literature and within historical debates. Chapter 1 explores the themes of rules indeterminacy and hegemonic technique, particularly in Martti Koskenniemi's work, that informs the investigation of the contemporary debate on universal jurisdiction over crimes against international law in Chapters 4 and 5. It explores the ideas of international law as a language and a 'site of politics' that illustrate the structural properties of international legal argument (indeterminacy) and the move to political discretion that accords to the structural biases of institutions. Here, the themes of hegemonic and counter-hegemonic technique are constructive and are explored along with the move to specialisms or regimes.

Chapter 2 explores narratives of justification from 1883 onwards that seek to locate those narratives within the larger professional, academic or political projects. Its aim is to briefly elucidate the 'paradoxes of [practitioner's] thought', their insights and their blindness.[41] It seeks to show how each narrative pulls from a set of multiple interpretations within historical debates that are then re-described within particular contemporary disciplinary style. We see each moment's hegemonic and counter-hegemonic positions and when we observe all the various junctures, we can recognize discontinuities, along with continuities.[42] Chapter 3 explores the conventional readings on the doctrine of jurisdiction and immunity of state officials within legal scholarship. We see how those conventional readings are constrained by the need to preserve paradoxical liberal assumptions of both freedom and order. We also see how each principle of jurisdiction is open-ended and compels a move to discretion through applying a principle of reasonableness and interest-balancing. We observe the opposing approaches over the doctrines

37 M Koskenniemi 'Between Impunity and Show Trials' (2002) 6 *Max Planck Yearbook for United Nations Law* 1.

38 D Robinson 'Inescapable Dyads: Why the International Criminal Court Cannot Win' (2015) 28 *Leiden Journal of International Law* 323, 347.

39 ibid.

40 D Kennedy 'Roll Over Beethoven' (1984) 36 *Stanford Law Review* 1, 42.

41 M Koskenniemi *Gentle Civilizer of Nations: International Law since 1870* (Cambridge University Press Cambridge 2005) 7.

42 ibid 9.

and the move to a 'middle ground' that attempts to navigate some reconciliation between the competing approaches.

The second part (Chapters 4 and 5) provides a chronological account of the development of 'hegemonic' control of a moralist approach that pulled on the *Eichmann* narrative to a formalist approach that seemed to be triggered by the *Arrest Warrant* case. This movement is best characterized as a sequence of hegemonic and counter-hegemonic positions of the competing positions. Chapter 4 explores the battle over the *Eichmann* narrative from the early 1990s to the litany of criminal complaints in national courts immediately prior to the *Arrest Warrant* judgment. In so doing, Chapter 4 explores a moralist position's hegemonic control that moves towards the outermost margins of the *Eichmann* narrative as evident in the Belgian and Spanish *Pinochet* judgments. Yet the *Javor* case and the *Pinochet III* dissent signalled a counter-hegemonic position within the discourse and therefore in *Pinochet III* judgment represents this tendency towards a middle ground, an attempt to draw from the 'valid' criticisms of the supplementary counter-point.

Chapter 5 explores the *Arrest Warrant* judgment and its aftermath that seemed to lead to the unravelling of the moralist position's hegemonic control. It discusses the formalist approach's hegemony within *Arrest Warrant* judgment, continuing with what appeared to be a contagion effect in the Belgian, Spanish and UK amendment laws. Yet the *Guatemalan Generals* case and the Committee against Torture's *Habré* decision signalled a counter-hegemonic position that tended towards a moralist middle. The *Obligation to Prosecute or Extradite* case illustrates how the formalist's hegemonic control moved towards a formalist middle, as the idea of universal jurisdiction has not been abandoned entirely.

References

Baars, G 'Making ICL History: On the Need to Move Beyond Pre-fab Critiques of ICL' in C Schwöbel (ed.) *Critical Approaches to International Criminal Law: An Introduction* (Routledge London 2014) 196.

Bassiouni, MC 'Universal Jurisdiction for International Crimes: Historical Perspectives and Contemporary Practice' (2001–02) 42 *Virginia Journal of International Law* 81.

Becker, S 'Universal Jurisdiction: How Universal is it?' (2003) 12 *Palestine Yearbook of International Law* 49.

Cassese, A 'Is the Bell Tolling for Universality? A Plea for a Sensible Notion of Universal Jurisdiction' (2003) 1 *Journal of International Criminal Justice* 589.

Davis, M (ed.) *The Pinochet Case: Origins, Progress and Implications* (Institute of Latin American Studies London 2003).

The Einsatzgruppen Trial: Trial of Otto Ohlendorf and Others (1948) IV Trials of War Criminals before the Nuremberg Military Tribunals Green Series (1946–49).

Henzelin, E *Le Principe de l'universalité en droit penal international* (Helbing & Lichtenhahn Bruylant 2000).

Jouannet, E 'Koskenniemi: A Critical Introduction' in M Koskenniemi *The Politics of International Law* (Hart Publishing Oxford 2011) 7.

Kaleck, W 'From Pinochet to Rumsfeld: Universal Jurisdiction in Europe 1998–2008' (2008–09) 30 *Michigan Journal of International Law* 927.

Kendall, S 'Critical Orientations: a Critique of International Criminal Court Practice' in C Schwoebel (ed) *Critical Approaches to International Criminal Law: An Introduction* (Routledge London 2014).

Kennedy, D 'Roll Over Beethoven' (1984) 36 *Stanford Law Review* 1.

Kennedy, D *The Dark Sides of Virtue: Reassessing International Humanitarianism* (Princeton University Press Princeton 2005).

Koskenniemi, M 'Letter to the Editors of the Symposium' (1999) 93 *American Journal of International Law* 351.

Koskenniemi, M 'Between Impunity and Show Trials' (2002) 6 *Max Planck Yearbook for United Nations Law* 1.

Koskenniemi, M 'International Law and Hegemony: A Reconfiguration' (2004) 17 *Cambridge Review of International Affairs* 197.

Koskenniemi, M *From Apology to Utopia: The Structure of the International Legal Argument* (Cambridge University Press Cambridge 2005) 570.

Koskenniemi, M *Gentle Civilizer of Nations: International Law since 1870* (Cambridge University Press Cambridge 2005) 7.

Koskenniemi, M *The Politics of International Law* (Hart Publishing Oxford 2011).

Koskenniemi, M 'What is International Law for?' in M Evans *International Law* 4th edn (Oxford University Press Oxford 2014).

Koskenniemi, M and Leino, P 'Fragmentation of International Law? Postmodern Anxieties' (2002) 15 *Leiden Journal of International Law* 553.

Lutz, EL and Reiger, C (eds) *Prosecuting Heads of State* (Cambridge University Press Cambridge 2009).

Macedo, S (ed.) *Universal Jurisdiction: National Courts and the Prosecution of Serious Crimes under International Law* (Princeton University Press Princeton 2004).

Reydams, L *Universal Jurisdiction: International and Municipal Perspectives* (Oxford University Press Oxford 2003).

Robinson, D 'Inescapable Dyads: Why the International Criminal Court Cannot Win' (2015) 28 *Leiden Journal of International Law* 323.

Roht-Arriaza, N *The Pinochet Effect: Transitional Justice in the Age of Human Rights* (University of Pennsylvania Press Philadelphia 2006).

Schwoebel, C 'The Market and Marketing Culture of International Criminal Law' in C Schwoebel (ed) *Critical Approaches to International Criminal Law: An Introduction* (Routledge London 2014).

Seyedin-Noor, S 'The Spanish Prisoner: Understanding the Prosecution of Senator Augusto Pinochet Ugarte' (2000) 6 *University of California Davis Journal of International Law and Policy* 41.

Simpson, G *Law, War and Crime* (Polity Press Cambridge 2007).

Tran, M 'CIA Torture Report sparks renewed calls to prosecute senior US officials', *The Guardian* (12 December 2014) URL: http://www.theguardian.com/us-news/2014/dec/12/cia-torture-report-prosecute-senior-us-officials.

UN Secretary General Ban Ki-Moon, Report of 'The scope and application of the principle of Universal Jurisdiction' (29 July 2010) UN Doc A/65/181 para 9.

Zahar, A and Sluiter, G *International Criminal Law* (Oxford University Press Oxford 2008).

1 The politics of international law

When we explore the debate surrounding the principle of universal jurisdiction in international criminal law, there appears to be intractable dichotomies at play. We observe competing positions over the justification for the principle that appear to pull from normative order or state liberty and produce multiple interpretations that range from rejecting to accepting the 'validity' of the principle.[1] The debate over the presence of the offender as a prerequisite to exercising jurisdiction has been contentious, as is evident in the separate and dissenting opinions in the International Court of Justice's *Arrest Warrant* case.[2] Similarly, the debate surrounding the immunity of state officials before foreign courts has produced competing legal outcomes in national courts.[3] There are opposing positions within the case law regarding the crimes over which universal jurisdiction can be asserted by states.[4] Numerous studies have produced different interpretations over the justification and content of the principle[5] and these multiple interpretations are more recently reflected in the United Nations General Assembly debates.[6] Seeking to make sense of these seemingly endless oppositions, scholars

1 Contrast KC Randall, 'Universal Jurisdiction in International Law', (1988) 66 *Texas International Law Journal* 785 and MC Bassiouni 'Universal Jurisdiction for International Crimes: Historical Perspectives and Contemporary Practice' (2001) 42 *Virginia Journal of International Law* 81, with M Henzelin *Le Principe de l'universalité en droit penal international* (Helbing & Lichtenhahn Bruylant 2000) and L Reydams *Universal Jurisdiction: International and National Perspectives* (Oxford University Press Oxford 2003).

2 Contrast *Case of the Arrest Warrant of 11 April 2000 (Belgium v. Democratic Republic of Congo)* (2002) ICJ Rep No. 121 (Guillaume, para 15) with (Van den Wyngaert, para 58).

3 Contrast *R v. Bow St. Metropolitan Stipendiary Magistrate, ex parte Pinochet Ugarte (No.3)* (1999) 2 All ER 97 with *Decision of the General Federal Prosecutor: Center for Constitutional Rights et al v. Donald Rumsfeld et al* (2006) 45 International Legal Materials 119.

4 Contrast *Javor and Others* (2002) 127 International Law Reports 126 (torture as crimes against humanity) vs *Bouterse,* ILDC 80 (NL 2001).

5 Report of AU-EU Technical Ad-hoc Expert Group on the Principle of Universal Jurisdiction (15th April 2009), para 34 and 40, International Law Association 'Final Report on the Exercise of Universal Jurisdiction of Gross Human Rights Offences' (London 2000), *Cairo-Arusha Principles of Universal Jurisdiction in Respect of Gross Human Rights Offences: An African Perspective,* URL: http://www.afla.unimaas.nl/en/act/uj.html and Princeton Project on Universal Jurisdiction 'Princeton Principles on Universal Jurisdiction' (Princeton University Princeton 2000).

6 United Nations General Assembly 'The Scope and application of the principle of universal jurisdiction (Agenda 86)' URL: http://www.un.org/en/ga/sixth/70/universal_jurisdiction.shtml

have captured the debate in terms of a binary naturalism-positivism dichotomy[7] or as a tripartite structure with two diametrically opposed positions and a middle ground.[8] Nevertheless, these studies are underpinned by one of the basic tenets of liberal rule of law: the concept of legal objectivity vis-à-vis political subjectivity.

In contrast, this book employs certain techniques drawn from Martti Koskenniemi's 'multiple points of thought' to deconstruct these seemingly competing legal positions.[9] This reads international law as a language system and uses an image of a deep structure (or grammatical rules) in international legal argument to illustrate legal style, that is, 'how the legal mind, in some special moment, navigates the field of legal materials'.[10] This illustration of legal style captures the internal inconsistency of the arguments and the capacity to deploy competing yet interdependent doctrinal styles that represent the formal conditions of possibility of legal argument. This approach simultaneously reads international law as a 'site of politics'[11] that illustrates how, rather than 'anything goes', legal outcomes accord with structural biases of institutions. These techniques of rule indeterminacy and structural bias are employed in later chapters to capture how the legal debate appears to be a movement of hegemonic and non-hegemonic positions, struggling for ('hegemonic') control, which ultimately tends towards a 'middle ground' position. Therefore, in this chapter, we explore the techniques of Koskenniemi's of rule indeterminacy, hegemonic positions and structural bias of institutions.

1 Generalizing the language model and its critique

Approaching international law as rhetorical technique draws on the Harvard School, which interrogates legal practice 'from the inside'.[12] This aims to make sense of 'one of the ways in which we experience law [which] is as a medium in which one pursues a project rather than as something that tells us what we have to do'.[13] This medium is a 'complex argumentative practice' where international lawyers (as the competent language speakers) connect rules with other rules 'at different levels of abstraction'.[14] In this way, the approach of the Harvard School corresponds to approaches in other disciplines that generalize the language

7 A Zahar and G Sluiter *International Criminal Law* (Oxford University Press Oxford 2008) and Henzelin (n 1).

8 S Becker 'Universal Jurisdiction: How Universal is it?' (2003) 12 *Palestine Yearbook of International Law* 49.

9 E Jouannet 'A Critical Introduction' in M Koskenniemi *The Politics of International Law* (Hart Publishing 2011).

10 J Desantels-Stein 'Back in Style' (2014) 25 *Law and Critique* 141, 145.

11 Jouannet (n 9) 7.

12 D Kennedy 'Freedom and Constraint in Adjudication: A Critical Phenomenology' (1986) 36(4) *Journal of Legal Education* 518 and D Kennedy *International Legal Structures* (Nomos Baden-Baden 1987) 7.

13 ibid 526.

14 ibid.

model of Saussure's semiotics and thus, view 'complex social phenomena' as akin to language in the sense of having the same internal structure.[15] Therefore, such approaches presuppose then that there is 'no more reliable *access* to those worlds [of physics and medicine] than what is provided by the languages of physics or medicine as spoken by the competent language-speakers of *those* disciplines'.[16] Similarly, there is 'no access to legal rules or the legal meaning of international behaviour that is independent from the way competent lawyers see those things'[17] and international law 'is what lawyers think about it and how they go about using it in their work'.[18] Accordingly, a 'particular utterance called legal argument' can be explored using the generalization of the language model. This academic style draws upon insights from Saussure's binaries and Derrida's deconstruction that breaks and displaces the binaries. We briefly explore these latter insights before turning to the legal literature. However, it is necessary to be mindful that as each critique has in general been the subject of critique, it undermines any claim by the critiques 'to get at the truth of the objects they represent'.[19] Instead of some possibility of a resolution, the competing critiques are in a 'complex relationship of mutual critique', each attacking the other.[20]

Saussure proposed sets of distinctions that he theorized from exploring the condition of spoken language in general (*synchronic*), rather than historical changes over time (*diachronic*).[21] One set of distinctions is the division of spoken language into an essential system that is a 'self-contained whole' (*langue*) and everything else after the essential system is abstracted (*parole*).[22] This means language is 'a vast network of differences where each word has a value that is determined by the other words',[23] that is, each linguistic sign (word/concept) is related to each other by differential values of linguistic signs.[24] The *langue* is located between linguistic signs and, as a 'special' social institution;[25] the set of relations (language as

15 D Kennedy 'A Semiotics of Critique' (2001) 22 *Cardozo Law Review* 1147, 1176.
16 M Koskenniemi *From Apology to Utopia: The Structure of International Legal Argument* (Cambridge University Press Cambridge 2005) 568, original emphasis.
17 ibid.
18 ibid.
19 D Kennedy *A Critique of Adjudication* (Cambridge University Press Cambridge 1998) 15 ('I don't believe that my object (adjudication) corresponds . . . only and truly to a representation made in the "correct" medium. It will transcend or surpass my representation . . . no matter what method(s) I adopt and that's fine with me').
20 Kennedy (n 15) 1148.
21 F de Saussure *Course of General Linguistics* R Harris (tr) (Bloomsbury London 2013) 94.
22 ibid 11 and 20. See also P Bouissac *Saussure: A Guide for the Perplexed* (Continuum London 2010) 86.
23 Bouissac (n 22) 98. Kennedy cautions against the common mistake that 'words get their meanings from their relationship with other words rather than the things they refer to'. Instead, 'the meaning of words depends, in Saussure's theory, *both* on other words and on the way reality presents itself from conceptual organization'. Using the price-value idea, it is that 'changing any price sends ripples through the system and may or may not affect every other price'. See Kennedy (n 15) 1152.
24 Saussure (n 21) 121.
25 ibid 18.

system) are not fixed permanently but rather are in constant movement between past and future conditions of the language.[26] The essential elements of the *langue* and all its changes develop from *parole*[27] and therefore, by studying *parole*, we can determine the essential elements of *langue*.[28] Another set of distinctions is the division of the linguistic sign itself into a two-sided entity (or dyad) composed of a *signified* (concept/meaning) and a *significant* (sound pattern).[29] Its importance is to recognize signified/significant as inseparable and incapable of being disassociated.[30] Saussure also argued that there is no natural link between the quality of one word (friend), its opposition (enemy) and a specific sound pattern.[31] We inherit our language by social convention when we grow up and therefore, while linguistic signs are arbitrary (as opposed to natural), there is no free choice – or at least there are degrees of motivation, with some words being arbitrary and others being less so, although implying 'analogical thinking'.[32]

Overall, Saussure read language as emerging from a process of articulation.[33] Each linguistic sign emerges from a system of differences and therefore, there are no 'ideas established in advance . . . before the introduction of the linguistic structure'.[34] Therefore, language takes shape with its linguistic units in between two shapeless masses' of thoughts and sound patterns.[35] Identities emerge retroactively from the process of articulation of differences and are unstable; they are only stable to the extent that they are suffused with differences.[36] In this way, terms are not independent from each other; rather, they have differential and reciprocal values with the language system both as sound patterns and as concepts.[37] Saussure argued that there must be at least four terms to a language system and therefore, scholars engage in minimal pair analysis to determine basic units that are within a given language to allow for creation of meaning.[38] As Kennedy explains, a language (as a system) possesses 'a set of resources available at a particular moment to compose utterances (parole or speech)', that involves 'picking and choosing, arranging and re-arranging, maintaining and modifying the given pieces'.[39]

26 ibid 85–7 ('a language alters, or rather evolves . . . after a certain time, changes can always be seen to have taken place') and Bouissac (n 22) 82 (a 'conceptual snapshot' of an essential system that makes communication possible at the moment when it takes place).

27 Bouissac (n 22) 87.

28 Desentels-Stein (n 10) 142.

29 Saussure (n 21) 76–7.

30 ibid 121.

31 ibid 78.

32 ibid 78–9 and Bouissac (n 22) 98 (but no specific agency that develops *langue*).

33 ibid 133 and S Luedemann *Politics of Deconstruction: A New Introduction to Jacques Derrida* (Stanford University Press Stanford 2014) 21.

34 ibid 141 and 131.

35 Saussure (n 21) 32.

36 Luedemann (n 33) 23.

37 Bouissac (n 22) 98.

38 Luedemann (n 33).

39 Kennedy (n 15) 1178. Note issue over relationship of linguistic sign and speaking subject, see B Stawarska *Saussure's Philosophy of Language as Phenomenology: Undoing the Doctrine of the Course of General Linguistics* (Oxford University Press Oxford 2015).

Derrida critiqued this linguistic turn in humanities and theorized that any set of binary oppositions can be subject to a deconstructive reading.[40] He was 'more concerned with the "rhetorical" tactics' used to privilege positions than the content and meaning of those arguments[41] and therefore, deconstruction discloses 'the essential uncertainty of human discourse'[42] (or the 'text') by revealing the 'self-contradictions and double binds that lie latent in any text'.[43] A deconstructive reading involves both an overturning and displacing that Derrida referred to as a 'double gesture'.[44] It both overturns and displaces a conceptual order and a non-conceptual order 'with which the conceptual order is articulated'.[45] Overturning recognizes that 'texts are structured around binary oppositions (e.g. good-bad, male-female)'[46] and the phase of overturning is 'to overturn the hierarchy at a given moment'.[47] What this shows is that 'an opposition of metaphysical concepts is never the face to face of two terms, but a hierarchy and an order of subordination.'[48] It allows us to recognize that the binaries are not in a 'peaceful coexistence' but rather it is a 'violent hierarchy'; 'one of the two terms governs the other (axiologically, logically etc.) or has the upper hand.'[49] Derrida cautions against merely overturning the hierarchy as the lower term 'becomes the "higher" term and is thus itself ripe for overturning'.[50] In this sense, it would merely 'operate on the terrain of and within the deconstructed system'[51] and therefore, deconstruction requires an unending or 'interminable' analysis as 'the hierarchy of dual oppositions always re-establishes itself.'[52]

It follows then that the second strategy is a 'general displacement of the system'[53] or breaking the binaries that Culler describes as working 'within the terms of the system but in order to breach it'.[54] Derrida reveals how there is an infinite double movement 'within the opposition' so that the dominant term is defined by contrast to its supplement (or inferior term) that 'continually threatens the former's sovereignty'.[55] Derrida used the metaphor of the shuttle, *la navette*, to convey the movement between two positions, that is, the 'to-and-fro' or back-and-forth movement of the shuttle.[56] In binary oppositions, there is a constant

40 J Derrida *Positions* A Bass (tr) (Continuum London 2004), 42.
41 R Cooper 'Modernism, Post-Modernism and Organizational Analysis 3: The Contribution of Jacques Derrida' (1989) 10(4) *Organizational Studies* 479, 480.
42 ibid, 481.
43 ibid.
44 Derrida (n 40), 38.
45 ibid.
46 Cooper (n 41) 483.
47 Derrida (n 40), 39.
48 ibid.
49 ibid.
50 Cooper (n 41) 483.
51 Derrida (n 40), 39.
52 ibid, 39–40.
53 J Derrida *Margins of Philosophy* A Bass (tr) (University of Chicago Press Chicago 1982) 329.
54 J Culler *On Deconstruction* (Routledge London 1983), 86.
55 Cooper (n 41) 483.
56 J Derrida *Negotiations: Interventions and Interviews, 1971–2001* E Rottenberg (tr) (Stanford University Press Stanford 2002) 12.

movement from one to another with 'the impossibility of establishing oneself anywhere'.[57] This double movement shows how binary oppositions are simultaneously separated and connected. Although they have binary differences, they are not as different as they seem. Rather the oppositions merge or fuse, contaminating one another, or what Derrida calls 'always already' as a 'trace'.[58]

This supplementarity (or 'delayed effect') is necessary to '*complete* some deficiency in the present state of things' and this reveals 'a subservient term to be (unconsciously) dominant'.[59] This shows that the apparent separate terms succumb to 'a process where opposites merge in a constant undecidable exchange of attributes',[60] a paradox in which 'a term is shown to be inhabited by its opposite.'[61] An undecidable is 'neither/nor' or 'simultaneously either *or*'.[62] In this way, 'the essence of undecidability is the existence of contradictory meanings *within a single term*'.[63] Deconstruction then simultaneously overturns the hierarchy (and the 'entire system attached to it') '*and* releases the dissonance' (or difference) of one binary within another 'thereby disorganizing the entire inherited order and invading the entire field'.[64] In this sense, this second phase of displacement marks 'the interval between inversion' (or overturning) that brings about the overturning and violently produces 'a concept that can no longer be . . . included in the previous regime'.[65] This new concept or 'undecidables' can no longer be within the binary opposition and at the same time, it 'inhabit[s]' the opposition 'resisting and disorganizing it, without ever constituting a third term, without ever leaving room for a solution'.[66]

Derrida applied the double gesture to law in its relationship to force and justice. In his view, 'every judicial contract . . . is founded on violence'[67] or as Cover argues, 'legal interpretation takes place in a field of pain and death.'[68] In this sense, interpretations 'signal and occasion the imposition of violence upon others' and they constitute 'justifications for violence which has already occurred

57 ibid. See also J Derrida *Writing and Difference* A Bass (tr) (Routledge London 1978) 278 (centred structure is a 'concept of a freeplay based on a fundamental ground, a freeplay which is constituted upon a fundamental immobility and a reassuring certitude, which is itself beyond the reach of the freeplay').

58 J Derrida *Of Grammatology* G Chakravorty Spivak (tr) (Johns Hopkins University Press Baltimore 1997) 7. See also Cooper (n 41) 486 ('later ideas or experiences always take precedence over what was initially there', or supplementarity).

59 Cooper (n 41) 486, original emphasis.

60 C Norris *Derrida* (Harvard University Press Cambridge 1987) 35.

61 Cooper (n 41) 486 (and the marginal is actually 'necessary and essential, as writing to speech').

62 Derrida (n 40), 40, original emphasis ('supplement' as 'neither plus nor minus, neither outside nor the complement of an inside').

63 Cooper (n 41) 486, original emphasis.

64 Derrida (n 40), 39, original emphasis.

65 ibid.

66 ibid 40.

67 J Derrida 'The Force of Law: The Mystical Foundation of Authority' in G Anidjar *Acts of Religion* (Routledge London 2002) 234.

68 R Cover 'Violence and the Word' (1986) 95 *Yale Law Journal* 1601 and 1604 ('law is the projection of an imagined future upon reality').

or which is about to occur'.[69] Derrida's point of departure then is that law is 'an authorized violence, a force that justifies itself or is justified in applying itself, even if this justification may be judged from elsewhere to be unjust or unjustifiable'.[70] A deconstructive reading exposes the paradox in the relationship between 'the force of law . . . and the allegedly originary violence that must have established this authority'.[71] That originary violence 'could not of itself have authorized itself by any anterior legitimacy so that, in this initial moment, it is neither legal nor illegal, just nor unjust'.[72] It is later paradoxically read as illegal based on law enacted after the originary violence,[73] like the revolutionary violence that establishes a nation state.[74] In this sense, judgements and interpretation 'cannot be understood independently of this inescapable implication in violent action' – they are a 'practical activity . . . designed to lead to effective threats –and often violent –deeds'.[75]

At the same time, law is 'conceptually and politically distinct from justice'.[76] Law can be deconstructed but 'justice itself, if such a thing exists, outside or beyond law, is not deconstructible.'[77] Rather deconstruction is justice in that justice 'takes place in the interval that separates the undeconstructibility of justice from the deconstructibility of *droit* (authority, legitimacy and so on)'.[78] Derrida sees justice as an 'impossible invention'[79] or 'possible as an experience of the impossible . . . where even if it does not exist (or does not yet exist or never does exist), *there is* justice'.[80] In this sense, law is not justice but an element of calculation 'and it is just that there be law but justice is incalculable, it demands that one calculate with the incalculable.'[81] Therefore, experiences of justice are 'moments in which the decision between just and unjust is never insured by a rule'.[82] When one makes an address, it is always singular – and justice, as law, 'seems always to suppose the generality of a rule, a norm or universal imperative'.[83] Here, Derrida notes a paradox in that an act of justice is singular yet the rule or norm is in general form: 'To address oneself to the other in the language of the other is both a condition of all possible justice, it seems . . . but it appears not only impossible . . . but even excluded by justice as law', because justice as law

69 ibid.
70 ibid 233.
71 ibid 234.
72 ibid.
73 E O'Brien 'The Force of Law in Seamus Heaney's Greek Translations' in L Fitzpatrick (ed) *Performing Violence in Contemporary Ireland* (Careysfort Press Dublin 2010) 31, 33.
74 C Douzinas 'Violence, Justice, Deconstruction' (2005) 6 *German Law Journal* 171, 175 (the French Revolution retrospectively legitimized by its *Declaration des droits de l'homme*).
75 ibid 173.
76 S Chesterman 'Beyond Fusion Fallacy: The Transformation of Equity and Derrida's 'The Force of Law' (1997) 24(3) *Journal of Law and Society* 350, 357.
77 Derrida (n 67) 243.
78 ibid.
79 Chesterman (n 76) 363.
80 Derrida (n 67) 243, original emphasis.
81 ibid 244.
82 ibid.
83 ibid 245.

appears to imply a measure of universality, that is, 'the appeal to a third party who suspends the unilaterality or singularity of the idioms'.[84]

Derrida then argues for a reconsideration of the 'thought of the just and unjust' through a double movement. There is a 'sense of responsibility without limits' in that we continually interrogate justice or be '*juste* with justice', that is, 'the first justice to be done is to hear it, to try to understand where it comes from, what it wants of us, knowing that it does so through singular idioms.'[85] In this sense, 'justice always addresses itself to singularity, to the singularity of the other, despite or even because it pretends to universality.'[86] Therefore, the responsibility requires a constant 'questioning of the origins, grounds and limits of our conceptual, theoretical or normative apparatus surrounding justice' and does not assume an 'inherited' or natural determination of justice.[87] Instead, both theoretical limits and 'concrete injustices' are continually challenged. This constant questioning produces a 'moment of suspense' that in turn, opens the interval in which transformations take place. Deconstruction finds its site between law's claim to 'exercise itself in the name of justice' and justice's demand for itself 'to be established in the name of a law'.[88] In this sense, justice demands freedom of action yet must follow the law, a calculation, and therefore, the judge must not only follow law but 'must assume it, approve it, confirm its value, by reinstituting act of interpretation'.[89] Derrida calls the decision of the responsible judge a 'new freshness', that is, for the decision to be 'just and responsible . . . it must preserve the law and also destroy or suspend it enough to have to reinvent it in each case, rejustify it, reinvent it, at least in the reaffirmation and new and free confirmation of its principle'.[90]

Consequently, in the judge's decision, there is a test of undecidability and the undecidable remains as an 'essential ghost in every decision',[91] which means the decision is no longer 'presently just, fully just'.[92] Derrida also reads a just decision as 'required immediately' in that the moment of the decision remains a 'finite moment of urgency and precipitation'.[93] Yet paradoxically, justice is 'yet-to-come (*avenir*)';[94] 'there is no justice except to the degree that some event is possible which, as event, exceeds calculation, rules, programs. . . .'[95] Justice is 'unpresentable but it is the chance of the event and the condition of history' and

84 ibid.
85 ibid, 247–8.
86 ibid, 248.
87 ibid 248.
88 ibid 250.
89 ibid 251.
90 ibid.
91 ibid 252 ('either [the decision] has not yet been made according to a rule and nothing allows one to call it just or has already followed a rule, which nothing guarantees absolutely and if it were guaranteed, the decision would have to turn back to calculation and one could not call it just').
92 ibid.
93 ibid 255.
94 ibid.
95 ibid 257

as there is a tendency towards the bad, the assurance against this risk is the idea that 'incalculable justice *commands* calculation'.[96] Chesterman describes Derrida's idea of justice as 'transformation in progress', which is 'not in the sense that it lies in a possible future, but that its future lies in the possible'.[97] This converts into an 'emancipatory politics premised on a self-critical methodology that is rigorous to the point of reinventing itself with each step that is taken'.[98]

2 Binary oppositions

Applying these critiques to legal phenomena, by generalizing the language model, law is read as a language system that is divided into a 'deep constitutive syntax' (*langue*) and a lexical or verbal 'surface' (*parole*).[99] There is a set of necessary elements of rule, facts, an application (*parole*) where one of those at least is in question, e.g. dispute over rule, facts, or how applied. Lawyers produce what Kennedy calls 'argument bites', that is, they 'select, arrange, modify and supplement in order to produce an argument for the choice of a rule, an argument recognizably spoken in legal *langue*'.[100] In this way, law as language system (of differential values) means that there is considerable discretion in producing legal argument at the surface level, yet the verbal usage (surface) is constrained by the underlying syntax or grammar.[101] In other words, legal arguers can produce an argument for any position, yet simultaneously, are constrained by limited patterns that govern what it is possible to say. Kennedy reads this simultaneous freedom and constraint as somewhat akin to a physical medium (such as bricks) in that the constraint is relative to your chosen project or what you want to make, similar to how 'building something out of a given set of bricks constrains you, controls you, deprives you of freedom'.[102] In this way, Kennedy sees the work of the judge as being 'free to deploy work in any direction but limited by pseudo-objectivity of the rule-as-applied, which he may or may not be able to overcome'.[103] As we noted, by studying the *parole*, we can determine the essential elements of the *langue*. Nevertheless, the language structure that is produced is seen as 'a pseudo object more amendable to [law's] internal requirements',[104] that is, 'an image of

96 ibid 257, original emphasis.
97 Chesterman (n 76) 362.
98 ibid 361.
99 Kennedy (n 15) 1175.
100 ibid 1178.
101 ibid.
102 Kennedy (n 12) 526.
103 ibid, 522.
104 D Kennedy 'A Semiotics of Legal Argument' (1991) 42 *Syracuse Law Review* 75, 89–90 (that the 'more of legal argument and the less semiotic invention . . . the more political it will be – the more capable of disquieting power'). See also D Kennedy 'Roll Over Beethoven' (1984) 36 *Stanford Law Review* 1, 17 (that 'the point of the fundamental contradiction . . . was against falsely mediated forms of unity among people that have to be broken through before people can in fact experience what's going on between them in a real, honest experiential way' yet has ceased to play this role and had to be renounced).

a set of ground rules' that 'provide formal conditions of a lexicon [verbal speech act]'.[105] This image of a language structure is 'a *style* of legal thought that is neither scientific nor imagined'.[106]

In the international law context, scholars have identified an *image* of language structure based on 'a particular historically conditioned discourse' that translates or reproduces 'some basic tenets of liberal political theory' to the international world.[107] These basic tenets form the basic units that are the essential system of the *langue*. Here, state liberty is considered to be a social fact that is atomistic and in turn, justifies the legal order. It is assumed that law's binding force emanates from the state's voluntary consent rather than descending from a natural or moral order.[108] The rejection of a higher normative order is necessary because under the liberal principle of subjectivity of value, it is assumed that value or 'justice' is either 'subjective or necessarily imposed'[109] that is, cloaking political preferences in an idea of universalism.[110] However, each state's liberty appears to be 'capable of quashing the liberty of the others and vice-versa', as a state is free to act in a way that entirely opposes other states.[111] Liberal theory then operates from an assumption that the legal order must constrain the individual freedom of all subjects in order to protect the freedom of all and that order is maintained through applying objective standards or rules.[112] This assumes legal rules 'are objective in some sense that political ideas, views and preferences are not'.[113]

It follows that international law involves an appeal to such 'historically conditioned discourse' 'so as to impose 'a particularist language upon others as if it were a universally accepted legal discourse',[114] and yet simultaneously modern international law 'provides no awareness of the political and moral nature of its hidden substantive commitments'.[115] By pulling on a critique of the liberal theory of law, we observe how basic liberal tenets are paradoxical and cannot be reconciled

105 Desantels-Stein (n 10) 144.

106 ibid.

107 A Carty 'Critical International Law: Recent Trends in the Theory of International Law' (1991) 2 *European Journal of International Law* 66.

108 N Purvis 'Critical Legal Studies in Public International Law' (1991) 32 *Harvard Journal of International Law* 81, 93–4.

109 N Onuf 'Book Review and Notes: *From Apology to Utopia: The Structure of the International Legal Argument* by Martii Koskenniemi' (1990) 84 *American Journal of International Law* 771, 774.

110 M Koskenniemi, 'The Politics of International Law' (1990) 1 *European Journal of International Law* 4, 8.

111 Purvis (n 108) 95.

112 R Unger *Knowledge and Politics* (Free Press New York 1975) 66–103 and A MacIntyre *After Virtue: A Study in Moral Theory* (3rd edn University of Notre Dame Press 2007).

113 Koskenniemi (n 110) 7.

114 Carty (n 107) 66 and D Kennedy 'International Law and the Nineteenth Century: History of Illusion' (1996) 65 *Nordic Journal of International Law* 385, 388 ('what we think of as the classical system, of both legal philosophy and doctrine, has never been as thoroughly rejected as [the] conventional picture suggests . . .').

115 Purvis (n 108) 102.

'for reasons internal to the [liberal] *ideal itself*'.[116] Here, the idea of the state as atomistic and the theory of objective rules are in contradiction with the principle of subjectivity of value. The concept of the state as atomistic is a normative position and this means that 'liberalism has accepted some norms, including liberty and sovereignty, while rejecting others.'[117] Adopting a theory of objective rules is also a normative position, yet liberalism cannot 'deny the existence of the objectivity of value and at the same time, claim to resolve conflict through the application of "objective legality" of law'.[118] If the law's origin rests upon state liberty, the law's neutrality remains endlessly challengeable because the so-called 'moral consensus' is drawn from conflicting state liberties.[119] 'To the degree that it exists, is only the sum of moral decisions made by sovereigns' and in turn, this means that logic of the rule of law is unable to reconcile their positions 'objectively'.[120]

In determining the essential system, international lawyers have ascertained a set of binary oppositions drawn from these dual (paradoxical) liberal assumptions of liberty and order. In Koskenniemi's thought, these oppositions are described as *normativity* and *concreteness*[121] and these twin criteria are 'left . . . on purpose ambiguous so as to allow maximal coverage'.[122] Normativity aims to ensure that law is opposable to the state (critical of state policy), that the norm/standard is ascertained without political value judgment and 'applies regardless of the political preferences of legal subjects'.[123] In this sense, it applies even if the state opposes the rules' application to itself. Concreteness aims to ensure that law is verifiable by the politics of the state (reflective of state policy), that the 'observable fact' may be ascertained scientifically and without political bias[124] and that law is 'not a natural but an artificial creation, a reflection of social circumstances'.[125] In other words, if law only reproduces what someone thinks the law should be like, it reproduces their political preferences and similarly, if law only applies against states who accept it, it reproduces 'those states' political views'.[126] Therefore, to be verifiable (and scientific), the law must reflect the social fact of state behaviour while at the same time distancing itself from both fact (power) and norm (morality), as these would only conceal political or moral preferences.

It follows that only when both binary oppositions are present simultaneously can international lawyers demonstrate law's independence from politics and

116 Koskenniemi (n 110) 7, original emphasis.
117 Purvis (n 108) 102.
118 P Kotiaho 'A Return to Koskenniemi; or the Disconcerting Co-Optation of Rupture', (2012) 13(5) German Law Journal 483, 487.
119 Purvis (n 108) 97.
120 ibid.
121 Koskenniemi (n 16) 19–20. See also D Kennedy 1987 (n 12) 8 ('hard' and 'soft' doctrines) and D Kennedy 'The Last Treatise: Project and Person (A Reflection on Martti Koskenniemi)' (2006) 7 *German Law Journal* 982.
122 ibid 513.
123 ibid 16–23 and 41–58.
124 ibid.
125 Koskenniemi (n 110) 7.
126 ibid 8.

meet the 'requirements of legal objectivity vis-à-vis political subjectivity'.[127] In this sense, these oppositions reflect the battle the legal mind fights 'on two fronts', that is, separating law from theories of natural order (concrete) and simultaneously separating law from actual state behaviour (normativity).[128] Theoretically, individual freedom is protected because no normative standard of justice is imposed (law reflects state policy) and at the same time, the freedom of all is guaranteed because there is no oppressive rule by a hegemon (law criticizes state policy).[129] However, proving the argument's 'validity' by being simultaneously concrete and normative is impossible. As the oppositions 'cancel each other out' when brought to their logical conclusion,[130] the argument structure 'both creates and destroys itself'.[131]

An argument about normativity purports to show the rule's 'distance' from state practice.[132] Yet the more normative the argument appears, the less related to the state practice it seems and may be 'validly' criticized as 'undemonstrable utopia'[133] and 'like theories of natural justice –manipulable at will'.[134] Any attempt to reflect state preferences creates an arbitrary distinction between states.[135] An argument about concreteness purports to show the rule's 'closeness' to state practice.[136] Nevertheless the more concrete (or reflective of the perceived 'facts') the argument is claimed to be, the less normative it appears and may be 'validly' criticized as apologizing for the interests of the powerful.[137] Any attempt to be normatively controlling (and binding non-accepting states) would be a claim to 'know better' what the state agreed to (objective interests) based on some 'non-acceptance-related criteria' upon which the existence of acceptance can be determined ('naturalistic theory of good faith, reasonableness, equity').[138] This argumentation reflects the 'two ways of arguing about order and obligation in international affairs' that are both exhaustive and mutually exclusive.[139]

Applying a deconstructive technique to the binary oppositions, Koskenniemi demonstrates how these binary oppositions are in constant movement with each other, between both positions, that is, *la navette* (or the 'to-and-fro').[140] The double gesture allows us to recognize the violent hierarchy, involving a 'hierarchy and an order of subordination', and demonstrates that 'the apparently dominant term in each binary opposition in fact depended on the secondary term for its

127 ibid.
128 ibid 7.
129 Koskenniemi (n 16) 63 and 309–24.
130 ibid 65.
131 Koskenniemi (n 110) 8.
132 ibid.
133 Jouannet (n 9) 7–8 and Koskenniemi (n 16) 58.
134 Koskenniemi (n 110) 8.
135 Koskenniemi (n 16) 64.
136 ibid.
137 Jouannet (n 9) 7–8.
138 Koskenniemi (n 16) 64.
139 ibid 58.
140 Koskenniemi 'Style as Method' (1999) 98 *American Journal of International Law* 352, 355.

meaning or force',[141] that 'continually threatens the former's sovereignty'.[142] In this way, each binary opposition acts as the necessary supplement to the other that is brought in to support the main position.[143] As we noted, 'the essence of undecidibility is the existence of contradictory meanings within a single term.'[144] This illustrates how binary oppositions are simultaneously separated and connected and that they merge or fuse, contaminating one another, or what Derrida calls, 'always already' as a 'trace'.[145] Therefore, normativity and concreteness merge or fuse and these dynamics are captured using Ullmann's ideas of 'descending' and 'ascending' patterns of argument that trace their patterns to norms/justice (normative code overrules state will) or social phenomena/fact (concrete, state will as determining).[146] Every legal argument preserves the descending/ascending patterns within itself and therefore, these patterns act as points of emphasis that privilege either normativity or concreteness, yet cannot remain fixed stably in either pattern.[147]

It follows that both patterns of normativity and concreteness need to draw from each other to avoid the criticisms of being subjective[148] and therefore, the structural properties operate 'so as to make them seem compatible'.[149] Yet any attempt to make the normative and concrete oppositions compatible only renders the argument self-contradictory. Any 'compatibility' is sustained so long as the argument is not challenged, but once it is challenged, it must defend itself by emphasizing either normativity or concreteness. It is also impossible to prefer one position absolutely over the other, as this would only expose the former to the 'valid' criticisms of the latter.[150] Therefore, the outcome is 'an incoherent argument which constantly shifts between the opposing positions while remaining open to challenge from the opposite argument'.[151] 'A middle position seems excluded', given the incompatibility of both patterns and the capacity of each position to 'validly' accuse the other of being too subjective.[152] What this means is that legal problem-solving is indeterminate, that is, it is unable to produce determinate results.[153] There is then no 'pure objectivity' or 'pure subjectivity' as the binaries are bound within the argumentative structure

141 ibid. See also Derrida (n 40) 39.
142 Cooper (n 41) 483.
143 See Koskenniemi (n 16) 308 (naturalism acknowledges the legitimacy of positivism as theories of justice only appear 'tangible . . . when linked to what states have thought them to mean – to what they have consented to' whereas similarly, positivism needs naturalism in order to justify how state behaviour 'creates binding obligations').
144 Cooper (n 41) 486.
145 Derrida (n 40) 7.
146 W Ullmann *Law and Politics in the Middle Ages: An Introduction to the Sources of Medieval Political Ideas* (Cornell University Press New York 1976) 30–31.
147 Koskenniemi (n 16) 226 and 60.
148 ibid 10, 68 and 513.
149 ibid 60.
150 ibid (for instance, naturalism appears to positivism as failing to reflect state policy while positivism appears to naturalism as failing to be critical of state policy).
151 ibid.
152 ibid 59.
153 ibid 62.

and subject to the play of argumentation.[154] Therefore, the structural properties of the language produce recurring irresolvable dichotomies (such as positivism/naturalism or consent/justice) that allow for multiple interpretations which on a structural level are indistinguishable from one other.

This concerns the interchangeability of each position (or interpretation) given the 'capacity of each legal concept to be projected with a meaning which links it both to ascending and descending conceptual scheme'.[155] 'A position . . . is recognized as descending or ascending only in its opposition to a deviating one', that is, as a 'result of projection from a contrasting view'.[156] Each position can pivot its acceptability on the claim that the opposing position is 'subjective', that is, either utopian (subjective theories of justice) or apologist (subjective expressions of power). This inclusion of both conceptual schemes in each position produces 'reversibility' because the 'available concepts themselves contain both principles within them' and therefore, we can 'reverse these initial associations', that is, justice/consent and vice-versa.[157] Consequently, the reversibility means that it is possible to connect the competing positions to any political project. In this book, this deconstructionist technique is used to illustrate that state and humanity (global) are in both logics of moralist and formalist. In other words, it does not read formalist as state and moralist as global; both logics are in each position. A single conflict arises when the position is identified temporarily and an opponent must evoke the opposite position to 'validly' accuse the former of subjectivity.[158] Once the competing positions are pushed into argument, both positions are seen to be self-contradictory as each position is both positions,[159] that is, both moralist and formalist. As a result, there is a move to the middle in an attempt to reconcile the irreconcilable. Yet as both positions are self-contradicting, there is no underlying conflict and there must be an ad hoc solution in the moment of the decision.[160] In this way, the choice between positions does not depend on their 'natural essence but on our (interpreter's) position in regard to some principle of justice'.[161]

Given the language's structural properties, international lawyers use different strategies or 'legal styles' to prove the relevance and validity of their doctrines that are captured as four competing doctrinal styles, which are mutually exclusive, vary in terms of how they privilege normativity and concreteness and dependent on each other to generate meaning.[162] These styles are employed to '[manage] the tension

154 Jouannet (n 9) 28. Note her criticism that argument structure can accord with neo-Kantian intersubjectivity, a formal universality integrating the linguistic turn. She notes that Koskenniemi 'is prepared to accept a degree of intersubjectivity', yet once play of argumentation begins, 'intersubjectivity becomes a simple argumentative strategy for claiming objectivity'. ibid 24.
155 Koskenniemi (n 16) 504.
156 ibid 511.
157 ibid 505.
158 ibid 511.
159 ibid.
160 ibid 508.
161 ibid 504.
162 Koskenniemi (n 16) 182–223 and Koskenniemi (n 110) 12 (rule-oriented (normativity emphasis), policy-oriented (concreteness emphasis), idealism and rule scepticism (as extreme challenges to other principal approaches)).

between scientific hopes and political ideals',[163] yet the choice of style cannot actually fulfil the assumed 'objectivity', that is, the setting aside of an international lawyer's perceptions and desires in order to be scientific. There is no scientific method that is unrelated to any method or non-method which can determine the persuasiveness of any style;[164] therefore, legal styles are 'normatively tinged', with some styles being preferred over other choices, because 'there was a story about progress in our discipline that one needed to learn in order to for one's science to get going.'[165] Therefore, the competing legal styles are all subject to the endless play of argumentation within the structure of the language.[166] In this sense, an international lawyer cannot set aside their 'politics' because their choice of style signals their chosen theoretical assumptions and 'what use the style is put to, depends on the fears and passions' of the lawyer:[167] 'The 'feel' of professional competence is the outcome of style, more particularly of linguistic style' and international law 'always involves a translation from one language to another'.[168] The raw materials of social conflict (power, desire and fear) are 'translated' into legal styles yet 'translation does not "resolve" those claims, but it makes them commensurate and susceptible to analysis in the professional and bureaucratic contexts in which it is used. But translation is not completely devoid of normative consequences, either'.[169]

2.1 A reading of texts on jurisdiction

The 'deep structural' binary oppositions (and the resulting incoherence) are detected in the many definitions of the concept of jurisdiction in international law. In early twentieth-century literature, Woosley defined jurisdiction as a rule that permits the individual state to decide 'what exceptions to territorial jurisdiction it supports', yet simultaneously requires that the state's decision must accord with 'the interests of other states'.[170] In a similar vein, Politis argued that the state's liberty is both 'limited by international law' and 'not regulated by international law'.[171] This means the content of (or the determination of) the state's liberty must be both 'capable of determination from a perspective which is external to it' and from the state's own perspective.[172] However, the resulting incoherence is evident. If the state's liberty is determined from an 'external (and overriding) normative' idea, the state loses its 'individuality' as a state and any

163 M Koskenniemi, 'International Law in a Post-Realist Era', (1995) 16 *Australian Yearbook of International Law* 1, 4.
164 Koskenniemi (n 140) 356.
165 ibid 353.
166 *ibid 352.*
167 ibid, 356.
168 ibid 357.
169 ibid.
170 LH Woolsey 'Extraterritorial Crime' (1926) 20 *American Journal of International Law* 726, 758.
171 N Politis 'Le Problème des Limitations de la Souverainetè et la thèorie de l'abus des droits dan les rapports internationaux' (1925) 6 *Recueil des Cours* 1, 47.
172 Koskenniemi (n 16) 225.

claim to independence and self-determination.[173] If the state's liberty is determined from the state's own perspective, the rule loses its normativity and any claim to objective binding force. Any attempt to reconcile the incoherence is futile – both oppositions cancel each other out. As we explore in Chapter 3, the legacy of these narratives on the concept of jurisdiction are endlessly repeated in modern international law literature. Koskenniemi explains the resulting incoherence as the oscillation between a 'pure fact' and a 'legal' approach towards the origin of international law,[174] that is, sovereignty as external to law (Schmitt)[175] or sovereignty as determined within law (Kelsen).[176]

An argument from a 'pure fact' approach is based on the assumption that the state is free unless its freedom is limited by rules. In this sense, the state is anterior to international law and therefore, sovereignty is 'a question of fact which the law can only recognize but cannot control'.[177] This characterizes the law as concrete, as the state possesses a wide discretion of sovereign power and any limiting rules originate in social fact or behaviour.[178] Its purpose is to protect state freedom from harm (or unwarranted and arbitrary interference). However, what the harm is in the circumstances depends upon the state's idea of harm, as if not, the idea of harm must be sourced to a value (or normative idea) beyond the state, which would appear to be the legal approach. When two disputing states allege harm to their liberties, 'the pure fact approach must protect both "harms" and cannot (without appeal to an external idea of harm) decide a preference or balance between them, a method which the "pure fact approach" has supposedly rejected.'[179]

An argument from a legal approach is based on the assumption that the state possesses liberty where legal rules have granted this freedom to the state. In this sense, international law is anterior to the state and therefore, sovereignty is a 'sum of rights, liberties and competences' granted by international law.[180] Sovereignty is then 'a description of the norms whose normative force is in their being incorporated in some legal act, not in their being inherent in statehood'.[181] This characterizes the law as normatively controlling and endeavours to restrict state freedom as far as possible.[182] Its purpose then is to constrain state liberty to protect all liberties. However, what is considered a 'just' constraint on liberty depends

173 ibid.

174 ibid 233.

175 C Schmitt *Political Theology* G Schwab (tr) (2nd edn University of Chicago Press Chicago 2005) 6 and 10–15.

176 H Kelsen *Introduction to the Problems of Legal Theory* BL Paulson and S Paulson (tr) (Clarendon Press Oxford 1992) 123.

177 Koskenniemi (n 16) 232 ('to be a state was to hold certain factual not evaluative properties').

178 ibid 233.

179 ibid 225.

180 ibid 229. See M Virally 'Panorama du Droit International Contemporain' (1983) 183 *Recueil des Cours* 5, 79.

181 ibid 231. See Virally (n 175) 78 (delimited and determined within the law and not external to it (or as a pre-existing fact).

182 ibid 233.

upon normative value[183] and this, in turn, is an external objective standard that liberal theory rejects under the principle of subjectivity of value. In a dispute between states, a legal approach cannot decide a preference based purely on an external standard or based 'the correctness of the pure fact view (and thus accepting self-contradiction)'.[184]

We noted above that structurally both approaches are in each position, as legal arguers must address both binary oppositions of concreteness and normativity in order to fight the battle on two fronts. Therefore, when states are in dispute over the extent of their jurisdiction, this contradictory mix of state discretion and rule limitation in each opposing argument compels the judge to turn to *context* that considers the 'character of the social relations which surround [the State]'.[185] We observe these 'surface' opposing positions (and their internal incoherence) in the debate surrounding the judgment in the *SS Lotus* case and its approach to the origin of principles of jurisdiction.[186] This latter dilemma traces through all jurisdictional debates in international law. In their judgement, the majority of the Court appeared to adopt the pure fact approach that assumes state liberty is prior to the legal order and as such, has normative content (or value) (an ascending pattern).[187] International law 'presupposes the State's existence' and therefore, any legal rights or competencies accrue to the state because of its statehood.[188] In this way, rules are merely a description of 'what was required to safeguard the anterior liberties'[189] and examples of such doctrines include requirement of 'clear and convincing evidence' of limitations of sovereignty and the inability to derive legal rules by analogy.[190]

Nevertheless, the Court's ascending pattern may be 'validly' accused of apology for power because it derives the rule of law from state preferences even though states conflict in their behaviour, which, in turn, conflicts with the premise of a legal order regulated by neutral rules.[191] The Court was then forced to move from an ascending to a descending pattern in order to decide between conflicting liberties (and in its attempt to avoid being accused of apologizing for power).[192] In its descending move, the Court had to appeal to theory; 'beyond liberty' as to what is just.[193] However, the resulting incoherence means that although a state is supposed to have a wide discretion, its liberty must be delimited by the liberties of other states. Yet to do so, this delimitation can only be presupposed on a higher

183 ibid 231 (values such as interdependence, common interests, a shared progressive morality or legal logic).
184 ibid 254.
185 ibid 225.
186 *Case of the SS Lotus (France v Turkey)* (1927) PCIJ Ser. A No 10, 18 and 19.
187 Koskenniemi (n 16) 232 and 256.
188 C De Visscher *Theory and Reality in Public International law* (PE Corbett tr, Princeton University Press Princeton 1957) 166.
189 Koskenniemi (n 16) 224.
190 ibid 257.
191 ibid 225 and 257.
192 ibid 225 and 256. See also Case of SS Lotus (n 181) 20.
193 ibid.

normative code, which undermines the original assumption that the state's liberty is anterior to the legal order.[194] Therefore, the Court moves back to an ascending pattern to avoid being accused of undemonstrable utopia and locates the rule in 'concrete' state behaviour. But this invariably was one of the disputing states' behaviour argued to be equitable or drawn from a consensus.[195]

In the dissenting opinion of Judge Loder, he seemed to adopt the legal approach that assumes the legal order (a higher binding code) pre-exists the sovereignty of the state and controls the state (***descending pattern***).[196]. This assumes that all rights, liberties and competences are conferred by law[197] and all sovereign activity must conform to law.[198] It is based upon the idea of the systematic character of international law or 'the completeness of the legal system'.[199] Here, international law can ascribe competences and 'legitimate spheres of action' to bodies which, it decides, are legal subjects. The state cannot be above or outside the law[200] and is bound by the law regardless of state voluntary will.[201] Therefore, exclusivity of territorial jurisdiction can only be trumped by a permissible rule to exercise extraterritorial jurisdiction – an exception to exclusive territorial jurisdiction. However, Judge Loder's descending pattern may be validly criticized as mere undemonstrable utopia because it derives the rule from 'objective' theories of justice, which, in turn, conflicts with the assumption of an order derived from liberty (and that rejects the idea of a higher moral order). Judge Loder is then compelled to move in an ascending pattern and provide empirical evidence of consent to the rule in state behaviour. The resulting incoherence is that even though the law is anterior to the state, the concept of 'justice' within the legal order is determined from state preferences (or voluntary will). Yet this determines the objective theory of justice according to state values which undermines the original assumption of a higher moral order prior to the state. Therefore, Loder moves back to a descending pattern and located the rule in a higher moral code but this was one of the contested theories of justice, based on equity or the common good.[202]

It is evident that the competing arguments of the Court's majority and Loder's dissent 'preserve the descending and ascending ideas within itself'.[203] Within the literature on jurisdiction, the resulting incoherence means that it is impossible to

194 ibid. See *Case of the SS Lotus* (n 181) 19–20 (noted the probable paralysis on the action of state courts if a permission was needed).

195 *Case of the SS Lotus* (n 181) 18–19 (noting objective territoriality in certain states' laws yet unable to find any protests among states towards such a jurisdictional claim).

196 ibid 34 (Judge Loder) and 52 (Lord Finlay) (rejected the notion that 'everything which is not prohibited is permitted').

197 JG Merrills *The Anatomy of International Law: A Study of the Role of International Law in the Contemporary World* (2nd edn Sweet and Maxwell London 1981) 45.

198 A Verdross 'Fondement du Droit International' (1927) 16 *Recueil des Cours* 1, 318.

199 Koskenniemi (n 16) 230.

200 HLA Hart *The Concept of Law* (Clarendon Press Oxford 1961) 216.

201 *Corfu Channel (Albania v. United Kingdom)* (1949) ICJ Rep No. 4, 43 (Judge Alvarez).

202 Koskenniemi (n 16) 239. See also *Case of SS Lotus* (n 18) 34–36.

203 ibid 226.

'determine' the normative content of sovereignty. Consequently, international lawyers turn to the doctrine of sources for a method to locate the law and justify the jurisdictional claims. Kennedy argues that the doctrine of jurisdiction has an uneasy relationship with the doctrine of sources because jurisdiction attempts to be distant from consensualism (or a consent-based approach). This is necessary because the purpose of the doctrine of jurisdiction is to delimit authority between sovereign equals.[204] However, any move to the doctrine of sources fails to overcome the problematic in the doctrine of sovereignty as the former illustrates similar competing approaches underpinned by a higher moral order (justice/non-consent) or by state liberty (consent). In the sources doctrine, it must be assumed that a rule is sourced neither to justice nor consent because either idea would force lawyers to revert back to the problematic of state liberty or a pre-existing legal code.[205]

Naturalism would be pure utopia, unless it seeks to connect justice or common interest to a meaning which states have ascribed to those concepts (consent). Whereas positivism would be pure apology, unless it can explain why behaviour creates obligations, and therefore, it turns to naturalism in order to provide an answer (justice).[206] Therefore, every argument pulls on both concrete and normative positions that describe both the processes within which states create law (social description) and provides an 'independent method' for finding rules and principles (political proscription).[207] The reason that there can be no reconciliation is because the positions are fundamentally opposed and cannot avoid falling foul of apology or utopia. Consensualism is needed to guarantee concreteness and non-consensualism is needed to justify the rule's binding force: 'Consensualism is justified only if non-consensualism is not and *vice versa*.'[208] Any attempt to decide a preference between consent and justice must be based on a higher theory, which would have to be either naturalistic or positivistic.[209]

3 A 'site of politics': Hegemonic techniques

Approaching international law through literary style demonstrates how the liberal project, with its notion of an objective rule of law, masks how 'social conflict must still be solved by political means and [that legal rhetoric] must, ***for reasons internal to the ideal itself***, rely on essentially contested – political – principles' in order to defend the outcomes to international law disputes:[210] 'Behind every notion of a universal international law, there is always some particular view, expressed by a

204 D Kennedy (n 12) 110 and 118 (jurisdiction (as derived from sovereignty) appears to be the 'hard' doctrine in opposition to the softness of the sources doctrine).

205 Koskenniemi (n 16) 303.

206 ibid 307.

207 ibid 305. Pure consensualism cannot explain the use of non-consensual principles (such as reasonableness or humanitarian values) because it would mean that those principles would be subject to changing state will, interest and behaviour when the International Court of Justice uses those principles as a constraint on state will. See Koskenniemi (n 16) 307 and 321 respectively.

208 ibid *321*.

209 ibid.

210 Koskenniemi (n 110) 7, original emphasis.

particular actor in some particular situation.'[211] There is a constant movement, an endless repetition of narrative, that appears to maintain the status quo, yet there is a transformation over time, incapable of being fixed on any one moment, that is, the chance of the event and the condition of history.[212] Here, a deconstructionist technique rejects the possibility of a meta-historical narrative or logic to explain why change (or the way the positions change) occurs. Rather, when change occurs, it is historically contingent and consequently, different every time.[213] We explore transformation over time in Chapters 4 and 5, and we see that it is impossible to capture the change of position in terms of some basic rule or law.

The need to accommodate both opposing logics in every argument indicates why no legal argument of itself can determine the legal outcome[214] and has compelled judges in international adjudication to move equitable standards or notions such as reasonableness in order to produce a legal outcome,[215] that is, an ad hoc solution. This is a move to political choice that cannot be reconciled with the role of the rule of law in liberal thought.[216] This decision making is not irrational, or a situation of 'anything goes'; rather, it is based on the particular rationality of the international legal profession that expresses the 'interplay' of ideology, politics, judges' perception and professional preferences.[217] Here, Koskenniemi conceives international law as having a 'degree of autonomy' from politics and morality (or separated and connected) based on an 'intuition' that legal arguments operate in some measure on a particular logic of the profession separate to their interest or that of the social group.[218] Therefore, the decision is not an extra-legal decision in the sense of eliminating or minimizing the role of law in relationship to power rather it is based on the particular rationality of the legal profession according to the structural bias of the deciding institution.[219]

211 M Koskenniemi 'International Law and Hegemony: A Reconfiguration' (2004) 17 *Cambridge Review of International Affairs* 197, 199. This is the art of reduction that appeals to either general or particular, reducing the event to either a singularity (requiring an exception) or a pattern. See M Koskenniemi 'Forward' in F Johns et al. (eds) *Events: The Force of International Law* (Routledge London 2010) xviii.

212 M Koskenniemi, 'A Response', (2006) 7 *German Law Journal* 1103, 1104–5 and Derrida (n 67) 257.

213 Kennedy (n 104) 42 ('an irreducible element of the absurd and the free in people's choices to fit themselves into these patterns . . . it's always a choice to be patterned according to false consciousness'). See also S Singh 'The Critic(al) Subject' in W Werner (ed) 'Koskenniemi and his Critics' (Draft paper) URL: http://www.academia.edu/15750896/The_Critic_al_Subject_2016_forthcoming_ (Singh argues that the critical subject involves 'absolute free choice to see the situation and its limits' yet the call for continual reimaging of the world is not a 'mastery' of the world and her situation but is more reflective of Derrida's 'ethic of responsibility', that is, doing justice to justice as discussed in section 1).

214 Koskenniemi (n 140), 356.

215 Koskenniemi (n 16) 258–303, 333–45 and 461–74.

216 ibid 65.

217 ibid 68.

218 ibid 67.

219 M Koskenniemi, 'The Politics of Law: Twenty Years Later', (2009) 20(1) *European Journal of International Law* 7, 9.

In other words, the politics at play is the hegemony of one legal argument over another that is dependent on how the rational of the argument accords with the structural bias of the institution.

This is the operation of the language of international law as a battleground or a 'site of politics' in which participants struggle for hegemony over their opponents.[220] In this sense, international law 'offers a defence for hegemonic and non-hegemonic practices equally'.[221] As Koskenniemi argues, international law debates suggest that two projects characterize international law; one project claims to transform from 'sovereign egoism into world unity' (descending) while the other from 'oppressive uniformity of global domination into self-determination' (ascending):[222] 'Each project starts from a negative characterization of the political present and seeks to override it with a legal blueprint conceived alternatively as a project of unity or a project of diversity.'[223] In this sense, each project is formal law that is politically open-ended, allowing 'any substances to fill the space that which appears to be either "unity" or "identity"'.[224] Neither project can trump the other 'in any general way'; rather they operate as 'surfaces' on which lawyers can 'reciprocally make and oppose hegemonic claims'.[225]

It means that when seeking to secure the hegemony, there must be an awareness of 'the moment's hegemonic and counter-hegemonic narratives'[226] in order to pitch the right argument at the right time to the right audience in order to be persuasive. This historical (diachronic) view demonstrates how the 'centre' moves within the discourse, so that today's hegemonic position is overtaken by the counter-hegemonic position tomorrow.[227] Of course, both hegemonic and counter-hegemonic positions fail to avoid the accusation of apology/utopia as they are either less normative/more concrete or less concrete/more normative.[228] It follows then that pitching the right argument means that the hegemony of any one argument depends upon how the legal argument accords with the structural bias of the institution in which the legal argument is pleaded.[229]

At this point, the move to specialization is significant and it is here where 'the world of legal practice is being sliced up in institutional projects that cater for special audiences with special interests and special ethos.'[230] Here, by framing the situation in terms of a particular specialism, the issue can be decided within that particular specialism's institutional setting and ensure the success of certain legal arguments

220 Jouannet (n 9) 7.
221 M Koskenniemi *The Politics of International Law* (Hart Publishing Oxford 2011) 241.
222 Koskenniemi (n 211) 200.
223 ibid 200.
224 ibid 200.
225 ibid 202.
226 ibid 202.
227 M Koskenniemi, 'Global Legal Pluralism: Multiple Regimes and Multiple Modes of Thought', (Harvard University March 2005), URL: http://www.helsinki.fi/eci/Publications/Koskenniemi/MKPluralism-Harvard-05d[1].pdf, 15.
228 Jouannet (n 9) 7.
229 Koskenniemi (n 219) 9.
230 ibid 9–10.

that follow the general bias of the deciding institution.[231] As any legal vocabulary is politically open-ended, it means that 'what gets read into it (or out of it) is a matter of subtle interpretative strategy.'[232] With ingenuity, lawyers can re-describe because there is no self-evident normative concepts and because every legal argument is fundamentally indeterminate and cannot be preferred over another.[233] This technique is the 'politics of redefinition' where these specialist vocabularies can be used to 'push forward' certain interests 'while leaving others in the shadows',[234] all of which is determined by the choice of language.[235] Because the ethos is essential for each specialism, it is irrelevant whether specialisms have the same or different rules as each rule would be 'applied differently' in accordance with the different ethos.[236] The specialisms are also not delimited between one another and this means that 'any international event may be described from any such perspective.'[237]

Nevertheless, specialisms do not develop as a progressive move, rather 'they grow spontaneously'; 'they emerge from field-construction of narration, of pinning informal labels on aspects of the world that describe them from the perspective of particular interests or objectives.'[238] Rather than a natural occurrence, the use of a particular specialism and its institutional bias is, in fact, ideological. Of relevance here are the competing ideas over the concept of war crimes trials that in turn reflects the image of the international criminal law regime. Simpson captures this as four interdependent positions over the 'political' whereas Simpson reads war crimes trials as a 'politics of compromise between liberal cosmopolitanism (procedural justice/equality before the law/individualism) and illiberal particularism (anti-formal, violent, sometimes chauvinistic/exceptional and collective)'.[239] The international criminal tribunals themselves seem to view their own practice as a formal institution that represents the international community in its struggle 'against impunity'.[240] This idiom struggles for hegemony against other idioms, such as the 'centre' and its preference for stability between sovereign equals. As Koskenniemi observes, the *Arrest Warrant* was a hegemonic struggle over human rights themes where the authority of human rights bodies was challenged by alternative preferences: 'rights were trumped by traditional rules of diplomatic law.'[241] However, indeterminacy reveals that every specialism is subject to the same oscillation between individual and community, normativity and concreteness.[242]

231 ibid 11.
232 ibid 9.
233 ibid.
234 ibid (re-definition means regimes may be transformed).
235 ibid 11. See also M Koskenniemi 'The Lady Doth Protest too Much: Kosovo and the Turn to Ethics in International Law' (2002) 65 *Modern Law Review* 159.
236 ibid 12.
237 ibid.
238 ibid.
239 G Simpson Law, War and Crime: War Crimes, Trials and the Reinvention of International Law (Polity Press London 2007).
240 See *Prosecutor v. Dusko Tadic* (Decision on Defence Motion on Jurisdiction) IT-94- 1 (10 August 1995), para 42.
241 Koskenniemi (n 211) 209.
242 Koskenniemi (n 219) 12.

Consequently, each specialism has its contentious positions with each group of experts 'divided among themselves . . . about how to understand the world and what to do with it', as the functional vocabulary is indeterminate.[243]

In light of the indeterminacy critique and in terms of 'a progressive choice', Koskenniemi advocates for a 'culture of formalism' that he sees as a 'culture of resistance to power, a social practice of accountability, openness and equality whose status cannot be reduced to [particular] political positions'.[244] Yet his choice to refer to 'law' in the administrative of international matters – instead of, for example, 'morality' or 'rational choice' – is not 'political[ly] innocent'.[245] It is based on the culture's ideals of 'accountability, equality, reciprocity and transparency' quite apart from 'whatever historical baggage, including bad faith, such culture entails'.[246] This demands that international actors think of their positions in universal or general terms, as part of a community, and may resist 'the pull towards imperialism' that views the social world in terms of their own idiosyncratic interests.[247] It is a demand to think in institutional terms as well as a community to accountability, binding oneself to the outcomes of the debate regardless of one's own preferences. Law's critical function then is the capacity to provide a process of justification that forces actors to submit 'to critique and dialogue with others about the proper understanding of the community's principles and purposes', that is, both justification and disputing the destination.[248] This culture is as against or in opposition to what is referred to as 'culture of dynamism', a culture that supports instrumentalism where certain idiosyncratic preferences are the starting point and any deviation is foreclosed.[249] It is in this sense (as against a culture of dynamism, in a relationship of mutual critique) that law's culture of formalism can be given meaning and is subject to the play of interpretations. Therefore, the culture of formalism's progressive choice (and its exclusion) is to be hegemonic over dynamism and a tendency towards managerialism (or expert rule). This means that its 'emancipatory politics' is assuring against a culture where only certain preferences are sponsored.

243 ibid 13.

244 M Koskenniemi, *The Gentle Civilizer of Nations: International Law 1870–1960* (Cambridge University Press Cambridge 2001) 500.

245 ibid 504. Kotiaho notes that this culture remains embedded within the 'same liberal theory of politics' yet we observed that this liberal theory contains both its inherited tradition ('naturalism') and the critique of that tradition ('positivism') so that the former appears to be a 'white ghost' in the latter. The culture of formalism then pulls on Derrida's idea that the double gesture reverses the prevailing distinctions (a structure we inherit and cannot avoid) and seeks to displace those concepts 'opening up [the text of the tradition] and pushing it beyond itself'. See Kotiaho (n 118) and Luedemann (n 33) 28.

246 ibid.

247 ibid. In this sense, rather than ensure international lawyers appear to avoid the 'depths of apology or highs of utopia' (as these are not fixed sensibilities), this culture serves to resist instrumentalism. See Kotiaho (n 118) 6.

248 M Koskenniemi, 'The Place of Law in Collective Security', (1996) 17 *Michigan Journal of International Law* 455, 479.

249 Koskenniemi (n 243) 496.

Conclusion

Modern international law is riddled with opposing doctrine where for every principle, there is a counter-principle and for every rule, there is an exception. The structural properties of legal argument account for the endless repetition of binaries that at a surface level permit any position to be put forward and counter-argued by an opposing approach. This illustrates how the competing positions in legal discourse are indistinguishable at the structural level of argument, because each position simultaneously draws on both positions and thus, they merge into one another. The bleeding or merging of the binary positions means that each position depends for meaning on its supplementary (or counter-) point. This produces a phenomenon of reversibility whereby each argument or position is reversible, because both positions can connect to either descending or ascending patterns. We noted that this interchangeability of positions occurs given the fluidity of the social context behind the competing logics. In this sense, both logics are associable with any political project and not fixed upon one particular political project. Consequently, as each position is self-contradictory, no legal argument can have preference over another and therefore, international law's indeterminacy compels a move to equitable standards and a political decision between opposing legal projects based on the particular rationality of the legal profession, according to the structural bias of the deciding institution. This is a move to political choice that cannot be reconciled with the assumption of the rule of law in liberal thought as politically neutral.

We noted then that the liberal project, with its notion of an objective rule of law, masks how 'social conflict must still be solved by political means [and] must, *for reasons internal to the ideal itself*, rely on essentially contested – political principles' in order to defend the outcomes to international law disputes.[250] We observed also how international law debates suggest that two projects characterize international law, one of unity and the other of diversity. In so doing, international law 'offers a defence for hegemonic and non-hegemonic practices equally'.[251] This is the operation of the language of international law as a battleground or a site of politics in which participants struggle for hegemony over their opponents.[252] In light of these observations, the move to specialisms is significant because each situation or event is described according to the preference and ethos of the particular specialism. Rather than a natural occurrence, the use of a particular specialism and its institutional bias is, in fact, ideological. Here, we noted the competing ideas surrounding war crimes trials and the clash of idioms over addressing issues involving post-conflict societies. Therefore, in particular, the techniques of indeterminacy and hegemonic positions inform the analysis of the rhetorical moves within the debate surrounding universal jurisdiction, as explored in Chapters 4 and 5.

250 Koskenniemi (n 110) 7, original emphasis.
251 Koskenniemi (n 221) 241.
252 Jouannet (n 9) 7.

References

Bassiouni, MC 'Universal Jurisdiction for International Crimes: Historical Perspectives and Contemporary Practice' (2001) 42 *Virginia Journal of International Law* 81.

Becker, S 'Universal Jurisdiction: How Universal Is it?' (2003) 12 *Palestine Yearbook of International Law* 49.

Bouissac, P *Saussure: A Guide for the Perplexed* (Continuum London 2010) 86.

Cairo-Arusha Principles of Universal Jurisdiction in Respect of Gross Human Rights Offences: An African Perspective, URL: http://www.afla.unimaas.nl/en/act/uj.html.

Carty, A 'Critical International Law: Recent Trends in the Theory of International Law' (1991) 2 *European Journal of International Law* 66.

Chesterman, S 'Beyond Fusion Fallacy: The Transformation of Equity and Derrida's 'The Force of Law'' (1997) 24(3) *Journal of Law and Society* 350.

Cooper, R 'Modernism, Post-Modernism and Organizational Analysis 3: The Contribution of Jacques Derrida' (1989) 10(4) *Organizational Studies* 479.

Cover, R 'Violence and the Word' (1986) 95 *Yale Law Journal* 1601.

Culler, J *On Deconstruction* (Routledge London 1983).

Derrida, J *Margins of Philosophy* A Bass (tr) (University of Chicago Press Chicago 1982).

Derrida, J *Negotiations: Interventions and Interviews, 1971–2001* E Rottenberg (tr) (Stanford University Press Stanford 2002).

Derrida, J *Of Grammatology* G Chakravorty Spivak (tr) (Johns Hopkins University Press Baltimore 1997).

Derrida, J *Positions* A Bass (tr) (Continuum London 2004).

Derrida, J 'The Force of Law: The Mystical Foundation of Authority' in G Anidjar *Acts of Religion* (Routledge London 2002).

Derrida, J *Writing and Difference* A Bass (tr) (Routledge London 1978).

Desantels-Stein, J 'Back in Style' (2014) 25 Law and Critique.

De Saussure, F *Course of General Linguistics* R Harris (tr) (Bloomsbury London 2013).

De Visscher, C *Theory and Reality in Public International law* (PE Corbett tr, Princeton University Press Princeton 1957).

Douzinas, C 'Violence, Justice, Deconstruction' (2005) 6 *German Law Journal* 171.

Hart, HL *The Concept of Law* (Clarendon Press Oxford 1961).

Henzelin, M *Le Principe de l'universalité en droit penal international* (Helbing & Lichtenhahn Bruylant 2000).

International Law Association 'Final Report on the Exercise of Universal Jurisdiction of Gross Human Rights Offences' (London 2000).

Johns, F et al (eds) *Events: The Force of International Law* (Routledge London 2010).

Jouannet, E 'A Critical Introduction' in M Koskenniemi *The Politics of International Law* (Hart Publishing 2011).

Kelsen, H *Introduction to the Problems of Legal Theory* BL Paulson and S Paulson (tr) (Clarendon Press Oxford 1992).

Kennedy, D *International Legal Structures* (Nomos Baden-Baden 1987) 7.

Kennedy, D 'International Law and the Nineteenth Century: History of Illusion' (1996) 65 *Nordic Journal of International Law* 385.

Kennedy, D 'The Last Treatise: Project and Person (A Reflection on Martti Koskenniemi)' (2006) 7 *German Law Journal* 982.

Kennedy, D 'A Semiotics of Legal Argument' (1991) 42 *Syracuse Law Review* 75.

Kennedy, D 'Roll over Beethoven' (1984) *Stanford Law Review* 1.

Kennedy, D 'Freedom and Constraint in Adjudication: A Critical Phenomenology' (1986) 36(4) *Journal of Legal Education* 518.

Kennedy, D *A Critique of Adjudication* (Cambridge University Press Cambridge 1998).
Kennedy, D 'A Semiotics of Critique' (2001) 22 *Cardozo Law Review* 1147.
Koskenniemi, M 'The Politics of International Law' (1990) 1 *European Journal of International Law* 4.
Koskenniemi, M 'International Law in a Post-Realist Era', (1995) 16 *Australian Yearbook of International Law* 1, 4.
Koskenniemi, M 'The Place of Law in Collective Security', (1996) 17 *Michigan Journal of International law* 455.
Koskenniemi, M 'Style as Method' (1999) 98 *American Journal of International Law* 352.
Koskenniemi, M *The Gentle Civilizer of Nations: International Law 1870–1960*, (Cambridge University Press Cambridge 2001).
Koskenniemi, M 'The Lady Doth Protest too Much: Kosovo and the Turn to Ethics in International Law' (2002) 65 *Modern Law Review* 159.
Koskenniemi, M 'International Law and Hegemony: A Reconfiguration' (2004) 17 *Cambridge Review of International Affairs* 197.
Koskenniemi, M *From Apology to Utopia: The Structure of International Legal Argument* (Cambridge University Press Cambridge 2005).
Koskenniemi, M, 'Global Legal Pluralism: Multiple Regimes and Multiple Modes of Thought', (Harvard University March 2005), URL: *http://www.helsinki.fi/eci/Publications/Koskenniemi/MKPluralism-Harvard-05d[1].pdf.*
Koskenniemi, M 'A Response', (2006) 7 *German Law Journal* 1103.
Koskenniemi, M 'The Politics of Law: Twenty Years Later', (2009) 20(1) *European Journal of International law* 7.
Koskenniemi, M *The Politics of International Law* (Hart Publishing Oxford 2011).
Kotiaho, P 'A Return to Koskenniemi; or the Disconcerting Co-Optation of Rupture', (2012) 13(5) *German Law Journal* 483.
Luedemann, S *Politics of Deconstruction: A New Introduction to Jacques Derrida* (Stanford University Press Stanford 2014).
MacIntyre, A *After Virtue a study in moral theory* (3rd edn University of Notre Dame Press 2007).
Merrills, JG *The Anatomy of International Law: A study of the Role of International Law in the Contemporary World* (2nd edn Sweet and Maxwell London 1981).
Norris, C *Derrida* (Harvard University Press Cambridge 1987).
O'Brien, E 'The Force of Law in Seamus Heaney's Greek Translations' in L Fitzpatrick (ed) *Performing Violence in Contemporary Ireland* (Careysfort Press Dublin 2010).
Onuf, N 'Book Review and Notes: *From Apology to Utopia: The Structure of the International Legal Argument* by Martii Koskenniemi' (1990) 84 *American Journal of International Law* 771.
Politis, N 'Le Problème des Limitations de la Souverainetè et la thèorie de l'abus des droits dan les rapports internationaux' (1925) 6 *Recueil des Cours* 1.
Princeton Project on Universal Jurisdiction 'Princeton Principles on Universal Jurisdiction' (Princeton University Princeton 2000).
Purvis, V 'Critical Legal Studies in Public International Law' (1991) 32 *Harvard Journal of International Law* 81.
Randall, KC 'Universal Jurisdiction in International Law', (1988) 66 *Texas International Law Journal* 785.
Reydams, L *Universal Jurisdiction: International and National Perspectives* (Oxford University Press Oxford 2003).
Schmitt, C *Political Theology* G Schwab (tr) (2nd edn University of Chicago Press Chicago 2005).

Singh, S 'The Critic(al) Subject' in W Werner (eds) *Koskenniemi and his Critics* (Draft paper), URL: http://www.academia.edu/15750896/The_Critic_al_Subject_2016_forthcoming_.

Simpson, G *Law, War and Crime: War Crimes, Trials and the Reinvention of International Law* (Polity Press London 2007).

Stawarska, B *Saussure's Philosophy of Language as Phenomenology: Undoing the Doctrine of the Course of General Linguistics* (Oxford University Press Oxford 2015).

Ullmann, W *Law and Politics in the Middle Ages: an Introduction the Sources of Medieval Political Ideas* (Cornell University Press New York 1976).

United Nations General Assembly 'The Scope and application of the principle of universal jurisdiction (Agenda 86)' URL: http://www.un.org/en/ga/sixth/70/universal_jurisdiction.shtml.

Unger, R *Knowledge and Politics* (Free Press New York 1975).

Verdross, A 'Fondement du Droit International' (1927) 16 *Recueil des Cours* 1.

Virally, M 'Panorama du Droit International Contemporain' (1983) 183 *Recueil des Cours* 5.

Woolsey, LH 'Extraterritorial Crime' (1926) 20 *American Journal of International Law* 726.

Zahar, A and Sluiter, G *International Criminal Law* (Oxford University Press Oxford 2008).

United Nations General Assembly 'The Scope and application of the principle of universal jurisdiction (Agenda 86)' URL: http://www.un.org/en/ga/sixth/70/universal_jurisdiction.shtml.

2 Narratives of justification from 1883

'Like other modern institutions, war crimes trials deploy narratives of justification' that refer to 'origins, struggles and ideals that led to the current status'[1] and within this practice is an attempt 'to actively construct the legitimacy of the trial'.[2] Simultaneously, those objecting to the tribunal's claim of legitimacy construct a counter-narrative that contests those same origins, struggles and ideals. This chapter explores those narratives at various junctures from the late nineteenth century onwards[3] and in so doing, it looks beyond the 'commonplace view that there are a single, homogeneous periods when "international law" has been either this or that'.[4] Instead, it aims at a reading of the history of international law as 'a complex set of practices and ideas . . . and the way we engage in them or interpret them cannot be dissociated from the larger professional, academic or political projects we have'.[5] As Berman argues, a legal history that is written with the aim of 'furthering linear progress . . . tend[s] to gloss over legal history's fundamental breaks and controversies' and isolate that history from other cultural developments.[6]

The practice of war crimes trials indicate how institutions have constructed particular 'history-making practices' that reflect the debate between 'two ways of thinking about history', which in turn has 'infected jurisdictional rules'.[7] There is the preference for 'linear arrangements' over chaotic histories despite 'a greater

1 M Koskenniemi 'The Preamble of the Universal Declaration of Human Rights' in G Alfredsson and A Eide (eds) *The Universal Declaration of Human Rights: A Common Standard of Achievement* (1999) 27 and 30.

2 S Stolk 'The Record on Which History will Judge Us Tomorrow': Auto-History in the Opening Statements of International Criminal Trials' (2015) 28(4) *Leiden Journal of International Law* 993, 994.

3 D Kennedy 'Primitive Legal Scholarship' (1986) 27(1) *Harvard International Law Journal* 1 (the end of the nineteenth century as a period considered to be instrumental in the turn towards a modern international legal profession).

4 M Koskenniemi *Gentle Civilizer of Nations: International Law since 1870* (Cambridge University Press Cambridge 2005) 7.

5 ibid.

6 N Berman 'Modernism, Nationalism and the Rhetoric of Reconstruction' (1992) 4 *Yale Journal of Law and the Humanities* 353.

7 G Simpson 'Linear Law: The History of International Criminal Law' in C Schwoebel (ed) *Critical Approaches to International Criminal Law: An Introduction* (Routledge London 2014) 169.

acceptance that histories are accounts of the past or interpretations of a set of materials about an existing past'.[8] Nevertheless, given the defence arguments, war crimes trials 'do produce pluralist histories' that form an 'unauthorized legacy' of the trials.[9] Another feature is how war crimes trials may prefer 'individual agency over structural causation'.[10] In other words, tribunals prefer the idea of the 'historical agency' of individuals during great historical crises (or the 'Great Man' theory of history) over materialist histories, that attribute change to structural forces or collective will 'against which individuals men and women are powerless'.[11]

In this sense, although international lawyers were 'interested in the same phenomena in particular periods', they approached those same phenomena from different positions 'that reflected national background, political preferences and personal idiosyncrasies'.[12] There is an overwhelming Eurocentrism yet Koskenniemi also notes how there are some exclusions and inclusions that reflect disciplinary struggles within the legal profession, with international law's others and 'with the production and reproduction of more general cultural hierarchies'.[13] As we observe in this chapter, debates over jurisdictional rules produces pluralist narratives that reflect competing accounts of the past and disciplinary concerns and struggles. Therefore, each narrative pulls from a set of multiple interpretations that are then re-described according to larger projects within particular contemporary disciplinary styles. We see each moment's hegemonic and counter-hegemonic positions and when we observe all the various junctures, we can recognize discontinuities, along with continuities.[14]

1 The move to 'positivism'

Kennedy argues that in the conventional story of the field's history, the nineteenth century is remembered in two ways: as the philosophical struggle between naturalism and positivism, and 'as a classical period' that established 'basic doctrinal and philosophical underpinnings for international law – sovereignty, the state – only to be eroded, rejected and replaced by twentieth century international law'.[15] It is 'an image of the pre-modern' against which the progress of the discipline is measured, seen as moving from 'coexistence to cooperation, from autonomy to community'.[16] Consequently, the discipline reads the nineteenth century as 'firmly a thing of the past'[17] and Kennedy suggests that this is considered the

8 ibid 166 (linear histories 'excludes or flattens some of the quirks or anomalies').
9 ibid 169.
10 ibid 170.
11 ibid 161–2.
12 Koskenniemi (n 4) 7.
13 ibid 9.
14 ibid 9.
15 D Kennedy 'International Law and the Nineteenth Century: History of an Illusion' (1996) 65 *Nordic Journal of International Law* 385, 386–7.
16 ibid.
17 ibid 387.

nineteenth century's main disciplinary contribution: 'turning itself into a past, a past related only obliquely to its own theoretical and doctrinal practices'.[18] In this sense, modern lawyers remember 'a diplomatic system' whose failures precipitated the move to institutions that 'rejected the nineteenth century system of power politics'.[19] Therefore, this 'Age of Empires' is remembered, in general, by the 'poisonous and mistrustful nature of nineteenth century European diplomacy'.[20] It is also really only viewed in its latter stage from 1870 onwards when empire, commerce and nationalism were at their apex – and 'as largely a European story' by isolating events that act as 'immature precursors for contemporary arrangements'.[21]

Accordingly, in one reading, the nineteenth century is recalled as a 'pre-legal international world of politics, war, religion and ideology' – a period dominated by developments in philosophy and theoretical struggles over foundations.[22] Here, the move to 'positivism'[23] among nineteenth-century international lawyers occurred due to the increasing criticism of the language style of natural law lawyers as 'suspect and unpersuasive'.[24] Positivism answered the field's key dilemma of how to justify a law between sovereigns, when sovereignty 'by definition admits no higher authority', by originating the law's binding force in consent of sovereigns.[25] In this way, 'international law rid itself of faith only by enshrining the state' and in turn, international lawyers 'became priests', simultaneously sceptical and deferential to absolute state authority that 'renders legal order among sovereigns *implausible* in the first place'.[26] Nevertheless, nineteenth-century texts demonstrate how international lawyers were less engaged in philosophical response to the field's key dilemma and rather sought to describe 'what seemed a self-evident system of rules'.[27] In terms of dominant disciplinary performance at the time, Kennedy calls the period 'a self-confident period of invention and renewal of what was then thought to have been a long-established tradition'.[28] In this sense, developments in the nineteenth century occurred 'in close relation' to the 'second globalization of legal thought', when lawyers across the legal world absorbed the idea of law as having a sociological base and function.[29] Therefore, Kennedy shows that it was

18 ibid 390 (the story of the nineteenth century is the story of twentieth century's 'originalism and the origins of that exceptionalism').

19 ibid 392.

20 Simpson (n 7) 167.

21 Kennedy (n 15) 391–2. See also Koskenniemi (n 4) 9 and A Martineau 'Overcoming Eurocentrism? Global History and the Oxford Handbook of the History of International Law' (2014) 25(1) *European Journal of International Law* 329.

22 ibid 397.

23 On a more nuanced understanding of positivism, see Chapter 1, section 2.

24 M Koskenniemi 'Into Positivism: Georg Friedrich von Martens (1756–1821) and Modern International Law' (2008) 15(2) *Constellations* 189.

25 Kennedy (n 15) 398.

26 ibid, 399–400 (failure to avert war read as 'futility of philosophy'), original emphasis.

27 ibid 401.

28 D Kennedy 'When Renewal Repeats: Thinking Against the Box' (2000) 32 *NYU Journal of International Law and Policy* 335, 340.

29 M Koskenniemi '"Not Accepting the Iroquois Themselves . . .": Sociological Thought and International Law', *Max Weber Lecture* (April 2007), 1.

early twentieth-century reinterpretations of the pre-1900 period which divided nineteenth-century lawyers into either positivists or naturalists, as opposed to this period of philosophy as remembered by later generations.[30]

According to the other reading, the nineteenth century produced a classical system with a particular notion of sovereignty as a pivoting point for a universal international law that organized the relations between 'civilized' and 'uncivilized' states.[31] This idea of a 'single sovereignty' was a 'scientific project' to late nineteenth-century lawyers, who were keen to establish a 'common sovereignty . . . a shared project of universalization . . . broader than national traditions [and] the difference between civil and common law'.[32] This 'shared project' was seen in the increased use of the private law analogy in international treaties and the acceptance of concepts of territoriality and state theory drawn from German private and public law tradition.[33] It was evident in the influence of German public law that conceived the image of the Holy Roman Empire as the 'ideal frame' for organizing European states.[34] It was reflected in the move away from different normative systems in the early nineteenth century to a single uniform order with a distinction drawn between private and public international law in legal consciousness.[35] It was also seen in how this 'single sovereignty' was shaped and defined through the colonial encounter in the late nineteenth century.[36] Legal rules defined, identified and categorized the 'uncivilized'[37] and institutions were established to whom membership was restricted to those societies willing to accept the legal rules of the European powers.[38] Sovereignty, delimited by territorial boundaries, was 'in the language of absolute rights to property and freedom of contract' and states had exclusive rights over their territory, 'treating the States on analogy with individuals'.[39] Law originated in and could only bind by consent of sovereigns.[40] Beyond sovereignty was either territory to be colonized or an outlaw (the pirate) to be subject of exceptional jurisdiction; it was an alternative of 'civilization and everywhere else, a space

30 Kennedy (n 15) 403.
31 ibid. See also L Obregon 'The Civilized and the Uncivilized' in B Fassbender and A Peters (eds) *Oxford Handbook of History of International Law* (Oxford University Press Oxford 2012).
32 ibid 405. S
33 A Carty *The Decay of International Law: A Reappraisal of the Limits of the Legal Imagination in International Affairs* (Manchester University Press Manchester 1986), 10.
34 Koskenniemi (n 24) 191.
35 Kennedy (n 15) 406 and 411 (noting the existence of many sovereigns and types of sovereignty).
36 A Anghie *Imperialism, Sovereignty and the Making of International Law* (Cambridge University Press Cambridge 2005).
37 H Kleinschmidt 'The Family of Nations as an Element of the Ideology of Colonialism' (2016) *Journal of the History of International Law* 1, 5.
38 ibid 4. See also Koskenniemi (n 4) 72–3 (international law as 'an effect of European culture, instead of habits of diplomacy', that is, 'based on the cultural processes of Europe, a process of "civilization" – in contrast to which the cultural process of other nations could be understood as half-civilized or savage').
39 Carty (n 33) 50–51.
40 ibid 16 (pulled on 'Vattel's system in which "nations" existed in a state of nature' with certain 'fundamental' legal qualities that may be modified by tacit or express consent).

beyond (or . . . before) international law'.[41] In this sense, international law no longer regulated behaviour within territories but rather delimited spheres of jurisdiction.[42]

1.1 The fugitive offender and the enemy irregular

Article 1 of the Institute of International Law's 1873 Statute spoke of the 'legal conscience of the civilized world' and therefore, 'to articulate and to represent this *conscience* became the task of the international law profession'.[43] The meaning of 'conscience' merged 'romantic sensibility with Enlightenment rationalism', that is, some kind of common moral attitude within European societies combined with an idea of an objective truth.[44] The Institute read law as science in a way that 'linked law to popular consciousness as represented by the legal profession'.[45] In its 1883 session, the Institute issued a resolution on criminal jurisdiction at a time when there remained conflicts between territorial states and jurisdiction founded on allegiance.[46] The dominant turn towards an absolute sovereignty (and international law as a regulator of jurisdiction) shaped the focus of the resolution. Territoriality was foundational and any jurisdiction outside its territory was narrowly conceived.[47] Therefore, on the latter, it recognized jurisdiction over acts causing effects in territory, jurisdiction over acts by nationals abroad and over acts against the security of the state (so long as the acts are not criminal in territorial jurisdiction).[48] It also recognized a right of every 'Christian state (or recognizing principles of Christian states)' to a complementary or subsidiary jurisdiction of the state with custody of the alleged offender.[49] This right was also narrowly conceived as it was triggered only when the location of the offence was unknown or where extradition was rejected or deemed dangerous.[50] Consequently, the absolute sovereignty of the state of location of the offence continues to be respected and in this sense, the resolution reflects the nineteenth-century disciplinary style of seeing a conflict between rights as only implicating one sovereignty.[51]

41 Kennedy (n 15) 412 and Carty (n 33) 52–3 (writers excluded the 'question of political legitimacy . . . from any consideration in law of territory').

42 Carty (n 33) 53 *et passim* (use of private property analogies was designed to 'make it conceptually impossible' to explore a people's right to self-determination').

43 Koskenniemi (n 4) 47, original emphasis.

44 ibid.

45 ibid, 48.

46 RE Mensel 'Jurisdiction in Nineteenth Century International Law and its Meaning in the Citizenship clause of the Fourteenth Amendment' (2012–13) 32 *St. Louis University Public Law Review* 331 and LA Benton *Law and Colonial Culture: Legal Regimes in World History 1400–1900* (Cambridge University Press Cambridge 2002).

47 Kennedy (n 15), 409 and Carty (n 33).

48 Institute of International Law 'Règles relatives aux conflits des lois pénales en matière de compétence' (1883–85) 7 *Annuaire de l'Institut de droit international* (Munich Session 1883) Articles 1–8.

49 ibid Article 10.

50 ibid.

51 Kennedy (n 15) 414.

It follows that this right applied only to those within the 'Family of Nations' or those on the semi-periphery that had assimilated to European legal culture. As noted above, the absolute notion of sovereignty was conceived by academic and professional culture of the Great Powers in a manner that declassified colonial territories as sovereign, justified by the colonizers' 'civilizing mission'.[52] In this sense, indigenous societies were no longer viewed as possessing sovereign power as had been assumed since Vitoria.[53] Indigenous legal institutions could not bind late nineteenth-century European colonial powers, and 'the Orient' was viewed as having the potential 'with increased civilization' to assimilate or conform to European states.[54] Nevertheless, Lorca draws on the practice of semi-peripheral states and underlines how non-Western jurists appropriated and internalized the "classical" system, reinterpreting the rules as applicable to non-Western states and in turn, being critical for the universalizing of international law.[55] The resolution also reflected jurisdiction recognized in continental legal traditions that dominated the Institute's outlook.[56] These continental legal traditions justified this subsidiary jurisdiction upon a historical tradition of surrender or try. This historical tradition was traced by de Vabres (and later Reydams) to the sixteenth-century jurist Covarruvias, who re-described the earlier notion of a jurisdiction of the place of arrest (*judex deprehensionis*) over all dangerous fugitive offenders, drawn from the Italian Lombard League city states in the Middle Ages.[57] In keeping with the disciplinary style of that period, Covarruvias's re-description presupposed that the law of nations descended from a pre-existing normative code, a cosmopolitan or natural law order that was universal and applied to all societies, whether European or non-European.

The heritage of this disciplinary style is obvious in the kind of language adopted to justify the jurisdictional claim under Article 10. The Institute assumed 'a kind of solidarity among civilized states' to punish serious offences threatening 'human society' and to avoid 'absolute impunity'.[58] They also assumed that this solidarity was reflected in the comparable (*yet diverse*) national laws that in turn, demonstrated consent by states to a jurisdictional rule of international law. In this way, the Institute presupposed a normative (or cosmopolitan) order among

52 A Anghie 'Finding the Peripheries: Sovereignty and Colonialism in Nineteenth Century International Law' (1999) 40 *Harvard International Law Journal* 1, 2.

53 A Anghie 'Francisco De Vitoria and the Colonial Origins of International Law' (1996) 3 *Social and Legal Studies* 321.

54 M Koskenniemi 'The Civilizing Mission: International Law and the Colonial Encounter in the late 19th Century' (Bonn 2004), URL: http://www.helsinki.fi/eci/Publications/Koskenniemi/Bonn.pdf.

55 See AB Lorca 'Universal International Law: Nineteenth-Century Histories of Imposition and Appropriation' (2010) 51(2) *Harvard International Law Journal* 475.

56 Harvard Research on International Law, *Draft Convention on Jurisdiction with Respect to Crime* (1935) 29 *American Journal of International Law* Supplement 439 (Austrian Penal Code of 1852 as the exemplary example).

57 See L Reydams *Universal Jurisdiction: International and National Perspectives* (Oxford University Press Oxford 2003) 29.

58 Institute of International Law (n 48) 141–2.

'civilized' Christian states originating in what appears to be a common or universal idea of retributive justice over so-called offences threatening 'human society'. Simultaneously, they assumed that law had a sociological base and derived by consent of states within the 'Family of Nations', as reflected in the principles adopted in their domestic laws. Therefore, the idea of 'solidarity' sought to *neatly* reconcile the competing normative justifications of the Institute's members, exemplified by de Bar's justification in 'universal justice'[59] and Brusa's in 'domestic state security', that seemed to presuppose law derived either from a higher moral code or from state liberty.[60] Nevertheless, similar to later debates, the Institute tried to offset accusations of validating politically motivated trials or dismissal of its jurisdictional principle as utopian and unrealizable. Therefore, this subsidiary jurisdiction should be narrowly defined to avoid 'abuses', such as ill-founded complaints and arbitrary arrests.[61] The 1883 Resolution was influential because from the late nineteenth century to the 1930s, this subsidiary jurisdiction was included in the legislation of most continental states.[62] In the *Eichmann* case, the Israeli Trial Court drew heavily on de Vabres's historical narrative of the principle of 'universality' since the 16th century,[63] in order to present universal jurisdiction over crimes against international law as another progressive move within a long-standing historical legal tradition, as opposed to than an entirely 'new' endeavour.

International lawyers in the late nineteenth century also engaged in efforts to codify the laws and customs of war. Here, Berman argues that law's role has been to construct war 'as a separate sphere of human activity in which the "normal" rules of social life . . . do not operate':[64] 'Rather than *opposing* violence, the legal construction of war serves to *channel violence* into certain forms of activity engaged in by certain kinds of people'.[65] It is also highly contingent in that the construction of war has been contested in each move to codify since the late nineteenth century.[66] In the case of *jus in bello* (or what is referred to as international humanitarian law), the rules around 'irregular' forces in the late nineteenth and early twentieth centuries developed out of disputes between 'large and small European powers'.[67] In the Lieber Code, there was a distinction made between enemy soldiers who commit acts within the soldiers' privilege, and enemy irregulars, who commit such acts 'without any commission, without being part and portion of the organized army. . . .'[68] Enemy soldiers (as *hostes*) were afforded

59 See A Mercier 'Le conflit des lois pénales en matiére de competence' (1931) *Annuaire de l'Institut de Droit International* 87, 134 as cited in Reydams (n 1) 30–31.
60 ibid ('territorial jurisdiction' as presence threatens public order).
61 ibid 143.
62 See Harvard Research (n 56), 574–6.
63 D de Vabres *Les Principes Modernes du Droit Pénal International* (Sirey Paris 1928) 135 et seq.
64 N Berman 'Privileging Combat? Contemporary Conflict and the Legal Construction of War' (2004–05) 43 *Columbia Journal of Transnational Law* 1, 4–5.
65 ibid 5, original emphasis.
66 ibid.
67 ibid 6.
68 Article 82 of the *Instructions for the Government of the Armies of the United States in the Field* (24 August 1863).

prisoner-of-war status on capture for commission of lawful acts of war during hostilities.[69] However, enemy irregulars that committed acts without commission were to be 'treated summarily as highway robbers and pirates'.[70] In other words, enemy irregulars were considered 'outlaws' and denied the protections of the laws of war by belligerents in a conflict because they were not acting on behalf of any state.[71] They were, in legal terms, private individuals engaged in acts of war and subject to the ordinary criminal law.[72] As such, the acts of enemy irregulars were within the jurisdiction of the capturing state.[73] In this sense, the Lieber Code, in making an analogy to piracy, sought to deny enemy irregulars any status under laws of war and to justify exercising an exceptional jurisdiction that would permit a state to punish the offender irrespective of nationality.[74] Therefore, in the American Civil War, without the consent of the Confederate forces, the Union Armed forces claimed to have the right to punish enemy irregulars for offences committed outside state territory (whether or not in active hostilities) irrespective of any legal nexus to the offence and offender.

Nevertheless, the Lieber Code's narrative of justification sidestepped the endless opposing positions within historical debates towards the claim of jurisdiction over piracy committed on the high seas. Therefore, it serves our purposes to explore some of those debates in order to appreciate to what extent the Lieber Code concealed these oppositions. In one controversy, lawyers attempted to untangle what was agreed to be piracy *jure gentium* from definitions of piracy under municipal statutes.[75] Of particular interest is the debate on the importance of the 'private ends' or *animus furandi* element.[76] The *animus furandi* element was used by lawyers to make a distinction between the practices of piracy and privateering (or state-licensed sea robbery).[77] In this sense, a definition of piracy was generated as against (or relative to) a similar practice of commercial warfare that was exploited by sovereign powers to secure military objectives.[78] For privateering, a sovereign issued a state license or letters of marque and reprisal that

69 Lieber Code (n 68) (article 49). On the notion of 'hostes' or enemy, see D Heller-Roazen *The Enemy of All: Piracy and the Law of Nations* (Zone Books New York 2009) 99–102.

70 ibid (Article 82).

71 AP Rubin *The Law of Piracy* (University Press of the Pacific Honolulu 2006) 295 and Heller-Roazen (n 69) 103–18 (treated as 'common enemy' and denied protections as *hostes* under the laws of war).

72 H Kelsen 'Will the Judgment in the Nuremberg Trial Constitute a Precedent in International Law' (1947) 1 *International Law Quarterly* 153, 160.

73 WB Cowles 'Universal Jurisdiction over Violations of the Laws of War' (1945) 33(2) *California Law Review* 177, 189.

74 W Rech 'Rightless Enemies: Schmitt and Lauterpacht on Political Piracy' (2012) 32(2) *Oxford Journal of Legal Studies* 235, 246.

75 Harvard Research on International Law 'Draft Convention on Piracy' (1932) 26 *American Journal of International Law* Supplement 739, 750–51 and 769–85.

76 Rubin (n 71) 82.

77 E Kontorovich 'The Piracy Fallacy: Modern Universal Jurisdiction's Hollow Foundation' (2004) 45(1) *Harvard International Law Journal* 183, 211 and 217.

78 ibid, 217 (privateering fell outside the laws of war, yet was not punishable under municipal criminal law).

permitted private vessels to interfere with recognized or unrecognized belligerents and validated post-seizure title in the sovereign's prize courts.[79] Therefore, sovereign maritime powers delimited what was the legitimate use of violence based on distinguishing state sanctioned from non-state violence. Otherwise, the practices were analogous, that is, conducted by privately financed vessels for profit.[80] Over time, the formality of a state licence became less significant and instead, the courts would place more emphasis on deducing whether there were political motives and thereby, implying state authorization.

It follows that the dominant style in the late nineteenth century was to describe piracy *jure gentium* as robbery committed on the high seas for 'private ends' and therefore, restricted the definition to non-state violence.[81] However, states operated inconsistently in their behaviour because two leading maritime powers applied the term 'piracy' in their domestic laws on counter-insurgency. The British and American governments applied domestic statutes to acts whether committed on the high seas or in the territory of non-European states that were politically motivated rather than purely commercial warfare.[82] For instance, Rubin explores Lushington's interpretation of the British Bounty Act 1850 in situation of the *Segredo* to demonstrate that he made no distinction between acts for private ends and those for public motives.[83] In this way, the non-European insurgents were described as pirates when their acts threatened imperial interests, despite the evident lack of private motive or *animus furandi*. The dominant position of early twentieth-century international lawyers was to criticize this British and American claim as unlawful.[84] In this view, the private ends element was considered critical. As Simpson argues, the *Republic of Bolivia* case suggests that the 'controlling feature' of being a pirate is the 'lack of politics'.[85]

Subsequent writers depict the controversy in line with the twentieth-century reinterpretation of the nineteenth century as a period of philosophy and therefore, the controversy stems from the 'jurisprudential split' between 'naturalists' and 'positivists'.[86] The dominant style that restricts piracy to non-state violence is considered to be an accurate reflection of state behaviour (positivist). However, the piracy/privateering distinction can be accused of merely serving imperial interests of powerful maritime states. Historically, the distinction justified state commission of 'lawful' sea robbery, which seems to merely excuse power politics. In this sense, the positivist analysis of state behaviour uncritically privileges certain

79 CK Marshall 'Putting Privateers in Their Place: The Applicability of the Marque and Reprisal Clause to Undeclared Wars' (1997) 64 *University of Chicago Law Review* 953, 959 (accused of piracy if did not possess a valid letter of marque).

80 ibid 958 and 954.

81 Rubin (n 71) 295. See WE Hall *International Law* (8th edn Clarendon Press Oxford 1924) 310–11.

82 *The Magellan Pirates* (1853) 3 BILC 796 as cited in Rubin (n 71) 232–5.

83 Rubin (n 71) 232–5.

84 Hall (n 8) 310–11.

85 G Simpson *Law, War and Crime: War Crimes, Trials and the Reinvention of International Law* (Polity Press London 2007), 165.

86 Rubin (n 71) 309–10.

behaviour in earlier historical periods, which, in turn, in the resolve to reflect state liberty as closely as possible, would deny law's normativity. From this positivist analysis, international lawyers then described the British and American practice in the nineteenth century as mere naturalistic interpretations or dismissed as purely serving imperial interests.[87] For our purposes, the conflicting behaviour of maritime powers in the nineteenth century was pulled upon in 1930s by Carl Schmitt and Hersch Lauterpacht in order to justify diametrically opposed definitions of piracy.

Another controversy among nineteenth-century lawyers was whether the definition of piracy involved an offence against the law of nations, for which there was direct liability of an individual under international law, or a municipal law offence that gave rise to an exception to the exclusive jurisdiction of the flag state. The former seemed to presuppose a pre-existing legal order, while the latter seemed to presuppose that law derived from a sociological base. This debate, in turn, affected jurisdictional rules and led to competing positions on justifying states exercising jurisdiction over acts committed on the high seas. One interpretation premised the jurisdiction on the nature of the offence and pulled upon the idea of an 'outlaw' or 'public enemy' that was adopted historically by natural law lawyers to justify the punishment (or execution) of certain persons as falling outside the laws of war.[88] Both De Vattel and Grotius considered that the crimes of the 'outlaw' gave rise to a right of a sovereign in whose territory the offender had fled to exact *punishment*,[89] that is, a situation arising post-conviction in the territorial jurisdiction.[90] This right was conditional in that it depended on whether the place of the commission of the crime sought the offender's return.[91] Both scholars appeared to emphasize one or other of what was identified as characteristics of the crime as justification for claiming jurisdiction. De Vattel described the crimes as 'by their character and frequency . . . a menace to public security everywhere',[92] whereas Grotius described the crimes as affecting 'human society'.[93]

During the eighteenth and early nineteenth centuries, these notions of an 'enemy of mankind'[94] or 'common danger (of mankind)'[95] were drawn upon by certain international lawyers to provide a normative justification for piracy as an offence against the law of nations, giving rise to this natural right of the sovereign. As such, all individuals were bound under the universal moral order and, if in breach, must be held directly individually responsible. In this sense, Lorimer contended that 'when the law of nations exercises criminal jurisdiction directly, it deals with persons whom

87 ibid (read 'valid' state practice as instances of acting against the material interests of that state).

88 Rubin (n 71) 18–19 (noting certain sixteenth-century interpretations that led to the loss of the pirate's law of war status).

89 E de Vattel *Law of Nations or the Principles of Natural Law* Book I, Chapter XIX CG Fenwick (tr) (Carnegie Institution Washington, DC 1916) paras 232 and 233.

90 H Grotius *De Jure Belli Ac Pacis Libri Tres* FW Kelsey (tr) (Clarendon Press Oxford 1925) 527.

91 ibid 526 and 533.

92 De Vattel (n 89) para 232 and 233.

93 Grotius (n 90) 527.

94 W Blackstone *Commentaries on the Laws of England* Vol 4 (Clarendon Press Oxford 1765–1769) 71.

95 *Case of the SS Lotus France v Turkey)* (1927) PCIJ Ser. A No 10, 95 (Dissent of Altamira).

it claims as its own citizens.'[96] Such 'cosmopolitan criminals' ceased to be state citizens because they had violated the 'laws of humanity as a whole, and become enemies of the human race'.[97] Lorimer's ideas seem to be a repetition of Molloy's position within the debate among English lawyers in the sixteenth century. Molloy considered that *under the law of nature*, English courts had jurisdiction over pirate vessels of non-nationals where the acts against English vessels or where victim and perpetrator were present in English territory and the victim's state did not proceed.[98]

Nevertheless, another interpretation justified the jurisdiction on the threat to the common interest of states in their maritime commerce. Harvard Research's 'Draft Convention on the Law of Piracy' constructed from the literature a meaning of piracy as a 'special, common basis of jurisdiction'.[99] In this sense, piracy was a municipal offence that gave rise to an exception to the exclusivity of territorial jurisdiction and therefore, international law was 'permissive only', allowing states to establish jurisdiction in their municipal law even though the crime was committed outside the territory of the state.[100] This was normatively justified on the collective interest in maintaining the safety of commerce on the high seas.[101] Harvard Research's interpretation seems to reflect Jenkins's position within the aforementioned debate in the sixteenth century, that justified the extension of English municipal law jurisdiction to non-national vessels for acts against non-national vessels when public peace and security of navigation required it. This was presupposed upon a jurisdictional lacuna in the normal jurisdictional rules.[102] Even so, Harvard Research referred to the inconsistencies in state behaviour, noting how many national law provisions based such jurisdiction on some nexus to the offence and how historical cases could be supported by one or other jurisdictional principles.[103] In so doing, they acknowledged that this comparative law analysis could justify the conclusion that piracy is not an exceptional basis of jurisdiction.[104] However, the Harvard Research's commentary dismissed the significance of these inconsistencies because of a common accord or consensus of states (the special jurisdiction was 'generally supported . . . by at least all seafaring states') and on normative grounds (the necessity of 'sea policing').[105]

It follows then that the Lieber Code's piracy analogy neither directly addressed debates within the literature over justifying jurisdiction over *piracy jure gentium* nor the definitional dilemma surrounding the concept.[106] With its reference to

96 J Lorimer *The Institutes of the Law of Nations: A Treatise of the Jural Relations of Separate Political Communities* Vol II (Blackwood & sons London 1883–84) 132.

97 ibid.

98 Rubin (n 71) 86–7.

99 Harvard Research (n 75) 757.

100 ibid 566 (normatively justified on communal interest in maintaining the safety of commerce on the high seas) and 760.

101 ibid.

102 Rubin (n 71) 88–9 (as pirates not subject to jurisdictional limits of European sovereigns).

103 Harvard Research (n 75) 760.

104 ibid 761.

105 ibid 760–61.

106 Rubin (n 71) 292.

the phrase 'without commission', it appears to read piracy as requiring *animus furandi* and in turn, pulled on the dominant disciplinary style in the nineteenth century. Yet, it also presupposed an analogy was justified based on this common characteristic and this appears to privilege an appeal to a normative higher order.[107] Nevertheless, the Lieber Code's analogy was influential in the late nineteenth century when the Institute of International Law addressed penal sanctions for violations of the laws of war in its 1880 *Manual of the Laws of War*. Under article 84, offenders against the laws of war would be liable under the ordinary criminal law of belligerents.[108] As the *Manual*'s commentary explained, this right could be invoked against an alleged perpetrator ('after a judicial hearing') by the belligerent 'into whose hands they are'.[109] This led to debate among American and French lawyers as to the parameters of this right of belligerents whether it was only over belligerents' own territory[110] or that it may extend to offences committed against nationals in enemy territory.[111] Similarly, the question of jurisdiction over offences committed during military occupation was contentious.[112]

The Institute's 1880 *Manual* appeared to have some influence on the Great Powers in revising *their* military manuals. The revised manuals stated that violations of the laws of war were to be treated as analogous to ordinary crime and prosecuted under domestic criminal law.[113] Nevertheless, the parameters of these jurisdictional claims were somewhat open-ended. There was a definite claim over national and enemy forces on the belligerent's own territory.[114] However, it was also possible to interpret the language within certain military manuals widely to encompass enemy nationals outside of the belligerent's territory. For instance, the French Code of Military Justice referred to 'every individual' and this could arguably have been interpreted broadly to include enemy nationals.[115] Simultaneously, the manuals provided counter-principles to their jurisdictional claims in the form of the doctrine of superior orders.[116] This meant that belligerents could only exercise their criminal jurisdiction over enemy irregulars (private persons) or enemy

107 Cowles (n 73) 177 (claiming support in state practice, citing United States' exercise jurisdiction over brigandage or piracy on land).

108 Institute of International Law 'Manual of the Laws of War on Land' (Oxford 1881–1882). See Project of an International Declaration concerning the Laws and Customs of War, Brussels, 27 August 1874 (influence of Lieber Code on substantive law).

109 Part III: Penal Sanctions.

110 JW Garner 'Punishment of Offenders against the Laws and Customs of War' (1920) 14 *American Journal of International Law* 70, 73–5.

111 Clunet cited in Garner (n 110) 78 (justifying belligerent's extraterritorial jurisdiction on security of the state).

112 ibid (acts of enemy forces during military occupation). Contrast L Renault 'De l'application du droit penal aux faits de guerre' (1918) 25 *Revue Général de Droit International Public* 5, 28.

113 Garner (n 110) 73–5.

114 Article 181 of the US Rules of Land Warfare and article 443 of the British Military Manual respectively.

115 Article 249 of the French Code of Military Justice as cited in Garner (n 110) 73.

116 Garner (n 110) 85 (no right to prosecute subordinates acting on orders of military superior, rather a right to prosecute captured enemy commanders).

commanders if they fell into the belligerent's hands.[117] As a result, failing capture of an enemy commander, the only resort was through lawful reprisals.[118]

2 The move to criminalizing war

It was during the inter-war period that nineteenth-century absolute sovereignty appeared to threaten the very possibility of international law and 'needed so earnestly to be rejected for law to be possible'.[119] It was a period filled with calls for modernizing the field that was read as producing an 'explosion break' from the nineteenth century and in this disciplinary practice, two agendas operated simultaneously: the desire for absolute sovereigns to be 'tamed, ruled and brought into institutions' and to engage in a 'systematic doctrinal assault' on absolute sovereignty of the nineteenth century.[120] In this sense, Kennedy argues that the doctrine ('in many ways the entire project') that arose in the post-war environment 'was both an act of recollection, revisiting, rewriting the nineteenth century and an act of innovative self-consciousness'.[121] Early twentieth-century lawyers projected back onto nineteenth century an image of absolute sovereignty as 'mystical' (when nineteenth-century lawyers had read their project as scientific) and then saw their reform as 'demystifying . . . reacting against a sovereignty which had been worshipped as absolute'.[122] It follows then that the post-war period is marked by international lawyers, who sought to reinvigorate or transform the practice of international law, whether liberal nationalists[123] or international legal Modernists.[124] For instance, in the sources doctrine, international lawyers constructed a 'style of argument that helped legitimize a project for the reconstruction of public international law'.[125] Through invoking the 'vocabulary of pragmatism', legitimacy was produced, a feeling of certainty created and 'all the different questions' that expose the indeterminacy were set aside.[126]

This 'intellectual posture' transformed 'international lawyers into polemicists for internationalism in a self-consciously evolutionary narrative, inaugurating a

117 GA Finch 'Superior Orders and War Crimes' (1921) 15 *American Journal of International Law* 440, 441–2 (an absolute rule of defence of superior orders would frustrate criminal prosecutions).

118 G Bower 'The Laws of War: Prisoners of War and Reprisals' (1915) 1 *Transactions of the Grotius Society* 23, 28.

119 Kennedy (n 15) 404.

120 ibid 389 and 403–4 respectively.

121 ibid 394–5.

122 ibid 405.

123 LV Smith 'The Wilsonian Challenge to International Law' (2011) 13 *Journal of the History of International Law* 179.

124 Berman (n 6) 354–7.

125 See T Skouteris 'The force of a doctrine: article 38 of the PCIJ Statute and the sources of international law' in F Johns, R Joyce and S Pahuja *Events: The Force of International Law* (Routledge London 2011), 78.

126 ibid.

disciplinary practice of progress narration'.[127] In the reforms, it is evident that international lawyers sought to distance themselves from sovereignty as normative and therefore, sovereign consent became the key ingredient of obligation. Yet due to the 'shrinking corpus of substantive doctrines', international lawyers deduced 'elaborations of sovereignty'[128] and in this way, deductions from sovereignty continued into the modern period. The formalist definition of the state, traced to the pre-war theory of the state, continued to be popular as international lawyers and politicians preferred to 'remain value-neutral towards democracy and dictatorship'.[129] However, Kennedy identifies a 'subtle shift' towards seeing two 'conflicting, if absolute, sovereignties' within a reciprocal system rather than a situation of only implicating one sovereignty.[130] This later leads to 'a fragmentation of sovereign rights which might then be balanced or exercised only where "reasonable"'.[131] In other words, rather than determining disputes based on a norm of exclusivity of jurisdiction of the location of the offence, there is a shift towards seeing the situation as two conflicting sovereignties between jurisdiction over territory and over extraterritorial acts.[132]

There was also a 'move to institutions' that contemporary international lawyers believed was a 'necessary and desirable' response to war – a progressive move towards peace.[133] Kennedy argues that the discipline's literature on origins of the institutions indicates three themes of break, movement and repetition. Reading the origin as a 'break' drew from diplomatic history and reads the war as punctuating 'an ambiguous difference between "old" and "new" order', a difference conceived as either a movement from chaos to order or from order to liberty.[134] Seeing the origins as movement treated pre-war institutions (such as arbitration) as scattered and thereby contrasted with the League as integrated and part of a 'mature' institutional regime.[135] Confirming and repeating the narrative of the League's origins, as part of its institutional practice, served to show the League to be 'able to continue the struggle against tyranny and chaos'.[136] Within the 'new' order, the Versailles settlement was the first time a state was subject to 'such intense levels of scrutiny [or to] a regime as punitive'.[137] It was the beginning

127 Kennedy (n 15) 390 (this 'continually resituates international law forward of what can then be remembered as the nineteenth century').

128 ibid 414.

129 A Carty 'Interwar German Theories of International Law: The Psychoanalytical and Phenomenological Perspectives of Hans Kelsen and Carl Schmitt' (1994–95) 16 *Cardozo Law Review* 1235 (theories responded to collapse of monarchical constitutional order and fear of power falling 'directly into the hands of the masses').

130 Kennedy (n 15) 414.

131 ibid.

132 ibid.

133 D Kennedy 'Move to Institutions' (1986–87) 8 *Cardozo Law Review* 841, 845.

134 ibid 854.

135 ibid 857–58.

136 ibid 867–8 (peace (providing order and liberty) is repeatedly juxtaposed against war ('radically different from organized life').

137 Simpson (n 85), 59.

of the notion of 'institutional oversight' of entire states and a move towards the Great Powers seeing themselves as representing an 'international community' with an underlying moral code, a move that Schmitt found intolerable. However, Simpson observes that this move meant the conditions for criminal law were met, that is, 'the self-consciousness (and self-righteousness) of a moral community (albeit one largely directed by the Great Powers)'.[138]

2.1 Submarine warfare and the 'piracy analogy'

It follows that a move to criminalize war infected the debates among lawyers at the Versailles Conference and during the inter-war period. This was motivated by the demand for war crimes trials in Germany and Allied states, which had originated from elites' either personal or political agendas that was then captured as a broader popular demand.[139] At Versailles, the Allies set up the Commission on the Responsibility of the Authors of the War whose deliberations ended up being particularly fractious.[140] The Commission was instructed to address whether there could be personal liability in the case of war either regarding authorship of the war or commission of violations of laws of war. Their conclusion that responsibility for initiating the war lay wholly with Germany and its allies had the advantage of offering an 'account of war that meshes with the judicial requirement that wars be the produce of an individual's criminal mind or a small elite's criminal conspiracy'.[141] However, Simpson notes how this account silences the structural forces at play in the build-up to the declaration of war, along with accidental factors or personal involvement of other actors. It also demonstrates a reticence about the idea of imposing *legal* responsibility for authorship.[142] As the Commission explained, this kind of inquiry 'must raise many difficulties and complex problems which might be more fitly investigated by historians and statesmen than by a tribunal appropriate to trial of offenders'.[143] Therefore, the Commission recommended that 'these gross outrages on the law of nations . . . should be the subject of a formal condemnation at the Conference' rather than criminal charges.[144] Simpson argues that in this sense, the Commission 'accepts and implicitly rejects' the Great Man theory of history; thereby, it reads the causes of war as multiple and structural.[145] At the very least, it considered law as incapable of 'offering definitive accounts of such histories'.[146]

138 ibid 60.

139 JF Willis *Prologue to Nuremberg: The Politics and Diplomacy of Punishing War Criminals of the First World War* (Greenwood Westport 1982).

140 Simpson (n 87) 167.

141 ibid.

142 ibid.

143 *Commission on the Responsibility of the Authors of the War* (1920) 14(1/2) *American Journal of International Law* 95, 118–19.

144 ibid 120.

145 Simpson (n 87) 164.

146 ibid.

The Commission's conclusion on personal liability for violations of the laws of war produced strong divisions with dissents from the United States and Japanese delegations. The majority countenanced the criminal liability of enemy forces, regardless of rank and disagreed that sovereign immunity would preclude liability, dismissing it as 'practical expedience in municipal law' rather than 'fundamental'.[147] They argued that if a tribunal is established with consent of the state of nationality of the defendant, a Head of State should not be able to invoke immunity as 'such a conclusion would shock the conscience of civilized mankind' and the vindication of laws would be incomplete if only the less ranked were tried.[148] On the contrary, the United States delegation argued that any proceedings against a sovereign would be contrary to sovereign immunity, as discussed in the US Supreme Court case *Schooner Exchange v. McFaddon*.[149] Rather the only law to which a Head of State is responsible 'is the law of his own country', albeit they viewed this as being subject to political authority.[150] However, they made a proviso for a Head of State, who has abdicated or been repudiated by people and although not definitively ruling on its merits, they noted that such a trial would be against 'an individual out of office'.[151]

In the end, the controversial recommendation to indict the former Kaiser was included under article 227 of the Versailles settlement.[152] Overall, the influence of the Institute's *Manual* and later revisions of military manuals of the Great Powers is evident in the acceptance by majority and dissents that lower-ranking enemy forces could be liable for violations of laws of war.[153] In the end, the Allies were forced to agree to the Weimar Republic's proposal to prosecute German officers before the Leipzig Supreme Court, as surrender of German rank and file would have been politically impossible.[154] However, the Leipzig trials were controversial and there were accusations of miscarriages of justice. After the trials, Commission of Allied Jurists publicly accused the German courts of giving lenient sentences to those convicted.[155]

Another dimension of this move to criminalize acts of government forces was the Allied Powers' negotiation of treaties to regulate submarine warfare against civilian shipping, which had been used most extensively by the German Navy during the First World War. In its practices, German U-boats had given neither a prior warning shot nor placed civilians in safety before attacking. At the time, rules relating to attacks on civilian shipping were drawn from the Institute of

147 *Commission on the Responsibility* (n 143) 116.

148 ibid and 117.

149 ibid 135 (also rejecting notion of liability for violating 'laws of humanity') and 152 (Japanese Delegation's Dissent).

150 ibid 136.

151 ibid.

152 Article 227 of the Treaty of Versailles (28 June 1919), Part VII. See also GG Battle 'The Trials Before the Leipsic Supreme Court of Germans Accused of War Crimes' (1921–22) 8 *Virginia Law Review* 1, 4 (official demand for Kaiser's surrender refused by the Netherlands and ultimately conceded by the Allies in March 1920).

153 See also article 228 of Treaty.

154 Battle (n 152) 4–5.

155 ibid 9–12.

International Law's *Manual of the Laws of Naval Warfare* and this provided that belligerents could only use force against civilian shipping if they were met with resistance. Even so, all persons on board an enemy civilian vessel must be 'placed in safety' before the vessel could be destroyed.[156] Therefore, the *Manual*'s rules were consistently flouted during the war and international lawyers were divided as to the legal consequences of engaging in such acts.[157] Notwithstanding, the British government argued that these practices were 'acts of piracy' and refused to afford prisoner-of-war status to captured German submarine crews.[158]

The opposing positions during the war were repeated during the 1930s in response to the 1937 Nyon Agreement that similarly referred such acts as 'acts of piracy'.[159] The wider context for the dispute was the Allied response to the Spanish Civil War that involved a non-intervention agreement and an arms embargo.[160] Britain and France entered into these agreements even though Nazi Germany and Fascist Italy were openly providing logistical support to Anti-Republican forces led by Franco.[161] The British government's policy sought to localize the Spanish Civil War, to protect geo-strategic interests in the Mediterranean and to thwart the spread of Bolshevism through applying a policy in a 'one-sided manner' that 'put a premium on Franco's victory'.[162] International lawyers clashed over the legality of these agreements as they were outside the 'institutional framework of the League of Nations' and 'cunningly neutralized the League's system of collective security'.[163] However, Morales explains how the non-intervention system reflected prior moves towards neutrality in response to earlier annexations,[164] while Berman demonstrates that theoretical precursors can be located in interwar international legal scholarship.[165] The idea emerged 'in the context of reform proposals of the system of collective security' and in this sense, the system 'cannot be simply dismissed as part of the general collapse of Versailles system'.[166]

It follows then that the Nyon Agreement was negotiated within a broader policy of neutrality and non-intervention, in response to Italian submarine attacks on commercial shipping.[167] Under the Nyon Agreement's preamble, acts of submarine

156 *Manual of the Laws of Naval War* (Oxford 9 August 1913) (article 104, destroying enemy vessels was restricted to 'exceptional necessity')

157 Bower (n 118) 26 (jurisdiction only over espionage, war treason and war crimes).

158 Anon 'Reply of the Allies: Mr Asquith's Speech' *The Times* (2 March 1915) 9.

159 See W Rech (n 74) 240 (exploring dispute between Holland and Harrison in 1915).

160 NP Padeldorf 'The International Non-Intervention Agreement and the Spanish Civil War' (1937) 31(2) *American Journal of International Law* 226, 234

161 I de la Rasilla del Morales 'In the General Interest of Peace? British International Lawyers and the Spanish Civil War' (2016) *Journal of the History of International Law* 1, 5.

162 ibid 16 and 40–41.

163 ibid and 12.

164 ibid 13–14.

165 N Berman 'Between Alliance and Localisation: Nationalism and the New Oscillationism' (1993–94) 26 *New York University Journal of International Law and Policy* 499, 464.

166 ibid.

167 WC Mills 'The Nyon Conference: Neville Chamberlain, Anthony Eden and the Appeasement of Italy in 1937' (1993) XV(1) *International History Review* 1, 2.

warfare were described as 'acts contrary to the most elementary dictates of humanity, which should be justly treated as acts of piracy'.[168] This clearly pulled on the earlier 1922 Treaty on Submarines and Noxious Gases that applied the *Manual*'s rules regarding civilian shipping to submarines and that any breach was a violation of the laws of war giving rise to liability 'as if for an act of piracy'.[169] This would permit trial of an accused within the civil or military jurisdiction of any state party 'of which he may be found' and extended the Lieber Code's approach to include both enemy irregulars and enemy armed forces.[170] In this way, the Nyon Agreement appeared to reproduce the late nineteenth-century British and American narrative that had described non-European insurgency as piracy in order to invoke extra-territorial jurisdiction. However, in its operative part, the Nyon Agreement departs from this key element of the earlier treaty. Instead, state parties constructed a scheme of joint policing or 'special collective measures' that permitted Britain and France to enforce the criminal sanctions on the high seas rather than a right of all treaty parties to exercise universal jurisdiction.[171] Rubin has described this as 'special military or political rights' justified upon 'the interests of general commerce' and controlling insurgency within territorial waters 'to the profit of third county merchants'.[172]

In the debates on the 1937 Nyon Agreement, Schmitt and Lauterpacht are illustrative of competing interpretations among lawyers over the "validity" of criminalizing submarine warfare using the piracy analogy. Schmitt recognized that the 'golden age of *jus publicum Europaeum* had gone'.[173] He opposed the 'new and authentic inter-State European order'[174] which certain developments are designed to bring into being, that is, the attempt to replace war with collective measures or in creating 'some power capable of acting "in the name of humanity"'.[175] In the midst of the rise of the 'total state', the 'empty space' for the non-political had become smaller and less significant and Schmitt feared that the use of the concept of the pirate was a means to impose a 'moralizing global politics'.[176] Schmitt's concept of the political assumed that only the state can be political; the state could never act in substantive terms like the 'outlaw'.[177]

168 Contrast article 22(1) of the Treaty for the Limitation and Reduction of Naval Armaments (22 April 1930) (without any analogy to piracy).

169 Article 1(2) and 3 of the Treaty in Relation to the Use of Submarines and Noxious Gases in Warfare (Washington 1922) See Rubin (n 71) 295(arguing that article 3 appears to prohibit privateering).

170 ibid.

171 The Nyon Agreement (14 September 1937) URL: http://www.icrc.org/ihl.nsf/FULL/310?OpenDocument. See Anon 'The Nyon Arrangements: Piracy by Treaty?' (1938) 19 *British Yearbook of International Law* 198, 202 ('prevailing view' that an officer under government orders could not be a pirate).

172 Rubin (n 71) 297.

173 Rech (n 74) 238.

174 Heller-Roazen (n 69) 144.

175 C Schmitt 'The Concept of Piracy (1937)' (2011) 2(1) *Humanity An International Journal of Human Rights, Humanitarianism and Development* 27, 28.

176 Rech (n 74) 248.

177 ibid 249 and 251.

According to Schmitt, the 'enemy of mankind' was an 'un-political entity', out of which one can construct the idea of humanity to be defended.[178] However, humanity must be itself an un-political construct as it depends upon the un-political pirate. As Simpson explains, the rise of the international community's self-consciousness 'required the identification of groups and states outside this community and, ideally, representing a threat to that community'.[179]

The 1922 and 1937 treaties located submarine warfare in a space where the state must be absent, despite the evident political motive.[180] Schmitt's ultimate call was to avoid adopting the 'English concept of piracy' or continental policing and using 'interim concepts', permitting the move into grey areas between war and peace.[181] Noting the unsettled history of the concept, he pulled on Paul Stiel's conceptually sound definition that stressed the private motive and citizenship-less of the pirate.[182] Therefore, rather than an offence against international law, piracy was merely an expanded competence of the state because of the pirate's citizenship-less.[183] Although Schmitt's concept of the political can be criticized,[184] writers observe Schmitt's contemporary insight into the 'irreversible change' in the laws of war 'where state vessels were no longer impervious to charges of criminality'.[185] This altered inter-state warfare into a situation of 'setting the representatives of a universal code of law against the stateless criminals who sought to transgress it'.[186] If one evoked 'humanity', then it opened the door to arguments justifying the use of criminal justice methods against the 'enemy'[187] or as Schmitt saw it, against an illegitimate idea of a political 'outlaw'.[188]

Conversely, Lauterpacht's contribution was his 'detailed construction of the argument that international law was not in fact a "special type", even less a "primitive form" of law'.[189] His programme, common with his mentor Lord McNair, was 'to bring international law out of its isolation as a branch of suspect moral or jurisprudential theory by presenting it as an object of legal technique no different from the domestic.'[190] He advocated for a re-engagement of the 'theoretical connection between international law and remnants of natural law'[191] and in this sense, to replace the dominant positivist sensibility (that he

178 Schmitt (n 175) 28.
179 Simpson (n 87) 142.
180 Schmitt (n 175) 28.
181 ibid 29.
182 ibid ('empty space in which the State was completely absent' was piracy's 'stage').
183 ibid 28. Contrast Rubin (n 71) 307.
184 Rech (n 74) 249 and 251.
185 Heller-Roazen (n 69) 145.
186 ibid.
187 ibid.
188 Schmitt (n 175) 28.
189 M Koskenniemi 'Hersch Lauterpacht' in J Beatson et al. *Jurists Uprooted: British Émigré Lawyers* (Oxford University Press Oxford 2004) 602, 617.
190 ibid.
191 See I Venzke *How Interpretation Makes International Law: On Semantic Change and Normative Twists* (Oxford University Press Oxford 2012), 204.

associated with aggressive nationalism and 'arbitrary dogma[s]' with no room for international law[192]) with a 'comprehensive and professionally administered system of cosmopolitan law and order in the image of a liberal state'.[193] Therefore, he believed that international law could be addressed as a complete system and international questions could be resolved by precedent or analogy from domestic law.[194] On the Nyon Agreement, Lauterpacht contended that acts of submarine warfare could rightly be termed acts of piracy as they were 'acts which no government was prepared to take responsibility for' and were 'contrary to the most elementary rules of humanity'.[195] This latter reference reiterates the language of moral outrage in the Nyon Agreement's preamble that in turn, pulls upon such language in the 1907 Hague Regulations. Lauterpacht's position on government agreement to liability is in keeping with his contemporary writing on the doctrine of immunity, where he described immunity as 'an anarchical principle of legal and moral irresponsibility' with the principle of individual criminal responsibility as the only solution.[196]

Nevertheless, his approach to the piracy analogy meant he had to play down (or overrule) the significance of the private-ends element of piracy because submarine warfare was solely politically motivated and incompatible with Schmitt's 'classic' definition. It follows then that, unlike Schmitt, Lauterpacht turned to the same controversial practice of the British and American governments declaring non-European rebels to be pirates in the nineteenth century. He considered that this 'trend' in practice demonstrated the division among jurists and made it doubtful whether the private-ends element was fundamental.[197] Taking the conflicting practice among states as a basis, he could then define piracy as an act of violence committed on the high seas with the legal consequences of universal jurisdiction.[198] In other words, piracy was characterized by the agreement of states to address the particular conduct with universal jurisdiction rather than distinguished by types of violence and their motive. This definition meant he could avoid the limitation imposed by private ends and at the same time, by focusing on the jurisdiction, he could avoid the debate on assimilating other offences to piracy that lack a treaty basis.[199] In this way, Lauterpacht 'took what he needed from municipal law' and considered the distinction between piracy and privateering as a fiction, given that the acts were in substance analogous.[200] He read the label 'universal enemy'

192 Koskenniemi (n 190) 617.
193 M Koskenniemi 'Lauterpacht: The Victorian Tradition in International Law' (1997) 2 *European Journal of International Law* 215, 217.
194 M Koskenniemi 'Hersch Lauterpacht and the Development of International Criminal Law' (2004) 2 *Journal of International Criminal Justice* 810, 812.
195 H Lauterpacht 'Insurrection et Piraterie' (1939) 46 *Revue générale de droit international public* 513.
196 H Lauterpacht 'General Rules of the Law of Peace', in E Lauterpacht (ed) *International Law. Being the Collected Papers of Sir Hersch Lauterpacht*, Vol 1 (Cambridge University Press Cambridge 1970) 392.
197 Lauterpacht (n 195) 523.
198 ibid 525.
199 ibid 528.
200 W Rech (n 74) 259.

as a mechanism for uniting 'an otherwise anarchical international society' and legitimizing 'collective security actions that conventional law had not managed to protect'.[201]

2.2 Completing the League system

Criminalizing submarine warfare was part of what Rech has described as radicalizing 'the trend towards moralizing warfare and discriminating against the public enemy'.[202] Rech believes that the use of the 'enemies of mankind' analogy shifted international lawyers' arguments to 'justifying war in humanity's name', which in turn broke the taboo of non-discrimination against the public enemy.[203] This trend was also reflected in the various proposals submitted by European international lawyers during the 1920s that sought to establish an international criminal court as part of the 'desire to complete the League system'.[204] These proposals were also underpinned by the goal of modernizing (and globalizing) penal codes of 'civilized states' in order to mount the same type of criminal prosecutions against nationals and foreigners 'regardless of where they were apprehended'.[205] At the League of Nations, Edouard Descamps proposed an international criminal court that would be part of a three-part international tribunal system and significantly, would be independent of belligerents with a purpose of securing international security. His proposal was rejected by the Assembly's Third Committee, based on the lack of harmonization of penal codes of all states and, as pointed to by the Committee's rapporteur Henri Lafontaine, a custom of using states' national jurisdictions.[206]

Lewis argues that Descamps' proposal lacked the 'preparatory intellectual work and the political agreement' that supported the proposal for a Permanent Court of International Justice.[207] Therefore, within the Advisory Committee of Jurists, there was uncertainty over the broadly defined offences within the proposed court's jurisdiction, a reluctance to endorse a court with a wide competence to specifically define crimes and determine penalties and an assumption that governments would not want to extradite those accused of political crimes and thereby, limit the right to grant political asylum.[208] There was also an evident preference among League members to use diplomatic or economic sanctions against governments rather than conducting criminal prosecutions of state officials or to go so far as criminal liability of states.[209] In fact, Western European states were sceptical

201 ibid 260.
202 ibid 236.
203 ibid 237.
204 M Lewis *The Birth of the New Justice: The Internationalization of Crime and Punishment 1919–1950* (Oxford University Press Oxford 2014), 78.
205 ibid.
206 ibid 88.
207 ibid 82.
208 ibid, 85 (concept could include attacks on League officials by revolutionary socialists).
209 ibid 80 and 86 (similar views were raised in the Advisory Committee).

of unifying criminal jurisdiction, seemingly to imply a 'civilized' and 'uncivilized' dichotomy.[210] Overall, League members were focused on multilateral disarmament, reform of existing League structures and the United States's adherence to the Permanent Court of International Justice.[211]

Nevertheless, the League's Assembly did recommend that non-governmental organizations should explore ways to codify international law.[212] Consequently, the International Law Association (ILA) and Association International de Droit Pénal (AIDP) produced proposals for the creation of an international criminal court over war crimes and over aggressive war respectively.[213] While both their proposals designed critical elements that would be repeated in later debates, Lewis identifies that prior experience in the League debates influenced the frame of the ILA and AIDP's proposals, along with internal dynamics within the organizations themselves.[214] The former included the awareness of how challenging it would be to convince states to endorse an international court with jurisdiction over senior civilian and military leaders for aggressive war, war crimes, or any other defined offences.[215] This was particularly difficult against a context where the Great Powers openly sidestepped the League's collective security through treaty negotiation outside of the League's framework.[216] By the end of the 1920s, the only successful codification project was the negotiation of an anti-counterfeiting currency treaty that focused on domestic jurisdiction and recognition of the acts as extradition crimes.[217] Given the lack of enthusiasm for an international criminal court, the AIDP turned towards a unification project that sought to harmonize criminal codes to ensure universal repression of certain crimes. The AIDP were influenced by Italian penal reforms' principle of 'social defence' that meant states criminalize acts as a means of social security rather than to secure some foundational moral principle.[218] In this way, there was a swing away from the ILA's normative idea of offences against international morality and towards an alternative notion of threatening public security.

It follows then that the AIDP's Third International Congress of Penal Law addressed the question of extraterritorial jurisdiction and explored what offences should give rise to universal jurisdiction. As we observed above, de Vabres had narrated a history of jurisdiction in his *Treatise* in the 1920s and therefore, within the debate, he advocated that *forum deprehensionis* (judge of the place of arrest) should apply to all offences (whether or not deemed international offences) as

210 ibid 79.

211 ibid.

212 Report of Committee No III, 764 as cited in Lewis (n 204) 90–95.

213 International Law Association, *Report of the Thirty-Fourth Conference, Vienna, 1926* (Sweet & Maxwell Ltd London 1927), 118.

214 Lewis (n 204) 97–8, 100.

215 League of Nations Acts de La Premiere Assemblee 327–8 as cited in Lewis (n 211) 98–100 (the ILA rejected proposal to including offences against minorities, within jurisdiction of League states (such as Eastern European Jews)).

216 Lewis (n 204) 98.

217 Convention for the Counterfeiting or Currency 1929. See Lewis (n 211) 117.

218 Lewis (n 204) 113–16.

establishing a specific category of *delicta juris gentium* would be challenging. His suggestion of a hierarchy of jurisdictions where the *forum deprehensionis* is the final resort would appear to avoid accusations of unwarranted interference or politically motivated trials.[219] In the end, the Third Congress's Resolution advocated the revision of existing treaties or negotiation of new treaties to 'ensure the universal repression of all offences which the states *would agree* to consider as harming their interests or as dangerous to international relations'.[220] In default of this harmonization of laws, it recognized that extradition was preferable to universality, although universality was highly desirable in the case of offences against 'the Common Law'.[221] Nevertheless, the Third Congress discerned a 'tendency towards a universal repression of certain of these offences . . . which endanger the common interests of States'.[222] This observation appears to emphasize the 'social defence' principle, seeming to reflect actual state will, yet it constitutes a normative principle assumed to bind all states.

Another attempt to reform criminal laws through a uniform model was the Institute of International Law's Resolution on Conflict of Penal Laws with respect to Competence.[223] This dramatically expanded the parameters of extraterritorial jurisdiction in its earlier 1883 Resolution. Under article 5, every state had the right to punish acts committed abroad by a foreigner, found on its territory, where the acts constituted an offence against the general interests protected by international law.[224] This interwove the subsidiary jurisdiction of the 1883 Resolution[225] with the notion of offences against the law of nations (drawn from the debates over piracy *jure gentium*). It also appeared to reflect jurisdictional claims in certain national codes that asserted extraterritorial jurisdiction over offences that had been defined in specific treaties in the instances where the state had custody of the alleged offender.[226] These treaties involved offences taking place across borders and provided that states parties could establish jurisdiction over the offence under various heads of jurisdiction.[227] The reference to 'general interests' could reflect both de Vabres's 'interests of humanity' or Travers's threat

219 D de Vabres 'Pour quells delits convient-il d'admettre la competence universelle' (1932) 9 *Revue International de Droit Penal* 315.

220 Section 1, para 1 of the Resolution of the Third International Congress of Penal Law, reprinted by International Association of Penal Law ('harmful to the interests common to all States'), URL: http://www.penal.org/sites/default/files/RIDP86%201-2%202015%20EN.pdf, emphasis added.

221 ibid section 2, para 1 and 2.

222 ibid (preamble).

223 Compare article 6 of the Resolution on International Penal Law (Warsaw, 1927) cited in Appendix 6, Harvard Research (n 56) 641.

224 Institute of International Law 'Resolution on the Conflict of Penal Laws with respect to Competence' (Cambridge 1931) (list included piracy, slavery and facilitating the spread of contagious diseases).

225 ibid (jurisdiction conditional on failure to demand or refusal of offer of extradition).

226 Harvard Research (n 56).

227 See article 2 of *International Convention for the Suppression of the White Slave Traffic*, May 4, 1910, 211 Consol. T.S. 45, 1912 GR. Brit. T.S. No. 20.

to security and domestic order and in this sense, appear both moralistic or formal positivist.

In academic literature, there were also contrasting interpretations as to whether universal jurisdiction could be asserted over offences against the law of nations. Mikliszanski contended that a 'universal right to punish' *delicta juris gentium* derived theoretically from the nature of the penal norm as an international crime.[228] Therefore, Mikliszanski distinguished the subsidiary basis of jurisdiction from jurisdiction over piracy, which was interpreted as an offence against the law of nations. He argued that as the penal norm constituted an 'expression of human justice', the 'universal right to punish' must be a primary right of the custodial state and not subsidiary to the territorial jurisdiction.[229] This was justified because the national courts represented human justice and not their state's own interests. In effect, international crimes triggered the jurisdiction of all courts.[230] However, his thesis was not entirely assumed to descend from a higher normative code, as he considered *delicta juris gentium* as the offences defined in treaties agreed by states, albeit this universal right could be imposed on treaty parties irrespective of their consent.[231]

Conversely, the Harvard Research's *Draft Convention on Jurisdiction* rejected the claim that *delicta juris gentium* should be assimilated to piracy for the purposes of jurisdiction. Instead, the commentary emphasized the disparity of national statutes and international resolutions[232] that rendered it impossible to draw 'common agreement as to which offences should fall into a class of *delicta juris gentium*'.[233] It further rejected the claim that universality should extend to all crimes proscribed in treaty law based on the implicit or explicit acceptance of international cooperation for the repression of treaty offences.[234] It cited the conclusion of the Third International Congress of Penal Law that further unification of national legislation was required along with better cooperation in matters of criminal proceedings.[235] It endorsed the view that until these developments, extradition would be preferable in situations of such offences.[236] Accordingly, if states sought to assert jurisdiction over 'international crimes' committed extraterritorially, they could use article 10 (other crimes) of the *Draft Convention* (although a state is not obliged to assert such jurisdiction) or alternatively, conclude an international treaty providing for universal jurisdiction

228 K Mikliszanski 'Le systéme de l'universalité du droit de punir et le droit penal subsidiare' (1936) *Revue de science criminelle et de droit pénal comparé* 331. See Reydams (n 1) 32 (divergences between Travers and Mikliszanski as moment for spilt between refusal of extradition and natural right to punish).

229 ibid 338.

230 ibid 339.

231 ibid.

232 Compare section 6 of the German Penal and article 9 of the Polish Penal Code cited in Harvard Research (n 56) 569.

233 Harvard Research (n 56) 569 (divergent state practice not influential).

234 ibid.

235 ibid 571.

236 ibid (using phrase 'universal jurisdiction').

over specific offences.[237] In this sense, article 10 appeared to be justified upon a wide measure of discretion on states to determine jurisdictional principles, combined with an analysis of behaviour that demonstrated a variety of rules.

3 The Nuremberg model

The Nuremberg model has become synonymous with the 'origins' of international criminal law and the affirmation of an individual liability for state-sponsored violence. It is paradoxically an origin and a non-origin, that is, an affirmation of what states already recognized and unprecedented.[238] 'Nuremberg' evokes a variety of meanings whether literal or figurative, whether by those interested in the trial process or the trials' political aftermath.[239] It is also largely perceived as 'an event, and by extension a symbol rather than a process'.[240] Bloxham argues that this is the most appropriate way for lawyers to interpret it 'since a tightly packaged event is more easily deployable as that all-important legal entity, the precedent'.[241] However, if Nuremberg is perceived as a 'process', it can allow for a critical look at the responses or aftermath of Nuremberg.[242] This demonstrates the failure of the International Military Tribunal (IMT) trial's moralizing effect as it was 'retrospectively discredited' when surveys in the early 1950s are considered, showing a dramatic drop in German perception of the trial as fair.[243] While the IMT trial was followed by the United States Nuremberg Military Tribunal (NMT) trials, those trials were markedly scaled back by the end of the 1940s prompted by both German opposition and a shift in US attitude towards Germany's role within the developing Cold War.

At the time of its establishment, the architecture constructed by the IMT appealed to 'metropolitan' sensibilities within what Kennedy called 'largely liberal mainstream international post-WWII intelligentsia'.[244] It had an institutional context as part of the 'outgrowths of a characteristically American approach to post-war multilateralism' with all the key United States negotiators being New Dealers.[245] Borgwardt argues that the post-war institutions may be read as 'an attempt to institutionalize a New Deal orientation, more specifically FDR's so-called "Four Freedoms" in the sphere of international relations'.[246] In

237 ibid 572.

238 Simpson (n 87) 84.

239 D Bloxham 'From the International Military Tribunal to the Subsequent Nuremberg Proceedings: The American Confrontation with Nazi Criminality revisited' (2013) 98(332) *History* 567.

240 ibid 568.

241 ibid.

242 ibid 569.

243 ibid.

244 D Kennedy 'The International Style in Post-War Law and Policy' (1994) 12 *Utah Law Review* 7, 13 ('characteristic of public international lawyers and institutions', 'beckons the intelligentsia to a personal commitment to public service with an international orientation').

245 E Borgwardt 'A New Deal for the Nuremberg Trial: The Limits of Law in Generating Human Rights Norms' (2008) 26(3) *Law and History Review* 679, 689.

246 ibid 690.

this way, the trial is 'an example of the kind of pragmatic administrative pastiche favoured by New Dealers', who, she argues, viewed their efforts 'as contributing to this new integrated idea of "security", encompassed all of Roosevelt's Four Freedoms'.[247] Therefore, the IMT came into being because of internal dynamics within the United States that secured dominant support for war crimes trials over Morgenthau's Versailles Settlement-type model.[248] This was then combined with support from the Soviet Union, and lastly, Britain, albeit with reluctance.[249] A move to war crimes trials has also been perceived as shifting responsibility from Germany and Japan, as states. A process Bloxham referred to as 'ridding Germany of guilt of nations' is evident in the NMT trials decision not to classify the Wehrmacht or the SA as criminal organizations.[250] However, even though it appears, as discussed below, that the Great Man theory of history won the intellectual battle, Simpson argues that collective responsibility was invoked via other means. He points to how elements of Morgenthau's discredited plan found their way into the JCS 1067 Directive and Potsdam Protocol.[251] The former established a 'highly intrusive economic control and complete military and industrial disarmament' while the latter set conditions for the Four Zone occupation that had elements of Morgenthau's plan.[252]

Accordingly, the IMT trial was seen as a morally more sound process and a way of aiding the 'democratization', demilitarization and denazification of post-war Germany through exposing the 'evils of the Nazi regime'.[253] It was about putting the 'very idea of lawlessness . . . on trial', 'a rebuke to the absence of law during the Third Reich'.[254] In this sense, the Nazi defendants' political project was on trial: for the Soviets, it was fascism and for the United States, France and Britain, it was Nazism.[255] In the trial, the Allied prosecutors' sought to frame all of the Nazi atrocities within one overarching idea for 'continental and world domination'.[256] This decision to frame the atrocities under this conspiracy means that 'aggressive warfare became the most significant act because it facilitated and encouraged further atrocities.'[257] The IMT referred to aggressive war as

247 ibid.

248 ibid 683 (noting the importance of FDR facing elections and the realization of having responsibility for administering Germany in wake of deteriorating relations with Soviet Union).

249 G Bass *Stay the Hand of Vengeance: The Politics of War Crimes Trials* (Princeton University Press Princeton 2000).

250 D Bloxham *Genocide on Trial: War Crimes Trials and the Formation of History and Memory* (Oxford University Press Oxford), 78.

251 Simpson (n 85) 62.Note also this period for the emergence of Morgenthau's realism and international relations theory that reduced international law to a tool of state power rather than a constraint on power, see H Morgenthau 'Positivism, Functionalism and International Law' (1940) 34 *American Journal of International Law* 260 and Koskenniemi (n 4) 459–74.

252 ibid.

253 J Tusa and AN Tusa *The Nuremberg Trials* (Macmillan London 1983).

254 Simpson (n 85) 13.

255 ibid.

256 D Bloxham (n 239)

257 ibid.

'the supreme international crime . . . that contains within itself the accumulated evil of the whole'.[258] There was also an attempt to prosecute defendants that would broadly reflect major political, military and economic institutions within the Nazi regime, alongside the surviving highest-ranking leadership.[259] In the end, the Nuremberg tribunal only considered the conspiracy charge in regards to aggressive warfare, which meant that pre-war atrocities, such as persecution, would not fall within conspiracy.[260] The tribunal also did not allow for mass summary trials in its approach to criminal organizations and this meant that the United States's desire to contend with what it called the 'military industrial complex' was only 'done in an attenuated way'.[261]

We noted that 'Nuremberg' signalled the affirmation of individual liability and this concept is 'wedded to the idea that men do make history of their own choosing'.[262] This theory is one that 'overstates the agency of elites . . . and has powerful associations with the orthodox concept of history as "a factual account of the past"'.[263] In this way, Simpson reads international criminal law as 'at least temperamentally, implicated in this sort of history'.[264] Therefore, at the International Military Tribunal, Allied Prosecutors justified individual criminal responsibility, drawing heavily on Lauterpacht's use of piracy as an appropriate precedent.[265] Earlier, Lauterpacht had argued that the laws of war were binding 'upon human beings' rather than 'impersonal entities' and this was by its 'very nature . . . a responsibility of a criminal character'.[266] His analysis of state behaviour pulled on an exception (espionage) and argued that by analogy, it becomes a general rule given the profound inconsistency if there was no responsibility for war crimes.[267] Therefore, in his opening address, Jackson referred to piracy and brigandage as acts 'long recognized as crimes punishable under international law' for which individual responsibility was 'old and well-established'.[268] Such liability was necessary for international law's function to maintain peace and in turn, it would be 'intolerable' for the 'legalism' of state collective responsibility to become personal immunity.[269] Similarly, Shawcross read sovereign immunity as

258 J Laughland *A History of Political Trials: From Charles I to Saddam Hussein* (Peter Lang Oxford 2008) 106.

259 ibid 103.

260 1 International Military Tribunal (1946), reprinted in (1947) 41 *American Journal of International Law* 172.

261 Bloxham (n 250) 22–5.

262 Simpson (n 7) 162.

263 ibid 164.

264 ibid.

265 See Closing Speech Part 1 reprinted in H Lauterpacht 'Draft Nuremberg Speeches' (2012) 1(1) *Cambridge Journal of International and Comparative Law* 72, 93 and 82 ('the State could be a pirate').

266 H Lauterpacht 'The Law of Nations and the Punishment of War Crimes' (1944) 21 *British Yearbook of International Law* 58, 64 and 61.

267 ibid 64.

268 RH Jackson 'Opening Address for the United States: Chapter V' (1946) 1 Office of the US Chief of Counsel for Prosecution of Axis Criminality, Nazi Conspiracy and Aggression 114, 167.

269 ibid.

pure comity and an 'arbitrary political doctrine(s) more appropriate to the sphere of power politics than [where] the rule of law prevails'.[270]

The International Military Tribunal concurred with Allied Prosecutors. Their justification implicitly pulled from the Prosecutors' discussion of law of piracy, along with explicit reference to espionage. Accordingly, 'individuals have international duties which transcend the national obligations of obedience imposed by the individual State.'[271] If an individual breached the laws of war on government orders, they cannot be immune as 'the State . . . moves outside its competence under international law'.[272] Of course, this analogy appears to be presupposed upon some universal moral code, seemingly agreed to by states, and this position, if brought to its logical conclusion, would fail to avoid accusations of mere idealism. In its desire to be normative and reflect moral outrage, this position appeared politically suspect, appearing to privilege a certain normative project ('naturalistic') over others and claiming to know better what such a normative code consists of. Conversely, the counter-position, as illustrated by Kelsen, was that international law only established collective responsibility unless criminal liability arose under a treaty agreed to by the defendant's state of nationality.[273] However, Kelsen's analysis of state behaviour ignored the open-endedness of the provisions within military manuals that admitted multiple possible interpretations and this former position, if brought to its logical conclusion, would fail to avoid accusations of merely condoning power politics. In its desire to be concrete and reflect state policy, this position appeared politically suspect, appearing to privilege certain states' will over others and claiming to know better what a state had consented to.

That both competing narratives of justification sidestepped the internal paradox was identified by Hannah Arendt. She argued that the crimes could not be separated from the collective guilt of the state, yet simultaneously the political responsibility of the government could not be the subject matter of a criminal trial pronouncing individual guilt.[274] Simpson also points out that collective and individual responsibility suffers the same defect, that is, 'they exonerate a large number of people':[275] 'If everyone is responsible, then perhaps no-one is. If individuals are capable of leading states to disaster . . . then perhaps only the (dead) leader is responsible.'[276]

270 H Shawcross 'Closing Address for the United Kingdom of Great Britain and Ireland' (1947) Supplement A: Office of the US Chief of Counsel 62, 93–4. See also Q Wright 'War Criminals' (1945) 39 *American Journal of International Law* 257, 269 (arguing for an exception yet distinguishing between a former Head of State (removing immunity) and an incumbent (retained due to 'symbolic significance')).

271 International Military Tribunal (n 262) 220–21.

272 ibid.

273 Kelsen (n 72) 160 and 159 (sovereign immunity applied unless an exception existed in custom or treaty)

274 H Arendt *Eichmann in Jerusalem: Report on the Banality of Evil* (Penguin Books New York 2006) 298.

275 Simpson (n 7) 165.

276 ibid.

3.1 Justifying jurisdiction

The IMT submitted an open-ended justification for the validity of its jurisdiction and this left room for international lawyers to provide multiple interpretations to expand upon the narrative of justification provided by the IMT.[277] Invariably, the IMT stressed that it was bound by its Charter yet this argument, of itself, could not answer whether the states acted lawfully in conferring jurisdiction on the Tribunal.[278] Therefore, the Tribunal attempted to justify the Charter as lawful exercise of authority by referencing the 'unconditional surrender' of Nazi Germany[279] and the capacity of states to jointly establish 'special courts'.[280] These two justifications were particularly ambiguous and could accommodate multiple interpretations whether justifying upon the 'unconditional surrender' or upon the special courts 'done together'.[281] Interpretations pulling upon the 'unconditional surrender' had a common theme that the Allied Powers were entitled to exercise powers normally appropriate to the territorial sovereign. Critical for Kelsen's interpretation was his view that the legal status of post-war Germany was neither a status of occupation nor annexation.[282] Rather the legitimate government had ceased to exist either because the surrender treaty indirectly recognized the transfer of sovereignty to the Allies or because the last central government was legally abolished by the surrender treaty.[283] According to Kelsen, the Allied Powers established a condominium or joint sovereignty in establishing their own sovereignty over Germany and this meant the Allies possessed 'unrestricted legislative competence' that included the authority to establish a military tribunal with jurisdiction over crimes committed prior to their 'supreme authority'.[284] As they were in effect Nazi Germany's successor, they were bound by the duty to prosecute their own armed forces, that is, Axis armed forces.[285]

277 G Schwarzenberger 'The Judgment at Nuremberg' (1946–47) 21 *Tulane Law Review* 329, 339. This section does not explore issues of jurisdiction in the Tokyo Trial as universal jurisdiction was not raised within the discourse; jurisdiction was claimed to arise from the surrender of the existing Japanese government, that is, an claim of state consent.

278 AR Carnegie 'Jurisdiction over Violations of the Laws of War' (1963) 39 *British Yearbook of International Law* 402, 415.

279 International Military Tribunal judgment (n 262) 216–17 (right of occupying powers to legislate over occupied territory).

280 ibid ('have done together what any one of them might have done singly').

281 See Schwarzenberger (n 277) 334 (that phrase meant IMT was joint military tribunal under municipal law).

282 H Kelsen 'The Legal Status of the Unconditional Surrender' (1945) 39 *American Journal of International Law* 518, 518 (occupation assumes continuing state of war between occupier and occupied) and 520 (based on express terms of Berlin Declaration). See also M Radin 'Justice at Nuremberg' (1945–46) 24 *Foreign Affairs* 369, 372.

283 ibid 518 (although rules seemed to require annexation for an enemy state to cease to exist, argued that once Germany ceased to exist, could intend to establish own sovereignty over territory).

284 ibid 523 and 525.

285 ibid 519 (using the Leipzig trials as a precedent).

In another interpretation, Lauterpacht viewed Nazi Germany's occupation of Europe and North Africa during hostilities as the usurpation of the Allied belligerents' authority over their own territory.[286] Therefore, at the end of hostilities, the sovereignty over Allied territory was restored to the Allied Powers who possessed the legal authority and could assert territorial jurisdiction over the crimes committed in occupied territories against nationals of the state under occupation and against nationals of other states.[287] Lauterpacht combined what he read as a right of belligerents to exercise jurisdiction over crimes wherever committed against the safety of the state and its nationals, which was 'claimed by some states and not denied by international law', and the capacity of belligerents to punish war criminals 'as may fall into [their] hands'.[288] He did not elaborate as to whether the phrase 'safety of the state' was the protective principle or was the subsidiary jurisdiction based on Travers's threat to the security of the state. The implication from Lauterpacht's stress on the belligerents' right on capture would suggest that he sought to imply the latter.

The interpretations pulling on 'acting jointly' had a common theme in that the phrase was read as meaning the Allied Powers were entitled to exercise extraterritorial jurisdiction, either universal jurisdiction or protective principle of jurisdiction.[289] Critical to Wright's interpretation was the presupposition that 'international law imposes few limitations . . .', explicitly drawing on the majority in the *Lotus* case.[290] He interwove universality over piracy with the threat to security of the state that seemed to combine the piracy analogy with justification for extraterritorial jurisdiction, based on a threat to the security or public order of the state.[291] Earlier, Wright had implicitly pulled upon Lorimer's justifications for piracy, as crimes against humanity under article 6 of the Nuremberg Charter were considered 'offences against the universal law' that have the 'character of conspiracy, rebellion or aggression against the world community'.[292] He linked back to the Allied Prosecutors' concept of all Nazi atrocities descending from a conspiracy for global domination and concluded that such offences against the universal law 'may be prosecuted by a tribunal with the authority of the international community'.[293]

In another variant, Cowles justified the US military trials on an analogy between brigandage and war crimes; in this way, he pulled on the Lieber Code's

286 Lauterpacht (n 266) 62.

287 ibid 63 (arguing immunity for armed forces only applied if present 'with permission of the lawful sovereign', noting exceptions in wartime (acts of an ally) and implication from idea of war crimes prosecutions of an exception to immunity).

288 ibid.

289 Memorandum by the Secretary General 'The Charter and Judgment of the Nuernberg Tribunal: History and Analysis' UN Doc A/CN.4/5, 79.

290 Q Wright 'The Law of the Nuremberg Trial' (1947) 41 *American Journal of International Law* 38, 49.

291 ibid (Wright did not qualify the 'state' as the belligerent party to a conflict only and could be interpreted as applying neutrals).

292 Q Wright, 'War Criminals', (1945) 39 *American Journal of International Law* 257, 282.

293 ibid 282 and 284.

idea of extraterritorial jurisdiction over acts of enemy irregulars and detailed trials before US courts as evidence of state practice. He argued that this practice demonstrated neither a sense of obligation to desist from exercising jurisdiction nor any protest by the State with primary interest.[294] In this sense, international law did not prohibit US courts from exercising jurisdiction and there was no evidence that such prohibition emerged through objections by other states. Instead, US courts exercised extraterritorial jurisdiction 'where ordinary law enforcement is difficult or suspended' to ensure the offence was prosecuted[295] that appeared to be normatively based on the prevention of 'scandalous impunity'. This practice could empirically support jurisdiction over war crimes by government order given the similarity of the crimes and as a 'matter of general interest and concern' (or, in other words, in the interests of justice).[296]

There was a possibility for a second IMT trial but this was set aside by an Allied decision in favour of zonal trials.[297] At the time, there were 100,000 German nationals in custody and this presented a considerable logistical problem, especially in light of the IMT's approach towards individual participation in criminal organizations. This was somewhat resolved when the US Denazification Board recommended that the vast majority of 'organization cases' be handled by its denazification programme.[298] Therefore, it was initially believed that the Nuremberg Military Trials (NMT) would involve around 266 defendants.[299] In the end, US internal dynamics led to a reduction in resources[300] and in turn, a much more limited trial programme of 12 trials with 185 defendants.[301] Even though the trials had less visibility than the IMT, Bloxham argues that as the trials dealt with the 'functional elites' of the Nazi regime, they dealt with issues 'a little closer to home for the majority of Germans who had served in some functional capacity during the war'.[302]

The NMT proceedings were based upon article III of the *Control Council Law No. 10* that empowered each occupying authority to arrest within their respective zones of occupation and if there is a *prima facie* case, to prosecute all persons before an appropriate tribunal.[303] Ordinance No 7 defined that an 'appropriate tribunal' meant military tribunals with the authority to prosecute crimes under article II of the *Control Council Law No. 10*.[304] Within its trial programme, certain trials involved the prosecution of enemy nationals for crimes that occurred beyond the territorial jurisdiction of belligerents or against their own forces (nationality

294 Cowles (n 73) 216.
295 ibid.
296 ibid 217.
297 KJ Heller *Nuremberg Military Trials and the Origins of International Criminal Law* (Oxford University Press Oxford 2011) 10 and 22 (strong opposition to trials of the industrialists).
298 ibid 12.
299 ibid 45.
300 Bloxham (n 239) 579–80.
301 Heller (n 297) 45.
302 Bloxham (n 239) 570.
303 Article III of the *Control Council Law No. 10* (20 December 1945), reprinted in Appendix D, T Taylor 'Final Report to the Secretary of the Army (Washington 1949) 250.
304 Heller (n 297) 25.

of the victim). In the trial reports, they adopted either the same 'ambiguous' stance as the IMT or the dual reasoning as presented by Kelsen's joint sovereignty and Cowles' universal jurisdiction.[305] In *Re List*, the United States tribunal took an 'ambiguous' stance on its jurisdiction over acts prior to and beyond the zone of Allied occupation. It stressed the nature of the crime as 'sufficient justification' for the jurisdiction of the capturing State over any claim of exclusivity of the territorial jurisdiction, combined with probable impunity due to the 'political upheavals' of the post-war environment.[306] Similarly, the introduction to the *Law Reports* argued that international law permits 'jurisdiction to punish pirates and war criminals in its custody regardless of the nationality of the victims or the place where the offence was committed'.[307] It endorsed the 'exhaustive treatment' by Cowles and was 'generally accepted as sound' in principle.[308]

In the alternative, the *Hadamar*,[309] *Almelo*[310] and *Zyklon B*[311] cases drew on the dual reasoning. The US court's judgment in *Hadamar* captures the underpinnings of the previous judgments when the court argued that jurisdiction was based on three avenues: universality of jurisdiction over war crimes, a common enemy and a supreme authority. On universality, it cited the support for the doctrine by the UN War Crimes Commission and described 'universality' as jurisdiction over pirates and war criminals in a state's custody irrespective of nationality of the victim or location of the offence, 'particularly where, for some reason, the criminal would otherwise go unpunished'.[312] On the 'common enemy', it claimed that the US could exercise jurisdiction over offences where the victims are 'nationals of allies engaged in a common struggle against a common enemy'.[313] This is indicative of the 'common enemy' notion within the literature on the law of piracy and brigandage. Finally, the unconditional surrender and assumption of full authority permitted US tribunals to assume jurisdiction based on territoriality and nationality of the accused.[314]

305 Note criticism of the Law Reports when trial documents did not in general refer to issues of jurisdiction, see M Garrod 'The Protective Principle of Jurisdiction over War Crimes and the Hallow Concept of Universality' (2012) 12 *International Criminal Law Review* 763, 777.

306 *List and Others (Hostages Trial)* (1949) 8 Law Reports of the Trial of War Criminals 34, 55 (US Military Tribunal, Nuremberg, 19 February 1948).

307 1 Law Reports of the Trial of War Criminals 26.

308 ibid.

309 *Klein and Six Others (Hadamar Trial)* (1947) 1 Law Reports of the Trial of War Criminals 46, 52 (offences committed by non-US nationals, outside US territory and against non-US nationals but trial justified upon US federal law, including jurisdiction over enemy combatants and civilians against non-enemy nationals and against own forces).

310 *Sandrock and Three Others (Almelo Case)* (1947) 1 Law Reports of the Trial of War Criminals 35, 41 (British trial of German soldiers for the murder of a British and Dutch national in the Netherlands).

311 *Tesch and Two Others (Zyklon B case)*(1947) 1 Law Reports of the Trials of War Criminals 93, 103 (British trial of German industrialists regarding allegations against non-nationals).

312 *Klein case* (n 309) 53.

313 ibid 53. Contrast Garrod (n 305) (reading post-war trials as Allied concern with 'common enemy', justified on rights of injured belligerent or Allied state to exercise protective principle).

314 ibid.

We observed how the Nuremberg Military Trials process had already been affected by the increasing distrust between the Allied Powers and therefore, any possibility of post-war momentum on the 1930s project to establish an international criminal court was stalled by the Cold War. There were attempts to maintain momentum in the guise of the major diplomatic conferences on the laws of war that culminated in the Four Geneva Conventions and in the difficult negotiations over the Genocide Convention in the United Nations. These great humanitarian treaties appeared to signal a continuing 'progressive' step on the road of legal humanitarianism that was initiated with the Nuremberg model. The General Assembly's 1950 Nuremberg Principles seemed to follow this progressive trend[315] and, in the case of the Geneva Conventions, there was considerable ratification amongst newly independent states in the 1950s and '60s.[316] However, the deepening of Cold War, the obvious failure of collective security and the emergence of many new independent states after liberation wars changed the context within which these treaties had to operate. Invariably, this had an influence on the treaty negotiations in the first instance and the extent of the treaty implementation by states parties. On the former, jurisdictional rules were impacted in that states were more cautious to reciprocally agree to extraterritorial jurisdiction over genocide that could involve the trial of their nationals by other states,[317] whereas they were willing to agree to such trials over grave breaches in international armed conflicts.[318] Similarly, the International Law Commission's stalled project on an international criminal court seemed inevitable by the end of the 1950s. The Korean War, the hardening of ideological differences between the superpowers and the many liberation wars heralded a future of proxy wars, political stalemate and the desire by newly independent states to consolidate their independence.

4 The Eichmann trial and beyond

The Eichmann trial before the Israeli Courts was a *cause célèbre* in international affairs in the early 1960s, given the dramatic abduction of Eichmann from

315 Principles of International Law Recognized in the Charter of the Nürnberg Tribunal and in the Judgment of the Tribunal (1950) *Yearbook of the International Law Commission 1950*, Vol II, para 97. Note the move during the 1950s and 1960s into retreating into pragmatism in an attempt to avoid the dilemmas by using the 'language of (State) consent as a representational language'; see A Carty 'Critical International Law: Recent Trends in the Theory of International Law' (1991) 2 *European Journal of International Law* 66, 67.

316 See International Committee of the Read Cross 'Treaties, State Parties and Commentaries', URL: https://www.icrc.org/IHL.

317 See WA Schabas *Genocide in International Law: the Crime of Crimes* (2nd edn Cambridge University Press Cambridge 2009) 417–25 (states referred to the potential for 'dangerous international tension').

318 JS Pictet *The Geneva Convention of 12 August 1949: Commentary* Vol 1 (Geneva 1952) (common repression regime is based on *aut dedere aut judicare* that he read as 'universality of jurisdiction'). Contrast BV Roeling 'Aspects of the Criminal Responsibility for Violations of the Laws of War' in A Cassese (ed) *The New Humanitarian Law of Armed Conflict* (Editoriale Scientifijica Naples 1979) 202.

Argentina and his status as one of the architects of the Holocaust. The trial became a more direct focal point for the attempts to capture the Holocaust within international legal vocabulary as opposed to primarily capturing the atrocities within context of an aggressive war.[319] This returned the discipline to the debates surrounding the adequacy of trials in the face of administrative massacres. Arendt believed Eichmann should be hanged, yet the trial and conviction were completely inadequate.[320] In her view, this served to demonstrate how the legal system was transcended and shattered by such crimes. To impute criminal intent to individuals in situations of administrative atrocities presupposes that like all 'normal persons', the perpetrators must have understood the criminal nature of the acts when 'under the conditions of the Third Reich only "exceptions" could be expected to act normally.'[321] As we noted in section 3, she articulated the core dilemma of such trials in that it is impossible to separate the collective guilt of the state from the crimes, yet a trial pronounced only individual guilt.[322] Most international lawyers sidestepped these dilemmas and instead, argued over whether such trials should become legal routine or should be an exceptional case that illustrates the necessity of an international criminal court.[323]

On jurisdictional rules, the Eichmann trial also returned to the debates surrounding the 'validity' of universal jurisdiction because the trial involved a non-national accused of acts committed against (arguably) non-nationals as the crimes occurred prior to creation of the state of Israel. In turn, the trial judgment and defence counsel mounted the same battle-lines as adopted in the post-war 1940s trials.[324] The courts' invocation of universal jurisdiction appealed to their idea of acting as an agent of the international community, responding to universal moral outrage at Eichmann's crimes. Yet Simpson notes that, similar to the practice of piracy, it was also a trial 'exercised by those with specific national interests'.[325] Israel had a particular interest in prosecuting Eichmann that was not an 'incidental consequence' of the moral outrage and this is evident by its invocation of other bases of jurisdiction.[326] In this sense, 'the imperatives of sovereignty dominated the trial' as the victim also was both the Jewish people and the Israeli state. The trial was then 'an act of reasserting sovereignty in the face of an international failure to save the Jewish people, global indifference to the capture of fugitive Nazis and regional enmity'.[327]

Eichmann's defence counsel argued that universal jurisdiction only arose where there was no competent territorial jurisdiction and an international tribunal with

319 E Russell *The Trial of Adolf Eichmann* (Pimlico London 2002) and Simpson (n 7) 168.

320 Quoted in M Koskenniemi 'Between Impunity and Show Trials' (2002) 6 *Max Planck Yearbook of United Nations Law* 1, 2.

321 H Arendt (n 274), 27.

322 ibid 294 and 298.

323 Contrast H Silving 'In re Eichmann: A Dilemma of Law and Morality' (1961) 55 *American Journal of International Law*, 307, and D Lasok 'Eichmann Trial' (1962) 11 *International and Comparative Law Quarterly* 355, 368.

324 The binary narratives are discussed in greater detail in Chapter 4, section 2.

325 Simpson (n 87) 41.

326 ibid.

327 ibid.

jurisdiction had not been established.[328] This pulled on the law of piracy debates and implied that territorial jurisdiction was exclusive unless exceptional circumstances were involved, such as an absence of sovereignty.[329] He argued that that the principle operated according to *aut dedere aut punire* and therefore, required a refusal of an offer to extradite to the state of location of the offence.[330] He also adopted Kelsen's critic of individual criminal responsibility in that an act imputable to a foreign state cannot be the subject of criminal jurisdiction in a foreign court.[331] In opposition, the Israeli Trial and Appeals Courts drew on Lauterpacht, Cowles and Wright and identified a lack of a prohibition against exercising jurisdiction. They then turned to demonstrate a permission under international law 'with respect to such crimes . . . in the absence of an international criminal court' based on the nature of the crime.[332] The trial judgment used de Vabres's legal history and presented this history as if it had developed in a linear, uninterrupted fashion and that the concept of universal jurisdiction was undisputed from that advocated by the courts, that is, universal jurisdiction over crimes against international law. Yet when it provided empirical support for universal jurisdiction over crimes against international law, it only cited the Allied trials under the *Control Council Law*.[333]

The courts agreed with the defence counsel that there was a precondition of a refusal of an offer to extradite, yet disagreed on the interpretation of the facts as West Germany had not sought Eichmann's extradition.[334] Both the courts and defence counsel sidestepped whether this subsidiary jurisdiction was preconditioned upon voluntary (as opposed to involuntary) presence, as their debate centred on Eichmann's abduction. Yet in their practice of exercising jurisdiction over piracy, imperial states legitimized their capacity to secure custody through forcible capture. The courts disagreed with the defence counsel that Israeli law was being applied retroactively. Rather, following the IMT's position, the Israeli courts found an exception in the 'extraordinary instance' of Nazi atrocities[335] and therefore, the social circumstances that have been addressed in immunity case law 'do not fit the realities of Nazi Germany'.[336]

Writing after the Eichmann Trial, Lasok considered that the IMT process confirmed that states could prosecute war crimes with custody of the accused as the exclusivity of territorial jurisdiction 'can hardly be sustained' in the face of such moral outrage.[337] Yet as we noted at the beginning of this section, international lawyers differed over whether such a trial should become a precedent. Parvikko

328 *Written Pleadings submitted by Counsel for the Appellant Adolf Eichmann*, para 2 (a) (linked to claims that jurisdiction was invalid as and was not internationally authorised (treaty based) but unilateral).

329 ibid para 2 (b). See section 1.1 above.

330 ibid.

331 ibid.

332 *AG v Eichmann* (1968) 36 ILR 5, 26 and 291.

333 ibid 29.

334 ibid 302.

335 ibid 12.

336 ibid 46 and 309–10.

337 Lasok (n 303) 355, 364–5 See also Fawcett (n 313) 208.

divides the literature into what she calls legal positivists and moralists and identifies a division into reducing the trial to an extraordinary (singular) event or to a necessary pattern in the face of extraordinary evil.[338] The legal positivists argued that the trial appears to have broken all formal barriers to arbitrariness, could 'encourage imitation in less meritorious cases' and therefore, the necessary policy is the creation of an international criminal court.[339] Moralists argued that the situation giving rise to the trial was 'extreme and unprecedented' and therefore, positive law should cede to natural law ethical principles 'in order to avoid flagrant injustice'.[340]

During the Cold War, Eichmann represented a dramatic trial that seemed unable to galvanize a greater willingness of either of the superpowers to search for and punish Nazi war crimes. Instead, the next two decades were more dominated with treaty drafting than trial proceedings. The 1970 Hague Convention on Unlawful Seizure of Aircraft is illustrative of this move to establish treaty regimes in which state parties are obliged to establish various bases of jurisdiction over treaty-defined offences.[341] Similar to the 1920s, international lawyers left the legitimacy of what seemed like an 'absolute' freedom to contract unquestioned and instead, debated over the 'appropriate' justifications for extra-territorial jurisdiction within those treaty provisions.[342] This treaty drafting was conducted within the ideological battleground of the Cold War and set against a move of a minority argument that had 'long been in circulation' into the mainstream of liberal capitalist ideas.[343] Neoliberalism (or the radicalization of Adam Smith's economic theory) became a mainstream ideology that underpinned what Klein calls the 'shock doctrine', which was applied in various situations such as Pinochet's Chile.[344] Neoliberalism 'sloughed off the notion of common good associated with the welfare state of the twentieth century in favour of an arrant individualism, which is relentlessly pursued through the market'.[345]

Yet the beginning of the undermining of the welfare state was also the period of the breakthrough of the human rights movement. Moyn argues that human rights vocabulary provided a 'minimalist utopia of anti-politics'[346] and given the ideological battles of Cold War, human rights' anti-politics was particularly attractive when many had lost faith in other utopias.[347] This moment of anti-politics did not last long and compelled human rights advocates to establish

338 Parvikko (n 5) 243.
339 Lasok (n 303) 373–4.
340 H Silving (n 323) 307, 309.
341 Convention for the Suppression of Unlawful Seizure of Aircraft, (1970) 10 ILM 133.
342 Y Dinstein 'Criminal Jurisdiction over Aircraft Hijacking' (1972) 7 *Israeli Law Review* 195.
343 D Harvey *A Brief History of Neoliberalism* (Oxford University Press Oxford 2007) 2.
344 N Klein *The Shock Doctrine: The Rise of Disaster Capitalism* (Penguin Press London 2008). See also Harvey (n 343) 2.
345 M Thornton 'The Demise of Diversity in Legal Education: Globalisation and the New Knowledge Economy'(2001) 8(1) *International Journal of the Legal Profession* 37.
346 S Moyn *Human Rights in History: The Last Utopia* (Harvard University Press Boston 2010), 218.
347 ibid 213.

a political agenda and a vision.[348] As we explore in Chapter 4, this included a creative mutation into a field of transitional justice, and human rights vocabulary supplanted other idioms in addressing post-conflict responses. Part of this movement involved negotiating the Torture Convention in the late 1970s and early 1980s against a context of military regimes in Latin America that were engaged in systematic use of torture and enforced disappearance.[349] In another dimension, human rights advocates successfully pursued civil remedies for an act of torture in Paraguay under the US's Alien Torts Act, a domestic statute that asserted extraterritorial jurisdiction over acts in breach of international law.[350] This was seen as a triumph for human rights litigants and was a critical story within the fight against impunity discourse.[351]

The early 1980s also saw a return of the International Law Commission to the examination of the idea of an international criminal court and, towards the end of the 1980s, Demjanjuk's extradition to Israel and the Barbie trial looked as if the ideal of ending impunity was being re-ignited. In particular, the outcome of the United States courts in *Demjanjuk* re-described the *Eichmann* judgments in terms of custody of the accused so that his extradition to Israel was justified.[352] Yet Demjanjuk's extradition appeared underscore how the Allied search for Nazi fugitives had been woefully inadequate. Both the witness testimony challenges in the *Demjanjuk* case and the infamous 'trial of rupture' in the Barbie trial sat uncomfortably with what the project initiated by Nuremberg model was meant to establish.[353] Even so, the end of the Cold War and the 'new world order' appeared to herald a new beginnings and renewal for what the field considered to be 'law's promise' in the face of mass atrocity.[354] It is this moment of new order that is our point of departure for the portrayal of the 1990s debate in Chapter 4.

Conclusion

We noted that war crimes trials produced narratives of justification and how trials produced pluralist histories in which the defence arguments form an 'unauthorized legacy' of the trial.[355] We noted Simpson's observation that the practice of war crimes trials reflected two ways of thinking about history' that 'infected jurisdictional rules'[356] and we observed this phenomenon resurfacing

348 ibid.

349 JP McSherry *Predatory States: Operation Condor and Covert War in Latin America* (Rowman & Littlefield Publishers Lanham 2005).

350 *Filartiga v. Pena Irala*, 630 F.2d 876 (2nd Cir, 1980).

351 K McLoughlin '"Dispute Incarnate": Philip Roth's Operation Shylock, the Demjanjuk Trial and Eyewitness Testimony' (2007) 3(2) *Philip Roth Studies* 115, 118–19.

352 *In re Demjanjuk*, 612 F Supp. 544 (ND Ohio) and *Demjanjuk v. Petrovsky*, 776 F. 2d. 571 (6th Cir, 1985) cert denied, 475 US 1016 (1986).

353 Koskenniemi (n 320) 26–7.

354 Simpson (n 85).

355 Simpson (n 7) 169.

356 ibid.

within the debates since the end of the nineteenth century. It is apparent that there were narratives and counter-narratives that reflected political preferences and disciplinary concerns and certain positions succeeded in securing the hegemony over an opposing approach. It is noteworthy how these persistent contestations can be captured by the two projects identified by Koskenniemi that because the appeals to a normative order through solidarity or to state individualism can be mapped onto either an appeal to world unity as against sovereign egoism or an appeal to self-determination as against oppressive homogeneity.

We see these pluralist histories in the competing narratives in the Eichmann trial where the Israeli courts and Eichmann's defence counsel delved back into earlier debates, isolated their preferences and conjured up what seemed to be compelling opposing legal narratives. We noted how the *Eichmann* narrative was drawn upon and re-described on the question of custody of the accused in the Demjanjuk trial, a trial set against the overwhelming failure of the Allied search for Nazi fugitives and the continuing escalation of the Israeli-Palestinian conflict.

The post-1989 'new world order' seemed to herald a triumph for Western liberalism and for human rights as the last utopia and within this wider context, the field of international criminal law emerged to supplant other idioms in dealing with past atrocities. The *Eichmann* narrative was brought into the space opened up by the international criminal tribunals as it provided the narrative to justify the full realization of what the *Einsatzgruppen* trial called a court of humanity that never adjourns. It was as if the *Eichmann* narrative could build an indispensable complement to international criminal tribunals that allowed those tribunals to self-identify as the 'real' sites of international criminal justice, yet simultaneously avoid their credibility being eroded by their incapacity to prosecute all those accused or even secure their custody. Of course, the opposing position of Eichmann's defence counsel shadowed the *Eichmann* narrative into the 1990s debates and was pulled upon at the stage when a court of humanity appeared to be realizable. Both positions cancelled each other out and this meant that certain avenues continued while others were discontinued in the debate.

References

Anghie, A *Imperialism, Sovereignty and the Making of International Law* (Cambridge University Press Cambridge 2005).

Anghie, A 'Finding the Peripheries: Sovereignty and Colonialism in Nineteenth Century International Law' (1999) 40 *Harvard International Law Journal* 1.

Anghie, A 'Francisco De Vitoria and the Colonial Origins of International Law' (1996) 3 *Social and Legal Studies* 321.

Anon 'The Nyon Arrangements: Piracy by Treaty?' (1938) 19 *British Yearbook of International Law* 198.

Anon 'Reply of the Allies: Mr Asquith's Speech' *The Times* (2 March 1915).

Arendt, H *Eichmann in Jerusalem: Report on the Banality of Evil* (Penguin Books New York 2006).

Bass, G *Stay the Hand of Vengeance: The Politics of War Crimes Trials* (Princeton University Press Princeton 2000).

Battle, GG 'The Trials Before the Leipsic Supreme Court of Germans Accused of War Crimes' (1921–22) 8 *Virginia Law Review* 1.

Benton, LA *Law and Colonial Culture: Legal Regimes in World History 1400–1900* (Cambridge University Press Cambridge 2002).

Berman, B 'Privileging Combat? Contemporary Conflict and the Legal Construction of War' (2004–2005) 43 *Columbia Journal of Transnational Law* 1.

Berman, N 'Modernism, Nationalism and the Rhetoric of Reconstruction' (1992) 4 *Yale Journal of Law and the Humanities* 353.

Berman, N 'Between Alliance and Localisation: Nationalism and the New Oscillationism' (1993–94) 26 *New York University Journal of International Law and Policy* 499.

Blackstone, W *Commentaries on the Laws of England* Vol 4 (Clarendon Press Oxford 1765–1769).

Bloxham, D *Genocide on Trial: War crimes trials and the formation of history and memory* (Oxford University Press Oxford), 78.

Bloxham, D 'From the International Military Tribunal to the Subsequent Nuremberg Proceedings: The American Confrontation with Nazi Criminality revisited' (2013) 98(332) *History* 567.

Borgwardt, E 'A New Deal for the Nuremberg Trial: The Limits of Law in Generating Human Rights Norms' (2008) 26(3) *Law and History Review* 679.

Bower, G 'The Laws of War: Prisoners of War and Reprisals' (1915) 1 *Transactions of the Grotius Society* 23.

Carnegie, AR 'Jurisdiction over Violations of the Laws of War' (1963) 39 *British Yearbook of International Law* 402.

Carty, A *The Decay of International Law: A Reappraisal of the Limits of the Legal Imagination in International Affairs* (Manchester University Press Manchester 1986).

Carty, A 'Interwar German Theories of International Law: The Psychoanalytical and Phenomenological Perspectives of Hans Kelsen and Carl Schmitt' (1994–95) 16 *Cardozo Law Review* 1235.

Carty A 'Critical International Law: Recent Trends in the Theory of International law' (1991) 2 *European Journal of International Law* 66.

Commission on the Responsibility of the Authors of the War (1920) 14(1/2) *American Journal of International Law* 95.

Cowles, WB 'Universal Jurisdiction over Violations of the Laws of War' (1945) 33(2) *California Law Review* 177.

De la Rasilla del Morales, I 'In the General Interest of Peace? British International Lawyers and the Spanish Civil War' (2016) *Journal of the History of International Law* 1.

De Vabres, D 'Pour quells delits convient-il d'admettre la competence universelle' (1932) 9 *Revue International de Droit Penal* 315.

De Vabres, D *Les Principes Modernes du Droit Pénal International* (Sirey Paris 1928).

De Vattel, E *Law of Nations or the Principles of Natural Law* Book I, Chapter XIX (Carnegie Institution Washington 1916).

Dinstein, Y 'Criminal Jurisdiction over Aircraft Hijacking' (1972) 7 *Israeli Law Review* 195.

Finch, GA 'Superior Orders and War Crimes' (1921) 15 *American Journal of International Law* 440.

Garner JW 'Punishment of Offenders against the Laws and Customs of War' (1920) 14 *American Journal of International Law* 70.

Garrod, M 'The Protective Principle of Jurisdiction over War Crimes and the Hallow Concept of Universality' (2012) 12 *International Criminal Law Review* 763.

Grotius, H *De Jure Belli Ac Pacis Libri Tres* FW Kelsey (tr) Clarendon Press Oxford 1925).
Hall, WE *International Law* (8th edn Clarendon Press Oxford 1924).
Harvard Research on International law, *Draft Convention on jurisdiction with respect to crime* (1935) 29 *American Journal of International Law* Supplement 439.
Harvard Research on International Law 'Draft Convention on Piracy' (1932) 26 *American Journal of International Law* Supplement 739.
Harvey, D *A Brief History of Neoliberalism* (Oxford University Press Oxford 2007).
Heller, KJ *Nuremberg Military Trials and the Origins of International Criminal Law* (Oxford University Press Oxford 2011).
Heller-Roazen D *The Enemy of All: Piracy and the Law of Nations* (Zone Books New York 2009).
International Committee of the Read Cross 'Treaties, State Parties and Commentaries', URL: https://www.icrc.org/IHL.
Institute of International Law 'Règles relatives aux conflits des lois pénales en matière de compétence' (1883–85) 7 *Annuaire de l'Institut de Droit International* (Munich Session 1883).
Institute of International Law 'Manual of the Laws of War on Land' (Oxford 1881–82).
Institute of International Law 'Resolution on the Conflict of Penal Laws with respect to Competence' (Cambridge 1931).
International Law Association '*Report of the Thirty-Fourth Conference Vienna, 1926*' (Sweet & Maxwell Ltd London 1927).
Kelsen, H 'Will the Judgment in the Nuremberg Trial constitute a Precedent in International Law' (1947) 1 *International Law Quarterly* 153.
Kelsen, H 'The Legal Status of the Unconditional Surrender' (1945) 39 *American Journal of International Law* 518.
Kennedy, D 'The International Style in Post-War Law and Policy' (1994) 12 *Utah Law Review* 7.
Kennedy, D 'Primitive Legal Scholarship' (1986) 27(1) *Harvard International Law Journal* 1.
Kennedy, D 'International Law and the Nineteenth Century: History of an Illusion' (1996) 65 *Nordic Journal of International Law*.
Kennedy, D 'When Renewal Repeats: Thinking Against the Box' (2000) 32 *NYU Journal of International Law and Policy* 335.
Kennedy, D 'Move to Institutions' (1986–87) 8 *Cardozo Law Review* 841.
Klein, N *The Shock Doctrine: The Rise of Disaster Capitalism* (Penguin Press London 2008).
Kleinschmidt, H 'The Family of Nations as an Element of the Ideology of Colonialism' (2016) *Journal of the History of International Law* 1.
Kontorovich, E 'The Piracy Fallacy: Modern Universal Jurisdiction's Hollow Foundation' (2004) 45(1) *Harvard International Law Journal* 183.
Koskenniemi, M 'The Preamble of the Universal Declaration of Human Rights' in G Alfredsson and A Eide (eds.) *The Universal Declaration of Human Rights: A Common Standard of Achievement* (Kluwer Law International Dordrecht 1999).
Koskenniemi, M *Gentle Civilizer of Nations: International Law since 1870* (Cambridge University Press Cambridge 2005).
Koskenniemi, M '"Not Accepting the Iroquois Themselves . . .": Sociological Thought and International Law', *Max Weber Lecture* (April 2007).
Koskenniemi, M 'Into Positivism: Georg Friedrich von Martens (1756–1821) and Modern International Law' (2008) 15(2) *Constellations* 189.

Koskenniemi, M 'The Civilizing Mission: International Law and the Colonial Encounter in the late 19th Century' (Bonn 2004), URL: http://www.helsinki.fi/eci/Publications/Koskenniemi/Bonn.pdf.

Koskenniemi, M 'Hersch Lauterpacht' in J Beatson et al. *Jurists uprooted: British émigré lawyers* (Oxford University Press Oxford 2004).

Koskenniemi, M 'Lauterpacht: The Victorian Tradition in International Law' (1997) 2 *European Journal of International Law* 215.

Koskenniemi, M 'Hersch Lauterpacht and the Development of International Criminal Law' (2004) 2 *Journal of International Criminal Justice* 810.

Koskenniemi, M 'Between Impunity and Show Trials' (2002) 6 *Max Planck Yearbook of United Nations Law*, 2.

Lasok, D 'Eichmann Trial' (1962) 11 *International and Comparative Law Quarterly* 355.

Laughland, J *A History of Political Trials: From Charles I to Saddam Hussein* (Peter Lang Oxford 2008) 106.

Lauterpacht, H 'Insurrection et Piraterie' (1939) 46 *Revue générale de droit international public* 513.

Lauterpacht, H 'The Law of Nations and the Punishment of War Crimes' (1944) 21 *British Yearbook of International Law* 58.

Lauterpacht, H 'General Rules of the Law of Peace', in E Lauterpacht (ed) *International Law. Being the Collected Papers of Sir Hersch Lauterpacht*, Vol 1 (Cambridge University Press Cambridge 1970).

Lauterpacht, H 'Draft Nuremberg Speeches' (2012) 1(1) *Cambridge Journal of International and Comparative Law* 72.

Lewis, M *The Birth of the New Justice: The Internationalization of Crime and Punishment 1919–1950* (Oxford University Press Oxford 2014).

Lorca, AB 'Universal International Law: Nineteenth-Century Histories of Imposition and Appropriation' (2010) 51(2) *Harvard International Law Journal* 475.

Lorimer, J *The Institutes of the Law of Nations: Vol II* (Blackwood & sons London 1883–84).

Marshall, CK 'Putting Privateers in Their Place: The Applicability of the Marque and Reprisal Clause to Undeclared Wars' (1997) 64 *University of Chicago Law Review* 953.

Martineau, A 'Overcoming Eurocentrism? Global History and the Oxford Handbook of the History of International Law' (2014) *European Journal of International Law* 329.

McLoughlin, K '"Dispute Incarnate": Philip Roth's Operation Shylock, the Demjanjuk Trial and Eyewitness Testimony' (2007) *Philip Roth Studies* 115.

McSherry, JP *Predatory States: Operation Condor and Covert War in Latin America* (Rowman & Littlefield Publishers Lanham 2005).

Memorandum by the Secretary General 'The Charter and Judgment of the Nuernberg Tribunal: History and Analysis' UN Doc A/CN.4/5.

Mensel, RE 'Jurisdiction in Nineteenth Century International Law and its Meaning in the Citizenship Clause of the Fourteenth Amendment' (2012–13) 32 *St. Louis University Public Law Review* 331.

Mercier, A 'Le conflit des lois pénales en matiére de competence' (1931) *Annuaire de l'Institut de Droit International* 87, 134.

Mikliszanski, K 'Le systéme de l'universalité du droit de punir et le droit penal subsidiare' (1936) *Revue de science criminelle et de droit pénal comparé* 331.

Mills, WC 'The Nyon Conference: Neville Chamberlain, Anthony Eden and the Appeasement of Italy in 1937' (1993) XV(1) *International History Review* 1.
Morgenthau, H 'Positivism, Functionalism and International Law', (1940) 34 *American Journal of International Law* 260.
Moyn, S *Human Rights in History: The Last Utopia* (Harvard University Press Boston 2010).
Obregon, L 'The Civilized and the Uncivilized' in B Fassbender and A Peters (ed) *Oxford Handbook of History of International Law* (Oxford University Press Oxford 2012).
Padeldorf, NP 'The International Non-Intervention Agreement and the Spanish Civil War' (1937) 31(2) *American Journal of International Law* 226.
Pictet, JS *The Geneva Convention of 12 August 1949: Commentary* Vol. 1 (Geneva 1952).
Radin, M 'Justice at Nuremberg' (1945–46) 24 *Foreign Affairs* 369.
Rech, W 'Rightless Enemies: Schmitt and Lauterpacht on Political Piracy' (2012) 32(2) *Oxford Journal of Legal Studies* 235.
Renault, L 'De l'Application du droit penal aux faits de guerre' (1918) 25 *Revue Général de Droit International Public* 5.
Reydams, L *Universal Jurisdiction: International and National Perspectives* (Oxford University Press Oxford 2003).
Rubin, AP *The Law of Piracy* (University Press of the Pacific Honolulu 2006).
Roeling, BV 'Aspects of the Criminal Responsibility for Violations of the Laws of War' in A Cassese (ed) *The New Humanitarian Law of Armed Conflict* (Editoriale Scientifijica Naples 1979).
Russell, E *The Trial of Adolf Eichmann* (Pimlico London 2002).
Schabas, WA *Genocide in International Law: the Crime of Crimes* (2nd edn Cambridge University Press Cambridge 2009).
Schmitt, C 'The Concept of Piracy (1937)' (2011) 2(1) *Humanity An International Journal of Human Rights, Humanitarianism and Development* 27.
Schwarzenberger, G 'The Judgment at Nuremberg' (1946–47) 21 *Tulane Law Review* 329
Shawcross, H 'Closing Address for the United Kingdom of Great Britain and Ireland' (1947) Supplement A: Office of the US Chief of Counsel 62.
Silving, H 'In re Eichmann: A Dilemma of Law and Morality' (1961) 55 *American Journal of International Law*.
Simpson, G *Law, War and Crime: War Crimes, Trials and the Reinvention of International Law* (Polity Press London 2007).
Simpson, G 'Linear Law: The History of International Criminal Law' in C Schwoebel (ed) *Critical Approaches to International Criminal Law: An Introduction* (Routledge London 2014).
Skouteris, T 'The force of a doctrine: article 38 of the PCIJ Statute and the sources of international law' in F Johns, R Joyce and S Pahuja *Events: The Force of International Law* (Routledge London 2011).
Smith, LV 'The Wilsonian Challenge to International Law' (2011) 13 *Journal of the History of International Law*. 179.
Stolk, S 'The Record on Which History will Judge Us Tomorrow': Auto-History in the Opening Statements of International Criminal Trials' (2015) 28(4) *Leiden Journal of International Law* 993.
Thornton, M 'The demise of diversity in legal education: Globalisation and the new knowledge economy'(2001) 8(1) *International Journal of the Legal Profession* 37.

Tusa, J and Tusa, A *The Nuremberg Trials* (Macmillan London 1983).
Willis, JF *Prologue to Nuremberg: The Politics and Diplomacy of Punishing War Criminals of the First World War* (Greenwood Westport 1982).
Wright, Q 'The Law of the Nuremberg Trial' (1947) 41 *American Journal of International Law* 38.
Wright, Q 'War Criminals', (1945) 39 *American Journal of International Law* 257.
Written Pleadings submitted by Counsel for the Appellant Adolf Eichmann (31 January 1962).
Venzke, I *How Interpretation Makes International Law: On Semantic Change and Normative Twists* (Oxford University Press Oxford 2012).

3 Conventional readings

Given the structural tendencies of international legal argument, conventional readings of the doctrines of jurisdiction and immunity are constrained by the need to preserve both paradoxical liberal assumptions of freedom and order. We earlier observed the structural tendencies at play within the endless recurring theoretical debate over the origin of the doctrine of jurisdiction as adeptly illustrated in the case of the *SS Lotus.* We also see these tendencies in the binary opposition of jurisdiction to prescribe and jurisdiction to enforce that reflect freedom (state liberty) and equality (normative order). When we address each principle of jurisdiction, it is apparent that they are open-ended and indeterminate and therefore, the dominant approach is to apply a principle of reasonableness and interests-balancing. Yet this is a move to political discretion where international lawyers decide whether the jurisdiction is reasonable in the circumstances. With these observations in mind, we explore how the debate surrounding the principle of universal jurisdiction reveals opposing approaches on the justification for and content of the principle. In a related vein, the doctrine of immunity of state officials, that is in contradistinction to universal jurisdiction, reveals similar competing approaches. We also explore how there is a move to a 'middle ground' that attempts to navigate some reconciliation between the competing approaches.

1 The doctrine of jurisdiction under international law

Etymologically, the term 'jurisdiction' combines *jus* (or *juris*) and *dicere* (or *diction*), which is translated as 'the statement of the law or power to determine the right'.[1] Under international law, the doctrine of jurisdiction is understood as a body of principles delimiting the competences of states in their mutual relations.[2] Mann conceives jurisdiction under international law as the right of the state to exercise 'certain of its powers'[3] pertaining to the determination and enforcement of legal

1 S Sucharitkul 'International Terrorism and the Problem of Jurisdiction' (1987) 14 *Syracuse Journal of International Law and Commerce* 141, 155–6.

2 FA Mann 'The Doctrine of Jurisdiction in International Law' (1964-I) 111 *Recueil des Cours* 9, 15.

3 ibid 15.

rules[4] or 'to affect the rights of persons'.[5] In other words, it denotes the 'authority to affect legal interests: to prescribe rules of law, to adjudicate legal questions and to enforce the judgments judicially made'.[6] This is a legal concept distinct from regulating the jurisdiction of courts and administrative bodies within municipal law;[7] rather, jurisdiction under international law is considered the sum of external competences of the state deriving from sovereignty.[8] Thus, jurisdiction has been consistently 'equated with "imperium" or sovereignty';[9] it is 'an aspect or an ingredient or a consequence of sovereignty'.[10] The content of jurisdiction (or sum of competences) is premised upon the maxim *par in parem non habet imperium* so that 'while a state is supreme internally . . . it must not intervene in the domestic affairs of another nation.'[11] On this premise, the state possesses and exercises absolute and exclusive rights within its own territory and any exception (to its internal supremacy) must derive from either express or implied consent.[12]

It follows, then, that while the state may legislate within its internal law, this freedom, as an attribute of sovereignty, depends upon 'the overriding question of entitlement'.[13] Therefore, if the state assumes jurisdiction 'outside the limits of its sovereignty', it conflicts with the sovereignty of other states.[14] Accordingly, the extent of a state's sovereignty is more complex than solely its geographical limits. As Mann argues, the issue of right of regulation appears 'fundamentally different from the physical extent of territorial rights or the range of . . . rights over persons'.[15] Therefore, it also concerns the scope of application of a state's domestic law to extraterritorial 'events and persons . . . in circumstances affecting the interests of the other states'.[16] Thus, the state may determine the scope of its criminal law[17] yet this determination should not arbitrarily interfere with the rights of other states. In other words, 'jurisdiction, which in principle belongs solely to the state, is limited by rules of international law.'[18] In light of these observations, it is clear that the extent of a state's jurisdiction is correspondingly a 'relative concept' and while the state's act of delimitation is 'a unilateral act' within its domestic

4 Sucharitkul (n 1) 156.
5 J Beale 'The Jurisdiction of a Sovereign State' (1923) 36 *Harvard Law Review* 241.
6 CL Blakesley 'United States Jurisdiction over Extraterritorial Crime' (1982) 73(3) *Journal of Criminal Law and Criminology* 1109.
7 M Henzelin *Le Principe de l'universalité en droit penal international* (Helbing & Lichtenhahn Bruylant 2000) 15.
8 ibid.
9 I Brownlie *Principles of Public International Law* (7th edn Oxford University Press Oxford 2008) 299.
10 Mann (n 2) 20.
11 MN Shaw, *International Law* (6th edn Cambridge University Press Cambridge 2008) 647.
12 *Schooner Exchange v McFaddon* (1812) 7 Cranch 116, 136.
13 Mann (n 2).
14 ibid 30.
15 ibid 16–17.
16 O Schachter *International law in Theory and Practice* (M Nijhoff Dordrecht 1991) 250.
17 L Gardocki 'The Principle of Universality' in N Jareborg *Double Criminality: Studies in International Criminal Law* (Almqvist Wiksell International Sweden 1989) 57.
18 *Nationality Decrees in Tunis and Morocco Advisory Opinion* (1923) PCIJ Rep Series B no 4, 24.

law, 'the validity of the delimitation' depends upon international law.[19] Here, Mann constructs the interaction between domestic and international law as one of a higher law, determining the existence of a power, and a subordinate law, where the state gives effect to the power allowed to it.[20]

These twin components of state internal supremacy and international law's limitations explain the descriptions of jurisdiction in criminal matters as 'the international aspect of domestic criminal procedure',[21] or the municipal law description of the 'ambit or spatial scope' of the state's criminal laws (temporal, material and geographical).[22] When we examine the relevant legal context or Mann's 'higher' law, criminal jurisdiction is primarily delimited under principles of customary international law, in addition to multilateral treaties governing specific international offences, which authorize or oblige states to establish criminal jurisdiction within their domestic laws.[23] Unlike the field of civil and commercial law,[24] there is no general convention that defines and delimits jurisdiction with respect to crime.[25]

The debate surrounding the origin of the doctrine of jurisdiction remains contentious and in turn, any determination, as to whether the state's claim to jurisdiction is permitted or prohibited, can be controversial. In the *Lotus* case, the parties disagreed whether a state must 'point to some title to jurisdiction' or alternatively, jurisdiction is permitted if it 'does not come into conflict with a principle of international law'.[26] The dispute arose from the prosecution of a French national in a Turkish court resulting from a collision between French and Turkish ships in the high seas, leading to the deaths of Turkish sailors.[27] In its judgment, the Permanent Court of International Justice (PCIJ) concluded that international law consisted of a general liberty of states, where 'rules of law binding upon states . . . emanate from their own free will as expressed in conventions or by usages . . .'.[28] The function of the rule of law then is 'to regulate relations between these co-existing independent communities or with a view to the achievement of common aims'.[29] In light of this general liberty, 'restrictions on

19 *Anglo-Norwegian Fisheries Case* (1951) ICJ Rep 116.
20 Mann (n 2) 16.
21 I Cameron *The Protective Principle of International Criminal Law* (Dartmouth Aldershot 1994) 11.
22 G Schwarzenberger *International Law Volume I* (3rd edn Stevens and Sons London 1957) 255 (rejecting international criminal law 'in any true sense').
23 RS Clark 'Offences of International Concern: Multilateral State treaty practice in the Forty Years since Nuremberg' (1988) 57 *Nordic Journal of International Law* 49.
24 See Convention on Jurisdiction and Recognition and Enforcement of Judgments in Civil and Commercial Matters (adopted 30 October 2007) OJ L 339.
25 See Harvard Research on International Law, *Draft Convention on Jurisdiction with Respect to Crime* (1935) 29 *American Journal of International Law Supplement* 439.
26 *Case of the SS Lotus (France v Turkey)* (1927) PCIJ Ser. A No 10, 18 and 42 (Dissent of Judge Weiss) and 59 (Judge Nyholm).
27 ibid 25.
28 ibid 32.
29 ibid.

the independence of States cannot be presumed' and therefore, this presumption is only rebutted by certain limitations imposed by international law.[30] States are then bound to remain within those limits when exercising their inherent independence. According to the court, one of the foremost of these limitations is the prohibition against exercising jurisdiction (or acts of sovereign authority) on the territory of another state without the latter's consent.[31] It follows, then, that international law requires criminal proceedings to be undertaken within the legislating state's own courts if the state has lawful custody of the accused.

The PCIJ did not consider that the limitation on jurisdiction to enforce necessarily limited the state from exercising jurisdiction 'in its own territory . . . which relates to acts which have taken place abroad'.[32] Here, the court felt unable to conclude that international law comprised of a general prohibition against extending the scope of laws to persons, property and acts outside the state's territory, unless there are specific permissions (or exceptions to the general prohibition). Rather the court concluded from its analysis of the behaviour of states that the 'great variety of rules which [states] have been able to adopt without objections or complaints' demonstrated the 'wide measure of discretion' left to states by international law 'which is only limited in certain cases by prohibitive rules'.[33] Outside of those limitations, 'every state remains free to adopt the principles, which it regards as best and most suitable.'[34] Thus, laws applying to acts committed extraterritorially are within the state's discretion deriving from its sovereignty, unless there is a limitation under international law, and as long as the enforcement of such proscriptions would be conducted on the prosecuting state's own territory.[35] However, the majority in the PCIJ were uncertain if criminal jurisdiction required a different approach, as the territorial character of criminal law is fundamental. Yet the court argued that even where a permissive rule must be established, the court is required to determine whether there is a rule of international law restricting the discretion of states to adopt principles regarding criminal jurisdiction. This is because the court noted that states extended their laws to acts committed outside their territory and did so in ways that 'vary from state to state'.[36] Consequently, it was evident from state behaviour that the 'territorial character of criminal law is not absolute'.[37]

Judge Loder disagreed with the court's assumption that international law is comprised of rules of law where 'everything which is not prohibited is permitted' or 'every door is open unless it is closed by treaty or established custom.'[38] Loder stressed the need for a 'general consensus of opinion' in the development of rules

30 ibid.
31 ibid 19.
32 ibid.
33 ibid.
34 ibid.
35 ibid 19–20 (noted the probable paralysis on the action of state courts if a permission was needed).
36 ibid 20.
37 ibid 21.
38 ibid 34 and 52.

and he disagreed that a consensus could be demonstrated by the 'absence of international disputes or diplomatic difficulties' in response to municipal laws 'which are at variance with generally accepted ideas'.[39] Instead, Judge Loder interpreted the independence of states as meaning that no law could apply or have binding effect outside the national territory. Accordingly, the criminal law could only apply to all persons within the state's territory.[40] Therefore, if the state extends its law to acts committed by non-nationals abroad, it would infringe the sovereign rights of the state of nationality of the defendant. In this instance, the prosecuting state has no right to exercise jurisdiction within the former state. This general postulate on the exclusivity of territorial jurisdiction was considered to be overruled only by an exception recognized by law or a contrary conventional rule that permits jurisdiction.[41] Similarly, Judge Nyholm criticized the majority's reasoning because they seemed to imply that without a rule of law, relations between states were governed by an 'absolute freedom'; rather, he concluded that there must be express consent that demonstrated the recognition of the jurisdiction as authorized by international law.[42]

It follows then that the *obiter* in the *Lotus* judgment appears to presuppose that state liberty precedes the rule of law (the state has a wide measure of discretion).[43] Conversely, the dissenting opinions appear to assume that the legal order preceded the state (territorial jurisdiction was exclusive unless permitted).[44] Whether the law originates in a prior legal order or state liberty remains unresolved in legal discourse. One approach accepts the *Lotus* majority's presumption against restrictions on liberty and thus, requires evidence of a prohibition.[45] Although acknowledging its criticisms, the Joint Separate Opinion in the *Arrest Warrant* case concluded that this presumption (despite certain 'attendant dangers') has a continuing potential 'in the context of jurisdiction over international crimes'.[46] Another approach accepts the *Lotus* dissenting opinions' exclusivity of territorial jurisdiction and thus, requires evidence of permission.[47] Noting that the PCIJ did not conclude whether its *obiter* applied specifically to criminal jurisdiction,[48] Judge Guillaume in his Separate Opinion argued that the combination of the UN Charter's recognition of sovereign equality and the 'impressive legal corpus' of international criminal law indicates a different situation.[49] On this basis, it must be necessary for the state to demonstrate that it is authorized by international law.[50]

39 ibid 34, 44 and 60.
40 ibid and 44–5 (noting exception of nationality jurisdiction).
41 ibid 35.
42 ibid 60 ('the necessity of some action' by states).
43 ibid 18–19.
44 ibid 35 and 44–5.
45 See *AG v Eichmann* (1968) 36 ILR 5.
46 *Case of the Arrest Warrant of 11 April 2000* (2002) ICJ Rep 121 (Joint Separate Opinion) para 50 and 51.
47 Mann (n 2) 35. See also M Akehurst, 'Jurisdiction in International Law' (1972–73) 46 *British Yearbook of International Law* 145.
48 *Case of the Arrest Warrant* (n 46) (Judge Guillaume) para 14.
49 ibid para 15–16.
50 See Brownlie (n 9) 303.

In other approaches, scholars either limit the significance of the *Lotus* judgment to the recognition of certain key concepts or attempt to reconcile the opposing positions. Reydams narrowly extrapolates certain notions as fundamental assumptions, that is, concurrence of jurisdictions and the emphasis within *Lotus* on limitations under international law.[51] Meanwhile, O'Keefe proposes a reconciliation of positions, given the practice of only tolerating exercises of jurisdiction if they come within the accepted categories. He contends that the principles can be conceived of as 'pockets of residual presumptive permission in the interstices of specific prohibitions'.[52] Notwithstanding the theoretical opposition, it is accepted in contemporary scholarship that 'in certain circumstances [permission] and within certain limits [prohibition], it is consistent with international law for a state to exercise criminal jurisdiction in respect of the conduct of aliens abroad.'[53]

2 The binary components of jurisdiction

It is evident then that the relevant framework is a combination of the principles of jurisdiction as limited by the principle of non-intervention, in accordance with reasonableness, mutuality and proportionality.[54] These twin elements of jurisdiction and non-intervention mean that jurisdiction is 'not a unitary concept'.[55] Rather, there are the binary components of jurisdiction to prescribe and to enforce.[56] Although international lawyers debate over the most appropriate terminology, Cameron contends that prescriptive and enforcement jurisdiction is more appropriate in criminal matters.[57] If the state does not have legislative competence (the act is not made criminal under the municipal law), its courts will not apply foreign law to prosecute an individual for the particular conduct.[58] In other words, 'judicial competence cannot be separated from legislative competence', to which it is subordinate to, and the issue of choice of law, the key element in conflict of laws, does not arise in criminal cases.[59] Of relevance here, it is generally assumed that it is necessary for the state to legislate in order to criminalize crimes under customary international law within its domestic legal order.[60]

It follows then that exercising jurisdiction to prescribe is a precondition for the lawfulness of an exercise of jurisdiction to enforce. This means that the

51 L Reydams *Universal Jurisdiction: International and National Perspectives* (Oxford University Press Oxford 2003) 15–16.
52 R O'Keefe 'Universal Jurisdiction: Clarifying the Basic Concept' (2004) 2 *Journal of International Criminal Justice* 735, 738.
53 RY Jennings and A Watts *Oppenheim's International Law* (9th edn London Longmans 1992) 468.
54 Brownlie (n 9) 308.
55 See O'Keefe (n 52) 736.
56 Mann (n 2) 13.
57 Cameron (n 21) 4.
58 ibid 7.
59 ibid 7 ('adjudicative jurisdiction' primarily refers to conflicts of laws).
60 C Kress 'Universal Jurisdiction over International Crimes and the *Institut de Droit International*' (2006) 4 *Journal of International Criminal Justice* 561, 564.

paramount rule is if the state's prescriptive jurisdiction goes beyond the lawful limitations imposed by international law, then any exercise of enforcement jurisdiction within its territory is similarly unlawful.[61] Hence, international lawyers, in general, argue that the claim of jurisdiction over the offence must not be too remote or lead to 'nonsensical or grossly unjust results'.[62] It is considered that if a 'meaningful point of contact' does not arise, the exercise of jurisdiction is excessive and an abuse of power.[63] In other words, this paramount rule is directed at the 'absence of abuse of rights or arbitrariness'[64] and engages state responsibility 'even in the absence of an intention to harm another state'.[65] For instance, states have protested against what they argue are violations of the immunity afforded to state officials under customary international law,[66] or protested against what they argue is a violation of the principle of non-retroactivity where the relevant domestic legal provision asserting universal jurisdiction was absent at the time the offence was committed.[67] However, as Mann argues, any attempt to identify an abuse of power may be challenging because the circumstances for applying non-intervention are 'not always clear'.[68] Thus, he considers that the judgment will be based on 'good faith and reasonableness', that is, an exercise of discretion.[69]

2.1 Jurisdiction to prescribe

We observed that jurisdiction to prescribe is generally understood as the right to create and apply laws,[70] that is, 'whether and in what circumstances a state has the right of regulation'.[71] It is not territorially restricted in contrast to jurisdiction to enforce. Rather, the state can claim the right to apply its criminal law to particular conduct yet without custody of the accused, it 'cannot [claim] to enforce it'.[72] Nevertheless, it is clear that the lawfulness of enforcement on the state's own territory does not automatically imply the lawfulness of its exercise of jurisdiction to prescribe. In other words, the state may not have the authority to arrest a national or foreign national in its own territory because the accused may have committed an act which is lawful in the state of location of the offence, even though it is criminalized under the arresting state's laws.[73] Thus, the validity of jurisdiction to prescribe must be determined by certain principles that are independent of

61 Brownlie (n 9) 308 (constitutionally valid yet breach of international law).
62 ibid.
63 ibid.
64 Mann (n 2) 47.
65 Brownlie (n 9) 316.
66 *Case of the Arrest Warrant* (n 46).
67 O'Keefe (n 52) 742 (prevents a state from prosecuting an accused for an offence that is not criminalized at the time of the offence).
68 Mann (n 2) 47.
69 ibid 48.
70 Mann (n 2) 14.
71 ibid 16.
72 O'Keefe (n 52) 740.
73 Mann (n 2) 90.

the state's own determination.[74] In this regard, the Harvard Research's *Draft Convention on Jurisdiction* with respect to crime identified principles of jurisdiction that it described as the 'greatest common denominator of national law and practice'.[75] These principles are also described as 'generalizations' from 'a mass of national provisions which by and large do not directly reflect [these] categories of jurisdiction in the same way'.[76] In fact, it is argued that the principles have 'strong similarities' and 'often interweave in practice'.[77]

For the most part, the principles of jurisdiction operate concurrently because international law has not developed a rule of exclusivity of particular jurisdictional claims.[78] In fact, there are only rare examples in treaty law where conflicts of jurisdiction have been explicitly referred to.[79] While Mann considers this a 'matter for regret',[80] most international lawyers favour (or at the very least do not disprove of) concurrency.[81] As the principles of jurisdiction are recognized as concurrent, this requires 'further balancing of interests of the states involved and the requirements of justice' in order to determine the validity of claims.[82] According to Reydams, this amounts to a 'delicate' balancing between sovereignty (state interests) and non-intervention (justice).[83] As a result, the principles provide 'no clear answer' or delimit a strict boundary line as to the extent of a state's jurisdiction.[84] Rather, the principles may be 'only evidence of the reasonableness of the exercise of jurisdiction' or, what Brownlie calls, a genuine or meaningful link.[85]

It follows then that international lawyers discuss the principles of jurisdiction in terms of identifying a 'substantial and genuine connection'[86] or 'meaningful link'[87] between the state claiming jurisdiction and the offence, offender, or victim. This concept of genuine connection requires an inquiry into whether the state 'has a "legitimate interest" in the subject matter of its legislation' and whether this 'can "outweigh" the interests of other states'.[88] This is the 'search for the state or states whose contact with the facts is such as to make the allocation

74 O'Keefe (n 52) 741.
75 Harvard Research (n 25) 445
76 Brownlie (n 9) 308.
77 ibid 308.
78 ibid. See also Mann (n 2) 10.
79 Article 31(d) of the 1998 Amsterdam Treaty Amending the Treaty on the European Union, (1998) 37 ILM 56, 74 and article 7(5) of the UN Convention for the Suppression of Financing Terrorism (adopted 9 December 1999, entered into force 10 April 2002) 2178 UNTS 197.
80 Mann (n 2) 10.
81 C Shachor-Landau 'Extraterritorial Penal Jurisdiction and Extradition' (1980) 29 *International and Comparative Law Quarterly* 294, 285.
82 Reydams (n 51) 24.
83 ibid 24. See also C Pappas *Stellvertretende Strafrechtspflege* (Max Planck Institut fuer auslaendisches und internationals Strafrecht Freiburg 1996) 87.
84 JG Merrills *Anatomy of International Law: A Study of the Role of International Law in the Contemporary World* (2nd edn Sweet and Maxwell London 1981) 51.
85 Brownlie (n 9) 308.
86 ibid 299.
87 Pappas (n 83) 85.
88 Mann (n 2) 46.

of legislative competence just and reasonable'.[89] Here it is contended that the state must have 'a close, rather than the closest, connection with the facts, a genuine link, a sufficiently strong interest'.[90] Mann considers that this determination involves a 'flexible and largely discretionary notion based upon the degree of connection'.[91] Invariably, there is a concern to avoid subjectivity and therefore, international lawyers speak of the objective standards of international law, rather than those of the prosecuting state.[92] Hence, the court must determine whether there has been excessiveness or arbitrariness in the claim of jurisdiction based on context or the aggregate of factors.

2.1.1. Jurisdiction over territory

Territorial jurisdiction or the right of the state to exercise jurisdiction over its territory is considered to originate in its sovereignty[93] and is undoubtedly accepted.[94] Nevertheless, the scope of the principle remains a matter of dispute.[95] With the gradual decline of the natural law approach from the seventeenth century onwards, the dominant view became a 'strict territoriality of criminal jurisdiction', that is, laws only have force within the boundaries of the state 'but not beyond'.[96] Nevertheless, there was already a move towards a flexible approach in the nineteenth century[97] and as Mann argues, the *Lotus* judgment rejects the 'strict territoriality' advocated by the dissenting opinions,[98] albeit within the parameters of the territorial principle.[99] The influential Harvard Research's 1935 *Draft Convention on Jurisdiction with Respect to Crime* followed the flexible approach adopted in the *Lotus* judgment,[100] and this move away from "strict territoriality" was increasingly endorsed. However, it remained uncertain whether this flexible approach was justified on state liberty preceding the rule of law (wide discretion) or a legal order preceding state liberty (territorial jurisdiction was exclusive unless prohibited), that is, the *Lotus* judgment's dilemma.

89 ibid 44.
90 ibid 46 and 49.
91 ibid. See also Brownlie (n 9) 308 (conceding that a 'proper law' approach would not necessarily resolve all conflicts of jurisdiction).
92 ibid.
93 *Island of Palmas Arbitration Award*, (1928) Vol XI Reports of International Arbitral Awards (RIAA) 839.
94 *Case of the SS Lotus* (n 26).
95 Mann (n 2) 37–8.
96 See DJ Llewelyn Davis (1937) 18 *British Yearbook of International Law* 49, 64–5.
97 *The Apollon* (1824) USSC 32, 22 US 362, 9 Wheaton 362 (17 March 1824).
98 Mann (n 2) 36.
99 *Case of the SS Lotus* (n 26) 18 ('the constituent elements of the offence' are located on the prosecuting state's territory). See JB Moore 'Report on Extraterritorial Crime and the Cutting Case' (Government Printing Office Washington, DC 1887) 22 (a subjective principle is where an offence is committed on the territory and an objective principle is where it is committed 'within the territory by persons outside'). See also *Al-Saadoon v UK*, Judgment of 2 March 2010 (Appl. No. 61498/08) and *Al Skeini v UK*, Judgment of 7 July 2011 (Appl. No. 55721/07).
100 Harvard Research (n 25).

Of relevance here, Cryer rationalizes why extraterritorial jurisdiction is justified specifically in regards to crimes against international law. He argues that there is a threat of either 'excessive willingness to convict' or 'excessive lenience or willingness to acquit'.[101] For instance, certain *in absentia* convictions are considered to have been based on a manifest desire for convictions, such as Pol Pot and Leng Sary in 1979.[102] In other examples, national courts emphasized the leniency or lack of prosecution in other courts despite *prima facie* evidence against the accused, such as the failure of Chilean courts to overrule the amnesty law prior to Pinochet's arrest.[103] As we observe below, although international lawyers prefer the flexible approach, the parameters of extraterritorial jurisdiction are contentious with conflicting positions across international treaties and within customary international law that appear to only be explained by the political context.[104] In their attempt to deduce a consensus, the Joint Separate Opinion argued that there is a preference for the territorial and nationality jurisdictions within the broader context of a complementary system of international and national jurisdictions.[105] This position appears to reflect state behaviour in treaty and customary practice where all or certain categories of the Harvard Research's *Draft Convention* are adopted, while simultaneously prioritizing territorial jurisdiction. Notwithstanding this apparent preference, international lawyers continue to debate whether certain principles are lawful and/or the extent of their scope.

2.1.2 Jurisdiction over extraterritorial offences

Nationality jurisdiction is the right to exercise jurisdiction over offences committed abroad by nationals.[106] International lawyers have justified this legal basis on different rationales such as the protections afford by the state of nationality abroad,[107] or because the state of nationality does not extradite its nationals due to constitutional constraints.[108] Nevertheless, the scope of the principle remains in dispute because international lawyers disagree over the exact meaning of the term 'national'.[109] As the exact meaning of the term 'national' is open to interpretation, states have asserted nationality jurisdiction beyond the standard scenario of being

101 R Cryer *Selectivity in International Criminal Law* (Cambridge University Press Cambridge 2005) 75.

102 N Jain 'Between the Scylla and Charybdis: Prosecution and Reconciliation: The Khmer Rouge Trials and the Promise of International Criminal Justice' (2010) 20 (2) *Duke Journal of Comparative and International Law* 247, 253.

103 *Chilean Investigation* (5 November 1998) *Audiencia Nacional*, para 8.

104 Compare article 12 of the Rome Statute of the International Criminal Court and article 4(2) of the Hague Convention on the Unlawful Seizure of Aircraft.

105 *Case of the Arrest Warrant* (n 46) (Joint Separate Opinion) para 51.

106 Brownlie (n 9) 303–4.

107 L Henkin, *International Law: Politics and Values* (Martinus Nijhoff Dordrecht 1995) 238 (national 'enjoys the benefits of nationality abroad').

108 Z Deen-Racsmany, 'The Nationality of the Offender and the Jurisdiction of the International Criminal Court' (2001) 95(3) *American Journal of International Law* 609.

109 ibid 606 and 611.

a citizen at the time of the offence. For instance, states have claimed jurisdiction to prosecute offences committed extraterritorially by nationals who were non-citizens at the time of the offence,[110] such as crimes committed during the Second World War[111] or the Rwandan conflict.[112] The 'meaningful link' is considered to be the acquired citizenship of the accused. However, this would appear to overlap with universal jurisdiction. Similarly, states have asserted nationality jurisdiction over those granted permanent residence[113] or refugee status,[114] and international conventions have included 'stateless persons with habitual residence' either or in the same category as nationality jurisdiction[115] or without specifying which principle of jurisdiction applies.[116] International lawyers continue to argue over the legality of such claims. While O'Keefe rejects such claims as 'a form of *ex post facto* criminalization',[117] Deen-Racsmány considers that nationality 'at time of prosecution or at the time of commission' as sufficient to justify jurisdiction.[118]

We noted that one rationale for extraterritorial jurisdiction is to avoid politically motivated trials within the state of location of the offence. Nevertheless, nationality jurisdiction can be also accused of 'unwarranted leniency or unjustified acquittals' because of the 'affinity between the courts and the accused, or political interference in the process on behalf of the accused'.[119] Among numerous examples are the Leipzig trials, within which there were six acquittals out of twelve trials and accusations of lenient sentences to those convicted,[120] or the Indonesian domestic trials for offences committed in East Timor, where twelve of the eighteen defendants were acquitted – of the six convicted, only one was sentenced to a term greater than the legal minimum and on appeal, all were released.[121]

When we turn to the protective and the passive personality principles, they have rarely been explicitly invoked over crimes against international law[122] and when they are invoked, it is usually simultaneously. The protective principle is

110 See Harvard Research (n 25) 440 (included nationality at the time of trial, justified by the *Lotus* judgment).
111 *Polyukhovich v. The Commonwealth of Australia and Another* (1991) 172 CLR 501, para 21.
112 Reuters Africa 'Sweden Indicts Man over Rwandan Genocide', URL: http://af.reuters.com/article/rwandaNews/idAFL5E8M58VS20121105.
113 Article 6(1) bis of the Belgian Code of Criminal Procedure: Preliminary Title.
114 Judgment No. 62/2005 (23 March 2005) (Cour d'Arbitrage).
115 Article 31(1)(d) of European Convention on Action against Trafficking in Human Beings (adopted on 16 May 2005, entered into force on 1 February 2008) ETS 197.
116 Article 7(2)(d) of the Financing Terrorism Convention (n 124).
117 O'Keefe (n 52) 743.
118 Deen-Racsmany (n 108) 615.
119 Cryer (n 138) 77.
120 GG Battle 'The Trials before the Leipsic Supreme Court of Germans Accused of War Crimes' (1921–22) 8 *Virginia Law Review* 1.
121 HD Bowman 'Letting the Big Fish Get Away: The UN Justice Effort in East Timor' (2004) 18 *Emory International Law Review* 371, 394. See *Report of the Commission of Inquiry into the Events at the Refugee Camps in Beirut* (The Kahan Commission) (8 February 1983) URL: http://www.jewishvirtuallibrary.org/jsource/History/kahan.html.
122 Cryer (n 101) 77.

a right to exercise jurisdiction over acts committed abroad which affect the vital or fundamental interests of the state.[123] Similar to dilemmas over nationality jurisdiction, there is an uncertainty over the scope of the principle, which hinges upon the meaning of 'vital interests' or 'national security'.[124] The passive personality principle is the right to exercise jurisdiction over offences committed abroad where the victim is a national. It has always been a matter of controversy.[125] Historically, the Harvard Research's *Draft Convention* and Judge Moore's dissent in *Lotus* are illustrative of the general rejection of the legality of the principle because it was read as too much of an encroachment within internal affairs of states and would lead to politically motivated trials. For our purposes, the *Eichmann* case is particularly illustrative of using both the passive and protective principles.[126] The Israeli trial court contended that Israel could assert jurisdiction based on how 'the crime very deeply concerns the "vital interests" of Israel' and given the 'special connection' between Israel and the Nazi atrocities, the latter of which was 'one of the major causes for the establishment of the state of the survivors'.[127] However, the defence counsel countered that Israel could not claim jurisdiction as it was not a state at the time of commission of the alleged offences, an observation that some international lawyers supported.[128] Despite this controversy, the passive personality principle is invoked as the justification for jurisdiction of belligerents over offences against nationals committed by enemy forces.[129] It has also been invoked over domestically prescribed terrorist offences[130] or over legal residents and persons with refugee status.[131]

2.1.3 The principle of universal jurisdiction

International lawyers read the principle of universal jurisdiction as the most remote form of extraterritorial jurisdiction. They distinguish the other forms of extraterritorial jurisdiction as possessing a link to the elements of territory or population and therefore, engage a direct link or interest to state as an entity. Rather, the prosecuting state claims to exercise jurisdiction over certain offences committed extraterritorially by foreign nationals against foreign nationals.[132] In this way, the principle justifies jurisdiction without the claim of a jurisdictional link or

123 Cameron (n 21) 79–82. See also Council of Europe 'Report on Extraterritorial Jurisdiction' (Strasbourg 1990) 13–14.

124 ibid 2 (devising the normative rationale of 'damaging to national security or other central state interests').

125 Moore (n 132) (alleged libel of a Mexican national, resident in Mexico, by a United States national in United States) and Harvard Research (n 25) 578–9.

126 *AG v. Eichmann* (n 45).

127 ibid 49, 53–4 and 306.

128 JS Fawcett 'The Eichmann Case' (1962) 38 *British Yearbook of International Law* 181, 190.

129 See Cryer (n 101) 77 (yet overlapping with universal jurisdiction).

130 *U.S. v. Yunis* (1988) 681 F Supp 896.

131 'Loi relative aux violations graves du droit international humanitaire', *Moniteur Belge* (7 August 2003).

132 Shaw (n 10) 652 and 668 (a right of 'any' or 'every' state).

legal nexus to the location of the offence (including the constituent element of the offence), nationalities of the perpetrator or victim or the state's security/vital interests,[133] or 'any other ground of jurisdiction'.[134] When international lawyers endeavour to describe universal jurisdiction over crimes against international law, they combine an idea of a lack of a jurisdictional link and an idea of a legal right to exercise jurisdiction over certain 'offences against the international community'[135] that are considered 'offensive to the international community as a whole'.[136] Therefore, there are multiple interpretations over the justification for and 'exact' parameters of the principle that privilege either the ideas of fundamental interests or individual liberty.

Writers describe the debate over universal jurisdiction in terms of various dichotomies that appear to fall within the naturalism-positivism dichotomy.[137] For instance, Henzelin categorizes the various legal arguments as deriving from either an 'absolute' theory or an (opposing) 'delegated' theory which we will return to later.[138] Under the absolute theory, the state derives a right from a transcendent duty, divine or natural law, or need for 'human justice'[139] and, in this way, the state acts as part of a *civitas maxima*.[140] This assumes that the state secures the common interest in repressing crime, assuming a 'genuine moral community comprising all humanity'.[141] In other words, this approach emphasizes the normative proscription (normative approach) that appears to fall into the natural law approach and is open to criticism from a positivist counterpoint. Randall and van den Wyngaert are illustrative of this more normative approach as they assume that the principle derives from a normative proscription (the nature of the offence and the common interest in suppressing the crime), albeit they differ in how they justify their assumption. Randall's position is illustrative of the use of legal analogy while van den Wyngaert's position is illustrative of the use of a hierarchy of norms. The use of legal analogy or a hierarchy of norms is then combined with what is argued to be observable state behaviour that demonstrates the existence of a legal rule.

133 Reydams (n 51) 5 and T Meron 'International Criminalization of Internal Atrocities' (1995) 89 *American Journal of International Law* 554, 568.
134 Institute of International Law 'Resolution on Universal Criminal Jurisdiction with Regard to the Crime of Genocide, Crimes Against Humanity and War Crimes' (Krakow 2005).
135 R Higgins *Problems and Process: International Law and How We Use It* (Clarendon Press Oxford 1994) 56–7.
136 Shaw (n 11) 668.
137 A Zahar and G Sluiter *International Criminal Law* (Oxford University Press Oxford 2008) 497 and S Seyedin-Noor 'The Spanish Prisoner: Understanding the Prosecution of Senator Augusto Pinochet Ugarte' (2000) 6 *University of California Davis Journal of International Law and Policy* 41, 76.
138 M Henzelin 'La Competence Penale Universelle: Une Question Non Resolue Par L'Arret Yerodia' (2002) 4 *Revue General de Droit International Penal* 819.
139 ibid 821.
140 ibid (assumes 'existence of a common social or moral order).
141 MC Bassiouni and EM Wise, *Aut Dedere Aut Judicare: The Duty to Extradite or Prosecute In International Law* (Martinus Nijhoff Dordrecht 1995), 22.

Randall adopts the approach of legal analogy in the *Eichmann* judgements,[142] which treats certain offences as similar in character to the 'prototypal offences' of piracy and slavery and in turn, gives rise to a claim of universal jurisdiction.[143] Similar to *Eichmann*, Randall justified universal jurisdiction on the nature of the crimes as 'grave offences' that are an 'affront to mankind' and where the alleged perpetrators are enemies of all humanity.[144] He then combined this legal analogy with what he argued was observable state behaviour that confirmed the rule,[145] in keeping with the approach used in the *Eichmann* judgments. Van den Wyngaert adopts a justification for the principle that derives from the status of the crimes and the goal of preventing impunity.[146] This assumes that the criminalization of itself gives rise to universal jurisdiction. Similar to Randall, she combined this position with what she argued was observable state behaviour that demonstrated states were permitted to exercise universal jurisdiction.[147] Nevertheless, interpretations underpinned by a normative approach, in general, do not address the criticisms that national courts are diverse in their practice and in some cases, adopt idiosyncratic definitions of crimes against international law within their jurisprudence.[148]

These normative approaches can be seen in analysis by scholars as to whether universal jurisdiction can be asserted over war crimes, crimes against humanity and genocide. However, such scholarship rarely includes the crime of aggression even though on its premise, aggression should logically be included. When we look at the discussion on universal jurisdiction over war crimes committed in international armed conflicts, those adopting a normative approach have produced three distinct interpretations of the common provisions of the 1949 Geneva Conventions[149] and article 85(1) of Additional Protocol I[150] as establishing universal jurisdiction.[151] In one interpretation, the validity of universal jurisdiction is derived from the criminalization of itself. Thus, as the Convention's grave breaches regime is considered to have crystallized under customary international law, this criminalization gives rise to universal jurisdiction.[152] Similarly, in justifying universal jurisdiction over

142 KC Randall, 'Universal Jurisdiction in International Law', (1988) 66 *Texas International Law Journal* 785. See also MC Bassiouni *Crimes against Humanity in International Criminal Law* (Kluwer Law International The Hague 1999) 227–40.

143 ibid 794.

144 Randall (n 142) 789 and *AG v. Eichmann* (n 45) 25 and 300 and 304.

145 ibid 800–815 (citing Allied military trials and the modern international treaties as expanding the list of crimes).

146 *Case of the Arrest Warrant* (n 46) (van den Wyngaert) para 46.

147 ibid para 51.

148 Contrast A Colangelo 'The Legal Limits of Universal Jurisdiction' (2006–07) 47 *Virginia Journal of International Law* 149.

149 See Convention (1), (11), (111) and (IV) (adopted Geneva 12 August 1949, entered into force 21 October 1950).

150 Article 85(1) of the Additional Protocol relating to the Geneva Conventions of 12 August 1949 (adopted 8 June 1977, entered into force 7 December 1979) 1125 UNTS 3.

151 J Pictet, *Commentary on the Geneva Conventions of 1949: Vol I* and *Vol IV* (ICRC Geneva 1952–60), 365–6 and 587 (interprets 'search' to mean 'is present' on the state's territory).

152 *Case of the Arrest Warrant* (n 46) (Joint Separate Opinion) para 61.

violations in non-international armed conflicts, this approach adopts the position that the validity of jurisdictional claims should be judged based on the nature of the crime rather than the classification of the armed conflict.[153]

In another interpretation, the criminalization of war crimes is combined with an interpretation of state consent to extraterritorial jurisdiction arising from the provisions of the Geneva Conventions. The treaty interpretations involve a textual analysis that argues the terms 'irrespective of nationality' or 'each High contracting party' imply consent to extraterritorial jurisdiction either irrespective of place of commission or applying to all state parties including non-belligerents to an international armed conflict.[154] This is then claimed to be supported by what is argued to be observable state behaviour in the form of treaty incorporation, *travaux preparatoire* and the leading scholarship.[155] In order to justify jurisdiction over non-party nationals, there is a turn back to a claim of validity of extraterritorial jurisdiction over analogous domestic offences under customary international law.[156] In a similar vein, the criminalization of violations in internal armed conflicts is combined with the normative justification for universal jurisdiction based on the nature of the crimes and a textual analysis of the Geneva Conventions, which draws on the obligation on states parties to ensure respect for humanitarian law and the obligation to suppress all violations.[157] In a third interpretation, the various post-Second World War Allied military trials are read as evidence of state behaviour that gave rise to a customary international law practice.[158] Within this evidence, scholars have cited trials where the tribunal did not refer expressly to universal jurisdiction, but the elements of the crime indicated a claim of universal jurisdiction.[159]

When we look at the discussion surrounding universal jurisdiction over crimes against humanity and genocide, the different interpretations derive a right to claim universal jurisdiction from the criminalization[160] or as a legal consequence of *jus cogens*.[161] Certain national courts' jurisprudence has followed the

153 T Meron, *The Humanization of International Law* (Martinus Nijhoff Publishers Leiden 2006) 118.

154 R O'Keefe, 'The Grave Breaches Regime and Universal Jurisdiction' (2009) 7 *Journal of International Criminal Justice* 811, 813–14 (implicitly refer to extraterritorial jurisdiction as states already have right to prosecute crimes on their territory irrespective of nationality).

155 ibid 814 (fn 9). See also Final Record of the Diplomatic Conference of Geneva of 1949, vol II, section B, 116.

156 O'Keefe (n 154) 812 and 817 (distinguishes *aut dedere aut judicare* from mandatory universal jurisdiction).

157 Meron (n 153) 569–70.

158 Randall (n 142) 800 and WB Cowles, 'Universal Jurisdiction over Violations of the Laws of War' (1945) 33(2) *California Law Review* 177.

159 AR Carnegie, 'Jurisdiction over Violations of the Laws of War' (1963) 39 *British Yearbook of International Law* 402, 422–3 (if one rejects jurisdiction based on Allied sovereignty over Germany and Japan or passive personality).

160 C Tomuchat, 'Preliminary Exposition and Report on the 'Resolution on Universal Jurisdiction over War Crimes, Genocide and Crimes Against Humanity' (2006) *Yearbook of the Institute of International Law*, para 26.

161 A Orakhelashvili *Peremptory Norms in International Law* (Oxford University Press Oxford 2006).

Eichmann judgments in which the Israeli courts deduced universal jurisdiction from the recognition of crimes against humanity in the post-war 1940s trials.[162] Another interpretation merges the criminalization of crimes against humanity with an interpretation of state party consent to the Torture, Apartheid and Enforced Disappearances Conventions to claim universal jurisdiction over crimes of torture and apartheid committed as part of a 'widespread or systematic attack'.[163] The terms of the Conventions oblige state parties to establish jurisdiction over an alleged perpetrator, who 'is present in any territory under its jurisdiction and it does not extradite . . .' by submitting the case to its competent authorities.[164] This has different variants. In one variant, the treaty provisions are read as either a codification of a norm of customary international law or, where there is no pre-existing rule of customary international law, the possibility of an agreement between the parties to refrain from objecting to any state party's exercise of jurisdiction over an accused.[165] Non-state parties have a right (as opposed to a duty) to exercise universal jurisdiction based on a combination of principles, notably individual criminal responsibility and *jus cogens*.[166] In another variant, 'any' or 'every' state component of the generic definition is not to be applied literally and therefore, it is not required that all states must be treaty parties. In this way, universal jurisdiction is simply jurisdiction without any other accepted nexus and can also be claimed under treaty law.[167]

Regarding genocide, there are different interpretations centring upon the Genocide Convention. One interpretation reads the criminalization of genocide under customary international law (as confirmed by article 1 of the Genocide Convention) as giving rise to the right of states to claim universal jurisdiction[168] or, in a related vein, deriving from the status of the crime as a *jus cogens* norm and an obligation *erga omnes*.[169] Another interpretation combines the criminalization with the provisions of the Genocide Convention, based on a particular reading of the *travaux*. It contends that state parties never intended to restrict jurisdiction over genocide to the territorial jurisdiction stipulated in article VI.[170] Rather the obligation to exercise territorial jurisdiction under article VI must be read as a 'compulsory minimum'.[171] Without any prohibitive rule then, universal jurisdiction

162 *R v. Bow St. Metropolitan Stipendiary Magistrate, ex parte Pinochet Ugarte (No. 3)* (1999) 2 All ER 97.

163 Bassiouni (n 142).

164 Article 5(2) of the Convention against Torture and Other Cruel, Inhuman or Degrading Treatment or Punishment (1984) 1465 UNTS 85.

165 Randall (n 142) 820 (noting references made to universal jurisdiction in the treaty drafting).

166 ibid 825–31 (combined with legal analogy to piracy as justified on nature of crimes).

167 O'Keefe (n 52) 746–7.

168 *Case concerning the Application of the Convention on the Prevention and Punishment of the Crime of Genocide (Bosnia and Herzegovina v Serbia and Montenegro* (1993) ICJ Rep 325, 443 (Lauterpacht).

169 Randall (n 142) 829–30 and *Case of the Arrest Warrant* (n 46) (van den Wyngaert) para 59.

170 Article VI of the Convention on the Prevention and Punishment of the Crime of Genocide (adopted on 9 December 1948, entered into force 12 January 1951) 78 UNTS 277.

171 *AG v Eichmann* (n 45) 38 (arguing a *consensus* exists that lack of universal jurisdiction was a 'grave defect').

is derived from the 'nature of the crime as a crime of utmost gravity'.[172] A third interpretation combines the criminalization with what is argued to be observable state behaviour. For instance, in *Jorgic v Germany*, the European Court of Human Rights contended that the concurrent jurisdictions of international and national courts under article 9 of the ICTY Statute demonstrated the recognition among states of universal jurisdiction over the crimes within the Statute.[173] Similarly, scholars refer to the Rule 11bis (A) transferrals, increasing number of national laws and certain national proceedings in order to conclude that state behaviour and judicial authority are sufficiently strong.[174]

One of the most controversial elements of the discussion has been whether custody of the alleged offender is a prerequisite to exercising universal jurisdiction over the crime. Here, the prosecuting state would secure custody through either voluntary presence of the accused prior to the trial stage,[175] or extradition sought from a third state in which the accused is found.[176] Notionally, these situations have been referred to as *in absentia* or 'pure' universal jurisdiction as distinguished from conditional.[177] One interpretation reads observable state behaviour as either too varied[178] or neutral to be conclusive because states are not required to legislate to the maximum permitted by international law.[179] Therefore, there can be no indication from state behaviour whether states are prohibited from exercising universal jurisdiction *in absentia*.[180] On the contrary, the purpose underlying the criminalization of these atrocities is read as not prohibiting 'co-operative overt acts' designed to secure the accused's presence for trial.[181] Other interpretations look at specific treaties such as the Geneva Conventions, and combine the criminalization (and its underlying purpose) with what is argued to be treaty consent from a textual analysis of the treaty. If the Geneva Conventions are interpreted schematically or purposefully, the treaty provisions can be interpreted to support a wide interpretation of 'search and punish' given the silence within the Convention

172 ibid 38.

173 *Jorgic v Germany* (App No. 74613/01) (12 July 2007) para 20 and 69. See also Article 9(1) and 9(2) of the Statute of the International Criminal Tribunal for the Former Yugoslavia, UN SC Res 827 Annex (25 May 1993).

174 WA Schabas *Genocide in International Law: The Crime of Crimes* (2nd edn Cambridge University Press Cambridge 2009) 435 and MC Bassiouni, 'Universal Jurisdiction for International Crimes: Historical Perspectives and Contemporary Practice' (2001) 42 *Virginia Journal of International Law* 81, 120–21. See also Amnesty International, 'Universal Jurisdiction: A Preliminary Survey of Legislation Around the World' (AI Publications London 2011).

175 C Tomuschat 'Issues of Universal Jurisdiction in the *Scilingo* Case' (2005) 3 *Journal of International Criminal Justice* 1074, 1075.

176 *Re Pinochet*, Tribunal de Premier Instance de Bruxelles (6 November 1998), para 3.2.1 and *Re Sharon and Yaron* (2002) 127 ILR 100.

177 A Poels, 'Universal Jurisdiction in Absentia' (2005) 23(1) *Netherlands Quarterly of Human Rights* 64 and R Rabinovitch 'Universal Jurisdiction *in absentia*' (2004–05) 18 *Fordham International Law Journal* 500.

178 *Case of the Arrest Warrant* (n 46) (van den Wyngaert) para 55–6.

179 ibid para 45.

180 ibid para 51.

181 ibid (Joint Separate Opinion) paras 58–9.

on the format of universal jurisdiction.[182] In the other treaties, the final sub-paragraph that is common to most treaty provisions provides that the treaty does not exclude state parties from asserting jurisdictional claims under their national law.[183] Overall, these provisions are read as indicating the lack of a prohibitive rule. Another interpretation involves reading universal jurisdiction through the lens of the doctrine of jurisdiction. This rejects the idea that *in absentia* is a distinct head of jurisdiction that must be separately justified as this conflates jurisdiction to prescribe and enforce.[184] Rather, if there is a permission to exercise universal jurisdiction, then the 'exercise of *in absentia* is logically permissible also'.[185]

We noted above that writers describe the debate in terms of dichotomies that appear to reduce into the naturalism-positivism dichotomy and we discussed, in particular, Henzelin's thesis of an absolute theory opposed by a delegated theory. Under the delegated theory, the state can only derive a legal right from the voluntary contract of legal subjects.[186] This opposing approach assumes that the state is part of a legal order of independent states whose rules derive from voluntary will and therefore, challenge interpretations underpinned by a normative approach as failing to reflect the 'actual' behaviour of states. In other words, this approach emphasizes the factual description (factual description approach) that appears to fall into the positivism approach and is open to criticism from a naturalist counterpoint as failing to be critical of state policy. Reydams and Henzelin are illustrative of this more factual or social description approach as they assume that the principle can only derive from what is argued to be the factual description of the voluntary will of states, albeit they differ somewhat in how they justify their assumption. Reydams's position is illustrative of an inductive study of state behaviour while Henzelin combines a theoretical study of scholarship with an inductive study of judicial authority. These inductive studies are then combined with what is argued to be the rationale for the rule.

Reydams's inductive study contrasts the numerous examples of legislation since the nineteenth century claiming the subsidiary basis of jurisdiction, with the limited examples of legislation claiming extraterritorial jurisdiction over crimes against international law, along with even more limited implementation of such laws.[187] He also notes the diversity of legislation on issues such as immunity or voluntary presence of the accused. Similarly, his historical narrative highlights the diverse (albeit intersecting) range of claims in order to demonstrate the history of the principle as a fragmented concept,[188] which is largely based within legal scholarship rather than state behaviour. His conclusion is that state practice only justified the claim of extraterritorial jurisdiction if there was a prior refusal of an

182 M El Zeidy, 'Universal Jurisdiction in Absentia: Is it a Legal Valid Option' (2003) 37 *International Lawyer* 835, 852–4. Contrast Pictet (n 151).

183 *Case of the Arrest Warrant* (n 46) (van den Wyngaert) para 61.

184 O'Keefe (n 52) 735–6.

185 ibid 748.

186 Henzelin (n 138) 836.

187 Reydams (n 51) 42.

188 ibid 28–42.

offer to extradite (subsidiary basis). However, universal jurisdiction over crimes against international law (as especially *in absentia*) is merely a political aspiration.[189] Henzelin's combined study contrasts the theoretical threads between the different claims regarding universal jurisdiction. He traces a unilateral form to Hobbes and his followers' concept of sovereignty, a delegated form to Italian and German legal traditions and an absolute form to natural law philosophy within Greek, Christian and the classical traditions.[190] This similarly highlights the diverse range of claims within legal thought. In regards to the inductive study, he reads the cases cited as empirical support for universal jurisdiction over crimes against international law as also potentially justified by other competences (such as passive personality), or as a delegation under treaty law.[191] His conclusion is that unilateral form must be rejected on normative grounds, that the absolute is not supported by the consent of states and that the delegated constitutes the only *reasonable* concept of universal jurisdiction.[192] Another interpretation challenges the hierarchy of norms argument because of insufficient state practice to clarify the legal consequences of *jus cogens*[193] or obligations *erga omnes.*[194]

These factual description approaches can be seen in analysis by scholars as to whether universal jurisdiction can be asserted over war crimes, crimes against humanity and genocide. When we explore the debate surrounding universal jurisdiction over war crimes, those adopting a factual description approach have produced four distinct interpretations of the 1949 Geneva Conventions as failing to reflect universal jurisdiction. Each interpretation separates the criminalization of war crimes from the particulars of the jurisdictional regime. In one interpretation, the separation of the jurisdictional regime is combined with an interpretation of state consent. It is argued that states did not intend for the Conventions to impose a positive obligation to establish jurisdiction[195] or alternatively, for the regime to govern the jurisdiction of national courts.[196] In another interpretation, the criminalization of war crimes, for which there is individual criminal responsibility under international law, is read as producing a conceptual distinction. Here, the jurisdictional regime of Conventions is considered a distinct regime from that governing state jurisdiction over acts criminalized under domestic law.[197]

In a third interpretation, the Conventions are read as an implementation of Grotius's concept of *aut dedere aut punire.* This is read as unable to support the claim that states may exercise jurisdiction regardless of any jurisdictional link,

189 ibid.
190 Henzelin (n 7) 66–7, 72–8 and 81–110.
191 ibid 423 and 448 (normatively rejects the unilateral theory).
192 ibid 447–8.
193 L Benavides, 'The Doctrine of Universal Jurisdiction: Its nature and scope' (2001) 1 *Annuaire Derechos International* 19, 29 (uncertainty over what effects *jus cogens* produces).
194 Higgins (n 135) 57–8.
195 AP Rubin 'Formal Statement on HR 2587' reproduced as Appendix 3, Hearing before Sub-Committee on Immigration (US Government Printing Office Washington, DC 1996).
196 *Case of the Arrest Warrant* (n 46) (Guillaume) para 6 and (Ranjeva) para 7.
197 Brownlie (n 9) 306.

that is, the voluntary presence of the accused.[198] This has also been combined with further interpretation of state consent, namely the improbability that drafters would adopt universal jurisdiction when the same drafters had rejected it during Genocide Convention negotiations.[199] In a similar vein, state behaviour in regards to jurisdiction over war crimes in internal armed conflicts is too inconsistent to conclude that a 'uniform set of rules applying to all conflicts' is recognized by states as law.[200] Rather, state behaviour is read as demonstrating a 'resistance' to this move and any claims of universal jurisdiction have been cautious and selective, 'limited to a series of fairly elementary prohibitions'.[201]

When we look at the debate surrounding universal jurisdiction over crimes against humanity and genocide, the different interpretations focus on what is argued to be observable state behaviour, whether in terms of national practice or interpreted as 'actual' treaty consent. Regarding crimes against humanity, the different interpretations focus on the sufficiency of state conduct. It is argued that while claims of universal jurisdiction may appear to be *opinio juris* 'taken at face value', actual state behaviour does not 'reveal sufficient evidence'.[202] As explored above, interpretations of certain treaties that oblige states parties to establish jurisdiction are relevant here. In one variant, the treaty provisions are modified versions of Grotius's concept of *aut dedere aut punire* in light of the development of law of extradition.[203] In Grotius's concept, a natural right to surrender or punish any offence is conditional on the prior conviction of the fugitive offender by the injured state ('he who has been found guilty').[204] In the contemporary treaty version, states are only required to submit the case for prosecution and the obligation is restricted to the specific treaty defined crimes.[205]

In another variant, the word 'universal' is stressed and as the treaty obligations can only apply *inter partes*, this cannot be universal jurisdiction.[206] In a related vein, it is considered impossible to conceive the crimes defined in these treaties as offences against international community, ignoring the possibility of certain crimes being committed as crimes against humanity.[207] Another variant

198 *Case of the Arrest Warrant* (n 46) (Guillaume) para 6 and 9.

199 L Reydams 'The Rise and Fall of Universal Jurisdiction' in WA Schabas and N Bernaz (eds) *Routledge Handbook of International Criminal Law* (Routledge New York 2011) 344–5.

200 S Boelaert-Suominen 'Grave Breaches, Universal Jurisdiction and Internal Armed Conflict: Is Customary Law Moving Towards a Uniform Enforcement Mechanism for All Armed Conflicts?' (2000) 5(1) *Journal of Conflict and Security Law* 63, 101.

201 ibid 102.

202 S Yee, 'Universal Jurisdiction: Concept, Logic and Reality' (2011) 10 *Chinese Journal of International Law* 503, 519.

203 Clark (n 27) 97 (noting how most states refused to extradite in the absence of an extradition treaty in the nineteenth century).

204 H Grotius *De Jure Belli Ac Pacis Libri Tres* Book II, Chapter XX FW Kelsey (tr) (Clarendon Press Oxford 1925) 527.

205 Bassiouni and Wise (n 141) 39–40.

206 Kress (n 60) 567. Contrast O'Keefe (n 52) 755.

207 ibid (excluding the 1949 Geneva Conventions) and Henzelin (n 3) 376 (rather, they imply universal jurisdiction as an ingredient of the treaty).

is to frame the provision in terms of inter-state relations and therefore, they are 'a delegation of jurisdiction by the states of primary jurisdiction to the state of custody'.[208] Any claim of jurisdiction over non-nationals would have to be valid under customary international law.[209] Regarding genocide, the different interpretations focus on what is argued to be treaty consent. In most interpretations, the final decision of negotiators to reject universal jurisdiction is stressed[210] and argued to demonstrate how states chose to restrict the obligation to establish jurisdiction to the territorial jurisdiction, albeit without affecting nationality jurisdiction.[211] In other words, this is read as the treaty drafters only recognizing the validity of territorial and nationality jurisdictional claims.

As noted earlier, one of the most controversial issues within the debate over universal jurisdiction has been over the necessity for voluntary custody of the accused. Those adopting the factual description approach criticize universal jurisdiction *in absentia* as invalid under customary international law. The different interpretations are underpinned by the assumption that the extent of observable state behaviour is insufficient to justify claiming jurisdiction without voluntary custody. In one interpretation, it is assumed that the concept of universal jurisdiction must accord with Grotius's notion of *aut dedere aut punire* and therefore, *in absentia* is invalid as voluntary custody is clearly envisaged in Grotius's writing.[212] The theoretical assumption is combined with the conclusion that state domestic case law, in general, requires an objective link to the offence and offender.[213] In another variant, relevant treaty law provisions are deemed immaterial for an analysis of universal jurisdiction under customary international law[214] and when turning to what is considered relevant state behaviour, national legislation is extremely limited.[215] In another interpretation, it is assumed that the legal argument justifying *in absentia* is premised upon the *Lotus* majority's presumption against limitations. However, it is noted that the *Lotus* majority's opinion would negate law if brought to its logical conclusion and therefore, the ICJ's jurisprudence may be interpreted as requiring evidence of a permissive rule.[216] On this basis, it is concluded that observable state behaviour does not evidence such a rule.[217]

208 D Akande 'The Jurisdiction of the International Criminal Court over Nationals of Non-Parties: Legal Basis and Limits' (2003) 1 *Journal of International Criminal Justice* 618, 623.

209 O'Keefe (n 52) 813 and Akande (n 208) 623.

210 Reydams (n 199) 343–4.

211 *Case concerning the Application of the Convention on the Prevention and Punishment of the Crime of Genocide* (n 240) 766–7 (Kreca). See also UN Doc. A/C.6/SR.130, UN Doc. A/C.6/SR.129, UN Doc. A/C.6/SR.131 and UN Doc. A/C.6/SR.132.

212 Reydams (n 199) 341 (in absentia is 'textually and contextually indefensible').

213 ibid 347–9.

214 *Case of the Arrest Warrant* (n 46) (Guillaume) para 9 (*aut dedere aut punire* requiring presence). See Rabinovitch (n 260) 506–10.

215 ibid para 12 (the only precedent is Israel's 1950 Act). See Zahar and Sluiter (n 186) 500 (referring to a trend in requiring custody in ICC state parties' incorporation laws).

216 Henzelin (n 7) 149–61.

217 ibid 235.

It is evident that the diametrically opposed positions of a more normative approach and a more social description approach are not the end of the discussion. There is also an attempt to draw from both approaches and move to a middle ground.[218] This accepts that universal jurisdiction may be claimed over war crimes, crimes against humanity and genocide on normative grounds (normative approach) yet at the same time, invokes certain limits on the parameters of the principle based on state behaviour (factual description approach), such as rejecting universal jurisdiction *in absentia*. Benavides, Bassiouni and Cassese are illustrative of this 'middle ground'. They all conclude that universal jurisdiction may be exercised over war crimes, crimes against humanity and genocide based on the nature of the crimes albeit in different ways.[219] Benavides uses an idea of double *opinio juris* whereby there is both the recognition of the criminalization of the act and the recognition of the application of universal jurisdiction.[220] The latter is judged against certain normative criteria rather than the extent of factual behaviour of such jurisdictional claims. Bassiouni uses the hierarchy of norms approach as justifying universal jurisdiction combined with an emphasis on *opinio juris* rather than observable behaviour.[221] This widens what is considered as potential observable data and this is read as cumulative evidence of the principle.[222] Cassese implicitly applies the piracy analogy as he speaks of an exception under customary international law whereby universal jurisdiction is justified over certain crimes that 'constitute attacks on the whole international community'.[223]

We noted that those attempting a 'middle ground' position explore certain limits on the parameters of the principle that is argued to be justified upon factual behaviour. On treaty law provisions, they support the view that as such, treaties can only be *inter-partes*; the relevant jurisdiction provisions cannot be considered a claim of universal jurisdiction.[224] On universal jurisdiction *in absentia*, there are different variants, either emphasizing the lack of factual behaviour or emphasizing a normative idea of inter-state relations as reciprocal and incapable of realizing 'universal values'.[225] On immunity of state officials, the dominant interpretation is premised upon the assumption that this prevents politically motivated trials.[226] In this interpretation, a serving senior official is immune from jurisdiction during

218 See S Becker 'Universal Jurisdiction: How Universal Is It? A Study of Competing Theories' (2002–03) 12 *Palestine Yearbook of International Law* 49 (frames the debate as diametrically opposed approaches and a middle third approach).

219 Benavides (n 193) 52–8 and Bassiouni (n 174).

220 Benavides (n 193) 40.

221 Bassiouni (n 174) 88 (identifying two normative threads).

222 ibid 117, 120, 121 and 150.

223 A Cassese, 'Is the Bell Tolling for Universality? A Plea for a Sensible Notion of Universal Jurisdiction' (2003) 1 *Journal of International Criminal Justice* 589, 591–2 (combining limited number of national and international decisions, with a normative rationale based on nature of crimes).

224 Benavides (n 193) 59. (rejects idea of Geneva Conventions as universal jurisdiction) and Cassese (n 223) 594 (exempts crimes subject to individual criminal responsibility).

225 Cassese (n 223) 593 (subsidiary to other jurisdictions).

226 Bassiouni (n 174) 82.

office but once they leave office, they may be tried before foreign tribunals.[227] In a related interpretation, an additional safeguard against political motivated trials is advocated, that is, a first offer to the states that are considered to have a primary interest in prosecuting the crime.[228] Nevertheless, it is evident that this move to a middle ground would appear unsatisfactory to either the normative approach or the factual description approach because the middle ground fails to avoid criticisms of prioritizing normative value over social fact and vice-versa.

2.2 *Jurisdiction to enforce laws*

Jurisdiction to enforce is generally defined as the enforcement of laws by the executive arm of the state using administrative measures permitted by law. In criminal matters, this includes the seizure of property and arrest or detention of persons.[229] We noted that the PCIJ in its *Lotus* judgment identified a fundamental prohibitive rule under international law, that is, '. . . failing the existence of a permissive rule to the contrary, it may not exercise its power in any form in the territory of another state . . .'.[230] Therefore, it was argued that enforcement jurisdiction is 'certainly territorial' and consequently, no state can exercise its competence outside its territory unless permitted by a rule of customary international law or by convention between respective states.[231] Therefore, if a state exercises enforcement jurisdiction in another state without the latter's consent, there is a breach of the prohibition against enforcement jurisdiction even if the jurisdiction to prescribe is valid.[232] For instance, a state's police force may not conduct investigations or arrest suspects on the territory of another state unless it has obtained the latter state's consent.[233] Any measures undertaken without consent constitute excessive jurisdiction by the enforcing state.[234] Consequently, cooperation mechanisms between states are required in order to facilitate the prosecution of certain domestic, transnational and international offences.[235]

One contentious issue that arises from certain states' assertion of universal jurisdiction has been the decision by magistrates to issue an arrest warrant for a suspect, who resides in the state of nationality or the state of location of the offence at the time of the issuing of the warrant.[236] We observed that executing

227 Cassese (n 223) 594.
228 ibid.
229 O'Keefe (n 52) 740.
230 *Case of the SS Lotus* (n 26) 18–19.
231 ibid 14.
232 O'Keefe (n 52) 741. See M Virally, 'Panorama du Droit International Contemporain' (1983) 183 *Recueil des Cours* 5, 91 (any enforcement measures (judicial inquiry or administrative injunctions) are invalid without consent).
233 ibid 740. See Akehurst (n 208) 146 ('acts illegal by nature').
234 Virally (n 232) 91.
235 See Articles 40, 41(1) and 41(3) of the Convention Implementing the Schengen Agreement of 14 June 1985 (consent by treaty to the exercise of investigative acts by other contracting States on their territory).
236 For instance, *Re Pinochet* (n 176) and *Cavallo* (2003) 42 ILM 888.

an arrest warrant is obviously an aspect of enforcement jurisdiction and therefore the *Lotus* principle against exercising any enforcement measures on the territory of another state without consent would apply.[237] Of course, where the suspect is voluntarily present in the state claiming universal jurisdiction over the alleged offence, there is no need for cooperative mechanisms because the arrest takes place in the territory of the prosecuting state. Though the state of nationality may protest against the arrest of its national, there is no breach of enforcement jurisdiction; instead the issue would turn to the validity of the jurisdiction to prescribe. It follows that in the contentious cases of issuing arrest warrants against suspects that are not present in the enforcing state's territory, the enforcing state is attempting to secure custody through extradition from the territorial jurisdiction or third states.

Extradition is a procedure of 'request and consent' or a form of judicial assistance that operates on the basis of reciprocity through extradition treaties.[238] Both extradition and mutual legal assistance evolved from the twin desires of facilitating domestic prosecution of fugitive offenders and overcoming distrust of foreign jurisdictions.[239] Of brief note, there has been dispute within scholarship as to whether extradition treaties are required in the situation of crimes against international law. Brownlie argues that there is an exception to the general rule whereby the accused may be surrendered as of right in the absence of an extradition treaty.[240] In opposition, Green focuses on inadequacy of the empirical data offered in support of an exception; for instance, he notes how General Assembly resolutions on the surrender of war criminals are recommendatory only and can in no way be interpreted as obligatory or directive.[241]

Although treaty law justifies the rendition, national courts determine under domestic law whether to surrender the fugitive in accordance with the extradition treaty and these domestic laws can differ over various matters such as the role of executive and judiciary and the extradition of nationals.[242] Of note here is the move away from a strict rule of non-inquiry and to investigate whether human rights guarantees in constitutional law or international human rights law treaties would be complied with by the requesting state.[243] Previously, in certain common law states, national courts had operated under a rule of non-inquiry, albeit this was not absolute. Under this rule, the courts would refuse to enquire

237 See *Certain Questions of Mutual Assistance (Djibouti v France)* (2008) IC Rep 177, para 171 (whether the act is a 'constraining act of authority').

238 Brownlie (n 9) 316. See also Harvard Research in International Law, Part I: Extradition, (1935) 29 *American Journal of International Law Supplement* 1, 32 and G Gilbert *Transnational Fugitive Offenders in International law: Extradition and Other Measures* (Martinus Nijhoff Dordrecht 1998).

239 IA Shearer *Extradition in International Law* (Manchester University Press Manchester 1971) 5.

240 Brownlie (n 9) 308 (implies that an exception emerged from General Assembly resolutions on surrender of war criminals, combined with the Four Geneva Conventions).

241 LC Green 'Political Offences' (1962) 11 *International and Comparative Law Quarterly* 348–9.

242 J Dugard and C van den Wyngaert 'Reconciling Extradition with Human Rights' (1998) 92 *American Journal of International Law* 187, 188.

243 ibid 188.

upon the 'standards of criminal justice to which the fugitive is likely to be subjected' because such an enquiry was an executive matter.[244] In contrast, civil law jurisdictions had earlier adopted the position that defendants could raise the issue of human rights standards and increasingly, bilateral extradition treaties contained reciprocal clauses where extradition is refused if the death penalty could be applied to the fugitive.[245]

The most dramatic developments have emerged within human rights law treaty interpretation. Both the European Convention on Human Rights and the Covenant on Civil and Political Rights have been interpreted as obliging state parties to determine whether, as a foreseeable consequence of the extradition, the accused would be subjected to torture or inhumane or degrading treatment in the requesting state and if so, not to accede to the request for surrender.[246] Similarly, certain regional treaties contain provisions preventing state parties from surrendering a fugitive when there are 'substantial grounds for believing' that the request is 'for the purpose of prosecuting or punishing a person on account of his race, religion, nationality or political opinion . . .'.[247]

Other matters of particular relevance to the universal jurisdiction cases are double criminality and the consent to conduct investigative measures. The rule of double criminality and the corresponding principle of specialty have been extracted as 'general principles of international law' from what are read as common to treaties and domestic legislation.[248] Double criminality is of particular note as it requires that the act is criminal under the laws of the requesting and requested states[249] and therefore, its function is to ensure respect for the principle of *nullem crimen sine lege*.[250] As a condition to extradition, double criminality requires the court of the requested state to judge whether the act is criminal under its laws. However, the assessment is in the reverse when judging double criminality as a condition for jurisdiction.[251] Second, at the trial stage, the criminal courts of a state may not conduct their proceedings in the territory of another state unless by agreement.[252] This restriction naturally extends to the subpoena

244 ibid 189.

245 ibid 190. See *Magee v O'Dea* (1994) 1 IR 500, 510–13 (regarding common law jurisdictions).

246 *Soering v. United Kingdom* (1989) 161 EHHR (ser A) para 91 and also *Ng v Canada*, UN Doc CCPR/C/49/D/469/1991.

247 Article 11 of the European Convention on Extradition (1957) ETS 24, article 4(5) of Inter-American Convention on Extradition (1981) 20 ILM 733 and article 33 Convention Relating to the Status of Refugees (1951) 189 UNTS 150 (dealing with deportation or return).

248 See Brownlie (n 9) 317 (the principle of specialty ensures that the accused is tried and punished solely for the offences for which extradition has been sought).

249 ibid.

250 Dugard and van den Wyngaert (n 242) 188.

251 C van den Wygnaert 'Double Criminality as a Requirement to Jurisdiction' in N Jareborg *Double Criminality: Studies in International Criminal Law* (Almqvist Wiksell International Sweden 1989) 50 (as a condition to jurisdiction, the issue is whether the act is criminal under the state of location of the alleged offence).

252 See Agreement between the Government of the Kingdom of the Netherlands and the Government of the United Kingdom of Great Britain and Northern Ireland (1999) 38 ILM 926 (*Lockerbie* case).

witnesses and persons of interests as well as other forms of evidence.[253] In civil legal systems, where the investigative and trial stages are conducted by investigative magistrates, it means that the latter cannot engage their judicial police in investigative measures and the arrest of suspects. [254] Instead, as conducted in universal jurisdiction cases, the investigating state must secure consent of the state where the witnesses and/or evidence is located, to have access to witness testimony and other evidence, usually by letters rogatory.[255]

3 Immunity of state officials from foreign jurisdiction

We noted in section 2.2 that the state's ability to enforce its laws within the physical extent of its own territory may be limited by international law. Such a limitation arises when the state does not possess jurisdiction over the subject matter of the dispute even if the alleged transgression was performed on its territory or the alleged offender is found within its territory and the state would ordinarily have jurisdiction. The key limitation here is the rule of immunity of the state and its officials from the jurisdiction of foreign national courts. This is a plea that 'bars the national court of one State from adjudicating the disputes of another State'.[256] Its function is to prevent private parties from seeking to 'enlist assistance of the courts of one state to determine the claim against another state' and thus, it avoids a 'stand-off' between states over the appropriateness of forum. [257] *Schooner Exchange v McFaddon* acknowledged the cardinal rule that no sovereign could be amendable to another and pronounced that states remain bound 'not to degrade the dignity' of other states through adjudicating the latter's legal rights.[258] This rule was justified in the 'common interest . . . mutual intercourse and an interchange of good offices . . .'.[259]

Of particular relevance to this examination are the personal and functional immunities of state officials.[260] Personal immunity derives historically from the personal immunities of the monarch or sovereign, while functional immunity developed historically from the immunity of foreign ambassadors.[261] Notwithstanding their distinct historical development, 'the immunity belongs to the state which alone may consent to its waiver.'[262] Rather than a broad discussion regarding immunity of state officials and crimes against international law, this section's key focus is on its contradistinction with the jurisdiction of foreign tribunals asserting universal

253 O'Keefe (n 52) 740.
254 ibid.
255 *R v Munesyara* (2009) QCCS 2201 para 15 and *H v Public Prosecutor* (2007) ILDC 636 (conducted rogatory missions to interview witnesses).
256 H Fox and P Webb *The Law of State Immunity* (3rd edn Oxford University Press Oxford 2013) 1.
257 ibid.
258 *Schooner Exchange v McFaddon* (n 12) 137.
259 ibid.
260 Fox and Webb (n 256) 537.
261 ibid 538.
262 ibid 222.

jurisdiction over crimes against international law. In this regard, a brief overview of the distinction between the two types of immunity is constructive.

Personal immunity (or immunity *ratione personae*) relates to status.[263] It attaches to the office in light of international law's recognition of the office as 'an attribute of statehood' that requires the respect of other states.[264] It is generally considered that its function is to secure 'the smooth conduct of international relations' including 'the unimpeded operation of other states' organs in conducting its public functions'.[265] Personal immunity is possessed by the office-holder for the duration of their term[266] and exempts the office-holder from the civil and criminal jurisdiction of foreign courts irrespective of whether the alleged acts were committed in an official or private capacity.[267] As a complete immunity, it precludes the instigation of criminal proceedings for official and private acts performed during office or such acts performed before assuming office.[268] In light of this, it is conferred only on 'officials with primary responsibility for the conduct of the international relations of the state'.[269] Hence, it attaches to a limited group of senior state officials[270] and applies to diplomatic staff on mission[271] and other officials on special mission in foreign states.[272]

Functional immunity (immunity *ratione materiae*) attaches to the act conducted in an official capacity, as opposed to the status of the office. It exempts the state official from criminal or civil jurisdiction regarding acts performed in an official capacity. As the immunity attaches to the act as opposed to the office of state, it applies to both serving and former state officials. However, the plea only bars jurisdiction from 'acts performed in their official capacity' and therefore, does not cover both official and private acts.[273] Of note, van Alebeek identified two

263 Ibid 535.

264 ibid 543 (note debate on whether the immunities attach to the person or are an aspect of state or diplomatic immunity). See article 2(b)(iv) of the UN Convention on Jurisdictional Immunities of States and their Property (adopted 2 December 2004, not yet in force) UN Doc. A/59/508.

265 Zahar and Sluiter (n 137) 504.

266 D Akande 'Immunities and the International Criminal Court' (2004) 98 *American Journal of International Law* 407, 409.

267 *Case of the Arrest Warrant* (n 46) para 55. See also article 2 of the Institute of International Law 'Resolution on the Immunities from Jurisdiction and Execution of Heads of State and of Government in International Law' (Vancouver 2001) (immunity 'regardless of [the crime's] gravity').

268 ibid para 56.

269 Akande (n 266) 409.

270 ibid (noting how the Court's normative argument on immunity's function combined with the phrase 'certain holders of high-ranking Office' could apply to other portfolios within central government). See *Families and Relatives of Persons Affected by Military Operations Conducted by the IDF in the Occupied Palestinian Territories v General Mofaz* (2004) ILDC 97 (making an analogy between foreign affairs and defence in terms of overseas representation).

271 Article 29, article 30 and article 31 of the Vienna Convention on Diplomatic Relations (adopted April 18 1961, entered into force 24 April 1964) 500 UNTS 95.

272 Article 21 and article 29 of the Convention on Special Missions (adopted on 8 December 1969, entered into force 21 June 1985) 1400 UNTS 231.

273 Akande (n 266) 412.

concepts of act of state within the doctrinal history, which she argues, influences the confusion among lawyers regarding functional immunity. The first concept is that the official is immune from suit when ordinarily the state would have been immune, had it been sued in the official's place (act of state as public act). The second concept is that the official is immune when the subject matter of the dispute is an act attributable to the state.[274]

When turning to the focus of this section, it is submitted that there are competing approaches and a move to the middle ground, similar to that which we observed in our examination of the debate over the principle of universal jurisdiction. At the outset, it is important to note that international lawyers have distinguished the removal of the defence plea of immunity from the procedural plea. The former is a defence against liability for the substantive allegations, whereas the latter is a procedural plea against the appropriateness of the tribunal's jurisdiction.[275] The undisputed acceptance of individual criminal responsibility for crimes against international law means that the defence against liability is no longer valid.[276] However, the issue of the appropriateness of the tribunal as a forum for the dispute remains a contentious matter.

Adopting a more normative approach, both personal and functional immunities are always inapplicable in the context of crimes against international law. There are four variants. First, the acts cannot be functions of the state because the conduct is outlawed by *jus cogens* prohibitions, which possess a hierarchically superior status. In this way, a violation of a *jus cogens* norm cannot be a sovereign act and thus, immunity of a state official does not arise.[277] Second and relatedly, the crimes cannot be ordinary state functions that a state alone can perform. Here, it is argued that there is recognition 'that State related motives are not the proper test for determining what constitutes public State acts'.[278] Third, as the crimes are *jus cogens*, criminal liability overrides the procedural plea of immunity; in other words, rules of *jus cogens* invalidate any conflicting rules of international law.[279] As Al-Khasawneh argues, 'when this hierarchically higher norm comes into conflict with the rules on immunity, it should prevail.'[280] In van den Wyngaert's view, the issue was the conflict between individual and state responsibility, where the former must prevail in event of crimes against international law.[281] Finally, there was Belgium's claim that the recognition of individual criminal responsibility combined with certain

274 R van Alebeek *Immunity of States and their Officials in International Human Rights Law and International Criminal Law* (Oxford University Press Oxford 2008) 222.

275 ibid 265.

276 See C Damgaard *Individual Criminal Responsibility for Core International Crimes: Selected Pertinent Issues* (Springer Berlin 2008) 85–126.

277 Orakhelashvili (n 161) 325.

278 *R v Bow Street Metropolitan Stipendiary Magistrate, ex parte Pinochet Ugarte (Pinochet I)* (1998) 4 All ER 897, 939–40 (Nicholls) and 944 (Steyn).

279 *Case of the Arrest Warrant* (n 46) (Joint Separate Opinion) para 85 (arguing that state behaviour is gradually recognizing this idea).

280 ibid (Al-Khasawneh) para 7.

281 ibid (van den Wyngaert) paras 30–35 (citing Draft Code of Crimes (n 230)).

national proceedings against former state officials for criminal offences demonstrated the acceptance of an exception to the rule of immunity in the context of crimes against international law.[282]

Adopting a more social description approach, personal and functional immunity must be applied as a bar to criminal jurisdiction regardless of the context including crimes against international law. In the *Arrest Warrant* case, the ICJ justified personal immunity on functional necessity, irrespective of the context of the alleged crimes.[283] The court implicitly rejected the *jus cogens* argument because it focused on and then dismissed evidence of an exception, including rejecting the view that treaty law obligations can affect immunities of state officials.[284] However, regarding functional immunity, the judgment's *obiter* is open to interpretation. It considered that once the Minister for Foreign Affairs has left office and personal immunity is no longer applicable, the former Minister may be prosecuted before foreign tribunals 'for acts committed before and subsequent to assuming office and during office in a private capacity'.[285] The court's position has been interpreted to mean that a serving and former Minister for Foreign Affairs are treated as analogous for the purposes of immunity. Therefore, the change of status does not admit a different framework rather both immunities remain applicable before national courts.[286]

Fox and Webb contend that the *Arrest Warrant* signifies how there are firm arguments for the classical position in regards to functional immunity because the immunities belong to the state and therefore, the change in status from serving to former state official is irrelevant. If functional immunity is removed, it could arguably impinge arbitrarily upon state officials in the exercise of their functions during office. It would also render the entire internal administration of a state to the jurisdiction of foreign tribunals.[287] On the *jus cogens* argument, they note the lack of guidance in the Vienna Convention on Law of Treaties to overriding effects of *jus cogens* except in the case of treaties. Although *jus cogens* may overrule other rules of substantive law, they argue that the effect of *jus cogens* on jurisdiction or procedural rules was left in doubt by the Convention.[288] They argue that *jus cogens* has 'largely lacked success in further restricting the bar of state immunity', yet they observe that procedural/substantive distinction has been impacted in other areas and cautions against 'too heavy reliance' on the distinction.[289] Based on their analysis of state practice, they argue that state behaviour indicates a removal of functional immunity for state officials before foreign tribunals (other than a former Head of State) in specific situations of

282 ibid para 56.
283 Van Alebeek (n 274) 267.
284 *Case of the Arrest Warrant* (n 46) paras 58 and 59.
285 ibid para 61 (note Judges Oda, Al-Khasawneh and van den Wyngaert dissented).
286 Fox and Webb (n 256) 552.
287 ibid 553.
288 ibid 40.
289 ibid 45 (given the flux in state practice, she likens the practice to 'swings of a pendulum').

'crimes for which by treaty states are under obligation to make penal offences and prosecute in their national systems'.[290]

We noted that there is also an attempt to draw from both approaches and move towards a middle ground. These middle-ground approaches accord with the conclusions of the social description approach regarding personal immunity, yet at the same time, they accord with the conclusions of the normative approach regarding functional immunity. The conclusion is that senior state officials afforded personal immunity would be exempt during office. However, on ceasing office, they would be amenable to prosecution similar to all lower-level officials, as functional immunity could not be invoked before foreign jurisdictions.[291] Two strategies will be explored here. Van Alebeek stresses the distinction that she identifies between personal and functional immunity where the former's immunity from personal responsibility is based on status rather than on the act. Therefore, even if the individual may be held personally responsible for the act, this does not remove immunity based on status. In her view, the necessary balancing of interests should be a policy decision of states and any change in law, as determined by the courts, must be through an inductive study of state practice.[292] Accordingly, she rejects the normative arguments, which she considers as a selective balancing act where 'preventing impunity outweigh[s] the interests protected by the rule of personal immunity'.[293]

Nevertheless, van Alebeek distinguishes the situation of functional immunity because the acceptance of individual criminal responsibility demonstrates the requisite policy decision that functional immunity should be inapplicable. She argues that national court practice indicates that courts only apply functional immunity 'if the foreign state is the nominal or factual defendant in the proceedings'.[294] In other words, the individual lacks personal liability for acts committed 'as an arm or as a mouthpiece of the home State' and in turn, the proceedings would involve 'impleading the foreign sovereign'.[295] Based on this concept, the situation of individual criminal responsibility can be distinguished because the individual is held responsible in their personal capacity and the state is not the factual defendant in the proceedings.[296] In this sense, the underlying rationale and purpose for the rule of immunity of state officials does not arise. This is then contrasted with the situation of personal immunity, where the immunity attaches to the office and the state is the factual defendant.[297]

290 ibid 553 and 554–5 (combing *jus cogens* status, individual criminal responsibility and the obligation to prosecute).

291 Princeton Project on Universal Jurisdiction 'Princeton Principles on Universal Jurisdiction' (Princeton University Princeton 2000) 51 and article 13(2) of the Resolution on the Immunities from Jurisdiction and Execution of Heads of State and Heads of Government in International Law (Institute of International Law Vancouver 2001).

292 Van Alebeek (n 274) 273.

293 ibid 272.

294 ibid 104–7.

295 ibid.

296 ibid.

297 ibid 223 and 267 *et passim*.

Akande and Shah reject the *jus cogens* and the 'official acts' arguments in a similar vein to the social description approach.[298] They argue that an obligation on third states to prosecute must itself be of *jus cogens* status and that the claim that the right to exercise universal jurisdiction is *jus cogens* as it derives from a *jus cogens* crime 'read[s] too much into *jus cogens* prohibitions'.[299] Yet they consider individual criminal responsibility as a significant development that challenges the classical view.[300] They contend that the recognition of extraterritorial jurisdiction over the alleged crime is crucial and it demonstrated state assent to the jurisdictional rule overruling a prior rule of immunity where these rules are co-extensive, that is, applying to the same set of facts.[301]

Conclusion

When we explore the doctrine of jurisdiction, we see binary oppositions that reflect liberal assumptions of liberty and order within ideas of prescribe/enforce, wide discretion/strict territoriality, or permission/prohibition. We also note how each principle of jurisdiction does not possess a fixed or stable meaning; rather, international lawyers apply a principle of reasonableness or interests-balancing. When we explore the debates surrounding universal jurisdiction and immunity of state officials, we observe multiple interpretations among international lawyers that are underpinned by competing projects that, Koskenniemi argues, characterize international law. We see how the competing interpretations over universal jurisdiction (and immunity of state officials) seem to suggest two diametrically opposing positions, characterized here as normative or social description approaches, and a move to a 'middle ground' in an attempt to reconcile these seemingly irreconcilable competing approaches. As we observed in Chapter 1, rule indeterminacy reveals that the structural properties of every legal argument preserve the ideas of liberty and higher order within itself. Each interpretation at a structural level is identical, albeit appearing at the surface level to be in opposition to other interpretations. Therefore, the arguments characterized as normative and social description are not stable internally. Rather, they privilege a particular project and yet are dependent on their supplement (whether normative or social fact) for their meaning.

It follows that each competing interpretation can seem subjective and political to its opposing position. To a more normative approach, mere social description approach appears to cement the status-quo and offer justifications for shielding state officials from accountability when the territorial jurisdiction fails to act. To a more social description approach, mere normative value appears to be a

298 D Akande and S Shah 'Immunities of State Officials, International Crimes and Foreign Domestic Courts' (2010) 21(4) *European Journal of International Law* 815, 833–4 and 830 (official character of the act is whether it is 'intrinsically governmental', depending on the nature and context of the act).

299 ibid 836.

300 ibid 840.

301 ibid 841.

fanciful utopia and offers justifications for the intervention by humanity, which can only result in arbitrary rule by the powerful. The middle ground can appear unacceptable to the competing approaches. By moving back and forth between normative ideal and state behaviour, it can appear inconsistent and arbitrary. An inevitable move to political discretion in which international lawyers decide whether the jurisdiction is reasonable (or just) in the circumstances is compelled by the argument's structural properties. Therefore, the multiple interpretations that appear to be grounded in the naturalism-positivism dichotomy can be viewed as mere surface oppositions and the legal outcomes (and dominant approaches) can be understood as a hegemonic claim. It follows then that the subsequent chapters narrate the debate as a series of hegemonic and counter-hegemonic positions that struggle for hegemony at every historical moment.

References

Akande, D 'The Jurisdiction of the International Criminal Court over Nationals of Non-Parties: Legal Basis and Limits' (2003) 1 *Journal of International Criminal Justice* 618.

Akande, D 'Immunities and the International Criminal Court' (2004) 98 *American Journal of International Law* 407.

Akande, D and Shah, S 'Immunities of State Officials, International Crimes and Foreign Domestic Courts' (2010) 21(4) *European Journal of International Law* 815.

Akehurst, M 'Jurisdiction in International Law', (1972–73) 46 *British Yearbook of International Law*.

Amnesty International, 'Universal Jurisdiction: A Preliminary Survey of Legislation Around the World' (AI Publications London 2011).

Bassiouni, MC *Crimes against Humanity in International Criminal Law* (Kluwer Law International The Hague 1999).

Bassiouni, MC 'Universal Jurisdiction for International Crimes: Historical Perspectives and Contemporary Practice' (2001) 42 *Virginia Journal of International Law* 81.

Bassiouni, MC *Crimes against Humanity: Historical Evolution and Contemporary Application* (Cambridge University Press Cambridge 2011).

Bassiouni, MC and EM Wise, *Aut dedere Aut Judicare: The Duty to Extradite or Prosecute In International Law* (Martinus Nijhoff Dordrecht 1995).

Battle, GG 'The Trials before the Leipsic Supreme Court of Germans Accused of War Crimes' (1921–22) 8 *Virginia Law Review* 1.

Beale, J 'The Jurisdiction of a Sovereign State' (1923) 36 *Harvard Law Review* 241.

Becker, S 'Universal Jurisdiction: How Universal Is It? A Study of Competing Theories' (2002–03) 12 *Palestine Yearbook of International Law* 49.

Benavides, L 'The Doctrine of Universal Jurisdiction: Its nature and scope' (2001) 1 *Annuaire Derechos International* 19.

Blakesley, CL 'United States Jurisdiction over Extraterritorial Crime' (1982) 73(3) *Journal of Criminal Law and Criminology* 1109.

Boelaert-Suominen, S 'Grave Breaches, Universal Jurisdiction and Internal Armed Conflict: Is Customary Law Moving Towards a Uniform Enforcement Mechanism for All Armed Conflicts?' (2000) 5(1) *Journal of Conflict and Security Law* 63.

Bowman, HD 'Letting the Big Fish Get Away: The UN Justice Effort in East Timor' (2004) *18 Emory International Law Review* 371.

Brownlie, I *Principles of Public International Law* (7th edn Oxford University Press Oxford 2008).

Cameron, I *The Protective Principle of International Criminal Law* (Aldershot Dartmouth 1994).

Carnegie, AR 'Jurisdiction over Violations of the Laws of War' (1963) 39 *British Yearbook of International Law* 402.

Cassese, A 'Is the Bell Tolling for Universality? A Plea for a Sensible Notion of Universal Jurisdiction' (2003) 1 *Journal of International Criminal Justice* 589.

Clark, RS 'Offences of International Concern: Multilateral State treaty practice in the Forty Years since Nuremberg' (1988) 57 *Nordic Journal of International Law* 49.

Colangelo, A 'The Legal Limits of Universal Jurisdiction' (2006–07) 47 *Virginia Journal of International Law* 149.

Council of Europe 'Report on Extraterritorial Jurisdiction' (Strasbourg 1990).

Cowles, WB 'Universal Jurisdiction over Violations of the Laws of War' (1945) 33(2) *California Law Review* 177.

Cryer, R *Selectivity in International Criminal Law* (Cambridge University Press Cambridge 2005).

Damgaard, C *Individual Criminal Responsibility for Core International Crimes: Selected Pertinent Issues* (Springer Berlin 2008).

Deen-Racsmany, Z 'The Nationality of the Offender and the Jurisdiction of the International Criminal Court' (2001) 95(3) *American Journal of International Law* 609.

Dugard, J and van den Wyngaert, C 'Reconciling Extradition with Human Rights' (1998) 92 *American Journal of International Law* 187.

El Zeidy, M 'Universal Jurisdiction in Absentia: Is it a Legal Valid Option' (2003) 37 *International Lawyer* 835.

Fawcett, JS 'The Eichmann Case' (1962) 38 *British Yearbook of International Law* 181.

Fox, H and Webb, P *The Law of State Immunity* (3rd edn Oxford University Press Oxford 2013).

Gardocki, L 'The Principle of Universality' in N Jareborg *Double Criminality: Studies in International Criminal Law* (Almqvist Wiksell International Sweden 1989).

Gilbert, G *Transnational Fugitive Offenders in International law: Extradition and Other Measures* (M Nijhoff Dordrecht 1998).

Green, LC 'Political Offences' (1962) 11 *International and Comparative Law Quarterly* 348.

Grotius, H *De Jure Belli Ac Pacis Libri Tres* Book II, Chapter XX FW Kelsey (tr) (Clarendon Press Oxford 1925).

Harvard Research on International Law *Draft Convention on Jurisdiction with Respect to Crime* (1935) 29 *American Journal of International Law Supplement* 439.

Harvard Research in International Law, Part I: Extradition (1935) 29 *American Journal of International Law Supplement* 1.

Henkin, L *International Law: Politics and Values* (M Nijhoff Dordrecht 1995).

Henzelin, M *Le Principe de l'universalité en droit penal international* (Helbing & Lichtenhahn Bruylant 2000) 15.

Henzelin, M 'La Competence Penale Universelle: Une Question Non Resolue Par L'Arret Yerodia' (2002) 4 *Revue General de Droit International Penal* 819.

Higgins, R *Problems and Process: International Law and How we use it* (Clarendon Press Oxford 1994).

Institute of International Law 'Resolution on the Immunities from Jurisdiction and Execution of Heads of State and Heads of Government in International Law' (Vancouver 2001).

Institute of International Law 'Resolution on Universal Criminal Jurisdiction with Regard to the Crime of Genocide, Crimes Against Humanity and War Crimes' (Krakow 2005).
Jain, N 'Between the Scylla and Charybdis: Prosecution and Reconciliation: The Khmer Rouge Trials and the Promise of International Criminal Justice' (2010) 20 (2) *Duke Journal of Comparative and International Law* 247.
Jennings, RY and Watts A *Oppenheims International Law* (9th edn London Longmans 1992).
Kress, C 'Universal Jurisdiction over International Crimes and the *Institut de Droit International*' (2006) 4 *Journal of International Criminal Justice* 561.
Llewelyn Davis, DJ (1937) 18 *British Yearbook of International Law* 49.
Mann, FA 'The Doctrine of Jurisdiction in International Law' (1964-I) 111 *Recueil des Cours* 9.
Meron, T 'International Criminalization of Internal Atrocities' (1995) 89 *American Journal of International Law* 554.
Meron, T *The Humanization of International Law* (Martinus Nijhoff Publishers Leiden 2006).
Merrills, JG *Anatomy of International Law: A Study of the Role of International Law in the Contemporary World* (2nd edn Sweet and Maxwell London 1981).
Moore, JB 'Report on Extraterritorial Crime and the Cutting Case' (Government Printing Office Washington, DC 1887).
O'Keefe, R 'Universal Jurisdiction: Clarifying the Basic Concept' (2004) 2 *Journal of International Criminal Justice* 735.
O'Keefe, R 'The Grave Breaches Regime and Universal Jurisdiction' (2009) 7 *Journal of International Criminal Justice* 811.
Orakhelashvili, A *Peremptory Norms in International Law* (Oxford University Press Oxford 2006).
Pappas, C *Stellvertretende Strafrechtspflege* (Max Planck Institut fuer auslaendisches und internationals Strafrecht Freiburg 1996).
Pictet, J *Commentary on the Geneva Conventions of 1949: Vol I* and *Vol IV* (ICRC Geneva 1952–60).
Poels, A 'Universal Jurisdiction in Absentia' (2005) 23(1) *Netherlands Quarterly of Human Rights* 64.
Princeton Project on Universal Jurisdiction 'Princeton Principles on Universal Jurisdiction' (Princeton University Princeton 2000).
Rabinovitch, R 'Universal Jurisdiction *in absentia*' (2004–05) 18 *Fordham International Law Journal* 500.
Randall, KC 'Universal Jurisdiction in International Law', (1988) 66 *Texas International Law Journal* 785.
Report of the Commission of Inquiry into the Events at the Refugee Camps in Beirut (The Kahan Commission) (8 February 1983) URL: http://www.jewishvirtuallibrary.org/jsource/History/kahan.html.
Reuters Africa 'Sweden Indicts Man over Rwandan Genocide', URL: http://af.reuters.com/article/rwandaNews/idAFL5E8M58VS20121105.
Reydams, L *Universal Jurisdiction: International and National Perspectives* (Oxford University Press Oxford 2003).
Reydams, L 'The Rise and Fall of Universal Jurisdiction' in WA Schabas and N Bernaz (eds) *Routledge Handbook of International Criminal Law* (Routledge New York 2011).
Rubin, AP 'Formal Statement on HR 2587' in Appendix 3, Hearing before Sub-Committee on Immigration (US Government Printing Office Washington, DC 1996).

Schabas, WA *Genocide in International Law: The Crime of Crimes* (2nd edn Cambridge University Press Cambridge 2009).

Schachter, O *International Law in Theory and Practice* (M Nijhoff Dordrecht 1991).

Schwarzenberger, G *International Law Volume I* (3rd edn Stevens and Sons London).

Seyedin-Noor, S 'The Spanish Prisoner: Understanding the Prosecution of Senator Augusto Pinochet Ugarte' (2000) 6 *University of California Davis Journal of International Law and Policy* 41.

Shearer, IA *Extradition in International Law* (Manchester University Press Manchester 1971).

Shachor-Landau, C 'Extraterritorial Penal Jurisdiction and Extradition' (1980) 29 *International and Comparative Law Quarterly* 294.

Shaw, MN *International Law* (6th edn Cambridge University Press Cambridge 2008).

Sucharitkul, S 'International Terrorism and the Problem of Jurisdiction' (1987) 14 *Syracuse Journal of International Law and Commerce* 141.

Tomuschat, C 'Issues of Universal Jurisdiction in the *Scilingo* Case' (2005) 3 *Journal of International Criminal Justice* 1074.

Tomuchat, C 'Preliminary Exposition and Report on the "Resolution on Universal Jurisdiction over War Crimes, Genocide and Crimes against Humanity"' (2006) *Yearbook of the Institute of International Law.*

Virally, M 'Panorama du Droit International Contemporain' (1983) 183 *Recueil des Cours* 5, 91.

Van Alebeek, R *Immunity of States and their Officials in International Human Rights Law and International Criminal Law* (Oxford University Press Oxford 2008).

Van den Wygnaert, C 'Double Criminality as a Requirement to Jurisdiction' in N Jareborg *Double Criminality: Studies in International Criminal Law* (Almqvist Wiksell International Sweden 1989).

Yee, S 'Universal Jurisdiction: Concept, Logic and Reality' (2011) 10 *Chinese Journal of International Law* 503.

Zahar, A and Sluiter, G *International Criminal Law* (Oxford University Press Oxford 2008).

4 Competing for hegemony

Identifying structural tendencies of the field, Simpson describes international criminal law as 'constituted by, and properly understood through, a set of dilemmas and relationships', rather than captured under 'single models or unified theories'.[1] It is a 'field of repetition and recurrence [of] unresolved arguments about the shape and fate of retributive justice in the international order'.[2] These unresolved arguments are structured by 'moral enthusiasms embedded, instrumentalized and institutionalized in the project of international criminal law'.[3] Some scholars have captured these moral enthusiasms within legal discourse in the sense of binary paradoxes,[4] while others have disentangled law and politics in terms of four concepts of the political that are all in mutual relationships of critique with one another.[5] The aim of this chapter is to explore the debate over universal jurisdiction as a tension of these competing moral enthusiasms that reflect the inner struggle among international lawyers between their commitment to realizing a 'court of humanity that will never adjourn'[6] and their cynicism that such a court can be realized.[7]

We observe this inner struggle in the debate over universal jurisdiction with a seemingly endless swing between advocacy for 'ending impunity' and for 'avoiding abuse'.[8] Therefore, it is argued that the debate is best characterized as a struggle for hegemonic control by contrasting positions (moralist/formalist) that tends

1 G Simpson *Law, War and Crime: War Crimes, Trials and the Reinvention of International Law* (Polity Press London 2007), 4 ('neither one thing (international) nor another (domestic)').

2 ibid.

3 ibid 2.

4 M Koskenniemi 'Between Impunity and Show Trials' (2002) 6 *Max Planck Yearbook for United Nations Law* 1.

5 Simpson (n 1) 4.

6 *The Einsatzgruppen Trial: Trial of Otto Ohlendorf and Others* (1948) IV Trials of War Criminals before the Nuremberg Military Tribunals Green Series (1946–49) 499, URL: http://www.loc.gov/rr/frd/Military_Law/pdf/NT_war-criminals_Vol-IV.pdf ('where the law exists a court will rise . . . the court of humanity, if it may be so termed, will never adjourn'.)

7 M Koskenniemi 'Between Commitment and Cynicism: Outline for a Theory of International Law as Practice' in M Koskenniemi *The Politics of International Law* (Hart Publishing Oxford 2011) 523.

8 Koskenniemi (n 4) 1 This mapping of the debate narrates the key points in the battle over the Eichmann judgments' narrative.

towards a 'middle ground' with its particular hegemonic choice.[9] In this chapter, we explore how international lawyers drew on the logic of the *Eichmann* narrative to construct a moralist horizon and how they were able to manoeuvre into a hegemonic position within the debate from the mid-1990s until International Court of Justice's judgment in the *Arrest Warrant* case.

1 Structural tendencies: Moralist and formalist

We explored how competing positions in legal discourse are indistinguishable at the structural level of argument, because each position simultaneously draws on both positions and therefore, they merge into one another. Each legal utterance moves in constant opposition, continually attempting to be either more normative, less concrete (descending) or more concrete, less normative (ascending) as against its other.[10] The bleeding or merging of the binary positions means that each position depends for meaning on its supplementary (or counter) point and this leads to the phenomenon of reversibility whereby each argument or position is reversible because both positions can connect to either descending or ascending patterns. We noted that this interchangeability of positions occurs given the fluidity of the social context behind the competing logics. Therefore, rather than a structuralist approach, associating the two logics with either the state or humanity, the deconstructionist technique illustrates how state and humanity are both a moralist and formalist position. In this sense, both logics are associable with any political project and not fixed upon one particular political project.[11]

We noted that a single conflict arises when the position is identified temporarily and an opponent must evoke the opposite position to 'validly' accuse the former of subjectivity. However, once the competing positions are pushed into argument, both positions are seen to be self-contradictory and as a result, there is a move to the middle in an attempt to reconcile the irreconcilable. As both positions are self-contradicting, there is no underlying conflict and there must be an ad hoc solution in the moment of the decision.[12] We noted how the decision is not irrational but rather is based on a particular rationality of the international legal profession that expresses the 'interplay' of ideology, politics, judges' perception and professional preferences.[13] It is the hegemony of one legal argument over another that is dependent on how the logic of the argument accords with the structural bias of the institution. We also took note of how a transformation occurs over time that is incapable of being fixed on any one moment and therefore, a deconstructionist technique rejects the possibility of a meta-historical

9 M Koskenniemi 'International Law and Hegemony: A Reconfiguration' (2004) 17 *Cambridge Review of International Affairs* 197.

10 E Jouannet 'Koskenniemi: A Critical Introduction' in M Koskenniemi *The Politics of International Law* (Hart Publishing Oxford 2011) 7–8.

11 See Chapter 1, section 2.

12 ibid.

13 M Koskenniemi *From Apology to Utopia: The Structure of the International Legal Argument* (Cambridge University Press Cambridge 2005) 68.

narrative or logic to explain why change (or the way the positions change) occurs. Rather when change occurs, it is historically contingent and consequently, different every time: 'There will always be an unresolved element of undecidability between dominant narratives and the events from which they are derived and about which they are supposed to speak.'[14]

We observed that this book addresses the debate over universal jurisdiction in international criminal law as bounded by the tension between contrasting political preferences or positions, labelled as moralist ('ending impunity') and formalist ('avoiding abuse'). This illustrates the competing logics at a surface level in a manner recognizable to the field. A moralist position challenges what it reads as the injustice of impunity, privileging the moral value of criminal accountability and stressing state consent to individual criminal responsibility and universal accountability. This prefers the trial of identified perpetrators before international and national tribunals irrespective of (and because of) the approval of the state of nationality of the defendant. Accountability cannot be thwarted by jurisdictional counter-claims, arguing an abuse of jurisdiction, that are viewed as concealing an attempt to shield identified perpetrators. Rather, individual criminal responsibility is a 'universal' standard accepted by all states in their customary practice (state consent) and its enforcement through criminal prosecutions cannot be frustrated by the arrogant intransigence of a delinquent state (regardless of that latter state's consent). As a consequence, a court of humanity has the possibility to never adjourn, because a court will always rule that the jurisdiction is justified, as to rule otherwise appears to be an (arbitrary) apology for power. This seems to move to transform the political present from sovereign egoism to world unity and conversely, any lack of accountability is read as mere sovereign egoism thwarting preferred global institutions and in turn, justice/stability. This seems to privilege an idea of cosmopolitan justice where international institutions 'mete out impartial, majestic justice on behalf of the international community', yet it also appears to seek both international institutions and forms of localized justice.[15]

A formalist position challenges what it reads as the injustice of politically motivated or 'show' trials,[16] privileging the moral value of maintaining order and stressing state consent to jurisdiction. This prefers the trial of identified perpetrators before international and national tribunals because of (and irrespective of) the approval of the state of nationality of the defendant. Accountability cannot be secured by jurisdictional claims, arguing for ending impunity, that are viewed as concealing an excessive exercise of jurisdiction behind the cloak of 'universal' interest. Rather, jurisdictional rules are 'universal' standards that are accepted by all states in their customary practice (consent) and their use through criminal prosecutions cannot be manipulated by the arrogant intransigence of a delinquent

14 See discussion in Chapter 1, Section 3. D Campbell 'Time is Broken: The Return of the Past in the Response to September 11' (2001) 5(4) *Theory and Event.*

15 Simpson (n 1) 30. On Koskenniemi's project of 'unity' and project of 'identity', see chapter 1, section 3.

16 ibid 108 (drawing out what show trials are perceived as in the literature 'show trials are defined as procedures that seem to have exceeded the limits of legality itself. Such trials are all show, no trial').

state (regardless of that latter state's consent). As a consequence, a court of humanity looks like a utopian ideal and therefore, rather than never adjourning, a court will always rule against jurisdiction where state consent is not manifest, as to rule otherwise appears to be an (arbitrary) utopia of 'universal' justice. This seems to move to transform the political present from 'oppressive homogeneity to self-determination' and conversely, any universalist programme of criminal justice is read as mere 'oppressive homogeneity', thwarting preferred sovereign autonomy over post-conflict mechanisms and in turn justice/stability. This also seems to privilege an idea of cosmopolitan justice, yet it appears to prefer certain forms of localised justice over global institutions.[17]

As both logics are in each position, each position can be read as both moralist and formalist. Therefore, a moralist position considers nothing more concrete than the doctrine and practice of universal jurisdiction as it reflects state consent to enforcing individual criminal accountability and to the principle of universal jurisdiction as evident in international legal history. Similarly, a formalist position considers nothing more normative than preventing arbitrary and unfettered state interference, violating state liberty, and ensuring 'universal' interests in securing the dignity and independence of each state within the 'international community'. Therefore, in mapping the structural properties of the competing positions, it must be remembered that the opposing approaches are not conceived of as fixed, stable identities. Rather the opposing positions of moralist and formalist can be associable with either project of ending impunity or show trial, and the resulting incoherence compels a move to the 'middle' position, albeit that prefers one particular political project over another. Overall, this exploration accords with the contours of the debate, tracing the moves of competing narratives by international lawyers, and therefore, the 'boundaries' of the debate are continually re-shaped by international lawyers' closing particular avenues and choosing to pursue others. It also reflects how international lawyers would assume as uncontroversial the meaning of legal concepts, such as particular crimes, even though these concepts remained contested within the literature. It follows then that our exploration begins by drawing out the structural properties of the *Eichmann* judgments and the counter-position of Eichmann's defence counsel that were pulled upon from the 1990s onwards.

2 Structural properties in the *Eichmann* case

As we briefly noted in Chapter 2, the *Eichmann* case provided pluralist histories of universal jurisdiction that delved into particular narratives of justification in international legal history in order to construct their portrayal in an attempt to persuade their audience. We can explore the competing interpretations submitted by the Israeli trial and appeals court and Eichmann's defence counsel as indicative of these competing positions and draw out the structural properties of each position. The Israeli trial and appeals court sought to justify the validity of universal

17 ibid 30.

jurisdiction over crimes against international law (descending-ascending). In the trial court judgment, it argued that the crimes 'offended the whole of mankind and shocked the conscience of nations' and therefore, they were international in character (and 'not under Israeli law alone').[18] This appealed to what Koskenniemi calls the language of moral outrage, 'as part of a discipline relearning the crusading spirit and the civilizing mission' (descending).[19] Nevertheless, to avoid seeming to be mere political utopia, the Israeli courts moved to support their moral naturalism in social behaviour (ascending) and viewed state behaviour through the lens of their moral naturalism. Here, they pulled on the *Lotus* judgment's wide measure of discretion and searched for a prohibitive rule against exercising jurisdiction over such crimes. Viewed from a standpoint of moral outrage, unsurprisingly, neither court found such a prohibition in state behaviour, as to do so would have negated jurisdiction of foreign courts.

As their analysis of state behaviour could be validly criticized, both courts moved back to a descending pattern and concluded that there was in fact a permissive rule for its jurisdictional claim, in the guise of universal jurisdiction.[20] As the Israeli trial court argued, 'far from . . . negating or limiting the jurisdiction of countries with respect to such crimes', international law *requires* the courts of every state to implement international law's criminal prohibitions in the 'absence of an international criminal court'.[21] In other words, the moral naturalism of the nature of the crimes justifies a jurisdictional claim to avoid an inevitable impunity when international jurisdiction is unavailable. Similarly, the appeals court's point of departure was normative, privileging the moral outrage that underpinned the criminality ('damage to vital international interests'),[22] and moved to reflecting state behaviour (ascending), albeit through its normative lens. Here, it pointed to the series of factual precedents in the 'developmental stage' of international criminal law namely piracy, assaults against diplomatic agents and war crimes.[23] Although the appeals court was ambivalent towards the *Lotus* judgment, it implicitly used a presumption against limitations in its analysis of state consent and at the same time, used the *Lotus* dissents that required a permission.[24]

The trial and appeals courts pulled out a linear history drawn from one side of historical debates over jurisdiction of the International Military Tribunal and jurisdiction over piracy (and brigandage), in order to provide a narrative of justification

18 *AG v Eichmann* (1968) 36 ILR 5

19 M Koskenniemi 'The Lady Doth Protest too Much: Kosovo and the Turn to Ethics in International Law' (2002) 65 *Modern Law Review* 159, 172.

20 See Chapter 3, section 2.1.2 (referring to the alternative claims of protective and passive personality in the trial judgement).

21 *AG v. Eichmann* (n 18), 26.

22 ibid 291 ('impair the foundations and security of the international community', 'violate universal moral values and humanitarian principles that are at the root of the systems of criminal law adopted by civilized nations').

23 ibid 292–3 (citing Lansing and Kelsen on piracy as a crime against mankind, and Lauterpacht on personal liability for war crimes).

24 ibid 286 (divided the literature into four competing approaches towards the judgment, noted a lack of consensus and deemed the Israeli 1950 Act as indicative of a lack of a prohibition).

for the validity of universal jurisdiction.[25] Pulling from the International Military Tribunal and in particular the Justice Trial, the trial court noted the combination of moral outrage, with the consent of the international community, and the 'extraordinary' circumstances of post-war Germany that permitted 'distinct' rules from an exclusivity of territorial jurisdiction.[26] Pulling from the debates on jurisdiction over piracy, both courts assumed that this derived from the moral outrage over the offences, similar to Molloy and Lorimer. As if in a linear thought, they implicitly followed the Lieber Code, the 1922 Washington Treaty and Cowles in justifying an analogy between crime of piracy (and brigandage) and war crimes of enemy irregulars and enemy forces on capture.[27] Specifically, they cited de Vabres's history of the medieval Italian city states, various sixteenth-century jurists' references to jurisdiction over offences against the 'human society', and contemporary writers such as Hyde and Cowles in their linear progressive history.[28]

In an alternative interpretation, the appeals court acknowledged the existence of multiple interpretations justifying a principle of universal jurisdiction,[29] yet concluded that a common theme existed that recognized universal jurisdiction could apply to offences against the law of nations based on the attack on 'vital interest, common to all civilized States, and of universal scope . . .',[30] that is, a normative position.[31] Therefore, although the appeals court was ambivalent towards the differing justifications, it appears closest to Wheaton's assimilation theory because it noted the piracy analogy applied to war crimes within the literature. It contended that such an analogy applied with even 'greater force' to crimes against humanity.[32] In this sense, the court accepted the capacity to produce a legal analogy to justify jurisdiction over other offences against the law of nations, and it considered such an analogy as justified over acts on government orders, given the recognition of individual criminal responsibility.

The jurisdictional claim over genocide presented a distinct difficulty given article VI of the Genocide Convention, which obliged state parties to exercise only territorial jurisdiction, alongside recognition of jurisdiction of an international criminal court when established. In the Israeli courts' descending pattern, the Genocide Convention could not be considered a prohibitive rule that would preclude a universal jurisdiction claim because such an interpretation would 'foil' the overall object and purpose of the Convention, that is, a

25 ibid 27–9.
26 ibid 41 and 295.
27 ibid 26.
28 ibid 26–9 and 298–300. See C Hyde *International Law (Chiefly as Interpreted and Applied by the United States)* Vol 1 (2nd edn 1947) 804 ('close and definite connection' when act is deemed unlawful under law of nations).
29 ibid 298–9 (identifying four schools of thought: Judge Moore and *sui generis* jurisdiction over piracy, Harvard Research and subsidiary jurisdiction over domestic offences, Wheaton and jurisdiction over offences against law of nations by analogy, and Lauterpacht and *de lege ferenda*).
30 ibid 299.
31 ibid (citing Kelsen and Glaser on 'acting on behalf of international community').
32 ibid.

non-consensual position.[33] The courts then analysed state behaviour through their lens of moral naturalism in an ascending-descending move. Here, the Convention could not be interpreted as limiting the capacity of states parties to determine the extent of their jurisdiction ('wide measure of discretion') as long as they remain within limits imposed by international law. No evidence of a prohibitive rule was located in state behaviour; of course, given the dearth of cases. Instead, the Nuremberg Military Trials were cited as evidence of a practice of exercising universal jurisdiction over genocide.[34] This was combined with a claim of a 'consensus of opinion' that the exclusion of universal jurisdiction and failure to establish an international criminal court were defects in the Convention; therefore, article VI was a 'compulsory minimum'.[35] Overall, the courts' justification for universal jurisdiction over crimes against international law and in particular, over genocide, appears to an opponent too subjective, too utopian and vulnerable to attack over its moral naturalism and its analysis of state behaviour through the lens of its moral naturalism.

It follows then that neither court countenanced the possibility of a lack of jurisdiction under international law nor did they respond to the opposing position within the literature that rejected the jurisdiction of the International Military Tribunal and dismissed jurisdiction over piracy as based on either the nature of the crime, as involving a political motive, or on a principle of universal jurisdiction *per se*. On article VI of the Genocide Convention, their interpretation shadows the reference in the drafting history of the treaty parties to their rejection of universal jurisdiction as a treaty obligation and their explicit reference to nationality jurisdiction as not being precluded by the Convention's obligations.[36] Rather, Eichmann's defence counsel provided the space for pluralist histories as he provided a competing position regarding the justification for universal jurisdiction that privileged state liberty, non-interference and exclusivity of territorial jurisdiction (ascending-descending). This read the practice of universal jurisdiction as involving situations where there was no competent territorial jurisdiction, that is, similar to the subsidiary jurisdiction evoked by imperial European states in the early twentieth century. This implicitly appeals to the idea of the exclusivity of territorial jurisdiction, unless an exception exists that was raised by France in the *Lotus* case and supported by dissenting judges. Eichmann's defence counsel then turned to a normative justification in a descending move that pulled on the idea of jurisdiction over piracy as based on the absence of sovereignty over the high seas.[37] This repeated Jenkins's justification for a broad jurisdiction over piracy that argued territorial jurisdiction extended to the area of the high seas to secure public peace in the situation of a jurisdictional lacuna within the normal jurisdictional rules. It also

33 ibid 38 and 304.

34 ibid 38.

35 ibid.

36 See Report of Sixth Committee, UN Doc. A/C.6/SR. 134, 5 ('in particular . . . does not affect the right . . . to bring to trial . . . any of its nationals for acts committed outside the State').

37 *Written Pleadings submitted by Counsel for the Appellant Adolf Eichmann*, para 2 (b).

reflected the Harvard Research's position that read piracy as a municipal offence that gave rise to an exception to the exclusivity of territorial jurisdiction.[38]

Another matter of controversy was the question of Eichmann's abduction and what relevance it had in regards to the court's ability to exercise jurisdiction over him. The question of whether Eichmann's abduction rendered his detention unlawful was one dimension of the defence counsel's pleadings.[39] Of relevance here is the dimension related to the parameters of universal jurisdiction, as the defence counsel raised the claim that universal jurisdiction was subject to a limitation whereby the state with custody of the accused must first offer to extradite to the territorial jurisdiction.[40] The defence claimed that this limitation was implicit in the maxim *aut dedere aut punire*.[41] This pulled on the competing positions of de Vabres and Travers from the early twentieth century, where both adopted this format of the principle, yet they appeared to divide into the naturalism-positivism dichotomy on their competing justifications for the principle itself.[42] This also reflected the form of a subsidiary jurisdiction evoked by certain European states in their national provisions.

The appeals court provided another interpretation that justified the requirement for custody of the accused based on normative values of efficiency and pragmatism, as most of the witnesses and evidence would be generally located in the state of location of the offence. Even so, the appeals court argued that territoriality was a rule of convenience and left open whether the priority of the territorial jurisdiction was a limiting rule of law.[43] In other words, the appeals court claimed that international law required every state to prosecute international crimes, yet argued that jurisdiction over such crimes operated in a way that the territorial jurisdiction was given preference for pragmatic reasons (ascending). In this way, the Israeli courts tried to be more concrete, less normative than what the logical conclusion of their underlying moral naturalism, that justifies the principle itself, would allow. This would justify a universal jurisdiction claim without any limitation in the form of a priority of the territorial jurisdiction. Yet at the same, the appeals court moved towards equitable standards based on a rule of convenience, for which it offered no rationale whether from a normative moral naturalism (descending) or some claim in state behaviour (ascending). When it applied this rule of convenience to Eichmann, it concluded that Israel was a more superior *forum conveniens* than West Germany, weighing the significance of certain facts.[44]

38 See Chapter 2, section 2.1.

39 See LC Green 'Legal Issues of the Eichmann Trial' (1962) 37 *Tulane Law Review* 641.

40 *Written Pleadings* (n 37) para 2 (b).

41 *AG v. Eichmann* (n 21) 302.

42 D de Vabres *Les Principes modernes du droit penal international* (Recueil Sirey Paris 1928) 135 and 136.

43 *AG v Eichmann* (n 21) 302 (rejected idea that its jurisdiction depended on actions of West Germany).

44 ibid (greater access to the evidence and witnesses, lack of extradition request and lack of objection to Israeli jurisdiction).

The courts in Eichmann 'resolved' the issue of custody of the accused by applying equitable principles to weigh the competing interests between the various states with a vested interest. Nevertheless, in the original *Demjanjuk* extradition proceedings, the United States's courts demonstrated the first example where a court brought the moral naturalism of the *Eichmann* judgments to their logical conclusion or outermost point.[45] Here, the United States Court of Appeal followed the *Eichmann* judgment's narrative that universal jurisdiction was a well-recognized claim that was 'not unique to Israel'.[46] It considered that state behaviour in the post-1945 period demonstrated a 'general recognition' of extraterritorial jurisdiction over certain crimes that permit a state to 'vindicate the interest of all nations by seeking to punish the perpetrators of such crimes'.[47] This appeal judgment in effect sanctioned Demjanjuk to be involuntarily surrendered to Israel for trial rather than being voluntarily present in Israel at the time of the proceedings.

Another relevant controversy was whether immunity of state officials could bar Israeli jurisdiction. The defence counsel pulled on Kelsen's position on sovereign immunity in the post-war period that moved in an ascending-descending pattern. Here, Kelsen argued that if immunity had not been waived by consent of the requisite state, a 'customary or contractual rule' had to establish an exception.[48] Therefore, Eichmann's defence counsel stressed the importance of landmark judgments that affirmed the immunity of the state and its officials before foreign jurisdictions and did not indicate any exception for criminal jurisdiction (ascending-descending).[49] This rejected the fact of the Nazi atrocities as so distinct as to extinguish immunity without evident state consent, and this was implicitly based upon a normative position that privileges consent and the prevention of what is read as arbitrary interference with the state's self-determination. Invariably, the *Eichmann* judgments attacked these arguments as apology and rooted their positions in the IMT judgments (and in the pleadings of the US and British chief prosecutors).[50] Here, the trial court reduced the Nazi atrocities to a singularity and distinguished the factual circumstances of immunity case law as incapable of fitting the 'realities of Nazi Germany'.[51] A regime that commits such atrocities is incapable of being treated as *par in parem non habet*; rather the Nazi regime was best characterized as 'a gang of criminals' (descending-ascending).[52] Therefore, the trial court considered that the interests of justice required an exception from the general rule given the extraordinary circumstances.[53]

45 M Inazumi *Universal Jurisdiction in Modern International Law: Expansion of National Jurisdiction for Prosecuting Serious Crimes under International Law* (Intersentia Antwerpen 2005) 81.

46 *Demjanjuk v Petrovsky*, 776 F.2d 571, 583 (6th Cir. 1985) 581.

47 ibid 582.

48 See Chapter 2, section 3.

49 *Schooner Exchange v McFaddon* (1812) 7 Cranch 116, 137.

50 *AG v. Eichmann* (n 21) 309 (sovereignty not absolute, must be an exception for crimes 'outside the sovereign jurisdiction of the state that ratified it').

51 ibid 46.

52 ibid 46 and 310.

53 ibid 12.

It follows then that the courts appeared to treat the Nazi regime as a state without legitimacy (an outlaw) for the purpose of immunity, an interpretation that was submitted by the majority in *Pinochet I* that will we return to in section 4. It is significant that the IMT and NMT proceedings did not contend explicitly with the issue of immunity as a procedural plea as opposed to as a defence to the liability. Neither did the Israeli courts in *Eichmann*. In all cases, a procedural plea of immunity was never explicitly raised by the defence counsel as their focus was on challenging the whole notion of crimes against international law committed under government order for which personal liability arose. Notwithstanding, in the 1990s, it seems to have been assumed that the IMT's arguments contended with both the removal of the defence against liability and the procedural bar of immunity before foreign tribunals. Here, multiple interpretations were open-ended and could justify this assumption through combining unconditional surrender by Nazi Germany (consent) and the interests of justice necessitating punishment given lack of an effective German criminal justice system (non-consent). Alternatively, perhaps the questioning of a procedural plea was unforeseen. In the end, apart from the 1996 Draft Code, the debate over the procedural rule of immunity before national courts was first raised in a national court by Pinochet's defence counsel in the United Kingdom's extradition proceedings.

3 The 1990s and the 'new international order'

We observed in Chapter 2 how political consciousness shifted during the twentieth century to view law as more suitable for resolving international disputes and 'more attractive as a tool of political retribution after war'.[54] This shift restructured (or adjusted) 'the relationship between law, crime and politics in international relations'[55] and in the conventional story, post-1989 is read as reinvigorating a project initiated by the Nuremberg Trials that had been immobilized by the 'geopolitical and international legal glaciation' of the Cold War.[56] After being 'one of the casualties of superpower rivalry', the end of the Cold War appeared to herald 'a surge of international legal creativity'[57] and in its immediate aftermath, it seemed like everything was to play for.[58] This 'new international order' was a reconstruction of the 1945 project, based on cooperation and universal values – 'the holy trinity of markets, democracy and human rights'.[59] This led to renewalist commentary yet Kennedy reads the dominant tendency of the 1990s as a return to a mainstream of confusion and anxiety, much like 1860, 1910 and

54 Simpson (n 1) 3.

55 ibid 4.

56 F Johns, R Joyce and S Pahuja *Events: The Force of International Law* (Routledge London 2011) 109. On concept of the Cold War, see F Romero 'Cold War Historiography at the Crossroads' (2014) 14(4) *Cold War History* 685, 688–7.

57 ibid 109.

58 S Marks 'Guarding the Gates with Two Faces: International Law and Political Reconstruction' (1998–99) 6 Indiana Journal of Global Legal Studies 457.

59 Johns et al (n 56) 107.

1950, rather than a confident renewal.[60] As Newton argues, 1989 'only made way for the colonization by the West of international institutional space' that led to economic and political liberalism becoming the dominant form of governance.[61]

We noted that the marginal argument of neoliberalism gradually moved into the majoritarian position in the 1980s and in the post-Cold War environment, neoliberalism became entangled with globalization to the extent that neoliberal ideas have globally 'become hegemonic as a mode of discourse'.[62] Here, Kennedy was sceptical of the international legal renewalism movement as there was 'a self-conscious repetition of well-worn structures, institutions, doctrines . . . with an equally strident sense of historical break, repeating the discipline's construction of its history in phases of continuity punctuated by rupture'.[63] Instead, he identified a 'darker side to the renewal story' that shows how the 'relaxation of [West Europe] hesitance about allowing the East "in" seems only possible once the conditions of chronological inequality has been stabilized'.[64] Here, there were two tracks in the discourse about new architectures, modern and modernizing. There was a sophisticated track for developed societies which 'are understood to need advanced forms of governmental regulatory cooperation to manage their interdependence', and a second less sophisticated track 'for determining which participants fall into this category and which do not'.[65] Similarly, Marks found a comparable two-track architecture in the democratic side of market democracy: 'a track for democratizers and a track for democracies'.[66]

Against this renewal movement, the 'triumph' of human rights discourse seemed confidently assured. We noted in Chapter 2 that the 1970s anti-politics of human rights went through transformative change and this compelled human rights advocates to produce a 'political agenda and programmatic vision'.[67] This forced the regime to produce a vision of the good life and offer a plan for achieving it, despite being ill-equipped by the 'suprapolitical birth'.[68] It was a move 'from morality to politics and . . . charisma to bureaucracy'.[69] Nevertheless, it is also evident that the discourse moved from anti-politics, a tradition challenging power, to a discourse of power.[70] Rather than providing a platform of 'non-political' standards that are opposable to the politics of the state, experience

60 D Kennedy 'When Renewal Repeats: Thinking Against the Box' (1999–2000) *NYU Journal of International and Policy* 335, 342.

61 Johns et al (n 56) 109.

62 D Harvey *A Brief History of Neoliberalism* (Oxford University Press Oxford 2007) 3.

63 D Kennedy 'Turning to Market Democracy: A Tale of Two Architectures' (1991) 32 *Harvard International Law Journal* 373, 379.

64 ibid 379.

65 ibid 395.

66 Marks (n 58).

67 S Moyn *Human Rights in History: The Last Utopia* (Harvard University Press Boston 2010), 213.

68 ibid 214.

69 ibid 219.

70 A Orford *Reading Humanitarian Intervention: Human Rights and the Use of Force in International Law* (Cambridge University Press Cambridge 2003).

showed that 'what rights mean and how they are applied can only be determined by the politics of the state.'[71] Of particular relevance is that although the political agenda at the outset focused on Eastern European dissidents and anti-authoritarian government in Latin America, there was a gradual fusing of human rights and humanitarianism and then a 'creative mutation forging transitional justice' that allowed the Latin American experience to become both an 'external moral criticism' and an 'internal political resource' for successor states.[72]

This fusing of human rights and humanitarianism led to the integration of genocide prevention as a human rights concern. In the 1990s, there was a 'monumental change', although it is 'unclear whether, when and how the popularization of Holocaust memory helped construct norms of universalist responsibility'.[73] 'Somehow' since Cambodia and 'certainly' by the mid-1990s, given the resurgence of ethnic cleansing in the European continent, there was a merging of human rights and genocide prevention.[74] This was part of a larger shift, a 'slow amalgamation of humanitarian concern for suffering with human rights as both a utopian idea and a practical movement'.[75] The creative mutation to transitional justice meant that human rights vocabulary became a key discourse of post-conflict transition from the 1980s onwards. One dimension was how the narrative of 'ending impunity' became a slogan for post-conflict agendas. In the mid-1990s, this narrative was pulled upon by Jewish survivors of the Holocaust to construct the 'first significant instance' of using civil litigation to mount restitution claims.[76] Although restitution claims were 'settled for unprecedented amounts' in US courts,[77] the 'ending impunity' narrative was (and continues to be) less effective in other states, such as Poland, due to particular historical legacies which have been a significant factor in a lack of a restitution process.[78] Therefore, the transitional justice narrative was evoked in different contexts that produced different outcomes and invariably, had its own exclusions, such as contending with certain structural forces in the form of an economic shock therapy designed to push through a neoliberal programme.[79] Such exclusions have similarly pervaded the fledging field of international criminal law, given its privileging of individual agency over structural forces.

It follows that the 'new international order' was brief and 'too dependent on US power following Somalia'; peacekeeping operations had limited traction in Bosnia and Rwanda, and the human rights regime failed to prevent gross human rights

71 M Koskenneimi 'Human Rights, Politics and Love' in M Koskenniemi *The Politics of International Law* (Hart Publishing Oxford 2011) at 153.
72 Moyn (n 67) 221.
73 ibid 219.
74 ibid 220.
75 ibid.
76 L Bilsky 'Transnational Holocaust Litigation' (2012) 23(2) *European Journal of International Law* 349.
77 ibid 350.
78 L Weissman 'A Moot Issue? Rethinking Holocaust Era Restitution if Jewish Confiscated Personal Property in Poland' (2011–12) 13 *Cardozo Journal of Conflict Resolution* 679.
79 N Klein *The Shock Doctrine: The Rise of Disaster Capitalism* (Picador London 2008) 119–20.

violations.[80] In this context, the emergence of a field of international criminal justice 'profited from the inadequacies' of other projects of human rights and collective security.[81] Schwoebel captures this move as part of a marketing culture where 'ICL makes a claim to maximizing on investments more efficiently than its competitors.'[82] It is a form of branding where the field is the 'primary discipline dealing with rogue political leaders . . . a discipline fighting impunity, a beacon of global justice, the heroic few internationalists who dare to fight big power-players'.[83] This 'discipline creep' has meant that international criminal lawyers advocate for more and more of the world to be described according to the regime's ethos to the point of 'arguably swallowing the entire discipline of transitional justice'.[84] In particular, the Former Yugoslav and Rwandan conflicts marked a critical turning point when legal experts came to the forefront with a range of resolutions to what was read as international crimes rather than post-conflict transition.[85] In fact, the field's name was 'virtually unheard until the late 1990s' when the field's flagship journal emerged.[86] This 'act of coining/staking' was an attempt to capture a practice involving 'that part of international criminal law that had by then become deeply institutionalized through international criminal tribunals'.[87] It was (and is) international criminal justice being produced by international criminal lawyers,[88] a field with its own Lauterpachts and Henkins to push the discipline towards a Kantian horizon.

Much like other modern institutions, international criminal law has an 'accepted' history that involves a linear, progressive 'coming of age story'.[89] This story involves an institutional progress that adopts Western concepts of criminal justice with consequentialist and utilitarian justifications. Its institutions use 'highly evocative language' in order to tell a story that begins with 'desperation and [ends] with salvation'.[90] This 'feel-good image of global justice' appears attractive against a context of economic inequality, intractable conflicts and a sense of injustice.[91] However, as Tallgren argues, its utilitarian motives, when set against political crises, seem 'out of place, artificial, even ridiculous' and that perhaps international criminal law's purpose is to give a sense that the international political world can be submitted to 'rational governance' of domestic societies.[92] Therefore, international criminal

80 F Mégret 'International Criminal Justice as a Juridical Field' (2016) XIII *Champ Pénal* 1, para 16.
81 ibid para 16.
82 C Schwoebel 'The Market and Marketing Culture of International Criminal Law' in C Schwoebel *Critical Approaches to International Criminal Law: An Introduction* (Routledge London 2014) 265.
83 ibid
84 ibid 267.
85 Mégret (n 80) para 18.
86 ibid para 8.
87 ibid para 9.
88 ibid.
89 Schwoebel (n 83) 266.
90 ibid 273.
91 ibid.
92 I Tallgren 'The Sense and Sensibility of International Criminal Law (2002) 13(3) *European Journal of International Law* 561, 590.

law may serve a purpose 'simultaneously both to reason and to mystify political control exercised by those to whom it is available in the current international community'.[93] This naturalizes and excludes 'from the political battle' some acts from jurisdiction of tribunals as opposed to others, and this excludes 'certain phenomena which are in fact the precondition for the maintenance of the existing governance; by the North, by wealthy states, by wealthy individuals . . .'.[94]

Similarly, Schwoebel argues that the practice of international criminal institutions tend to depoliticize victims, forcing victims to ascribe to a particular model of justice.[95] She maps the field's central ideas onto the logic of neoliberalism that she believes pervades the logic of the field. This means that the complicity and involvement of Great powers is suppressed and international criminal law responses are managed according to efficiency; where expansion occurs if success is probable, yet simultaneously limits occur if failure is likely.[96] Therefore, the Great powers and their financiers are never prosecuted and instead, are 'heroes, rarely victims and never perpetrators'.[97] We can see that war crimes trials are political in the sense that the 'concept of the political is perpetually in play'.[98] Here, the trials are filled 'with conservations about what it means to engage in politics or law, as well as a series of projects that seek to employ these terms in the service of various ideological preferences'.[99] Simpson reads the politics as 'politics of compromise' between 'liberal cosmopolitanism and illiberal particularism that frames and distorts the discourse'.[100] Koskenniemi reads the formalism/anti-formalism as an ambivalent oscillation between ending impunity for humanitarian crises and the danger of becoming a show trial.[101] This inescapable and irreconcilable oscillation means that 'when criminal law and diplomacy meet . . . any middle ground is both narrow and slippery.'[102] In this chapter, we observe the moralist/formalist oscillation in every position, leading to an inevitable tendency towards a middle ground that is 'both narrow and slippery'.[103]

Turning to the 1990s, the international criminal tribunals were established by the UN Security Council in order to avoid having to engage in a military response to both Former Yugoslav and Rwandan conflicts.[104] The financial and

93 ibid 594.
94 ibid 594–5.
95 Schwoebel (n 83) 277. See S Kendall and S Nouwen 'Representational Practices at the International Criminal Court; The Gap Between Juridified and Abstract Victimhood' (2014) 76 *Law and Contemporary Problems* 235.
96 ibid 274
97 ibid 278.
98 Simpson (n 1) 11.
99 ibid.
100 ibid 12.
101 Koskenniemi (n 8) 1.
102 M Koskenniemi and P Leino 'Fragmentation of International Law? Postmodern Anxieties' (2002) 15 *Leiden Journal of International Law* 553, 579.
103 ibid.
104 G Bass *Stay the Hand of Vengeance: The Politics of War Crimes Tribunals* (Princeton University Press Princeton 2001) 206 *et passim*.

institutional backing of the United States, alongside cooperation with certain European and African states, permitted the tribunals to establish themselves.[105] This structured the discourse surrounding the tribunals in a cost/benefit analysis that explained to donors how international criminal justice was good for business, creating security in otherwise dangerous conflict zones. Kendall argues that this blurs boundaries between justice, security and development because 'recipient states are beneficiaries of funding that aligns with donor states' foreign policy objectives.[106] Another dimension was a serious challenge posed by state cooperation when key actors, particularly Serbia and Rwanda, failed to cooperate during those tribunals' formative period.[107] The *Tadic* and *Akayesu* judgments produced mixed responses among international lawyers over the tribunal's discussion of customary international law; yet at the same time, both judgments were perceived as significant moments that appeared to establish the field's identity as having a major role in post-conflict justice. There seemed to be a sense that individual criminal responsibility was being freed from its unfortunate immobilization during the Cold War and finally allowed to further the purposes of international community in constructing a world without impunity.

The validity of its customary status went largely unquestioned, even though scholars struggled to produce a universally agreed narrative from the limited evidence of state behaviour since the post-war trials of the 1940s. Their evidence did list the statutes of international tribunals, the International Law Commission's draft code and its Principles of Nuremberg and General Assembly resolutions, yet there was an underwhelming number of domestic prosecutions and national implementation of treaties.[108] This was a small number of treaty-based instruments combined with limited implementation. Notwithstanding, the Nuremberg model was unquestioned in the 1990s, even though it had been persistently questioned in the literature during the post-war 1940s trials and later. Repeating the model of the NMT, it was believed that individual criminal responsibility's customary status operated regardless of whether the trial takes place in an international or national tribunal. As we observe below, when the same argument pattern was applied to the issue of jurisdiction, international lawyers debated whether it established a customary rule.

3.1 The Eichmann judgments' *narrative in play*

The *Eichmann* narrative informed the debate surrounding the 'fight against impunity' and the drive for securing universal accountability, including through criminal trials. Literature in the 1990s could pull on interpretations that explained

105 ibid.

106 S Kendall 'Donors' Justice: Recasting International Criminal Accountability' (2011) 24(3) *Leiden Journal of International Law* 585, 592.

107 See generally V Peskin *International Justice in Rwanda and the Balkans: Virtual Trials and the Struggle for State Cooperation* (Cambridge University Press Cambridge 2008).

108 R van Alebeek *The Immunity of States and Their Officials in International Criminal Law and International Human Rights Law* (Oxford University Press Oxford 2008) 209.

the experience of advocates using the United States Alien Torts Act.[109] Therefore, the *Eichmann* narrative was repeated in the 1980s in regards to civil remedies and later in the 1990s surrounding criminal trials, yet in this repetition, it was transformed to engage notions of *jus cogens* and *erga omnes.* The narrative was not initially challenged within national courts, especially as the early 1990s case law involved Nazi atrocities.[110] Yet within the emerging field of international criminal law, the *Eichmann* narrative was read as applying by analogy to situations outside of the Nazi atrocities. As we observed in Chapter 2, the Nuremberg model's narrative pulled on the moral naturalism of the nature of the crimes (justice) combined with unconditional surrender and joint sovereignty (consent). This similar pattern was adopted in the *Eichmann* judgments that combined the nature of the crimes (justice) with its analysis of state behaviour (consent). In the early 1990s, when the Commission of Experts examined alleged war crimes and crimes against humanity in the conflict in Former Yugoslavia, they also explored the possibilities for conducting criminal trials. Among their proposals, there was an implied reference to the *Eichmann* narrative on universal jurisdiction as the Commission's Report assumed that the nature of the crimes gave rise to universal jurisdiction over crimes against humanity and genocide under customary international law and over grave breaches under treaty law and custom.[111] *Obiter* in the *Tadic*[112] and *Furundzija*[113] decisions similarly made an implied reference to the *Eichmann* narrative and, in effect, this repeated a similar narrative structure used to justify the tribunals themselves.[114]

In another interpretation, the International Law Commission addressed an aspect of the *Eichmann* narrative that the Israeli courts had not directly addressed, that is, the issue of voluntary presence of the accused. The work on the 1996 Draft Code of Crimes included an exploration of enforcement through universal jurisdiction in the form of an obligatory *aut dedere aut judicare.* Article 8 imposed an obligation on states to establish jurisdiction over war crimes, crimes against humanity and genocide, irrespective of location of the offence or nationality of the offender or victim.[115] It was premised on a political project that sought to establish the broadest jurisdiction through concurrent national and international jurisdiction. The obligation would be triggered when the accused is 'present' on the state's territory, yet the International Law Commission left politically

109 For instance, *Filartiga v Pena Irala* (1980) 630 F.2d, 890, *In re Demjanjuk*, 612 F Supp. 544 (ND Ohio).

110 See *R v. Finta*, 82 ILR, *Polyukovich v. Commonwealth of Australia*, (1990) HCA 40, *R v Wagner* (1993) SASC 4508. See also *Report of the War Crimes Inquiry* (HMG Stationary Office, CM 744).

111 *Final Report of the Commission of Experts*, UN Doc. S/1994/674 (27 May 1994), paras 107, 42, 45 and 105.

112 See *Prosecutor v. Dusko Tadic aka "Dule" (Decision on the Defence Motion on Jurisdiction)*, IT-94-1 (10 August 1995) para 42.

113 *Prosecutor v. Furundzjia*, IT-95-17/1-T (10 December 1998) para 156.

114 See *Prosecutor v. Milan Milutinović et al.*, IT-99-37-AR72 (21 May 2003).

115 *Draft Code of Crimes Against Peace and Security of Mankind* (1996) Vol II *Yearbook of the International Law Commission* Pt II, 28.

open-ended the meaning of the word 'present'. It also did not conceive the format in absolute form and therefore, this obligation was read as an alternative between prosecution and extradition, neither of which has priority.[116] While this regime applied to three of the 'core crimes', the draft code deemed the crime of aggression as requiring a distinct regime, exclusively under the jurisdiction of an international criminal court, and this distinctiveness has never been since questioned.

The International Law Commission also followed the *Eichmann* narrative on immunity of state officials, which privileged the moral outrage against the crimes and analysed social behaviour through that normative lens (descending-ascending). Its analysis appeared more concrete as it cited post-war 1940s trials along with the Former Yugoslav and Rwandan tribunals.[117] However, this analysis could be accused of being too apologist, attacking its selection of evidence of state practice and therefore, there is a move back to the moral naturalism of the crimes that justified the removal of the procedural bar as the 'essential corollary' of the lack of a substantive defence of immunity.[118] It utilized the same logic as regards the removal of the substantive defence, which read as paradoxical having rules of law that preclude invoking an 'official position to avoid responsibility for a crime only to permit him to invoke this same consideration to avoid the consequences of this responsibility'.[119] The International Law Commission also addressed the issue of non-retroactivity of laws, a rule that prohibits criminal prosecution of an individual for an act which was not criminal at the time of its commission.[120] Given the above positions, it argued against the application of non-retroactivity that would prejudice the prosecution of acts committed before the Draft Code's entry into force.[121] It used a combination of human rights treaties and the *Eichmann* narrative to provide the justification for the inapplicability of non-retroactivity.[122]

From the mid-1990s, war crimes trials began in various national courts that addressed alleged crimes in Former Yugoslavia. All these cases involved accused who had fled the Yugoslav conflict to other states in Europe and the proceedings were initiated either by civil party procedure[123] or by the state

116 ibid 28–30.

117 ibid 27. See also *Final Report of the Commission of Experts* (n 77) para 99 (noting, under culpability, that alleged perpetrators could not 'hide behind the shield of immunity').

118 ibid. See H Fox *The Law of State Immunity* (Oxford University Press Oxford 2008) 677 (arguing that where a properly constituted tribunal (established with consent of the state), no issue of a waiver of immunity).

119 ibid.

120 R O'Keefe 'Universal Jurisdiction *in absentia*' (2004) 2 *Journal of International Criminal Justice* 735, 742.

121 *Draft Code of Crimes* (n 115) 39.

122 Article 15(2) of the Covenant on Civil and Political Rights and see chapter 2, section 4.

123 A civil party procedure involves the submission of a complaint by a victim or on behalf of a victim to an investigating magistrate who is obliged to determine whether she has jurisdiction to proceed and if so determined, to engage a prosecutor to investigate the criminal complaint. In common law jurisdictions, the decision to initiate an investigation is in the sole discretion of the state prosecutor. See S Sule *German Legal System and Laws* (4th edn Oxford University Press Oxford 2010) 383.

prosecutor, depending on the state's criminal procedure. Each national court faced the dilemma over the validity of criminal jurisdiction, as had the previous post-war 1940s trials, and therefore pulled on the repetition of narratives since the 1960s. The *Saric* case involved an accusation of breaches of the Geneva Conventions that were alleged to have been committed in a camp in Dretelj, Bosnia-Herzegovina. The Danish trial court implicitly evoked the *Eichmann* narrative in that the crimes descend from a moral naturalism, and therefore it held that the claim of extraterritorial jurisdiction under article 8(5) of the Danish Penal Code could apply to war crimes under the Geneva Conventions without the specific implementation of those offences in domestic law.[124] Here, section 8(5) provides that the courts will have jurisdiction over extraterritorial offences committed by a non-national where the 'act is covered by an international rule, according to which Denmark is required to have jurisdiction'.[125] In other words, the court implicitly accepted the idea that universal jurisdiction over grave breaches was valid despite opposing positions as discussed in chapter 3, section 2.1.3 and could be invoked by Danish courts. However, this did not extend as far as to apply the treaty-defined offences, despite that fact that the logical conclusion of the moral naturalism would deem this to be so. Consequently, *Saric* was charged with committing domestic offences[126] and this seemed inconsistent in that jurisdiction could descend from moral naturalism, yet the crimes, recognized as crimes under customary international law, could not apply domestically.

This outcome was also adopted by the German courts in the *Djajic* case that involved allegations of genocide for the killing of Bosnian Muslims.[127] The Bavarian State Supreme Court combined the Geneva Convention's grave breaches repression regime with section 6(9) of the Strafgesetzbuch (Criminal Code) that asserted extraterritorial jurisdiction over offences 'which on the basis of an international agreement binding on the Federal Republic of Germany must be prosecuted even though committed abroad'.[128] Its logic pulled more directly from the *Eichmann* narrative as it rejected the existence of a prohibitive rule, yet simultaneously confirmed a permissive rule. Here, its descending move justified jurisdiction of German courts on the 'legitimate interest not to be seen by the international community as sheltering international criminals'.[129] International law was read as favouring war crimes trials over 'the limiting principle of non-interference'.[130] This repeated de Vabres's

124 L Reydams *Universal Jurisdiction: International and National Perspectives* (Oxford University Press Oxford 2003)126 *et seq.*, and A Laursen 'A Danish Paradox? A Brief Review of the Status of International Crimes in Danish Law' (2012) 10 *Journal of International Criminal Justice* 997.

125 See Penal Code, URL: https://www.retsinformation.dk/Forms/R0710.aspx?id=121398#Kap2.

126 Controversially, the Danish court classified the alleged acts as grave breaches without analysing whether the acts had been committed during an international armed conflict.

127 *Prosecutor v Djajic*, Bayerisches Oberstes Landesgericht, 23 May 1997, excerpts reprinted in Reydams (n 124) 151.

128 See German Criminal Code, URL: http://www.gesetze-im-internet.de/englisch_stgb/englisch_stgb.html.

129 C Safferling '*Public Prosecutor v Djajic*' (1998) 92 American Journal of International Law 528, 531.

130 ibid 533.

position that read a state intervening in default of all other states, to prevent in the interests of humanity 'a scandalous impunity'.[131]

Another similar decision is in the *Jorgic* case that involved allegations of killing Bosnia Muslim civilians and ill-treating detainees in the Doboj region in Bosnia Herzegovina. Here, the German Federal Supreme Court pulled on the *Eichmann* position on article VI of the Genocide Convention that dismissed the interpretation of article VI as a prohibitive rule for treaty parties.[132] The Israeli courts in *Eichmann* offered two justifications for their position, yet the first of these was too historically contingent to be pulled upon by German courts in *Jorgic*. It would have compelled the court to readdress whether article VI was a prohibitive rule.[133] Therefore, in *Jorgic*, the court only referred to the argument that the Convention's object and purpose would be thwarted if treaty parties were prohibited from asserting extraterritorial jurisdiction over genocide.[134] The court then produced a contemporary interpretation that drew on the International Law Commission's normative justification. We observed that the draft code included universal jurisdiction on the assumption that universal accountability needed concurrent national and international tribunals given the limited capacity of the latter.[135]

Through this normative lens, the court interpreted what it read as the meaning of article 9 of the Statute of the International Criminal Tribunal for Former Yugoslavia (ICTY). It concluded that the phrase 'national jurisdictions' could only mean both territorial and extraterritorial jurisdiction of UN Member States, as otherwise the obligation to exercise jurisdiction would be limited to the courts of the states of the Former Yugoslavia.[136] It bolstered its position with an invocation of the *erga omnes* obligation to prevent and punish the crime of genocide,[137] along with situations where the ICTY prosecutor declined to exercise jurisdiction and the prosecution was conducted by national courts exercising universal jurisdiction. On appeal, the German Constitutional Court recognized a need for a 'sensible nexus' that must depend 'on the particular nature of the subject of regulation'.[138] Here, the nature of the crime of genocide as 'the most severe violation of human rights' is significant in that the crime attacks 'important legal interests of the international community of states'.[139] Therefore, the principle of universal jurisdiction

131 D de Vabres (n 42) 135.

132 *Jorgic*, Bundesgerichtshof (30 April 1999) 6.

133 It seemed to be a neat position in *Eichmann* to pull on the rule in law of treaties that precluded treaty obligations applying to acts prior to the treaty's entry into force. However, if Jorgic had used *Eichmann*'s first argument, when the acts were committed after the Genocide Convention's entry into force, it would be forced the court to reassess whether article VI is a limiting rule.

134 *Jorgic* (n 132) 5–6 (limitation as 'irreconcilable with the obligation imposed by article 1').

135 ibid 6.

136 ibid 7.

137 See also *Case concerning Application of the Convention on the Prevention and Punishment of the Crime of Genocide (Bosnia v Serbia) (Preliminary Objections)* (1996) ICJ Rep 595, para 31.

138 Bundesverfassungsgericht (12 December 2000), para 3(a), URL: http://www.bundesverfassungsgericht.de/entscheidungen/rk20001212_2bvr129099en.html.

139 ibid para 3(b).

'constitutes such a sensible nexus'[140] and regardless of the lack of a treaty law obligation, states have permission to exercise if they so decide.[141] This repeats Hyde's 'close and direct connection' along with a move to reasonableness where universal jurisdiction is what appears reasonable in achieving universal accountability.

In the *Cvjetkovic* case, the Austrian Supreme Court evoked its claim of subsidiary jurisdiction, as discussed in Chapter 2 that was referred to by Eichmann's defence counsel. It then justified universal jurisdiction in the circumstances where the territorial jurisdiction's criminal justice system is not functioning and an international criminal court is not established or the state has not consented to its jurisdiction.[142] In other words, it re-described the idea of an absence of sovereignty (or jurisdiction) where the lacuna can be filled through an extraordinary jurisdictional claim. This then reframed the Eichmann defence counsel's position to support an opposite conclusion that justified rather than criticized universal jurisdiction.

3.2 An outermost point

Similar to the outcome in *Demjanjuk*, the Spanish and Belgian *Pinochet* judgments brought the *Eichmann* narrative to its logical conclusion and in turn, to what seemed to be the margins of a narrative that privileged the moral naturalism underpinning the crimes. Their position reflected the implications of Demjanjuk's extradition because the term 'presence' was considered to include situations of involuntarily surrender or extradition from another state. In this sense, the content of jurisdiction did not depend on voluntary presence; rather, presence was actively sought as part of the commitment of universal accountability. This seemingly outermost point of the *Eichmann* narrative is the moralist approach's horizon as the court of humanity that never adjourns is fully operational and the campaign to 'fight against impunity' has the widest possible jurisdiction. Yet to the opposing formalist position, this horizon seemed too utopian and merely oppressive homogeneity that violated self-determination.

Evidently the Belgian *Pinochet* judgment provided what it read as concrete state behaviour.[143] The investigating magistrate explored Belgian parliamentary intent and produced an interpretation of the preamble to the 1993 Law, that the 1993 Law applied regardless of whether the alleged offender is found on Belgian territory.[144] Therefore, he argued that the Belgian Parliament evoked the obligation to search for and punish grave breaches under the Geneva Conventions, regardless of the voluntary presence of the accused. Of course,

140 ibid para 3(a) (meaning of 'universal jurisdiction' as only applicable to specific crimes).

141 See *South West Africa* case (1962) ICJ Rep 319, 336 (teleological interpretation of treaties can be prioritized in *justifiable* cases).

142 *Cvjetkovic*, Obersten Gerichtshofes (13 July 1994).

143 *Re Pinochet*, Tribunal de Premier Instance de Bruxelles (6 November 1998). For a detailed historical account, see N Roht-Arriaza *The Pinochet Effect: Transitional Justice in the Age of Human Rights* (University of Pennsylvania Press Philadelphia 2006) 118 *et seq.*

144 *Projet de loi relatif à la répression des infractions graves*, Doc Parl. Senate 1317-1, 1990–91.

the phrase 'search for' is invariably politically open-ended and permits multiple interpretations. Alongside their move to the margins, both judgments submitted further alternative interpretations to the *Eichmann* narrative on justifying universal jurisdiction over genocide and crimes against humanity.[145]

In the Spanish *Pinochet* decision, the court provided an idiosyncratic version of an earlier argument that had accommodated domestic constitutional principles. Under article 96 of the Spanish Constitution, treaty law obligations prevail over domestic statutes.[146] Therefore, it was argued that Spanish courts are subject to a form of subsidiarity when exercising extraterritorial jurisdiction over genocide, as article VI of the Genocide Convention obliges treaty parties to exercise the territorial jurisdiction. This subsidiarity looks similar to nineteenth-century subsidiary jurisdiction, as it is triggered when the territorial jurisdiction has failed to prosecute.[147] This logic merged two positions. It approved the *Jorgic* position that the Genocide Convention did not prohibit treaty parties from exercising universal jurisdiction, and it added *Cvjetkovic*'s normative position that justified subsidiary jurisdiction based on preventing an impunity gap.

In the Belgian *Pinochet* case, the investigating magistrate followed the 1980s re-description of the *Eichmann* narrative that justified jurisdiction on nature of crimes as *jus cogens* and a fundamental interest of the international community to repress.[148] He also adopted Randall and the International Law Commission's position that the format of extradite or prosecute ensures punishment of the crimes 'regardless of where they were committed'.[149] Here, he was required to explore whether the norm of crimes against humanity could transcend national law, as the 1993 Belgian Law only provided for universal jurisdiction over war crimes in international and internal armed conflicts.[150] He implicitly followed the logic from the *Saric* decision in that, as crimes against humanity were norms of customary international law, the acts could be prosecuted under domestic criminal statutes as if analogous to domestic crimes. Support in state behaviour was traced to the statutes of post-war 1940s tribunals and the Former Yugoslav and Rwandan tribunals [151] Even though both Belgian and Spanish courts accorded

145 The Spanish decision also produced a controversial interpretation of the concept of terrorism under article 23(4). However, this chapter focuses on how courts and tribunals re-described the *Eichmann* narrative and therefore, it narrows its analysis to the discussion of genocide within the decision.

146 Article 23(4)(a) states that Spanish jurisdiction arises over listed acts 'committed by Spanish citizens or foreign nationals outside national territory where they are liable to be classified, under Spanish penal law'. See URL: http://www.poderjudicial.es/cgpj/en/Subjects/Compendium-of-Judicial-Law-/Laws/Organic-Law-6-1985-of-1-July--on-the-Judiciary.

147 *Chilean Investigations* (5 November 1998) Audiencia Nacional para 2.

148 *Re Pinochet* (n 143), para 3.3.2 ('either the crimes do not transcend borders . . . or crimes are of magnitude that repression is shared by all').

149 ibid, para 3.3.3.

150 See Chapter 3, section 2.1.3.

151 Re Pinochet (n 143) para 3.3.2 (noting recognition of crime as custom in post-war instruments, along with Belgian recognition that genocide is part of domestic law due to its customary status, despite lack of treaty incorporation).

with the *Eichmann* narrative on the issue of non-retroactivity, the Spanish court re-described that narrative.[152] It argued that article 23(4) of the Organic Law of Judicial Power is a jurisdictional (procedural) provision rather than substantive. Therefore, proceedings are not *ex post facto* as long as the act was criminal under Spanish law at the time of its commission (even if Spanish jurisdiction did not extend extraterritorially at the time of commission).[153]

An alternative counter-position was submitted to Spanish courts that had no legacy in the post-war or Eichmann trials. The Chilean and Argentinean amnesties had been concluded in the transition to market democracy in order to ensure political stability during the transition. Therefore, the national amnesties were invoked to challenge the validity of Spanish jurisdiction, that is, any exercise of Spanish jurisdiction would violate the political independence of Chile and Argentina. Turning to 1990s post-conflict transition literature and jurisprudence, the court confirmed the validity of its jurisdiction in keeping with its moralist position. It cited 1980s human rights litigation that had consistently concluded that national amnesties are incompatible with human rights treaty law obligations. Therefore, the Chilean Decree Law 1978 was not binding because amnesties for crimes against international law violated *jus cogens.*[154]

Another counter-argument posited that an exercise of Spanish jurisdiction would violate the principle of *non bis in idem* as Chilean courts had already dismissed a criminal complaint involving the same allegations.[155] However, the court privileged the nature of the crimes and the normative project of securing justice in the interest of the international community, which trumped post-conflict dialogue that did not permit criminal accountability. As the interests of the international community were being secured, Spanish jurisdiction did not involve arbitrary and unwarranted interference in a state's domestic affairs. To a formalist position, both judgments seemed even more normative, less concrete than *Eichmann*, particularly given the stance on presence of the suspect. To a moralist position, these decisions would epitomize the horizon of a preventing impunity project.

3.3 A counter-hegemony of the formalist position

Although the dominant position during the 1990s was the re-described *Eichmann* narrative, there was an inevitable counter-hegemonic position that

152 *Chilean Investigations* (n 147) para 3.22 (as long as the crime was criminal in domestic law at the time of its commission, it does not violate non-retroactivity and deemed part of domestic law through cooperation obligation with ICTY).

153 ibid para 3.

154 ibid para 8. See *FIDH v Ould Dah*, Court of Cassation No 02-85379 (23 October 2002), URL: http://www.asser.nl/upload/documents/DomCLIC/Docs/NLP/France/Ely_Cassation_23-10-2002.pdf (upheld French jurisdiction over torture committed extraterritorially, based on the Torture Convention yet applied to acts committed prior to French domestic implementation, as the Convention codified a customary crime, and rejected Mauritanian amnesty law as precluding French jurisdiction).

155 ibid (Chilean courts' dismissal did not amount to 'acquittal, pardon or conviction' as the facts were not adjudicated upon).

repeated Eichmann's defence counsel's narrative. This narrative was repeated yet re-described for a contemporary audience because in the 1990s, the dominant position that was embedded in legal consciousness was an acceptance of the validity of the personal liability for the crimes. As we explored in Section 3, it would have been inconceivable to adopt the defence counsel's rejection of personal liability. Therefore, the 1990s counter-hegemonic position drew on the Eichmann defence counsel's narrative that challenged the validity of universal jurisdiction over the crimes, and on the International Law Commission's reference to the procedural bar of immunity, albeit reaching an opposite conclusion. This renders the court's jurisdiction entirely dependent on the state's consent to the trial of its nationals that, of course, trumps the moral naturalism that underpins the criminal liability.

This counter-hegemonic position tapped into an unease over universal jurisdiction that arose from the moralist position's hegemonic control, as it could stand accused of being political motivated trials through 'jurisdictional imperialism'.[156] This is a familiar rhetorical move that is recognizable from the legal discourse of the late nineteenth century that noted the need for conditions to avoid arbitrary interference. This paradox would mean that the field of international criminal law emerged as a challenge to what was seen to be sovereign egoism, yet the entire political project would depend entirely on consent of the state of nationality of the defendant. This can be accused of bringing the legal argument to the vanishing point of power and, to a moralist position, would appear to override the moral naturalism that justifies liability and crime (beyond any treaty). This moral naturalism is a means of expressing moral outrage at the unthinkability of the atrocities.

We observed above how arguments adopting the formalist position privileged state independence and non-interference and the need for demonstrable state behaviour, that is, for the rule of law to reflect the voluntary will of states. The emphasis was on social fact and the search for evidence of state consent to the principle of universal jurisdiction in regards to crimes against international law. It criticized the moralist hegemonic position by citing infrequent historical cases and inconsistencies in state behaviour, which undermined any validity of universal jurisdiction *per se* and with respect to each of the crimes.[157] This position found more support in the literature after the UK *Pinochet* case.[158] As a counter-hegemonic position, the *Javor* case acts as a counter-point against what was the dominant position in national courts until the dissents in the UK's *Pinochet* case. The *Javor* case pertained to allegations of crimes against humanity in Serb forces-controlled detention camps in Bosnia Herzegovina. The investigating magistrate

156 International Law Association 'Final Report on the Exercise of Universal Jurisdiction of Gross Human Rights Offences' (London 2000) 19.

157 Reydams (n 124) and L Benavides 'The Doctrine of Universal Jurisdiction: Its Nature and Scope', (2001) 1 *Annuaire Derechos International* 19, 58 (rejecting *jus cogens* yet preferring nature of the offence).

158 See M Henzelin *Le Principe de l'universalité en droit penal international* (Helbing & Lichtenhahn Bruylant 2000).

found jurisdiction based on the Torture Convention and Geneva Conventions, with the latter considered self-executing.[159]

The magistrate rejected *Jorgic*'s interpretation on universal jurisdiction over genocide, as the cited evidence was either temporally limited or unratified by France, implying that a customary rule did not exist.[160] Yet he also concluded that presence of the suspect was not a prerequisite for exercising jurisdiction under Torture Convention because otherwise the treaties' object and purpose would be frustrated by being dependent on the chance of arresting the perpetrator.[161] In other words, the magistrate pulled from the same moral naturalism that was used in *Jorgic* in order to justify universal jurisdiction over genocide, despite the jurisdictional provisions of the Genocide Convention. Overall, this appears to a moralist opponent to be too apologist, as the magistrate cannot avoid an apparent inconsistency where he rejects universal jurisdiction over crimes against international law under custom and accepts the notion of universal jurisdiction by treaty. It leaves unexplained how states can consent to establishing universal jurisdiction by treaty and at the same time, avoid seeming to extinguish law's normativity because states appear to have some sort of absolute freedom to contract.

On appeal by the public prosecutor, the Court of Appeal rejected the idea that the treaties provided a basis for universal jurisdiction and therefore, French courts did not have any jurisdiction over the allegations. The Geneva Conventions were not self-executing; this seemed too utopian. Rather there must be domestic implementation for the French courts to possess jurisdiction as this seemed more concrete.[162] It supported this position with its interpretation of the 'wording of these texts' that indicated the obligations 'only [bind] State parties and are not directly applicable under domestic law'.[163] No justification was tendered for this particular textual meaning, yet it appeared to accord with a classical nineteenth-century notion of sovereignty, where international law merely delimited territorial boundaries. The court's conclusion on the meaning of search and punish in the Geneva Conventions was that those words were inseparable, with the implication that presence must be on the state's territory. When it turned to the meaning of 'is present in France' in article 689–2 of the French Code of Criminal Procedure, it argued that this requires voluntary presence in French territory and therefore, without presence of the accused, French courts lack jurisdiction over the alleged crimes.[164] Overall, the *Javor* case appeals to the project of stability and non-intervention, yet to a moralist position, it appears to be merely shielding alleged perpetrators from facing justice, hidden behind a so-called 'political project of stability' in international affairs. *Javor*'s legal outcome was similar to the

159 *Javor and Others* (2002) 127 International Law Reports 126.

160 ibid 127 (post-war instruments temporally limited, General Assembly resolutions did not have binding force and other treaties cited were not ratified by France).

161 ibid 129 ('empty the Convention of its substance and prevent victims from having case brought before competent tribunal . . .').

162 ibid 131–2.

163 ibid ('provisions . . . are of too general a character to create directly rules of extraterritorial criminal jurisdiction. Such rules must necessarily be drafted in a detailed and precise manner').

164 ibid 129 and 133 (upheld this meaning of presence on appeal to the Court of Cassation).

Danish *Pinochet* case[165] and to the German *X v. SB and DB.*[166] It was also applied in the German court's reasoning in *Tadic*[167] and *Djajic.*[168]

4 The late 1990s and *Pinochet III's* triumph

The late 1990s felt like a coming-of-age moment. In July 1998, the Statute of the International Criminal Court was finalized at a stunningly energetic diplomatic conference in Rome.[169] It featured 160 state delegations watched over by the leading NGOs in transitional justice and the 'Who's Who' of the field. Platitudes over the significance of the moment appeared to be issued all round.[170] A return was made to the field's agreed history in order to show what progress had been made.[171] It seemed for a moment as if there may be some truth to the 'new order' as this idea of a permanent international criminal court that had been immobilized in the Cold War was re-ignited spectacularly only a decade after 1989. Then something happened that would have been impossible years earlier. Former Chilean Head of State Augusto Pinochet was placed under house arrest in London pending his extradition to face trial in a Spanish court. An ally of past Conservative (Tory) governments in the United Kingdom, Pinochet was meant to simply access medical treatment in London and return home days later. Instead, after a provisional warrant was issued by the magistrate, Pinochet's counsel sought an order of *habeas corpus* and judicial review of the legality of the warrants. Pending the outcome of his challenge, he was prevented from returning to Chile.[172]

This was not meant to happen because, as we noted earlier, even in Spain, the Chilean/Argentine investigations were not seriously considered likely to proceed; they were believed to be 'doomed'.[173] As Megret reminds us, earlier

165 See 'Opinion of the Director of Public Prosecution', reprinted in (2000) 3 *Yearbook of International Humanitarian Law* 26–9 (argued that Danish courts lacked jurisdiction if the suspect was not present in Denmark, based on the DPP's reading of international treaty law, drafting history of the Danish Penal Code and legal scholarship).

166 Bundesgerichtshof, 11 December 1998, excerpt reprinted in Reydams (n 124) 151–2 (Federal Supreme Court argued 'without a meaningful point of contact, respect for the sovereignty of other states can hardly be assured', rejecting prosecutorial discretion as sufficient).

167 Bundesgerichtshof, 13 February 1994, excerpts reprinted in Reydams (n 124) 149 (arguing that Tadic's long-term residency and arrest in Germany was a legitimizing link, although would not decide whether such preconditions are 'always sufficient').

168 *Prosecutor v Djajic*, Bayerisches Oberstes Landesgericht, 23 May 1997, excerpts reprinted in Reydams (n 124) 151. See also Safferling (n 130) 528.

169 WA Schabas 'International Criminal Court: The Secret of its Success' (2001) 12 *Criminal Law Forum* 415, 416.

170 ibid.

171 MC Bassiouni 'The International Criminal Court in Historical Context' (1999) *St. Louis-Warsaw Transatlantic Law Journal* 55.

172 See D Woodhouse, 'The Progress of Pinochet through the UK Extradition Procedure: An Analysis of the Legal Challenges and the Judicial Decisions' in M Davis (ed) *The Pinochet Case: Origins, Progress and Implications* (Institute of Latin American Studies London 2003) 87. On the Home Secretary's discretion, see sections 8(4), 7(1), 7(4) and 8(4) of the Extradition Act 1989.

173 Roht-Arriaza (n 143) 15. See also Reydams (n 124) (discussing earlier attempt to arrest Pinochet in the Netherlands).

periods illustrated how state cooperation is 'radicalized' in the field even though paradoxically, the regime is 'a criminal law without a state'.[174] Yet despite unlikely cooperation from Chile, a Spanish arrest warrant was executed by a British magistrate and the possibility of Pinochet facing trial in a European domestic court seemed realizable. Set against the Rome Conference negotiations and judgments before the Former Yugoslav and Rwandan tribunals, it seemed like a bright moment, a moment of confident renewal within a wider style of anxiety and confusion.

Nevertheless, the intuition that international criminal law excludes certain phenomenon also returned. The NATO bombing of Kosovo led to a 'turn to ethics' as many international lawyers concluded that the bombing was illegal but morally necessary.[175] This 'turn to ethics' captured 'within law a great crisis that under the old, "realistic" view would have fallen beyond its scope'.[176] However, this was 'profoundly conservative in its implications' and indicated how the field struggled 'to find credibility and critical voice in the conditions of increasingly imperial politics'.[177] The NATO bombing also sharply illustrated how the field naturalized and excluded from the political battle 'certain phenomena which are in fact the precondition for the maintenance of the existing governance'.[178] The ICTY's decision not to investigate the NATO bombing demonstrated how powerful states are unlikely to be subjected to the field's institutions.[179] When Milosevic fell from power and was delivered to The Hague, it presented another serious test for the field and, uncooperatively at such a momentous juncture, Milosevic invoked the qualified right to self-represent[180] and from the outset, accused the tribunal of being in effect a political show trial.[181] The Milosevic trial reminded the field that criminal trials remain structured by tension between prosecutors' and defendants' truth, with each struggling to supplant the other.[182]

4.1 The UK's Pinochet case

The *Pinochet* decisions have been disparaged as failing to possess 'any degree of common understanding' on international law relevant to their decisions.[183] Approached through literary style, the decisions represent an inevitable multitude

174 Megret (n 80) para 12.
175 Koskenniemi (n 19) 159.
176 ibid 160.
177 ibid.
178 Tallgren (n 92) 594–5.
179 Simpson (n 1) 17 and 47.
180 NHB Jorgensen 'The Problem of Self-representation at the International Criminal Tribunals' (2006) 4 *Journal of International Criminal Justice* 64.
181 T Krever 'Unveiling (and Veiling) Politics in International Criminal Trials' in C Schwoebel *Critical Approaches to International Criminal Law: An Introduction* (Routledge London 2014) 117.
182 See Koskenniemi (n 4) and Simpson (n 1).
183 C Warbrick, EM Salgado and N Goodwin 'The Pinochet Cases in the United Kingdom' (1999) 2 *Yearbook of International Humanitarian Law* 91, 105, van Alebeek (n 108) 226 ('impossible to derive common *ratio decidendi*') and also JC Barker 'The Future of Former Head of State Immunity after ex parte Pinochet' (1999) 48 *International and Comparative Law Quarterly* 937.

of possible interpretations due to structural properties of the language, and show the general tendency in legal discourse to move to the middle. As all positions are seen to be self-contradicting when pushed into argument, the majority in *Pinochet III* attempted to forge a moralist middle. The case itself centred on whether the procedural bar of immunity of state officials extinguished any potential criminal jurisdiction of an English court over the crime of torture. Pinochet's defence counsel followed *Javor*'s scepticism over universal jurisdiction (in contradistinction with the doctrine of immunity of state officials) and in effect, re-described the International Law Commission's draft code in a sense that procedural immunity should be inapplicable only in ***appropriate*** judicial proceedings.[184] As this position stressed the distinctness of substantive defence of immunity vis-à-vis the procedural bar, it could reduce the question of the appropriateness of jurisdiction of national courts to a singularity as against the pattern of the Nuremberg model and therefore, the procedural bar before national courts requires a distinct rule. In other words, the nature of the crimes do not of themselves (as a singularity or extraordinary circumstance) necessitate a distinct regime, removing the procedural bar before national courts, and as a result, all immunity case law (regardless of subject matter of dispute) is relevant as a pattern of what occurs in situations when the procedural bar is invoked. This pattern shows that immunity of state officials under customary international law applies, regardless of the nature of the crime, and only if a waiver is given by the respective state or an exception exists under customary international law, could the procedural bar be removed.

The High Court upheld Pinochet's contention that functional immunity of state officials continued to apply, irrespective of the nature of the crimes alleged.[185] It interpreted the UK's Extradition Act as meaning that the relevant time for assessing whether English law has jurisdiction over the offence was the time of extradition rather than the time when the offence is committed.[186] This mirrored the Spanish courts' position on non-retroactivity and its jurisdiction. The High Court's focus was on the State Immunity Act 1978 as opposed to the domestic incorporation of the Torture Convention under the Criminal Justice Act 1988, because immunity was a preliminary matter, prior to questions of the tribunal's basis of jurisdiction.[187] When applying s20 of the State Immunity Act 1978 with 'any necessary modifications', the High Court contended that immunity from suit 'continues' after a Head of State ceases office in respect of acts 'in

184 *Draft Code of Crimes* (n 115) 27.

185 See *R v. Evans and Bartle and the Secretary of State for the Home Department ex parte Augusto Pinochet* (1998) EWHC Admin 1013 (28 October 1998), para 31, 34 and 42 respectively (upheld second warrant on offences of torture, hostage taking and murder). Hereinafter *Pinochet I*. See also Extradition Act 1989 ('extradition crime' includes 'an extraterritorial offence against the law of the foreign State', if extraterritorial offence would be punishable in UK by at least 12 months' imprisonment and is an extraterritorial offence either on the basis of the nationality of the offender or on another basis of jurisdiction asserted in UK law).

186 ibid (n 185) para 44 (argued that textually section 2(1) of the Extradition Act would have to include the reference 'have constituted' and section 2(2), 'would have constituted' if the relevant time would be the time of the offence).

187 Warbrick et al. (n 183) 91.

the exercise of [their] functions'.[188] This position adopted the argument that the legal position of a Head of State under customary international law is assimilated to the immunity afforded to a Head of Mission under diplomatic immunity. In other words, the Head of State is afforded absolute immunity while in Office (from civil or criminal proceedings whether in regard to official or private acts) and a limited immunity subsisting indefinitely (over acts executed in an official capacity while in Office) (ex-Head of Mission). The High Court rejected the contention that the offences alleged in the arrest warrants cannot be official functions, discussing the case law in the US and UK as failing to demonstrate an exception to the rule of immunity.[189] This reiterates Kelsen's post-war writing where he spoke of the need for an exception to the doctrine of immunity, rather than some notion that the nature of the crimes extinguished immunities under customary international law.

4.2 More concrete than **Eichmann?**

On appeal to the House of Lords, the majority took the notion of 'official acts' as a point of departure and questioned whether crimes against international law may be official acts or functions 'in a public capacity' of the Head of State. Both Lords Nicholls and Steyn read the meaning of 'official functions' according to the object and purpose of the Torture Convention.[190] Therefore, they privileged the moral naturalism of the crime and the normative project of securing criminal accountability (descending-ascending). They implicitly endorsed the re-described *Eichmann* narrative that immunity (whether defence or procedural bar) is removed, given the moral outrage at the nature of the crimes and the universal agreement that such acts should be punished.[191] Therefore, acts that contravened the Torture Convention could not be official functions as the acts cannot be attributable to the state.[192] This assumed that the concept of official functions was determined by the state parties through the Torture Convention (consent) and simultaneously through the moral naturalism of the crime (regardless of consent). This was necessary in order to bind Chile regardless of its own interpretation of its consent.

In an ascending move, Lord Nicholls sought to find evidence of his interpretation in state consent. He considered that parliamentary intent to remove act of state doctrine stemmed from Parliament's decision to criminalize torture

188 *Pinochet I* (n 185) para 75. See s1 of 1978 Act ('a state is immune from the jurisdiction of the courts of the UK'), s14(1) ('state' includes 'a sovereign or other head of that State in his public capacity') and s20 (Diplomatic Privileges Act 1964 subject to 'any necessary modifications' applies to a sovereign of other Head of State' as 'it applies to the Head of a Diplomatic mission').

189 ibid paras 70–73.

190 *Convention against Torture and Other Cruel, Inhuman or Degrading Treatment or Punishment* (adopted 10 December 1984, entered into force 26 June 1987) 1465 UNTS 85 (purposes of the Convention, described as 'is intentionally inflicted on a person . . . when such pain or suffering is inflicted by or at the instigation of or with the consent or acquiescence of a public official or other person acting in an official capacity').

191 *Pinochet I* (n 185) 939–40 (Nicholls) and 944 (Steyn).

192 ibid 940 and 944.

under domestic law. In other words, the 1988 Act provided English courts with the authority to exercise jurisdiction over acts of torture and thus, the claim that such acts are non-justiciable cannot reflect parliamentary intent.[193] He also contended that neither the Torture nor Hostages Convention could be interpreted as exempting a former Head of State from the respective accountability regimes.[194] However, this could be accused of failing to reflect actual state consent (given Chile's objections) and therefore, there was a move back to the underlying moral naturalism. Lord Steyn argued that no distinction was being drawn between acts purported to be functions of a Head of State and those which are criminal under international law. Though acknowledging the complexities, he considered that international law already provided a legal test, that is, whether the act is denounced by international law.[195] Hence, both Law Lords concluded that the crime of torture, as defined under the Criminal Justice Act 1988, could not be considered an official function because of its criminalization under treaty and custom combined with the treaty obligation to investigate and prosecute, and this extinguished the application of immunities within the framework of the Torture Convention.

A moralist position reads *Pinochet I* as normatively sound and concrete in reflecting what the treaty parties clearly agreed to, when they created a treaty regime for the suppression and punishment of torture. However, a formalist approach would criticize the court's interpretation of official functions as being too subjective, too political and too utopian. The court, in effect, unilaterally determined whether certain acts of the state officials can qualify as official functions or are outside the scope of immunity under international law, and presented this analysis as an account of treaty party consent. There is also an obvious inconsistency in that the acts are deemed private acts even though they are carried out on behalf of the state.[196] Of course, this inconsistency was familiar rhetoric in post-war 1940s trials as prosecutors spoke of the Nazi defendants acting outside of the state (an outlaw), yet acted within the state (subject to humanity's law). However, *Pinochet I* was set aside due to the automatic disqualification of Lord Hoffmann that led to a third and final ruling of the House of Lords.[197]

In *Pinochet III*, the majority in the House of Lords similarly explored the terms of the State Immunity Act 1978 based on the presumption that the 'statute must

193 ibid 939 (interpreting High Court's decision as erroneously applying the 'act of State' doctrine, that is, where acts are under the purported sovereign authority of another state, the dispute is not justiciable and instead, is a matter of judicial discretion whether adjudication is reasonable in the circumstances).

194 ibid (discussing the irrelevance of official capacity since Nuremberg Trials).

195 ibid 944.

196 ibid 928 (Lord Lloyd). See also van Alebeek (n 108) 223 (arguing that the inconsistencies between national courts on concept of immunity stems from competing notions of 'acts of State as public acts' or 'acts attributable to the State' that could support the removal of immunity, either within the rationale of the rule (not public acts) or in spite of the rationale of the rule (exception/not attributable to the state)).

197 Pinochet's counsel accused him of failing to recuse himself from the bench given his association with one of the interveners, Amnesty International. See (1999) 1 All ER 577.

be read in light of the United Kingdom's international obligations'[198] and yet the Law Lords, in their reading, produced a number of alternative interpretations. Only Lord Millet traced the origin of the crime of torture to customary international law and in turn to part of national law. The rest of the majority traced the origin of the crime of torture to the United Kingdom's ratification of the Torture Convention.[199] Although they produced multiple interpretations, most of the majority dismissed the official functions argument of *Pinochet I*. Warbrick argues that the absence of a specific limitation in the 1978 Act assisted the judges in adopting a wide understanding of official functions. Therefore, according to the Law Lords, the functions were defined by national law (determined by the state), were not confined to location of their exercise (in the state and abroad), and were not restricted to the Head of State's diplomatic role (international and internal affairs).[200] In so doing, the majority opinions either adhered to a concept of immunity as acts of state as public acts, or as a combination of the latter with the theory of acts attributable to the state.[201]

The majority in different ways accorded with the re-described *Eichmann* narrative on justifying jurisdiction over the crime of torture based on a moral naturalism of the nature of the crime (descending-ascending). Lords Brown-Wilkinson and Hutton implicitly traced the justification for torture as a crime to custom and Lord Millet did so expressly.[202] Although all the Law Lords accepted that the implementation of the Torture Convention criminalized the crime of torture domestically, Lord Millet appeared to presuppose that torture as a crime under customary international law was part of UK law.[203] Lord Browne-Wilkinson considered the crime of torture as a crime against humanity to be a *jus cogens* crime (under customary international law)[204] and its *jus cogens* nature 'justifies states in taking universal jurisdiction over torture whenever committed'.[205] This implicitly traces the justification for the crime to customary international law (beyond the treaty), in order to demonstrate how state parties had the legitimate authority to conclude a treaty that criminalizes acts of torture. Otherwise, the criminalization would appear to be only justified by treaty consent, which would appear to jeopardize the concept of torture being contrary to fundamental interests.

Browne-Wilkinson then merged the nature of crimes justification with an idea of an absence of sovereignty. As a 'totalitarian regime would not permit adjudication

198 Warbrick et al. (n 183) 105.

199 *R v. Bow St. Metropolitan Stipendiary Magistrate, ex parte Pinochet Ugarte (No.3)* (1999) 2 All ER 97. Hereinafter *Pinochet III*.

200 Warbrick et al. (n 183) 104 (unlike the rest of the majority, Phillips distinguished the functions of Head of Mission and therefore, argued that immunity could only be afforded when the Head of State visited the UK).

201 Van Alebeek (n 108) 224.

202 Warbrick et al. (n 183).

203 *Pinochet III* (n 199) 109 (Browne-Wilkinson) and 163 (Hutton). Warbrick et al. argued that the extension of criminality by the Convention to single acts of torture applied 'if only in the laws of the State parties'. See Warbrick et al. (n 183) 108.

204 ibid 108.

205 ibid 109 (be punishable by any state as the offenders are 'enemies of mankind').

in its courts', it was necessary to construct 'some international machinery' to avoid a dependency on local courts.[206] In another interpretation, Lord Millet justified the court's jurisdiction upon the systematic character of crimes evoking the Nuremberg model's moral outrage and described the crimes as of a scale as 'to attack the international legal order'.[207] Lord Hope assumed that torture 'on a widespread basis' was a crime under customary international law by the time of the Torture Convention, while Lord Hutton considered a single act of torture could be a crime against international law, that is, irrespective of a systematic character.[208]

These different variants seem more concrete, less normative than the *Eichmann* narrative, as they appear to imply that the jurisdictional claim was not a codification of custom and therefore, the claim in domestic law does not originate in custom but rather only in treaty law. However, the Law Lords need to reference a customary crime in order to suggest that state parties had a legitimate authority to conclude such a treaty in the first instance and avoid an implication that states possess 'pure' contractual freedom. When the majority turned to address the issue of immunity in the context of the Torture Convention, they did not endorse the more normative, less concrete argument that the *jus cogens* status of the crime extinguished immunity of state officials. From this position, there are two variants: either the crime as a norm of *jus cogens* invalidates any conflicting rules of international law,[209] or a violation of a *jus cogens* norm cannot be a sovereign act and thus, immunity of a state official does not arise.[210] However, if the Law Lords had adopted the *jus cogens* arguments, functional (and personal) immunity would always be overruled by certain crimes against international law that were deemed *jus cogens* prohibitions. This outcome would be deemed justified regardless of whether it could be established that the obligation to prosecute offences committed extraterritorially was *jus cogens*.[211] As we observed earlier, this would be the ultimate triumph for the moralist approach, because the court of humanity would never adjourn and the court would always rule that the foreign court's jurisdiction was justified (and reasonable).

Rather the Law Lords searched for an intention of the state parties to the Torture Convention that demonstrated the consent to the non-application of immunities within the context of the convention.[212] However, this consensualism (or ascending move) was viewed through the lens of their moral naturalism that underpinned the *jus cogens* status of the crime of torture and the normative function of the convention in making 'more effective the struggle against torture and other cruel,

206 ibid 110.

207 *Pinochet III* (n 199) 177.

208 ibid 151 (Hope) and 164–6 (Hutton).

209 *Case of the Arrest Warrant of 11 April 2000 (DRC v Belgium)* (2002) ICJ Rep 121 (Joint Separate Opinion), para 85 (that state behaviour is gradually recognizing this idea, citing the *Eichmann* judgment).

210 A Orakhelashvili *Peremptory Norms in International Law* (Oxford University Press Oxford 2006) 325.

211 Van Alebeek (n 108) 220 (arguing that 'for the [*jus cogens*] argument to work it must be established that the obligation to prosecute crimes against international law is of *jus cogens* nature').

212 *Pinochet III* (n 199) 114 (Browne-Wilkinson), 150 (Hope) and 189 (Philips).

inhuman and degrading treatment'.[213] Therefore, the majority either appeared to derive the meaning of the Torture Convention in light of its object and purpose (to which all state parties agree), or to assume subjective intent from the terms of the Torture Convention (by interpreting its terms schematically). Both the object and purpose (descending-ascending) and the subjective intent (ascending-descending) were addressed through the majority's moral naturalism. The majority did not conclude that there was a general exception to functional immunity in the situation of the crime of torture, although there is a dispute as to whether Lord Millet did so.[214] Instead, they interpreted the provisions of the Torture Convention as either expressly or impliedly waiving immunity in the context of systematic practice of torture and therefore, in their ascending move, the majority sought to demonstrate state consent to remove functional immunity in different ways.

Lord Saville considered that the *express* terms of the Torture Convention demonstrated a clear (subjective) intent that state parties agreed to the exercise of extraterritorial jurisdiction over 'alleged official torturers'.[215] However, he was not discounting the need for an express waiver, which appeals to Kelsen's position that an exception is necessary. Rather Saville considered that the express waiver was fulfilled by the express and unequivocal terms of the Convention. As the Torture Convention sought solely to address torture that has been carried out for state purposes, functional immunity that attaches to the conduct of the state official cannot coexist with the terms of the Torture Convention.[216] He placed more significant weight upon the jurisdictional provisions and the crime's definition than the silence on the issue of immunities within the text of the Convention and its drafting history.

In an alternative interpretation, Lord Hope appears to have dismissed any express or implied waiver in the Torture Convention.[217] He combined individual criminal responsibility for crimes against humanity (and its rejection as political crimes for purposes of extradition) with the acceptance of extraterritorial jurisdiction.[218] In so doing, he 'returned to considerations of customary international law'.[219] There were 'remnants of an allegation' that without doubt constituted crimes against international law and the prohibition under customary international law was 'so strong' as to override any immunity.[220] After the entry into force of the Torture Convention, it was 'no longer open to state parties to invoke immunity' in the face of allegations

213 Preamble of the Convention against Torture and Other Cruel, Inhuman or Degrading Treatment or Punishment (1984) 1465 UNTS 85.

214 *Pinochet III* (n 199) 148–51.

215 ibid 168 (Saville) (fits with his position that immunity could only be inapplicable if there was an agreement, qualification, or exception).

216 ibid.

217 ibid 148–51 (citing Burgers and Danelius's leading commentary in support of continuation of immunity combined with rationale that treaty parties would not have agreed to risk a former Head of State being detained for a single act of torture).

218 ibid 152. See also van Alebeek (n 108) 231–2.

219 ibid 151 and 189–90 (Lord Phillips, who seems to draw on both Saville's express agreement and Hope's extinguishing of immunity through combination of liability and extraterritorial jurisdiction).

220 ibid 152.

of systematic practice of torture.[221] In other words, functional immunity had already been removed in custom and could no longer be invoked by treaty parties.

Lords Millet, Hutton and Browne-Wilkinson in different ways placed significance on the official capacity as the 'essential ingredient' of the offence.[222] This means official capacity is necessary for engaging in the act as defined, yet torture cannot be committed in 'any capacity that gives rise to immunity'.[223] Lord Millet contended that the definition of torture must be 'inconsistent with the plea of immunity' because the crimes, as defined, could only be committed in official capacity and with toleration of state authorities.[224] The Torture Convention would be rendered a 'dead letter' and therefore, it is not a matter of a waiver, rather functional immunity is extinguished.[225] This noted how functional immunity and extraterritorial jurisdiction cancelled one another out or, as Millet put it, international law cannot establish a crime of *jus cogens* status and at the same time, provide for functional immunity from criminal jurisdiction.[226]

Lords Hutton and Brown-Wilkinson hinged their arguments on the international community's desire for universal accountability and the evident *jus cogens* status of the crime of torture.[227] As Brown-Wilkinson argued, the Torture Convention's purpose would be frustrated if there could not be any prosecution outside Chile unless the latter waived the functional immunity of its officials. [228] In this sense, 'the whole elaborate structure of universal jurisdiction over torture committed by officials [would be] rendered abortive.'[229] Lord Hutton followed *Pinochet I* and concluded that acts could not be functions under international law after the entry into force of the Torture Convention.[230] Lord Brown-Wilkinson argued that in the limited confines of treaty law, where acts are recognized as crimes against international law, functional immunity may be extinguished irrespective of the lack of an express waiver of immunity by the requisite state.[231]

Notably, some of the majority argued *obiter* that the personal immunity of a Head of State was unaffected by the Convention.[232] Yet as Fox argues, there is 'nothing in the wording of article 1 [of the Torture Convention] to support'

221 ibid 152.

222 ibid 179.

223 ibid 114–15. See van Alebeek (n 108) 230 (noting the internal inconsistency).

224 ibid 178–9.

225 ibid 179 (discussing *Eichmann*'s justification for jurisdiction and lack of immunity at length).

226 ibid.

227 ibid 115 and 163.

228 ibid 115.

229 ibid 114–15.

230 ibid 165–6 ('cannot be regarded as functions of a head of state . . . when international law expressly prohibits torture . . . in any circumstances whatsoever and has made it an international crime').

231 ibid 115.

232 ibid 164 (Hutton), 168 (Saville) and 189 (Phillips). See Princeton Project 'Princeton Principles on Universal Jurisdiction' (Princeton University Princeton 2000) 51 and 'Resolution on the Immunities from Jurisdiction and Execution of Heads of State and Heads of Government in International Law' (Institute of International Law Vancouver 2001).

the status versus conduct distinction. Rather, if a Head of State is construed as a 'public official' for the purposes of article 1, there is no basis on which to confine the removal of immunity to a former Head of State.[233] However, this distinction was made in other cases in civil law jurisdictions, albeit involving other offences.[234] Overall, the majority's outcome on functional immunity seemed to be undermined by the objection by Chile (a state party) that their official's immunity had been waived or extinguished by state consent to the Torture Convention.[235] To a formalist position, the majority's different interpretations appear to claim to know better what the state has consented to, that can only depended upon abstract justice.

Another important dimension was the determination as to what allegations in the arrest warrant could be deemed extradition crimes under English law[236] and their findings narrowed the list of crimes considerably, namely two charges in 1988 and 1990. This led to the unusual situation where lawyers had to urgently find and document cases that occurred during this two-year period to bolster the allegations against Pinochet and excluded the most egregious crimes committed during Pinochet's regime.[237] The majority considered that the temporal moment for the purposes of extradition was the date of incorporation of the Torture Convention by the Criminal Justice Act 1988. In this way, the majority interpreted its treaty obligations in terms of its domestic extradition law. This considered the UK's jurisdiction over the crime of torture (as a crime against humanity) as temporally limited to the entry into force of the Torture Convention. In fact, Warbrick et al. criticized the Law Lords' decision to interpret section 2 of the Extradition Act 1989 in accordance with the language of the Extradition Act 1870. Instead, the language of the latter statute could have been confined to its narrow scope within UK extradition law as opposed to becoming a lens through which to interpret UK extradition law as a whole.[238] In his criticism within the majority, Lord Phillips argued that extradition could proceed irrespective of when the crime was criminalized in UK law,[239] and Lord Millet claimed that torture was a crime under international law prior to the Convention against Torture and therefore UK courts had extraterritorial competence prior to the Criminal Justice Act 1988.[240]

This outcome in *Pinochet III* was a moderate success because it was more concrete, less normative than the *Eichmann* narrative. It seemed to narrow the instances where immunity may be inapplicable to treaty law regimes, except perhaps

233 H Fox 'The Pinochet Case No. 3' (1999) 48 *International and Comparative Law Quarterly* 687, 700.

234 *Gaddafi* (2001) International Law Reports 490, 507 and 509. See also Roht-Arriaza (n 143) 170 (referring to *Castro*, *Hassan II* and *Nguema* complaints).

235 See S Brett and C Collins 'The Pinochet Effect: 10 Years from London 1988' (Universidad Diego Portales, Santiago de Chile 1998) 11 (noting that Chile issued a diplomatic passport to former president Patricio Aylwin when he visited Spain, to shield him from being called to testify).

236 Pinochet III (n 199) (Lord Hope) See Warbrick et al. (n 183) 101 (ordinarily only England and Wales but the 1988 Act was extended by Parliament to other regions).

237 See Brett and Collins (n 235) 11.

238 Warbrick et al. (n 183) 91.

239 *Pinochet III* (n 199) 923.

240 ibid 912.

Lord Millet's position. Therefore, the issue over whether universal jurisdiction in customary international law extinguishes functional immunity continued to be debated. Notwithstanding their attempt to steer a middle ground, the opinions of the majority could be accused of leading to 'international chaos' where, as Lord Goff maintained, the 'courts of different state parties to a treaty reach different conclusions on the question whether a waiver of immunity was to be implied.'[241]

4.3 Far too concrete . . .?

The dissent in *Pinochet III* provides a counter-hegemonic position that would transform what appears to a formalist position as the oppressive outcome into respect for state independence and self-determination. From this position, the legal effect of *jus cogens* is uncertain and, when observing state behaviour through a formalist lens, states are moving cautiously and national judiciary must follow suit.[242] The *Pinochet* case demonstrated that there was evident disagreement among state parties regarding the content of their legal obligations and therefore, the majority's outcome contravenes the consent of the state party that does not agree with their interpretation. Lord Goff sought to determine the subjective party intent (ascending-descending) and he implicitly pulled on Kelsen's view that a waiver or exception was necessary, as concurred in certain 1990s literature.[243] Therefore, a waiver of immunity must 'always' be an express waiver, whether by submitting to the foreign jurisdiction in advance, by consent in a treaty, or clearly implied by behaviour, and he considered that this position was confirmed by Chile's assertion of immunity on behalf of Pinochet.[244] In particular, an advanced waiver by treaty must be expressed in a treaty provision and cannot be implied into the treaty. Instead, an implied waiver can only exist where it would explain a recognized exception (such as actual submission to jurisdiction of the courts of another state).

Lord Goff drew particular significance from the need for an express waiver to a treaty according to article 32(2) of the Vienna Convention on Diplomatic Relations[245] and from the silence on the question of immunity of state officials within the *travaux preparatoire* of the Torture Convention. The latter, in particular, indicated that the state parties did not agree to waive their immunity in the Convention.[246] In his view, an express waiver is what is expected under the UK's State Immunity Act 1978 and the Torture Convention cannot be interpreted as having an implied waiver. In his

241 ibid 861 (this criticism also applied to Saville's position of an express waiver).

242 *Pinochet I* (n 185) 913 (Slynn).

243 *Pinochet III* (n 199) 861 (citing *Oppenheim's International Law* and the International Law Commission's 1991 Draft Articles on Jurisdictional Immunities of States and their Property).

244 ibid. See also RY Jennings and A Watts *Oppenheim's International Law* (9th edn Longmans London 1992) 351–5 (if a state participates in proceedings to assert its immunity, it cannot be deemed to have waived its immunity).

245 Article 32(2) of the Vienna Convention on Diplomatic Relations (adopted 18 April 1961, entered into force 24 April 1964) 500 UNTS 95.

246 *Pinochet III* (n 199) 862 (presuming that as many states were unprepared to remove immunity, they felt the issue was 'not worth pursuing' during the drafting).

descending move, he assumed that the Torture Convention was intended to address a single act of torture and therefore, states would continue to assert immunity in order to avoid politically motivated or unmerited allegations, particularly when 'a former Head of State is concerned and political passions are aroused'.[247] He also assumed that immunities serve to avoid interfering with post-conflict reconciliation, because states may decide in the circumstances to grant an amnesty or other form of settlement.[248]

Any attempt to deduce subjective party intent faces the same problem as the schematic or teleological approach, because presumed subjective intent must somehow bind a state party that does not agree. In other words, Lord Goff's opinion reflected only the Chilean interpretation of its obligations under the Torture Convention and not the Spanish interpretation. There can also be an opposite interpretation of state behaviour that points to the implicit removal of the procedural bar in the extraordinary instances of crimes against humanity, as seen in the NMT and the Eichmann trials, leading to exercises of extraterritorial jurisdiction. The majority in *Pinochet III* consistently emphasized that their conclusions pertained to a systematic practice of torture, which is left unaddressed by Lord Goff. As the majority argue, there is an evident state consent to recognize the extraterritorial jurisdiction of other state parties over acts of torture committed by public officials of state parties and this could be read as a clear and reasonable implied waiver, that is, as necessary to ensure the effectiveness of the Convention's regime.

Lord Goff then turned to examine whether there is an exception under customary international law in regards to crimes against international law, and drew heavily from Lord Slynn's judgment in *Pinochet I*.[249] The latter argued that the nature of official functions could only be determined by national law and the test is whether the act had involved actual or ostensible authority of the state.[250] Therefore, if executive power is used in the planning and executing of the act, it must be deemed an act in official capacity,[251] and it can only be recognized as not being a function of state through an exception in treaty or custom.[252] This means that the commission of a crime cannot render the activities of the official

247 ibid.

248 ibid and 863 (that if personal and functional immunities were completely removed in all circumstances, Burgers and Danelius would have expressly stated it).

249 ibid 907 and 917. Lord Slynn in *Pinochet I* interpreted the meaning of 'public official' by making an analogy to other treaties that separate provisions between the Head of State and other state officials and concluded that 'public official' could not include the Head of State. Yet despite its appearance of concreteness in regards to other treaty consent, an analogy is normative and contextual. In all factual analyses, the language of international law permits both analogy and distinction to be made.

250 *Pinochet I* (n 185) 908 and 910. See A Watts, 'The Legal Position in International Law of Heads of States, Heads of Governments and Foreign Ministers', (1994) 247(III) *Recueil des Cours* 56.

251 ibid 908.

252 ibid 928. Another inconsistency (that will not be detailed in this section) is Slynn's interpretation of article 39 of the Vienna Convention on Diplomatic Relations. Rather than a literal interpretation that would mean immunity only arises within the Home State, article 39 should be interpreted in light of its object and purpose (descending pattern) to afford immunity in the Forum State. This descending move stresses the normative function of immunity as protection from legal process that would adjudicate state responsibility, which is 'most needed' in visits to foreign states.

outside the scope of official functions because, if it did, immunity from criminal jurisdiction 'would be deprived of much of its content'.[253] As the alleged acts of torture had been done in an official capacity, Lord Slynn examined whether an exception to functional immunity had emerged.

Overall, he argued that the trend in international criminal tribunals must be distinguished from the practice before national courts (ascending-descending) yet his examination of state behaviour was through a formalist lens, underpinned by a privileging of the normative value of state independence and non-interference.[254] He rejected the *Eichmann* narrative on the basis that definition of crimes against humanity was by no means universally accepted and there was little evidence that the legal consequence of *jus cogens* give rise automatically to universal jurisdiction.[255] Rather he rejected evidence of the recognition before national tribunals that all crimes against international law were justiciable. In this view, state behaviour signalled a lack of an exception under customary international law and arguments of an exception were 'aspirational'.[256] At this juncture, he made a distinction between international and national courts because he interpreted the statutes of the former as merely removing the defence against liability (permitting individual criminal responsibility). Therefore, these statutes must be interpreted as removing defence against liability *before tribunals with jurisdiction* and in his view of international practice, there has been a developing trend in recognizing the removal of functional immunity before international tribunals.[257]

Nevertheless, we noted that this distinction is being made even though both courts are prosecuting individual criminal responsibility, which privileges a moral naturalism and it assumes that an international court's jurisdiction is unquestionably valid, even though there have been challenges by defence motions in the international criminal tribunals.[258] Ultimately, the dissent in *Pinochet III* is based on an assumption that the subjective intent of the parties is objectively determinable from state behaviour, when states conflict over the content of their legal obligations and justify their claims on their sovereignty (and consent). Overall, unless the moral naturalism of the crimes is privileged, for instance, in cooperation with international tribunals, then any exception in the situation of crimes against international law could never emerge.[259]

253 ibid 908. See also van Alebeek (n 108) 223 (a concept of immunity as acts attributable to the state).

254 ibid 909–10.

255 ibid 913 and 188 (Lord Phillips in the majority was also sceptical, suggesting universal jurisdiction was still 'an open question').

256 ibid 913.

257 ibid 910.

258 Among the relevant examples, see *Prosecutor v. Dusko Tadic* (n 112) para 4 and *Prosecutor v. Milutinović et al.* (Decision on Motion Challenging Jurisdiction), IT-99–37 PT, para 36.

259 This essentially repeats the narrative over distinguishing piracy and privateering that cannot avoid the accusation of apology for power. States condoned a practice of comparable acts to piracy by validating those acts legally through the state's commission or authority. Similarly, the Joint Separate Opinion argued that there was 'an increasing realization that State-related motives are not the proper test for determining what constitutes public State acts'. See *Case of the Arrest Warrant* (n 209) (Joint Separate Opinion) para 85.

Lord Goff's position is based on the assumption that the treaty parties only intended to define the crimes of torture and impose obligations to establish and exercise jurisdiction. As a normative outcome, every criminal proceeding on the basis of extraterritorial jurisdiction (that states parties are obliged to undertake) would be preconditioned on an express waiver by written declaration, or by submission to proceedings.[260] This would result in substantially narrowing the potential for repression of torture through ordinary criminal law when the treaty expressly was designed to broaden that potential.[261] In all likelihood, extraterritorial jurisdiction would only be operable if there was regime change in the state where the alleged crimes were committed. Yet this appears to sit uncomfortably with the context for the Torture Convention's negotiations in the 1970 and 1980s, which was to construct a legal regime to address systematic practices of torture and enforced disappearances in situations, such as Pinochet's Chile and other military regimes.

5 A moralist horizon within reach

Pinochet III became a watershed moment. It galvanized victims and their representatives to submit criminal complaints under universal jurisdiction laws primarily in civil law jurisdictions.[262] Many of these complaints involved non-resident, former, or incumbent foreign state officials who were not in the territory of the prosecuting state at the time of the complaint. This dramatic upsurge in criminal complaints came to be referred to as the 'Pinochet Effect'.[263] Given *Pinochet III*'s move to the moralist middle, there was an evident tempering effect within the literature. As illustrative, Bassiouni had evoked the re-described *Eichmann* narrative in the mid-1990s.[264] Yet he turned to pull more towards the *Pinochet III*'s moralist middle in 2001,[265] that seemed more concrete, less normative than his earlier material. Overall, there was more noticeable interest in uncovering the 'exact' parameters of universal jurisdiction.[266] Rather than an exhaustive study of criminal complaints, this section addresses the judgments that are most illustrative of the narrative of the Pinochet Effect in play, along with seemingly shifting tides within the debate.

In the late 1990s, one of the significant trials among these complaints was the *Butare 4* trial, which came to be seen as one of the major success stories.[267]

260 Compare Browne-Wilkinson's point noted in section 4.1, see *Pinochet III* (n 199) 114–15.

261 *Pinochet III* (n 199) 862.

262 N Roht-Arriaza 'The Pinochet Precedent and Universal Jurisdiction' (2000–01) 35 *New England Law Review* 311 and R Brody 'The Prosecution of Hissène Habré: An "African Pinochet"' (2000–2001) 35 *New England Law Review* 321. However, Pinochet himself was deemed unfit to stand trial in Spain and allowed to return to Chile.

263 Roht-Arriaza (n 143) and Brett and Collins (n 235).

264 MC Bassiouni 'Searching for Peace and Achieving Justice: The Need for Accountability' (1996) 59(4) *Law and Contemporary Problems* 9, 17.

265 MC Bassiouni 'Universal Jurisdiction for International Crimes: Historical Perspectives and Contemporary Practice' (2001) 42 *Virginia Journal of International Law* 81.

266 See Benavides (n 157).

267 For a detailed analysis of trial, see L Reydams 'Belgium's First Judicial Application of Universal Jurisdiction: The Butare Four Case' (2003) 1 *Journal of International Criminal Justice* 428 (noting use of Minister for Justice's exceptional power to open criminal proceedings).

To a moralist position, the trial is illustrative of how universal jurisdiction can function most effectively in securing universal accountability. The defendants were alleged to have participated in the Rwandan genocide and were convicted under the Belgian 1993 Law that claimed universal jurisdiction over grave breaches of the Geneva Conventions and Additional Protocol I, common article 3 of the Conventions and fundamental breaches of Additional Protocol II.[268] The 1993 Law asserted such claims even though the Geneva Conventions and Protocols were silent on the issue of criminal responsibility for common article 3 and fundamental breaches[269] and the *Tadic* judgment on criminal liability for the former had yet to be delivered.[270] The Belgian Chamber's Commission of Justice justified this extension to common violations of article 3 by privileging the moral naturalism of universal accountability for 'the frightful violations of international humanitarian law which are committed in the purely internal armed conflicts, such as Bosnia-Herzegovina, Somalia. . . .'[271]

The 1999 Law extended universal jurisdiction to genocide, as defined in article II of the Genocide Convention, and crimes against humanity that reflected nearly all of those acts listed in article 7 of the Rome Statute.[272] It also expressly removed immunities attaching to official capacity that Belgium Chamber's Commission of Justice read as conforming to a similar provision under Article 27(2) of the Rome Statute.[273] According to Ongena and Daele, the terms of the 1999 Law were broad enough to disregard constitutional immunities and those granted by international law that could permit '*quasi* unlimited jurisdiction',[274] that is, its open-endedness permitted opposing positions. Therefore, the Commission of Justice made an analogy between international and national courts and rejected the distinction made in the counter-hegemony of *Pinochet III* dissent. This analogy assumed that individual criminal responsibility and

268 Article 7 of Law Relative to the Repression of Grave Violations of the Geneva Conventions of 12 August 1949 and of Protocols I and II of 8 June 1977, No. 877/1 (25 January 1993) (independent of the location where the offences had been committed'). See also *Cour D'Assises de Bruxelles*, URL: http://www.asf.be/AssisesRwanda2/fr/fr_VERDICT_verdict.htm (convictions of four defendants for violations of common article 3 and fundamental breaches of Protocol II upheld on appeal in 2001).

269 See T Meron 'International Criminalization of Internal Atrocities' (1995) 89 *American Journal of International Law* 554, 554–77 and T Graditzky 'Individual Criminal Responsibility for Violations of International Humanitarian Law Committed in Non-international Armed Conflicts' (1998) 80 *International Review of the Red Cross* 29.

270 *Prosecutor v Tadic (Decision on the Defence Motion for Interlocutory Appeal on Jurisdiction)* IT-94-1-AR72 (2 October 1995) para 134.

271 See Chamber of Representatives 'Report for the Commission of Justice', Doc 877/2-9293 (27 May 1993), URL: http://www.lachambre.be/FLWB/PDF/48/0877/48K0877002.pdf.

272 *Act Concerning Grave Breaches of International Humanitarian Law* (1999) 38 ILM 918. Note that 1999 Law did not address relationship with the International Criminal Court.

273 ibid (article 5(3)). See also Chamber of Representatives 'Report of the Commission of Justice' Doc. 1863/1/98/99 (7 December 1998) (citing other international tribunal statutes). Note similar position in *In re Pinochet* (1998) in section 3.2. See also article 27(2) of Rome Statute of the International Criminal Court ('immunities . . . which may attach to the official capacity of a person').

274 T Ongena and I van Daele 'Universal Jurisdiction for International Core Crimes: Recent Developments in Belgium' (2002) 15(3) *Leiden Journal of International Law* 687, 691.

universal jurisdiction extinguished any possible immunities. Alongside the 1999 Law, the Belgian Parliament inserted article 12bis into the Code of Criminal Procedure in 2001 that asserted jurisdiction over offences which Belgium was obliged to exercise jurisdiction under international treaties. In this sense, Belgium was seen as providing for the widest possible criminal jurisdiction, comparative to other states.

Alongside the *Pinochet III* and *Butare 4* victories, activism by human rights organizations led to the opening (or continuation) of numerous investigations. The Spanish Central Court's investigation into Argentina's 'Dirty War' led to two extradition requests being made to Argentina in 1999 and 2001 that involved 66 suspects accused of crimes against both Argentinian and Spanish nationals.[275] Both requests were rejected by Argentinian authorities at that time; and to a formalist position, the Spanish requests seem too utopian, ignoring Argentina's legitimate determination of its own national reconciliation policy as evident through maintaining its amnesty law.[276] In another investigation, a Spanish court issued an arrest warrant and extradition request against Ricardo Miguel Cavallo, former military officer and operative in the infamous ESMA or the Navy School of Mechanics.[277] On this occasion, the Mexican authorities extradited Cavallo at a time when the Mexican government sought to give greater standing to human rights law in its foreign policy.[278]

In justifying jurisdiction, the Spanish Central Court of Instruction drew upon the re-described *Eichmann* narrative on the principle of non-retroactivity vis-à-vis crimes under customary international law. While the discussion of the Spanish penal and procedural code appears idiosyncratic, the magistrate implicitly privileged the nature of the crimes. He contended that extra-territorial jurisdiction over domestic offences under the protective principle could be combined with domestic criminalization of genocide and a later claim of universal jurisdiction over crimes under customary international law to support jurisdiction over crimes committed in the 1970s.[279] He also pulled on the idea of an exception to non-retroactivity for crimes under customary international law as illustrated by article 15 of the Covenant on Civil and Political Rights.[280] Both arguments assume that

275 For a detailed historical account of various national proceedings, see Roht-Arriaza (n 143) 118–39.

276 On the Amnesty law, see Roht-Arriaza (n 143) 139.

277 ibid 143 (when Cavallo was identified in Mexico, Spanish lawyers sought an immediate arrest warrant that was then issued by Spanish magistrate, and executed by Mexican authorities who detained Cavallo, pending judicial review of extradition).

278 ibid 147 (Mexican extradition on allegations of torture with non-statutory limitations for crimes against humanity).

279 *Auto solicitando la extradición de Ricardo Miguel Cavallo* (12 September 2000) para 9, URL: http://www.derechos.org/nizkor/arg/espana/cavallo2.html (combining the 1870 Organic Law of Judicial Power (procedural law) that asserted protective principle with incorporation of the Genocide Convention in Penal Code in 1971 and assertion of jurisdiction 'irrespective of nationality of offender over genocide and torture in the 1985 Law, that is, a continuing jurisdiction from 1870 Law').

280 International Covenant on Civil and Political Rights (adopted 16 December 1966, entered into force 23 March 1976), 999 UNTS 171.

the nature of the crimes justifies a lack of non-retroactivity in barring jurisdiction. At the same time, he seems to have pulled on *Cvjetkovic* and Brown-Wilkinson in *Pinochet III* that justified universal jurisdiction on an absence of sovereignty.[281] This reshapes the ideas from the piracy debates and a lack of territorial sovereignty by using the terminology of the Rome Statute to denote a failure by the territorial jurisdiction to genuinely exercise its sovereign power to fulfil its commitment to individual criminal responsibility.

This seems concrete in grounding jurisdiction on domestic implementation (as opposed to direct applicability) and simultaneously, it seems normative in justifying the inapplicability of non-retroactivity based on the nature of the crimes. This position appears more concrete, less normative to a moralist position, yet too normative to a formalist position because Spanish jurisdiction applied to acts committed prior to its procedural law of 1985 and could be accused of utopia, eroding state consent. As we observed, Mexico executed the extradition request against Cavallo. In the judicial review of Cavallo's extradition, the Mexican Federal Criminal Court justified Mexican and Spanish jurisdiction over the crimes of genocide and terrorism on their reciprocal international treaty obligations, adopting the same position (more concrete, less normative) as *Pinochet III*. At the same time, it accorded with the *Eichmann* narrative on an exception to non-retroactivity in instances of crimes against international law, following a more normative, less concrete approach than *Pinochet III*.[282]

In a sign of shifting tides, the *Bouterse* case offers sharp disagreement between lower and higher courts over the justification for universal jurisdiction over torture in Dutch law. The Court of Appeal followed the hegemony of the moralist horizon and concluded that jurisdiction over the alleged acts of torture committed in Suriname in the 1980s could be established under the Torture Implementation Act 1988, combined with the criminalization of torture under custom.[283] The Court endorsed Dugard's opinion to the court in which he argued that the Convention against Torture 'is declaratory of existing customary international law in so far as prohibition, punishment and definition of torture are concerned',[284] which follows the pattern of the *Pinochet III* majority. In this sense, torture was 'an independent crime by 1982', and mostly likely punishable under custom as a species of crimes against humanity.[285] Therefore, the 1988 Torture Act could be applied retrospectively to alleged acts prior to 1989 and prosecuted under analogous domestic

281 *Cavallo* (n 279) para 9.

282 *Texto de Las Conclusiones Del Juez Natural Sobre la posible extradicion de Miguel Angel Cavallo A España*, Decision of 11 January 2001, Judge Jesús Guadalupe Luna Altamirano, URL: http://www.derechos.org/nizkor/arg/espana/mex.html.

283 Wijngaarde and Iloost, Court of Appeals of Amsterdam, reprinted in (2001) *Netherlands Yearbook of International Law* 266, 278–9. See also L Zegveld 'The Bouterse Case' (2001) 32 *Netherlands Yearbook of International Law* 97.

284 See J Dugard 'Opinion', URL: http://zoeken.rechtspraak.nl/detailpage.aspx?ljn=AA8427 (citing as evidence of custom: human rights law treaties, 1970s General Assembly resolutions, concept of *jus cogens* and preamble of the Torture Convention).

285 ibid.

offences as an enforcement of custom rather than an implementation of treaty.[286] Dugard distinguished retroactive and retrospective applications of a statute drawn from Canadian literature and considered this situation to be a retroactive application, that is, to retrospectively give courts' jurisdiction over criminal offences committed outside of the state.[287] On seeking extradition, he argued that presence was not a precondition for jurisdiction because in this regard, *Pinochet III* demonstrated the operation of the European Convention on Extradition.

Nevertheless, while the Court of Appeal reaffirmed the moralist margins of the *Eichmann* narrative, it simultaneously sought to avoid appearing too utopian by applying a principle of reasonableness and a balancing of interests. Those interests combined what appeared as both normative and concrete; the court listed the lack of proceedings in the territorial state, the public outrage at the crimes and the Dutch nationality or residency in the Netherlands of some of the victims.[288] However, the Supreme Court adopted the counter-hegemony of the formalist position and moved away from the *Eichmann* narrative.[289] It determined that the Torture Convention does not oblige the application of the Convention with retrospective effect, as any possible retroactive effect under custom would conflict with the Dutch implementation law.[290] This position would have cancelled out the Nuremberg model if it had been applied to the London Agreement, establishing the Nuremberg Charter. The Supreme Court also concluded that article 5 of the Torture Convention required an interest by way of presence of the suspect in the Netherlands at time of arrest.[291] This interpreted the word 'found' as voluntary presence and therefore, rejected *Demjanjuk*'s interpretation of *Eichmann*'s political open-endedness.

There seemed to be a dominant (cautious) optimism within legal literature. Some international lawyers embraced the contemporary position[292] while others disparaged those moves within the debate.[293] Many unconsciously accepted the justification for universal jurisdiction over crimes under customary international law drawn from the *Eichmann* narrative, even if they produced variant strands of that narrative. Simultaneously, some disputed the 'origins' of universal jurisdiction, reading the dominant position as too utopian, and submitted an alternative interpretation that was presented as being more concrete.[294] Overall,

286 ibid.

287 ibid.

288 Wijngaarde and Iloost (n 283) 272.

289 Contrast *Knesevic* case, Netherlands Supreme Court (11 November 1997) Judgment No. 3717 (upholding jurisdiction over violations of common article 3 of the 1949 Geneva Conventions).

290 *Bouterse*, ILDC 80 (NL 2001), paras 4.5–4.7 (statute prevails under article 94 of the Dutch Constitution).

291 ibid para 8.5.

292 K Roth 'The Case for Universal Jurisdiction' (2001) 80(5) *Foreign Affairs* 150.

293 H Kissinger 'The Pitfalls of Universal Jurisdiction: Risking Judicial Tyranny' (2001) 80(4) *Foreign Affairs* 86 and J Goldsmith and SD Krasner 'The Limits of Idealism' (2003) 132(1) *Daedalus* 47.

294 M Henzelin (n 158) and AP Rubin '*Actio Popularis, Jus Cogens* and Offences *Erga Omnes*' (2000–01) 35 *New England Law Review* 265.

there was a sense that greater attention to the parameters of the principle was needed, given the general acceptance of the validity of universal jurisdiction. Of course, the discussion of the scope of universal jurisdiction was through the lens of the moral naturalism of the nature of the crimes.[295] We also observe the influence on the debate on state parties' implementation of the Rome Statute of the International Criminal Court, as a number of state parties passed laws that established universal jurisdiction in different ways over the crimes defined in the Rome Statute.[296] Certain legal reports endorsed the content of universal jurisdiction as involving jurisdiction over core crimes, seeking extradition to secure custody (*in absentia*) and distinct rules between personal and functional immunity.[297] Hence, there was some optimism that the hegemony of a moralist approach would be assured.

Conclusion

In the 1990s, the *Eichmann* narrative fitted neatly into the field of international criminal law's move to supplant the dominance of transitional justice in the 'fight against impunity'. The re-shaping of the *Eichmann* narrative by the *Demjanjuk* extradition meant that Spanish and Belgian courts could draw on what appeared to be margins of the *Eichmann* narrative. This led to the controversial idea of securing custody through extradition to face trial in the prosecuting state and in turn, push the moralist's horizon out to what seemed like its farthest possibility. When Pinochet was placed under arrest in 1998, it felt like a transformative moment. His counsels' decision to invoke functional immunity was seen by a moralist position as cynical political ploy to threaten and undermine the political project of accountability underpinning the field.

Pinochet III came to be seen as a powerful reaffirmation of a moralist horizon. Notwithstanding, the judgments accommodated many of the positions tendered in the debate surrounding universal jurisdiction and immunity of state officials: the hierarchy of norms, the nature of official functions and the exception (either by treaty or custom). Moving to a moralist middle ground, the majority attempted to be more concrete and less normative than the *Eichmann* narrative. *Pinochet III* caused a sensation and led to a stream of complaints in Belgium, Spain, France and Senegal. These complaints were fairly rapidly depicted as reaching monumental

295 Bassiouni (n 265) 81, MC Bassiouni *Crimes against Humanity in International Criminal Law* (Kluwer Law International The Hague 1999) and R Brody and M Ratner (ed) *The Pinochet Papers: The Case of Augusto Pinochet in Spain and Britain* (Kluwer Law International The Hague 2000) 104.

296 See Crimes Against Humanity and War Crimes Act (2000, c 24) (presence in Canada after the alleged offence) and section 8 of the New Zealand International Crimes and International Criminal Court Act 2000 (No. 26).

297 Princeton Project on Universal Jurisdiction (n 232) 37 (argued to be combination of *lex lata* and *lex ferenda*) and 50 (Principle 5 provides that 'a head of state, diplomat or other official . . . may be immune . . . while in office, but once they step down any claim of immunity becomes ineffective').

proportions and it seemed that the moralist's horizon, a court of humanity, may actually have been realized.

Nevertheless, from each angle (moralist and formalist), the judgment is politically suspect and inadequate. To a formalist approach, the majority's outcome was too normative and could easily be accused of violating state sovereignty under a dubious guise of determining 'actual' state party consent. The majority's outcome claimed that treaty parties consented to any treaty party interfering in delicate national reconciliation when, from its formalist position, the limited treaty practice thus far could not give credence to such an interpretation. In this sense, the moralist approach can be accused of seeing a global moral community instead of state party consent to merely pooling jurisdiction. However, from a moralist position, *Pinochet III* limited the scope of universal jurisdiction over torture in domestic law to treaty party consent and reduced the potential of the *Eichmann* narrative. More worryingly, the dissents would reduce the possibilities of enforcement to the territorial jurisdiction, yet that runs completely counter to the treaty parties establishing an international dimension in the first place.

In the literature, international lawyers seemed to be wary of the full implications of this moralist horizon and there was a more obvious reference to 'avoiding abuse' and 'jurisdictional imperialism'.[298] Lawyers stressed need for safeguards when proceedings are not undertaken at the place of commission of the offence, which was a familiar rhetorical move in the 1920s and 1930s.[299] As the Princeton Project advised, 'insofar as universal jurisdiction is exercised, and seen to be exercised, in a reasoned, lawful and orderly manner, it will gain wider acceptance.'[300] This turn to a policy of reasonableness and restraint meant that the counter-hegemony of *Javor* and *Pinochet* dissents could take on more significance. Their counter-hegemonic position appealed to the preference for a return to what was read as the status quo and this wary concern for stability became the crucial context for the *Arrest Warrant* case. This increasing influence of a formalist counter-hegemonic position in the literature demonstrated a distrust of the *Eichmann* narrative that seemed to be read as an oppressive utopian ideal that was being used recklessly to destabilize international society.

After the stream of complaints submitted to Belgian magistrates, the focus turned to stressing the varieties in national practice, even though the practice of national courts in the 1990s could at the time have been dismissed as idiosyncratic. Belgium became the site of struggle over the construction of an imagined utopia or court of humanity in which a court never refuses to apply the laws of humanity. Here, there were complaints involving some of the most intractable political conflicts, past and

298 International Law Association (n 156) 19–20.

299 MT Kamminga 'Lessons Learned from the Exercise of Universal Jurisdiction in Respect of Gross Human Rights Offences' (2001) 23(4) *Human Rights Quarterly* 940, 963, Princeton Project on Universal Jurisdiction (n 232) 43 and 'Cairo-Arusha Principles of Universal Jurisdiction in Respect of Gross Human Rights Offences: An African Perspective', URL: http://www.afla.unimaas.nl/en/act/uj.html.

300 Princeton Project on Universal Jurisdiction (n 232) 43.

present.[301] Yet the state of nationality of the defendants did not support foreign court proceedings against their nationals and in some cases, took divisive diplomatic measures to register their outrage.[302] From a formalist position, criminal investigations into political conflicts in foreign states looked more like political motivated trials, particularly when they were prompted through a civil party complaint by victims. The 'bell tolling' for the moralist's horizon seemed a 'natural' inevitability within a context of contentious legal disputes and the diplomatic fallout between states engaged in otherwise: 'friendly relations'.[303] This space made the formalist position's bias towards non-interference appear more attractive, paving the way for the shift in hegemonic control.

References

Barker, JC 'The Future of Former Head of State Immunity after ex parte Pinochet' (1999) 48 *International and Comparative Law Quarterly* 937.

Bass, G *Stay the Hand of Vengeance: The Politics of War Crimes Tribunals* (Princeton University Press Princeton 2001).

Bassiouni, MC 'The International Criminal Court in Historical Context' (1999) *St. Louis-Warsaw Transatlantic Law Journal* 55.

Bassiouni, MC 'Searching for Peace and Achieving Justice: The Need for Accountability' (1996) 59(4) *Law and Contemporary Problems* 9.

Bassiouni, MC 'Universal Jurisdiction for International Crimes: Historical Perspectives and Contemporary Practice' (2001) 42 *Virginia Journal of International Law* 81.

Bassiouni, MC *Crimes against Humanity in International Criminal Law* (Kluwer Law International The Hague 1999).

Benavides, L 'The Doctrine of Universal Jurisdiction: Its Nature and Scope' (2001) 1 *Annuaire Derechos International* 19.

Bilsky, L 'Transnational Holocaust Litigation' (2012) 23(2) *European Journal of International Law* 349.

Brett, S and Collins, C 'The Pinochet Effect: 10 Years from London 1988' (Universidad Diego Portales, Santiago de Chile 1998)

Brody, R 'The Prosecution of Hissène Habré: An "African Pinochet"' (2000–01) 35 *New England Law Review* 321.

Brody, R and Ratner, M (ed) *The Pinochet Papers: The Case of Augusto Pinochet in Spain and Britain* (Kluwer Law International The Hague 2000).

'Cairo-Arusha Principles of Universal Jurisdiction in Respect of Gross Human Rights Offences: An African Perspective', URL: http://www.afla.unimaas.nl/en/act/uj.html.

Campbell, D 'Time is Broken: The Return of the Past in the Response to September 11' (2001) 5(4) *Theory and Event.*

301 See Ongena and van Daele (n 274) 693 (provides a comprehensive list of complaints against former and current foreign Heads of State, Minister for Foreign Affairs and leaders of opposition, including from the DRC, Rwanda, Republic of Congo, Israel and Palestine, Morocco and the Ivory Coast).

302 Here, Rwanda had expressly called on states to prosecute any alleged perpetrators on their territory; this echoed the policy of the ICTR Prosecutor.

303 A Cassese 'Is the Bell Tolling for Universality? A Plea for a Sensible Notion of Universal Jurisdiction' (2003) 1 *Journal of International Criminal Justice* 589.

Cassese, A 'Is the Bell Tolling for Universality? A Plea for a Sensible Notion of Universal Jurisdiction' (2003) 1 *Journal of International Criminal Justice* 589.
Chamber of Representatives 'Report for the Commission of Justice', Doc 877/2-9293 (27 May 1993), URL: http://www.lachambre.be/FLWB/PDF/48/0877/48K0877002.pdf.
Chamber of Representatives 'Report of the Commission of Justice' Doc. 1863/1/98/99 (7 December 1998).
De Vabres, D *Les Principes modernes du droit penal international* (Recueil Sirey Paris 1928).
Draft Code of Crimes Against Peace and Security of Mankind (1996) Vol. II *Yearbook of the International Law Commission* Pt II.
Dugard, J 'Opinion', URL: http://zoeken.rechtspraak.nl/detailpage.aspx?ljn=AA8427.
Final Report of the Commission of Experts, UN Doc. S/1994/674 (27 May 1994).
Fox, H *The Law of State Immunity* (Oxford University Press Oxford 2008).
Fox, H 'The Pinochet Case No. 3' (1999) 48 *International and Comparative Law Quarterly* 687.
Goldsmith, J and Krasner, SD 'The Limits of Idealism' (2003) 132(1) *Daedalus* 47.
Graditzky, T 'Individual Criminal Responsibility for Violations of International Humanitarian Law Committed in Non-international Armed Conflicts' (1998) 80 *International Review of the Red Cross* 29.
Green, LC 'Legal Issues of the Eichmann Trial' (1962) 37 *Tulane Law Review* 641.
Harvey, D *A Brief History of Neoliberalism* (Oxford University Press Oxford 2007).
Henzelin, M *Le Principe de l'universalité en droit penal international* (Helbing & Lichtenhahn Bruylant 2000).
Hyde, C *International Law (Chiefly as Interpreted and Applied by the United States)* Vol 1 (2nd edn 1947).
Inazumi, M *Universal Jurisdiction in Modern International Law: Expansion of National Jurisdiction for Prosecuting Serious Crimes under International Law* (Intersentia Antwerpen 2005).
Institute of International Law 'Resolution on the Immunities from Jurisdiction and Execution of Heads of State and Heads of Government in International Law' (Institute of International Law Vancouver 2001).
International Law Association 'Final Report on the Exercise of Universal Jurisdiction of Gross Human Rights Offences' (London 2000).
Jennings, RY and A Watts *Oppenheim's International law* (9th edn Longsman London 1992).
Johns, F, Joyce, R and S Pahuja *Events: The Force of International Law* (Routledge London 2011).
Jorgensen, NHB 'The Problem of Self-representation at the International Criminal Tribunals' (2006) 4 *Journal of International Criminal Justice* 64.
Jouannet, E 'Koskenniemi: A Critical Introduction' in M Koskenniemi *The Politics of International Law* (Hart Publishing Oxford 2011).
Kamminga, MT 'Lessons Learned from the Exercise of Universal Jurisdiction in Respect of Gross Human Rights Offences' (2001) 23(4) *Human Rights Quarterly* 940.
Kendall, S 'Donors' Justice: Recasting International Criminal Accountability' (2011) 24(3) *Leiden Journal of International Law* 585.
Kendall, S and S Nouwen 'Representational Practices at the International Criminal Court; The Gap Between Juridified and Abstract Victimhood' (2014) 76 *Law and Contemporary Problems* 235.
Kennedy, D 'When Renewal Repeats: Thinking Against the Box' (1999–2000) *NYU Journal of International and Policy* 335.

Kennedy, D 'Turning to Market Democracy: A Tale of Two Architectures' (1991) 32 *Harvard International Law Journal* 373.

Kissinger, H 'The Pitfalls of Universal Jurisdiction: Risking Judicial Tyranny' (2001) 80(4) *Foreign Affairs* 86.

Klein, N *The Shock Doctrine: The Rise of Disaster Capitalism* (Picador London 2008).

Koskenniemi, M *From Apology to Utopia: The Structure of the International Legal Argument* (Cambridge University Press Cambridge 2005).

Koskenniemi, M 'Between Impunity and Show Trials' (2002) 6 *Max Planck Yearbook for United Nations Law* 1.

Koskenniemi, M 'Between Commitment and Cynicism: Outline for a Theory of International Law as Practice' in M Koskenniemi *The Politics of International Law* (Hart Publishing Oxford 2011) 523.

Koskenneimi, M 'Human Rights, Politics and Love' in M Koskenniemi *The Politics of International Law* (Hart Publishing Oxford 2011) at 153.

Koskenniemi, M 'International Law and Hegemony: A Reconfiguration' (2004) 17 *Cambridge Review of International Affairs* 197.

Koskenniemi, M 'The Lady Doth Protest too Much: Kosovo and the Turn to Ethics in International Law' (2002) 65 *Modern Law Review* 159.

Koskenniemi, M and P Leino 'Fragmentation of International Law? Postmodern Anxieties' (2002) 15 *Leiden Journal of International Law* 553.

Krever, T 'Unveiling (and Veiling) Politics in International Criminal Trials' in C Schwoebel *Critical Approaches to International Criminal Law: An Introduction* (Routledge London 2014).

Laursen, A 'A Danish Paradox? A Brief Review of the Status of International Crimes in Danish Law' (2012) 10 *Journal of International Criminal Justice* 997.

Marks, S 'Guarding the Gates with Two Faces: International Law and Political Reconstruction' (1998–99) 6 *Indiana Journal of Global Legal Studies* 457.

Mégret, F 'International Criminal Justice as a Juridical Field' (2016) XIII *Champ Pénal* 1, para 16.

Meron, T 'International Criminalization of Internal Atrocities' (1995) 89 *American Journal of International Law* 554.

Moyn, S *Human Rights in History: The Last Utopia* (Harvard University Press Boston 2010), 213.

O'Keefe, R 'Universal Jurisdiction *in absentia*' (2004) 2 *Journal of International Criminal Justice* 735.

Ongena, T and van Daele, I 'Universal Jurisdiction for International Core Crimes: Recent Developments in Belgium' (2002) 15(3) *Leiden Journal of International Law* 687.

'Opinion of the Director of Public Prosecution' (2000) 3 *Yearbook of International Humanitarian Law* 26.

Orakhelashvili, *A Peremptory Norms in International Law* (Oxford University Press Oxford 2006).

Orford, A *Reading Humanitarian Intervention: Human Rights and the Use of Force in International Law* (Cambridge University Press Cambridge 2003).

Peskin, V *International Justice in Rwanda and the Balkans: Virtual Trials and the Struggle for State Cooperation* (Cambridge University Press Cambridge 2008).

Princeton Project 'Princeton Principles on Universal Jurisdiction' (Princeton University Princeton 2000).

Report of the War Crimes Inquiry (HMG Stationary Office, CM 744).

'Resolution on the Immunities from Jurisdiction and Execution of Heads of State and Heads of Government in International Law' (Institute of International Law Vancouver 2001).

Reydams, L *Universal Jurisdiction: International and National Perspectives* (Oxford University Press Oxford 2003).

Reydams, L 'Belgium's First Judicial Application of Universal Jurisdiction: The Butare Four Case' (2003) 1 *Journal of International Criminal Justice* 18.

Roht-Arriaza, N *The Pinochet Effect: Transitional Justice in the Age of Human Rights* (University of Pennsylvania Press Philadelphia 2006).

Roht-Arriaza, N 'The Pinochet Precedent and Universal Jurisdiction' (2000–01) 35 *New England Law Review* 311.

Romero, F 'Cold War Historiography at the Crossroads' (2014) 14(4) *Cold War History* 685.

Roth, K 'The Case for Universal Jurisdiction' (2001) 80(5) *Foreign Affairs* 150.

Rubin, AP '*Actio Popularis, Jus Cogens* and Offences *Erga Omnes*' (2000–01) 35 *New England Law Review* 265.

Safferling, C '*Public Prosecutor v Djajic*' (1998) 92 *American Journal of International Law* 528.

Schabas, WA 'International Criminal Court: The Secret of its Success' (2001) 12 *Criminal Law Forum* 415.

Schwoebel, C 'The Market and Marketing Culture of International Criminal Law' in C Schwoebel *Critical Approaches to International Criminal Law: An Introduction* (Routledge London 2014).

Simpson, G *Law, War and Crime: War Crimes, Trials and the Reinvention of International Law* (Polity Press London 2007).

Sule, S *German Legal System and Laws* (4th edn Oxford University Press Oxford 2010).

Tallgren, I 'The Sense and Sensibility of International Criminal Law (2002) 13(3) *European Journal of International Law* 561.

van Alebeek, R *The Immunity of States and Their Officials in International Criminal Law and International Human Rights Law* (Oxford University Press Oxford 2008).

Watts, A 'The Legal Position in International Law of Heads of States, Heads of Governments and Foreign Ministers', (1994) 247(III) *Recueil des Cours* 56.

Warbrick, C EM Salgado and N Goodwin 'The Pinochet Cases in the United Kingdom' (1999) 2 *Yearbook of International Humanitarian Law* 91.

Weissman, L 'A Moot Issue? Rethinking Holocaust Era Restitution if Jewish Confiscated Personal Property in Poland' (2011–12) 13 *Cardozo Journal of Conflict Resolution* 679.

Woodhouse, D 'The Progress of Pinochet through the UK extradition procedure an analysis of the legal challenges and the judicial decisions' in M Davis (ed) *The Pinochet case: Origins, Progress and Implications* (Institute of Latin American Studies London 2003).

Zegveld, L 'The Bouterse Case' (2001) 32 *Netherlands Yearbook of International Law* 97.

5 Returning to the status quo?

In the post-*Pinochet* environment, the discipline appeared as if, for a moment, to cautiously embrace the moralist's horizon. To many activists and lawyers, it appeared that the horizon was close to being reached and that universal accountability was realizable so long as the 'fight against impunity' continues. However, this triumphalism waned as states reacted sharply to the increasing list of former and current political and military leadership that were being accused before national courts. The threat to the ideal of collective security and the counter-terrorism measures after 9/11 generated a renewalist spirit and a simultaneous agony among international lawyers. In the midst of this, the imagined horizon of a court of humanity that never adjourns appeared for a moment and then became perceived cynically as politically motivated rather than as securing universal commitments. The powerful rallying cry of ending impunity appeared to be drowned out by its opponent theme of avoiding abuse and this move, once it occurred, felt to many international lawyers as inevitable, given the irrationality of so many foreign state officials being accused in a Belgian court.

In this chapter, we explore this transformation from a moralist position's hegemonic control to a formalist position that appeared to be both triggered and confirmed by the International Court of Justice's *Arrest Warrant* judgment. Multiple interpretations were put forward by the judges that covered many of the competing narratives within the existing literature. Much was made in the literature of the Belgian Parliament's series of changes to its universal jurisdiction laws, given its status as one of the principle sites of the struggle. When the Spanish constitutional court produced a more normative (moralist) position in counter-hegemonic move, its judgment was located within a formalist hegemony and it felt as if the court had misread the moment. The formalist position's hegemonic control even infiltrated the state parties' relationship towards the International Criminal Court, as some of the incorporation acts included universal jurisdiction that accorded with the formalist narrative. We noted the general tendency in legal discourse to move to the middle ground, as evident in *Pinochet III*, because once the positions are put in argument, they are seen to be self-contradicting. Of course, this move towards the middle privileged the formalist position and this was also reflected in the literature. Finding a formalist middle ground meant distinguishing situations into what appeared to be just in the circumstances according to formalist concerns. However, from a moralist lens, it could be accused of being based merely on arbitrary subjective preferences. We appear to be at a moment where universal jurisdiction over crimes against international law is acknowledged by most international lawyers. Yet it is largely reduced to situations under investigation with the International Criminal Court or other international criminal tribunals, as well as refugee communities fleeing conflicts outside the jurisdiction of the ICC, that is, leaving the powerful and their allies outside its scope.

1 The post-9/11 legal environment

The events of 9/11 and its aftermath are read as a rupture that 'intensified the unilateralist agenda [of the United States] and paved the way for a more overt exercise of US state power'.[1] Scholars point to the wars in Afghanistan and Iraq and the dominant discourse on a 'war on terror' as illustrative of this unilateralist turn.[2] However, Okafor challenges the perception of 9/11 as unique, because this can only occur 'through a deliberate or mistaken displacement of the experience of most of the globe'.[3] Rather the 'newness' of 9/11 can be debunked when situated against the complicity of powerful states in conflicts in the Global South. Once 'Third World suffering is foregrounded (rather than backgrounded as usual)', it demonstrates how we 'construct, sell and buy an inaccurate picture of the nature of this historical moment and the severity of the kinds of international or domestic reform measures that are required in response'.[4] In this sense, the 'war on terrorism' morphs into 'a re-run of the Cold War' in that it is a struggle exceeding the military threat (like that of Soviet Union) and a struggle against a range of entities 'regardless of their strategic capacity to be a threat' that are lumped together under the one threat.[5] There is repetition of a structure that survived in the post-1989 environment, including 'zero-sum analyses, a sense of endangerment' to all activities of the Other and a division into civilized/uncivilized.[6]

We see this same structure in responses to the Iraq War. During the Cold War, each geo-political bloc struggled for hegemonic control in their narrative on use of force. The Eastern bloc invoked the principle of non-interference in internal affairs as a 'legal shield of socialism'.[7] The newly independent states appealed to sovereignty to consolidate their self-determination, and the United States and its allies read the international rules on the use of force as 'a protective cordon against the spread of communism and attempts to undermine its economic

1 R Kiely *Empire in the Age of Globalisation: US Hegemony and Neoliberal Disorder* (Pluto Press London 2005), 67.
2 ibid.
3 O Chinedu Okafor 'Globalism, Memory and 9/11: A Critical Third World Perspective' in F Johns et al. *Events: The Force of International Law* (Routledge London: 2011), 240.
4 ibid 242.
5 D Campbell 'Time is Broken: The Return of the Past in the Response to September 11' (2001) 5(4) *Theory and Event.*
6 ibid.
7 ibid 250.

system'.[8] This struggle 'produced and reproduced' the dominant narrative that pulled on the classical system of late nineteenth century with its colonial origins.[9] In the post-9/11 situation, the idea of civilization was pulled upon in order to divide the world in civilized and terrorist/failed states and to construct rhetoric that reduces war to 'the status of police action'.[10] Therefore, although some held onto the attractive appeal of constructing a uniform understanding of international law post-1989, legal practice demonstrates how this 'underestimated . . . the difficulty of overcoming both contingency and indeterminacy (and consequent dependence on sovereign state determination) in delivering international law from the "propaganda battlefield"'.[11] It meant that 'while civilization could be gained during colonialism, it could be lost in the post-colonial period.'[12]

The same reaffirmation/agony was evident in the discipline's response to the United States Torture Memos. Johns argues that the Torture Memos 'invited international lawyers to see the site of violent detention as a law-making site', which was 'profoundly destabilizing', as it equated international law with 'unmitigated self-interested violence'.[13] She identifies two simultaneous reactions within the discipline, a 'reaffirmation of established positions' and a 'breakdown in the discipline's claim to conscience' or the 'failure of the affirmation . . . claims'.[14] The field's attempt to empathize yet remain distant from the terror-suspect detainee was undermined because the latter was 'actively resistant and participating in a process recognized by all involved as law-making'.[15] In this sense, the response of international lawyers to the post-9/11 'war on terror' involved both a renewalist spirit and an agony as the discipline's ideal of collective security was once more eroded, as the potency of the human rights vocabulary in challenging the politics of the state faced a serious threat and as law-making operated at sites of detention and at points of resistance by terror-suspect detainees.

The field of international criminal law responded by broadening its reach 'from the fight against impunity to a general idea of global justice'.[16] The International Criminal Court's operations were continually justified on the existence of global justice and the Court was 'imagined as a way of removing from the field the local peculiarities and prejudices of national criminal justice systems, putting in their

8 ibid.
9 ibid.
10 M Hardt and A Negri *Empire* (Harvard University Press Cambridge 2000) 12–13. See also G Agamben 'The Sovereign Police' in B Massumi (ed) *The Politics of Everyday Fear* (University of Minnesota Press Minneapolis 1993).
11 J Strawsom 'Provoking International Law: War and Regime Change in Iraq' in F Johns et al. *Events: The Force of International Law* (Routledge London: 2011), 249.
12 Campbell (n 5) 253.
13 F Johns 'The Torture Memos' in F Johns, R Joyce and S Pahuja *Events: The Force of International Law* (Routledge London 2011) 270 and 261 respectively.
14 ibid.
15 ibid 271.
16 C Schwoebel 'The Market and Marketing Culture of International Criminal Law' in C Schwoebel (ed) *Critical Approaches to International Criminal Law: An Introduction* (Routledge London 2014) 265.

place a unified system of transnational justice'.[17] Yet the Court's structure is 'a typical, if sometimes imaginative, compromise between cosmopolitan desire and nationalist or statist pride'.[18] Negotiations at the Rome Conference illustrated a retreat from the utopian ideal of a court of humanity because the proposal to empower the Court with a global reach of its jurisdiction was rejected by most states. In this way, the negotiations reflected how 'we are in Nuremberg every single day',[19] or as Simpson observes, the Rome Statute 'resembles Nuremberg in its deference to sovereignty, and hegemony too'.[20] Notwithstanding its lack of global reach, the International Criminal Court's early years seemed to confirm the Court's status as being what 'many observers [viewed] as the brightest star in the cosmopolitan firmament'.[21] From 2004, the International Criminal Court began to receive situations from a number of African state parties under the mechanism of state referral and it also received, not long after, a United States Security Council referral.[22] Even so, the impossibility of reconciling international/ local produced a continual struggle that among other challenges undermined the 'feel good image'.[23]

One dimension is a privileged site of knowledge that Kendall identifies in a binarism between the ICC's institutional centre in The Hague and its field offices.[24] This has created a core-periphery dynamic whereby the core of international criminal law production at its privileged site is transferred to the periphery. This means the Court's practice addresses the 'industry of the ICL field' rather than the affected communities despite the Court's rhetoric on local ownership.[25] Kendall argues that this produces effects on victims and local communities that are read as ethical rather than legal and in turn, outside the Court's mandate.[26] Another dimension is what seems to be 'sovereignty as the unbreachable barrier to jurisdiction of international criminal machinery'.[27] It structures the field's response to the international/local hybridity that has been produced beyond the ICC's jurisdictional reach, such as the Iraqi Special Tribunal and the Special Court for Sierra Leone. This oscillates between the desire to avoid violating sovereignty and the preference for international criminal machinery.[28]

17 ibid.
18 G Simpson *Law, War and Crime* (Polity Press Cambridge 2007) 35. See also Schwoebel (n 4).
19 M Koskenniemi 'International Justice: Between Impunity and Show Trial' (SOAS, University of London, 4 January 2013), URL: https://www.youtube.com/watch?v=2QTBdPyQtEw.
20 Simpson (n 18) 35.
21 ibid.
22 WA Schabas 'Complementarity in Practice: Uncomplimentary Thoughts' (2008) *Criminal Law Forum* 19 (criticizing the Office of the Prosecutor's policy of actively seeking out investigations, a policy that did not accord with the dominant reading of the complementarity scheme of the Rome Statute).
23 Schwoebel (n 16) 273.
24 S Kendall 'Critical Orientations: A Critique of International Criminal Court Practice' in C Schwoebel (ed) *Critical Approaches to International Criminal Law: An Introduction* (Routledge London 2014), 63.
25 ibid 63.
26 ibid.
27 Simpson (n 18) 50.
28 ibid 31.

It also structures the tendency towards certain exclusions that Tallgren identifies.[29] When the jurisdictional reach seemed beyond the Great Powers and the vast majority of states after the post-war 1940s trials of Nazi defendants, it seems that personal liability (despite its supposed universal essence) 'was to remain, for some time, highly attenuated'.[30] Simpson contends that this pattern of 'particularization' is repeated 'in more implicit forms' in contemporary practices so that the issue becomes the 'inhumanity of specific categories of [people] (Serbs in Bosnia but not Americans or Iraqis in Falluja). . . .'[31] In this regard, the accusation of anti-African bias in opposition to the claims of global justice became powerful rhetoric that was deployed against the International Criminal Court's practice and against European states over their universal jurisdiction laws.[32] The arrest warrants against Al-Bashir and Gaddafi provoked a strong rebuke from African governments and the African Union.[33] The latter also demanded an end to the proceedings against Kenyatta and Ruto in 2013, a trial that collapsed in the face of witness intimidation and lack of cooperation.[34] A similar rhetorical move occurred after the Rwandan government leadership, including President Kagame, was indicated by a Spanish investigating magistrate.[35] Krever reads the Court's 'selective and highly politicized interventions' as institutionalizing the 'de facto impunity long enjoyed by the powerful' and in turn, reproducing 'one-sided narratives of complex conflicts'.[36] It was within this move to global justice (and its discontents) that there was a shift to a formalist position's hegemonic control.

2 Change of the event? The *Arrest Warrant* case

The *Arrest Warrant* case emerged out of the many criminal investigations in Belgian courts and against a backdrop of an increasing number of challenges against jurisdiction by defendants and more broadly, high-profile diplomatic incidents as outlined in Chapter 4. The judgment itself was rendered soon after 9/11 and the United States-led bombing of Afghanistan that re-ignited again the debates

29 I Tallgren 'The Sense and Sensibility of International Criminal Law' (2002) 13(3) *European Journal of International Law* 561.

30 Simpson (n 18) 50.

31 ibid 51. This is also apparent in the fact of the United States' opposition to becoming a state party to the Rome Statute, see N Roht-Arriaza *The Pinochet Effect: Transitional Justice in the Age of Human Rights* (University of Pennsylvania Press Philadelphia 2006) 198.

32 KD Magliveras and GJ Naldi 'The International Criminal Court's Involvement with Africa: Evaluation of a Fractious Relationship' (2013) 82 *Nordic Journal of International Law* 417 and African Union 'Decision on the Abuse of the Principle of Universal Jurisdiction' Assembly/AU/Dec. 292(XV) (25–27 July 2010) para 3. Note the South African withdrawal from the ICC, see Statement of President of the Assembly (22 October 2016) URL: https://www.icc-cpi.int/Pages/item.aspx?name=pr1248.

33 ibid 423.

34 SD Mueller 'Kenya and the International Criminal Court (ICC): Politics, the Election and the Law' (2014) 8(1) *Journal of Eastern African Studies* 25.

35 Commentator 'The Spanish Indictment of High-ranking Rwandan Officials' (2008) 6 *Journal of International Criminal Justice* 1003.

36 T Krever 'Dispensing Global Justice' (2014) 85 *New Left Review* 67, 97.

over collective security, counter-terrorism and international law's role, as discussed above. In its application to the Court, the Democratic Republic of Congo accused Belgium of violating its sovereignty by issuing an arrest warrant against Yerodia Ndombasi, who, at the time of the warrant, was the DRC's Minister for Foreign Affairs.[37] The arrest warrant was issued in order to secure Yerodia's extradition to Belgium from any third state, to face trial for inciting crimes against humanity and grave breaches of the Geneva Conventions.[38] In the Belgian investigation, the investigating magistrate continued to interpret Belgian law to mean that voluntary presence was not a requirement for exercising universal jurisdiction and that custody could be secured through extradition from third states or a practice that was captured under the phrase 'universal jurisdiction *in absentia*'.[39] The DRC claimed that the arrest warrant violated immunity of its Minister for Foreign Affairs from foreign criminal jurisdiction[40] and amounted to arbitrary interference in its domestic affairs, violating the maxim *par in parem non habet*.[41] It was a clash of idioms or, as Koskenniemi observes, a struggle over human rights themes where the authority of human rights bodies was challenged by alternative preferences; 'rights were trumped by traditional rules of diplomatic law'.[42]

Famously, the Court decided not to contend with universal jurisdiction *in absentia* in its judgment even though both universal jurisdiction and immunity are principle and counter-principle to one another. Each principle in contradistinction to the other is significant because the competing principles cancel one another out. Therefore, by avoiding the universal jurisdiction *in absentia* issue, the Court's judgment seems somewhat artificial, with the *in absentia* issue casting a long shadow over the judgment. The Court's stance may have been driven by the parties' attitude during the proceedings. The DRC was ambivalent on whether the Court should address the issue while Belgium seemed determined to avoid the Court ruling it. Yet this appears from a moralist standpoint to be too state-centric and political; it allowed the parties' own positions to dictate the parameters of the Court's assessment. Conversely, to a formalist position, the

37 See *Application to Institute Proceedings Arrest Warrant of 11 April 2000* (Democratic Republic of Congo v. Belgium) See also *Counter-Memorial of Belgium*, Part 1, paras 2.26–2.38 (there was subsequently a cabinet reshuffle, with Yerodia becoming Minister for Education).

38 *Counter-Memorial of Belgium*, Part 1, paras 1.3–1.5 (civil party complaints were lodged at the Brussels Court of First Instance; all complainants were resident in Belgium and five were of Belgian nationality) and paras 3.2.22 and 3.2.27 (allegations that public speeches made by Yerodia, then Director of the Office of the President Kabila, involved the incitement of ethnic hatred against those of Tutsi origin and led to the instigation of widespread 'unlawful arrests, detentions and summary executions').

39 *Re Yerodia Ndombasi*, Tribunal de Premier Instance de Bruxelles (11 April 2000), para 3.4. On defendant's attempts to challenge the investigation, see *Counter-Memorial of Belgium*, Part 1, para 1.14.

40 *Application to Institute Proceedings* (n 37) 2.

41 *Par in parem non habet* translates as 'has no equal'. See MN Shaw *International Law* (6th edn Cambridge University Press Cambridge 2008) 647 (the state is 'supreme internally' but obliged not to intervene in the internal affairs of other states).

42 M Koskenniemi 'International Law and Hegemony: A Reconfiguration' (2004) 17 *Cambridge Review of International Affairs* 197, 209.

compartmentalizing of the competing principles is unproblematic – after all, a foreign state's claim of jurisdiction can be valid yet simultaneously barred by immunity or, as the Court put it, immunity does not mean impunity.[43] It follows then that the Court only addressed the issue of Yerodia's immunity from criminal jurisdiction in its ruling and left the disagreement over the validity of Belgian claim of universal jurisdiction to the academic practice of separate and dissenting opinions.

2.1 More concrete than Pinochet III?

One of the first contentious issues to be addressed was whether personal immunity applied to a Minister for Foreign Affairs. Its application to Heads of State and Heads of Government was roundly acknowledged and unquestioned.[44] However, the idea that personal immunity applies to a Minister for Foreign Affairs was controversial and the Court's logic has been since criticized[45] as it appears too political and arbitrary. The Court's judgment illustrates the margins of the formalist position that privileges state liberty and non-interference. Therefore, the Court's logic focused on determining if there could be an analogy made between the Minister for Foreign Affairs and Head of State (descending-ascending). In examining the 'essential nature' of the office of Head of State, the Court found a similarity with a Minister of Foreign Affairs in that both represent the state abroad and are seen as representative of the state by other states. The Court assumed that, given the greater frequency of international travel, this portfolio involved a greater level of state representation abroad than other cabinet portfolios. On this basis, the Court considered that there was a greater risk to the effective performance of ministerial duties if the Minister could be deterred from travelling internationally because he or she would be exposed to foreign criminal proceedings[46] and it noted how the function of immunity of state officials was to ensure 'the effective performance of their functions on behalf of their respective States'.[47] However, the analogy only seems suitable if the Court's position on the normative value of the Head of State's role is accepted. Otherwise, the normative position can be challenged by an opponent; for instance, the Head of State as a personification of the state, an idea that returns to the pre-classical notion of the sovereign. From this angle, an analogy to the Minister for Foreign Affairs is impossible.

When the Court turned to analyse state consent through its normative lens, it had to rest its position entirely on its analogy, as it did not cite any instance of state

43 *Case of the Arrest Warrant of 11 April 2000 (Democratic Republic of Congo v Belgium, Judgement)* (2002) ICJ Rep No. 121, para 60. See also *Counter-Memorial of Belgium*, para 0.25 and Memorial of the DRC, para 97.

44 See also A Watts 'The Legal Position in International Law of Heads of States, Heads of Governments and Foreign Ministers' (1994-I) 247 *Recueil des Cours* 13, 108–9.

45 D Akande and S Shah 'Immunities of State Officials, International Crimes and Foreign Domestic Courts' (2010) 21(4) *European Journal of International Law* 815, 833–4.

46 *Case of the Arrest Warrant* (n 43) para 55.

47 ibid para 53. See also Preamble of the Vienna Convention on Diplomatic Relations (adopted 18 April 1961, entered into force 24 April 1964) 500 UNTS 95.

behaviour in terms of national legislation or criminal proceedings. The Court's turn to referring to Belgium and the DRC's agreement that a Minister for Foreign Affairs is personally immune adds to the suspicion of being politically suspect.[48] It was attempting to show state consent of the disputing parties but it made the law seem incapable of being normatively controlling. It also failed to explain how such a rule could bind a state that did not agree to extend personal immunity to a Minister for Foreign Affairs. Here, the Court's outcome cannot avoid being accused of apology, preferring the particular voluntary will of the disputing parties over any normative controlling rule.

Turning to examine whether personal immunity under customary international law applied, the Court maintained its formalist position as there was an obvious privilege of a normative project underpinning the Convention on Diplomatic Relations in ensuring effective relations between states (descending-ascending) and this provided the Court with a lens for its analysis of state behaviour. This normativity was necessary to bind Belgium regardless of its lack of consent because the Court chose the DRC's interpretation of its sovereignty (over that of Belgium). This descending move followed a formalist position on distinguishing rules for substantive defence and procedural bar that we explored in Chapter 4. Therefore, Belgium made an analogy to the justification for the removal of the substantive defence (normative), whereas the Court made a distinction between rules applicable to international and national courts (sociological fact). In other words, Belgium reduced the practices of international and national courts in prosecuting crimes against international law to a pattern because each court is imposing a criminal liability that descends to bind all individuals regardless of nationality or official capacity. Yet the Court reduced the practice of international tribunals to a singularity based on the international composition of the Court, even though the proceedings pertain to individual criminal liability rather than inter-state disputes. This allowed the Court to side with the DRC's argument that, like Pinochet's defence counsel, rejected the 1990s re-description of the *Eichmann* narrative.

It follows that based on its normative project, Kelsen's position was the most appropriate and therefore, immunity could only be removed by waiver of the state[49] or by an exception under custom. The Court then searched in state behaviour for an exception to personal immunity in regards to crimes against international law.[50]

48 *Counter-Memorial of Belgium*, para 3.4.1 and *Case of the Arrest Warrant, Oral Hearings Monday 15*th *October 2001*, 27.

49 *Case of the Arrest Warrant* (n 43) para 52 (concluding that the Vienna Convention on Diplomatic Relations' provision on the waiver of immunity by the Sending State constituted a codification of customary international law). See also *Re Pinochet* Tribunal de Premier Instance de Bruxelles (6 November 1998), para 3 (rejecting acts as being legitimate functions of state and normal functions of Head of State).

50 ibid 58. See also *Counter-Memorial of Belgium*, (n 38) para 3.5.26 and 3.5.27 (justifying an exception through descending pattern by privileging norm of accountability, citing the International Law Commission's draft code in support, and ascending pattern in referring to exclusion of immunities either implicitly (Versailles) or explicitly (Nuremberg) as being justified on the nature of the offence, as opposed to the international character of the tribunal, citing statutes of international tribunals as transposable to national courts under custom).

As the Court reduced the practice of international criminal tribunals to a singularity, their statutes became an irrelevance. It also argued that personal immunity is unaffected by international treaties obliging states to prosecute or extradite, in effect, adopting *Pinochet III*'s position.[51] The Court identified only three cases that contended with whether personal immunity should be removed in cases involving allegations of crimes against international law.[52] In those cases, personal immunity was considered to continue to apply regardless of the nature of the crimes either in the *obiter* or *ratio*. To a formalist position, the Court's decision accurately reflects state behaviour and demonstrates the lack of state consent to an exception. Simply put, there are no precedents of prosecuting Heads of State before foreign courts and there is a clear indication that states are unwilling to countenance such an exception.

To avoid appearing to be too apologist, the Court attempted to illustrate how its outcome does not jeopardize entirely the possibility of prosecuting a Head of State, with four avenues for securing accountability. It is evident that these scenarios are identified through the lens of the judgments' normative project of maintaining stability. The first and second scenarios are clearly underpinned by state liberty, that is, the territorial jurisdiction (where no immunity under *international law* is available) and a foreign court exercising extraterritorial jurisdiction where the immunity of an incumbent or former Minister for Foreign Affairs has been waived.[53] Although the meaning of both the third and fourth scenarios has become a matter of controversy, only the third will be addressed. This scenario arises where on ceasing office, the Minister for Foreign Affairs may be prosecuted before a foreign tribunal 'provided it has jurisdiction' in regard to 'acts committed before and subsequent to assuming Office and acts committed during Office in a private capacity'.[54]

Fox and Gaeta interpreted this phrase as treating a serving and former Minister in the similar manner. Therefore, the change of status does not admit a different framework; rather both personal and functional immunities remain applicable.[55] This would mean functional immunity must be applied before foreign national courts over acts of both serving and former lower-level state officials. This would mean proceedings undertaken in various European states against lower-level officials in regards to alleged crimes committed in the Former Yugoslavia and

51 *Case of the Arrest Warrant* (n 43) para 58.

52 *R v. Bow St. Metropolitan Stipendiary Magistrate, ex parte Pinochet Ugarte (No.3)* (1999) 2 All ER 97, 164 (Hutton), 168 (Saville) and 189 (Phillips), *Gaddafi* (2001) International Law Reports 490, 507 and 509 and *Castro* as cited in Roht-Arriaza (n 31) 170.

53 *Case of the Arrest Warrant* (n 43) para 61. This would be a waiver of either personal immunity or on ceasing office, functional immunity. It appears to be distinct from the third scenario on the notion that a Minister would no longer enjoy all immunities accorded under international law to other states.

54 ibid para 61. The fourth scenario was 'may be subject to criminal proceedings before certain international criminal courts, where they have jurisdiction'.

55 Fox, H and Webb, P *The Law of State Immunity* (3rd edn Oxford University Press Oxford 2013) 552. See Chapter 3, section 2.2 (if functional immunity is removed, it could impinge arbitrarily upon state officials in the exercise of their functions during office). See also P Gaeta 'Ratione Materiar Immunities of Former Heads of State and International Crimes: The Hissène Habre Case' (2003) 1 *Journal of International Criminal Justice* 186, 189.

Rwanda could only be justified on an implied waiver.[56] In this way, the entire international criminal law project rests on the consent of the state of nationality of the defendant. As Akande and Shah argue, this is contrary to the 'extensive' post-war state practice.[57] Alternatively, the Court could have been referring to the 'private acts' argument, namely that such crimes cannot be functions of the state.[58] As we addressed in Chapter 4, strong criticisms of this position have been raised by Lord Lloyd and Lord Slynn in *Pinochet I*.[59]

Nevertheless, a moralist position would read the Court's judgment as apologist, fixated on certain states' failure to prosecute those accused of atrocities. From this position, it feels more like shielding those accused from facing justice than an outcome that is just in the circumstances. Here, the limited extent of prosecutions of Heads of State seems better explained as a failure by states to fully implement individual criminal responsibility (and produce the court of humanity) than evidence that immunity has not been removed. Here, van den Wyngaert's dissenting opinion illustrates the margins of the moralist position in a counter-hegemonic position. Through her moralist's lens, the Court's analogy and balancing act in justifying personal immunity of a Minister for Foreign Affairs produces a problematic legal outcome. The Court made a supposedly 'equitable' judgment call, yet if another cabinet post involves extensive foreign travel, there is nothing to prevent an analogy from being made to that cabinet post.[60] This potential outcome is facilitated by the Court's politically open-ended description that suggests the list is not exhaustive.

Van den Wyngaert's lens also leads her to a competing interpretation of state behaviour because the infrequent instances of criminal proceedings[61] and the uncertainty within legal scholarship is read as either courtesy (as opposed to sense of obligation) or political or practical considerations (ascending-descending).[62] In her view, state practice did not demonstrate a 'conscious decision' among states to generate a rule of customary international law that applied personal immunity to Ministers for Foreign Affairs.[63] Overall, the Court's position ends up constructing

56 See Chapter 4, section 4.2 (Lord Goff's critic of an implied waiver argument).

57 Akande and Shah (n 45) 839.

58 *R v Bow Street Metropolitan Stipendiary Magistrate, ex parte Pinochet Ugarte (Pinochet I)* (1998) 4 All ER 897, 939–40 (Nicholls) and 944 (Steyn). See also Akande and Shah (n 45) 839.

59 ibid 928 (despite the acts' commission within system criminality; would mean minor offences are official acts while grave offences are private acts) and 908 (if under actual or ostensible authority of the state, that is, if governmental in nature).

60 *Case of the Arrest Warrant* (n 43) (Wyngaert) para 21 and D Akande 'Immunities and the International Criminal Court' (2004) 98 *American Journal of International Law* 407, 412.

61 ibid paras 11 and 12 (referring to the few cases cited before the Court that involved Heads of State and a single case involving a Minister for Foreign Affairs). See also Akande (n 80) 412 and R van Alebeek *Immunity of States and their Officials in International Human Rights Law and International Criminal Law* (Oxford University Press Oxford 2008) 191–2 (widely accepted as protected by form of diplomatic immunity).

62 ibid para 13 (noting distinguishing features between diplomatic agents and Ministers for Foreign Affairs and how both the International Law Commission's *Draft Code of Crimes* and the Institute of International Law's 2001 *Resolution on Immunities* only assimilate Heads of Government with Heads of State).

63 ibid.

'a signpost for the guilty'[64] that van de Wyngaert explains could lead '*male fide* governments [to] appoint suspects of serious human rights violations to Cabinet posts' and in turn, shield them from prosecution in other states.[65] Nevertheless, her empirical analysis is vulnerable to accusation of being political because it concealed its normativity of universal accountability. In her analysis, she assumed that an analogy was unjustified, that infrequent practice must be interpreted as she outlined and that cabinet appointments would be made based on avoiding foreign prosecutions.

When van de Wyngaert turned to whether immunity applied, she stressed the international advocacy on accountability for war crimes and crimes against humanity (descending-ascending). She assumed that the *jus cogens* status of the crimes was hierarchically superior and overruled immunity of state officials. [66] From this approach, the infrequency of criminal proceedings was a failure to implement individual criminal responsibility rather than a confirmation of immunity. She drew significance from provision on the irrelevance of official capacity in statutes of international criminal tribunals[67] as the debate was 'about individual versus State responsibility' rather than procedural or substantive rules of immunity of state officials.[68] In fact, she observed that 'most authorities do not mention the distinction at all or even reject it.'[69] In other words, the Court read a pattern from all immunity jurisprudence regardless of subject matter of dispute whereas the Belgian position followed the *Eichmann* narrative (and in turn, the Nuremberg model), that reduced the crimes to a singularity which necessitated a distinct rule. If there is no such rule as determined by the Court, it seems to stifle any potential transformation because any claim of jurisdiction will always be trumped by the *Arrest Warrant* outcome. It straitjacketed the issue and closed an avenue.

Moving towards a moralist middle, the Joint Separate Opinion captured the trends developing within international criminal law as a 'balancing of interests' between the interest of mankind in preventing impunity and the interest of the community of states in protecting state liberty from arbitrary interference.[70] However, 'the weights on the two scales are not set for all perpetuity', rather a 'discernible' trend exists that rejects impunity and in turn, makes possible the wider assertions

64 British Prime Minister Anthony Eden as cited in M Koskenniemi 'The Lady Doth Protest Too Much: Kosovo and the Turn to Ethics in International Law' (2002) 65 *Modern Law Review* 159, 167.

65 *Case of the Arrest Warrant* (n 43) (Wyngaert) para 21. See Akande and Shah (n 45) 825 (that rationales for personal immunity (that justify immunity on private visits to Heads of State) does not fit for other senior officials on private visits).

66 ibid para 26.

67 ibid para 28. She considers the Court to have taken a 'minimalist' approach, a narrow interpretation of 'no immunity clauses' in statutes of international criminal tribunals.

68 ibid para 21.

69 ibid para 30 (citing the Princeton Principles as one of the few that endorsed the distinction and noted how the statutes of the international criminal tribunals 'do not address the question of procedural immunity').

70 ibid paras 75 and 77. See also A Slaughter 'Defining the Limits: Universal Jurisdiction and National Courts' in S Macedo (ed) *Universal Jurisdiction: National Courts and the Prosecution of Serious Crimes Under International Law* (University of Pennsylvania Press Philadelphia 2004) 168.

of jurisdiction and the limited availability of immunities.[71] They agreed with the Court's judgment on the application of personal immunity regardless of the gravity of the offences. However, they argued for a different framework for functional immunity and though they raised the same criticism of the four scenarios as van den Wyngaert,[72] they argued that immunities were not merely unavailable where impunity would occur. Rather immunities served 'their own intrinsic value' and it cannot be a situation where one value trumps another. Instead, there must be a balancing or weighing of interests and in exercising this balancing act, the commitment to accountability meant that immunities must be 'recognized with restraint'.[73]

It follows, then, that though they approved of inviolability during office, they distinguished the situation on ceasing office based on the 'not official functions' argument; in fact, they explicitly cited *Eichmann*.[74] This attempt to steer a middle course (similar to *Pinochet III*) appears to be more concrete, less normative than van den Wyngaert, but too normative and not concrete enough in comparison to the Court's judgment. Invariably, this move to reasonableness would appear to the polar ends of the moralist or formalist approaches as inconsistent and arbitrary; a political choice cloaked as law. Nevertheless, though van den Wyngaert position was reflected in scholarship,[75] the Joint Separate Opinion's template found particular favour in scholarship given its move to equity and its attempt to accommodate both moralist and formalist goals.[76]

2.2 It's got a name now: Universal jurisdiction in absentia

We observed that the Court did not address the validity of universal jurisdiction *in absentia* and how this failure casts a shadow over the judgment. Instead, the judges in their separate and dissenting opinions produced competing interpretations that spanned the width of contrasting opinions within the literature and jurisprudence. Van den Wyngaert adopted the margins of the moralist approach and assumed that universal jurisdiction derives from the 'international reprobation for certain very serious crimes' and its normative purpose is 'to avoid impunity' (descending-ascending).[77] In keeping with the *Eichmann* narrative, international

71 *Case of the Arrest Warrant* (n 43) (Wyngaert) para 75.
72 ibid para 78 (noting the improbability of trials with regime change or possibility of shielding an accused by keeping the Minister in office for an indeterminant period).
73 ibid para 79.
74 ibid para 85 ('state-related motives are not the proper test for determining what constitutes public state acts').
75 A Winants 'The Yerodia Ruling of the International Court of Justice and the 1993/1999 Belgian Law on Universal Jurisdiction' (2003) 16 *Leiden Journal of International Law* 491 and J Wouters and L De Smet 'The ICJ's Judgment in the *Case concerning the Arrest Warrant of 11 April 2000*: Some critical observations' (2003) 16(2) *Leiden Journal of International Law* 253.
76 A Cassese 'When may Senior State Officials be Tried for International Crimes? Some Comments on the Congo v Belgium Case' (2002) *European Journal of International Law* 853, 866–70 and Akande and Shah (n 33) 841. See also Q Wright 'War Criminals' (1945) 39 *American Journal of International Law* 257, 269.
77 *Case of the Arrest Warrant* (n 43) (van den Wyngaert) para 46.

law granted the right to exercise universal jurisdiction from the nature of the offence yet the content of this right was determined from state behaviour in punishing piracy committed on the high seas.[78] Again, this interwove the piracy analogy[79] and the *jus cogens* argument.[80] Through her moralist lens, she searched for a prohibitive rule and implicitly invoked the *Lotus* majority's presumption.[81] Here, she dismissed the dominance of national legislation requiring custody and how limited examples of proceedings constituted a prohibition. This could only be a prohibition if there had been a 'conscious decision' of states to prohibit jurisdiction unless the suspect was voluntarily present on the state's territory.[82]

On the contrary, she tendered the Belgian and Spanish legislation as evidence of the lack of a prohibition.[83] Similarly, the 1949 Geneva Conventions[84] and other multilateral treaty obligations do not explicitly indicate that presence of the suspect is required and may be interpreted as not prohibiting (permitting) a broader jurisdiction than provided in the treaty.[85] Of course, van den Wyngaert's moralist lens cannot explain how the DRC could be bound when it objected to Belgian legislation being excessive and violation of its sovereignty. It clearly did not consent to such a position. Therefore, she justifies her analysis of state behaviour (to bind the DRC regardless of consent) by returning to her normative position, privileging the moral outrage underpinning the desire for accountability. She presupposes the desirability of a wide discretion on states in determining the scope of extraterritorial jurisdiction in order to secure greater criminal accountability.

Guillaume adopted the margins of the formalist approach and drew somewhat upon the Eichmann defence counsel's arguments. Guillaume explicitly rejected the *Lotus* majority's presumption and searched for a permissive rule (ascending-descending).[86] Through his formalist lens, his analysis of state behaviour is diametrically opposed to van den Wyngaert's. He considered the requirement of voluntary presence of the accused in most national legislation as significant and concluded that only Israel's Nazi and Nazi Collaborators Act 1950 would qualify as similar to the Belgian legislation.[87] In treaty practice, he considered the Hague

78 *AG v. Eichmann* (1968) 36 ILR 5, 26–8 and 299–300.

79 MC Bassiouni 'Universal Jurisdiction for International Crimes: Historical Perspectives and Contemporary Practice' (2001) 42 *Virginia Journal of International Law* 81, 108 and K Randall 'Universal Jurisdiction in International Law' (1988) 66 *Texas Law Review* 785, 798.

80 A Orakhelashvili *Peremptory Norms in International Law* (Oxford University Press Oxford 2006) 288.

81 *Case of the Arrest Warrant* (n 43) (van den Wyngaert) para 51.

82 ibid para 56.

83 ibid para 55. See Chapter 2, section 4 for similar argument in the Eichmann appeal court's judgment.

84 *Case of the Arrest Warrant* (n 43) (van den Wyngaert) para 54.

85 ibid para 61.

86 *Case of the Arrest Warrant* (n 43) (Guillaume) paraS 14 and 15 (rejects 'wide measure of discretion' in *Lotus* judgment given the UN Charter's reference to sovereign equality and use of *uti possenditis* rule during the decolonization period).

87 ibid para 12 (refers to Article 689 I of the French Penal Code, Article 6 of the Strafgesetzbuch and Dutch implementation of the Convention against Torture but did not refer to the Spanish provision, Article 23(4) of the Organic Law of Judicial Power).

Convention's jurisdictional clause as an incorporation of Grotius's doctrine of *aut dedere aut punire*.[88] Therefore, he concluded that there is a near complete lack of state behaviour to justify the Belgian claim. It follows, then, that the only true instance of universal jurisdiction under customary international law, according to Guillaume, is the crime of piracy committed on the high seas.[89] Here, he considered the jurisdiction to be based on the absence of sovereignty over the location of the offence as opposed to the nature of the offence, similar to what was presented by Eichmann's defence counsel ('absence of a competent court').[90]

Guillaume's analysis implicitly assumed a wide measure of discretion of states, despite his express rejection of *Lotus* because his conclusions claimed to be the true reflection of the content of state liberty. Yet his formalist lens cannot explain how Belgium is bound when it objected to the claim of excessive jurisdiction and argued that its legislation was a legitimate exercise of its sovereignty. It clearly did not consent to such a position. Therefore, he justifies his analysis of state behaviour (to bind Belgium regardless of consent) by returning to his normative project that privileges state liberty and non-interference. It is apparent from the tenor of his analysis that he emphasized the territorial character of the criminal law as fundamental and the recognition of sovereign equality in the UN Charter that strengthened the territorial principle.[91] While he acknowledged the corpus of international criminal law and treaty obligations regarding extraterritorial jurisdiction,[92] he argued that 'at no time' has universal jurisdiction *in absentia* been envisaged; 'to do this would, moreover, risk creating judicial chaos.'[93]

The Joint Separate Opinion produced a moralist middle ground that emphasized how state practice cannot be solely determinative of jurisdictional claims, that is, state liberty cannot determine the exact scope of the state's legal rights (descending-ascending).[94] As states were not required to legislate as far as permitted in international law, it was evident that international law may permit a wider scope than that adopted by states.[95] However, this would no longer be reflective of state behaviour and thus, the Joint Separate Opinion conducted a detailed exposition of state legislation and criminal proceedings. Yet the Joint Separate Opinion's assessment did not adopt van den Wyngaert's absence of prohibition or Guillaume's absence of permission approach. Rather, the Joint Separate Opinion concluded that state behaviour was inconclusive (or 'neutral') and they dismissed the relevance of international penal conventions because those obligations involved

88 ibid para 9 (read as requiring presence on the prosecuting state yet Grotius's concept also required a prior conviction, unlike the 1970 Hague Convention).

89 ibid para 5.

90 ibid. See also *Written Pleadings submitted by Counsel for the Appellant Adolf Eichmann* (31 January 1962), Part II(b)(2)(b).

91 ibid para 15.

92 ibid.

93 ibid.

94 *Case of the Arrest Warrant* (n 43) (Joint Separate Opinion) para 45.

95 ibid.

exercising jurisdiction over a suspect present on state party territory.[96] Rather these were considered 'sensible realities' in light of the extradition component.[97] They similarly discounted national legislation, as national legislation only divulged what states have decided to establish.[98] Unlike Guillaume, they discounted the usefulness of the punishment of piracy, given its distinction in terms of the location of the offence.[99] The Joint Separate Opinion implicitly represented state behaviour as providing evidence of a possible permission under international law (because states are not required to legislate as far as permitted). Yet at the same time, the Joint Separate Opinion explicitly considered that treaty or national practice cannot evidence a prohibition against extradition to secure custody.

The inability to identify a permission or prohibition forced the Joint Separate Opinion to move back to a descending pattern. More obvious than van den Wyngaert, it stated that its assessment of state behaviour fits the 'underlying purpose of designating certain acts as international crimes [which] is to authorize a wide jurisdiction to be asserted over persons committing them'.[100] Given the irreconcilability between van den Wyngaert and Guillaume, the Joint Separate Opinion turned to the normative principle of reasonableness in order to balance the conflicting 'valid' liberties of the states exercising universal jurisdiction *in absentia* and the state of location of the offence.[101] This balancing of interests between preventing impunity and stability can be ensured through various safeguards, including the prior offer 'to the national State of the prospective accused person the opportunity itself to act upon the charges concerned'.[102] Therefore, *in absentia* may be theoretically valid but it must be exercised in accordance with reasonableness. In the end, it is apparent that van den Wyngaert's moralist approach was diametrically opposed to Guillaume's formalist approach and Joint Separate Opinion once more tried to steer a middle ground. These competing approaches were replicated in scholarship, dividing among those who approved van den Wyngaert,[103] Guillaume[104] or the Joint Separate Opinion.[105]

96 ibid para 32.
97 ibid para 57.
98 ibid paras 21 and 45 (that idea of universal jurisdiction is where there is no legal link to the prosecuting state and therefore, laws in Australia, the UK, France, the Netherlands and Canada do not provide for universal jurisdiction, as classically understood, which implies that the doctrine of universal jurisdiction does not require presence of the suspect (any link to the prosecuting state)).
99 ibid para 54.
100 ibid para 58.
101 ibid para 59.
102 ibid.
103 A Poels, 'Universal Jurisdiction in Absentia', (2005) 23(1) *Netherlands Quarterly of Human Rights* 64, 76–8 and M El Zeidy, 'Universal Jurisdiction in Absentia: Is it a Legal Valid Option', (2003) 37 *International Lawyer* 835, 852. Contrast R O'Keefe 'Universal Jurisdiction: Clarifying the Basic Concept' (2004) 2 *Journal of International Criminal Justice* 735, 748–9 (criticizing all opinions as conflating jurisdiction to prescribe and enforce).
104 R Rabinovitch 'Universal Jurisdiction *in absentia*' (2004–05) 18 *Fordham International Law Journal* 500, 506–10.
105 Institute of International Law 'Resolution on Universal Criminal Jurisdiction with Regard to the Crime of Genocide, Crimes Against Humanity and War Crimes' (Krakow 2005).

3 A formalist hegemony post-*Arrest Warrant*

The immediate outcome of *Arrest Warrant* was the cancellation of Yerodia's arrest warrant. However, its more seemingly totalizing effect was the series of moves that attempted to accommodate the *Arrest Warrant* judgment while salvaging universal jurisdiction *in absentia*. These interpretations became a model argument for re-describing the moralist position that made the *Eichmann* narrative appear more concrete. In *Re Sharon*, the Belgian Court of Appeal implicitly accorded with Guillaume's formalist approach and observed how treaty law provisions, and the requisite Belgian incorporation of same, did not demonstrate the recognition of *in absentia*.[106] Without evidence that the alleged perpetrators were either present or their presence was immediately anticipated,[107] the exercise of Belgian jurisdiction was excessive. However, the Court of Cassation disagreed. It drew from *Re Pinochet*'s moral naturalism and concluded that presence of the suspect prior to an investigation was not required.[108] It then interpreted the parliamentary intent of the 1993/1999 Law as intending to exclude the precondition of presence, because the crimes under the Law were excluded from the list of offences that required presence as stipulated in article 12 of the Belgian Code of Criminal Procedure.[109]

The Court then applied the *Arrest Warrant* judgment and dismissed the complaint against the then Israeli Prime Minister Ariel Sharon.[110] However, it did not adopt Fox and Gaeta's interpretation of the *Arrest Warrant*'s judgment's third scenario. Instead, it proceeded with the complaint against Commander Amos, which implied that functional immunity was inapplicable in the circumstances of crimes against humanity.[111] In this sense, the Court's position moved to a moralist middle ground that privileged 'ending impunity', much like the Joint Separate Opinion. However, its latter interpretation caused continued outrage from other states whose nationals were the subject of criminal complaints. Israel withdrew its ambassador and the United States warned that Belgium risked its status as a diplomatic capital and host state to NATO.[112] Faced with considerable international pressure to change its laws, the Belgian Parliament repealed 1993/1999 Law and made substantive amendments to the Code of Criminal

106 *Re Sharon and Yaron* (2002) 127 ILR 100, 115 and 117 ('so long as section 12 was not amended or repealed', presence must be required and noting article 12bis (regarding international treaty obligations) requires presence of the accused which was considered to have general application, justified normatively on THE principle of territoriality as A 'corollary . . . of sovereign equality').

107 ibid 121.

108 *Re Sharon et al* (2003) 42 ILM 596, 598.

109 ibid (that the Genocide and Geneva Conventions could not come within the scope of article 12bis regarding multilateral treaties because neither Convention had an obligatory rule to extend jurisdiction that derogates from the principle of territoriality, that is, claiming a distinction from other treaties).

110 ibid 599 (that the Genocide Convention removes immunity only before the territorial jurisdiction while the Geneva Conventions did not provide any obstacle to the application of immunity).

111 ibid 600.

112 SR Ratner 'Belgium's War Crimes Statute: A Post-mortem' (2003) 97 *American Journal of International Law* 888, 889.

Procedure in August 2003.[113] The transitional provisions of the 2003 Law facilitated the dismissal of a range of criminal complaints, including *Yaron* and *Bush et al.*,[114] and signalled a dramatic retreat from a moralist horizon by one of the states that seemed to be a standard-bearer for the construction of the court of humanity.

This retreat had what seemed like a contagion effect. In the *Guatemala Generals* case, the Spanish High Court upheld the public prosecutor's appeal against the investigating magistrate's finding of jurisdiction. The case involved allegations of genocide, torture, terrorism, murder and illegal detention in Guatemala, particularly between the years 1980 and 1984, against certain former civilian and military leaders in Guatemala. It also involved allegations of the murder of Spanish, Guatemalan and foreign nationals in the Embassy of Spain in 1980.[115] The magistrate had decided that Spanish courts had jurisdiction over the allegations of genocide committed in Guatemala against Guatemalan and Spanish victims as the Guatemalan justice system was inactive. However, the High Court disagreed. We observed the idiosyncratic interpretation in the Spanish *Pinochet* decision that constructed a form of subsidiarity;[116] here, the Court interpreted subsidiarity as an examination of whether Spanish jurisdiction infringed the rights of the territorial state and pulling on the *Eichmann* narrative, argued that any extraterritorial jurisdiction could only be exercised in the absence of effective exercise of jurisdiction by the territorial state.[117] It considered the exclusion of genocide from the Guatemalan amnesty law as significant and noted the limited time since the publication of the Truth Commission's report recommending criminal investigations by Guatemalan authorities. It concluded that Guatemalan courts could not be considered inactive *at this time* and Spanish jurisdiction was inoperable.[118]

On appeal to the Spanish Supreme Court, the majority of a divided court dramatically changed what had been considered as parameters of universal jurisdiction under article 23(4) of the OJLP.[119] The Supreme Court echoed the move

113 See Belgian Amendment Law (2003) 42 ILM 1258, 1265, 1266 and 1267 respectively. For a careful study, see L Reydams 'Belgium Reneges on Universality: The 5 August 2003 Act on Grave Breaches of International Humanitarian Law' (2003) 1 *Journal of International Criminal Justice* 679, 684–8 (observing how a 'lack of clarity remains' on the scope of universal jurisdiction).

114 ibid 1269 (article 29(3) obliged the Prosecutor to set aside those complaints, which were only pending in the investigation phrase while article 29(4) obliged the Federal Prosecutor to set aside the complaints pending in prosecution phase unless at the time of entry into force of the law, an investigative measure had been taken and at least one civil party is a Belgian national or at least one of the alleged suspects has a principal residence in Belgium).

115 For an historical account, see H Ascensio 'Are Spanish Courts Backing Down on Universality? The Supreme Tribunal's Decision in Guatemalan Generals' (2003) 1 *Journal of International Criminal Justice* 690, 691.

116 On article 23(4) and subsidiarity, see Chapter 4, section 3.2.

117 *Guatemalan Generals case* (2000) Judgment No. 15/2000 (13 December 2000) para 3.

118 ibid.

119 See also *Guatemalan Generals* case (2003) 42 ILM 686, 691–2 and 694–5 (controversially contended that due to the public importance, it was reasonable to adjudicate the matter even though the Prosecutor challenged its powers of review). See Ascensio (n 115) 692 (that the judicial review 'went beyond the scope of the legal questions raised by the plaintiffs [and thus], acted *proprio motu* on the ground that jurisdiction is a matter of public order).

to a more formalist position, privileging the avoidance of jurisdictional conflict and inter-state tension. From their particular normative project, they justified the test of subsidiarity as priority criteria needed to resolve 'supposed effective and real concurrence' of active jurisdictions[120] and therefore, Spanish jurisdiction was only justified 'as a default to tribunals initially competent' under the Genocide Convention.[121] This normative position informed their interpretations of article VI of the Genocide Convention that seem underpinned by the *Lotus* case's dissenting opinions, because they considered that any limit must recognize the territorial state as the natural primary jurisdiction to the exclusion of all others.[122] The Supreme Court reshaped the priority criterion from 'inactivity' to a prohibition against intervention.[123] It read the inactivity test as allowing Spanish courts to probe whether another state's criminal justice system was effective when such a determination would pass judgment on the judicial capacity of a foreign sovereign state.[124] Consequently the inactivity condition involved an encroachment on Spanish executive powers to conduct foreign relations, especially in situations where a judicial pronouncement could have a destabilizing effect.[125]

Although this appeared to be more concrete, relative to the *Pinochet* decision, it was a move towards a formalist middle, as it would be the *Eichmann* narrative if the Israeli courts paid greater deference to the territorial jurisdiction. Or it is Eichmann defence counsel's argument on presence of the accused combined with recognition of individual criminal responsibility and validity of universal jurisdiction over crimes against international law. In other words, the Court accepted the existence of universal jurisdiction over genocide (nature of the crimes),[126] yet entangled or interwove the subsidiary form of jurisdiction from the late nineteenth century. In this sense, it moved away from the outermost moralist's position that the nature of the crimes is the necessary 'close connection' (Hyde) and towards the idea of supplementary or subsidiary jurisdiction that justifies 'some point of connection' (Harvard Research).[127] Of course, a notion of 'legitimizing link' is politically open-ended and can accommodate both Hyde and Harvard Research. From a moralist position, its justification upon certain state decisions cannot avoid looking apologist[128] and its claim that presence of the suspect or nationality of the

120 ibid 695.

121 ibid.

122 ibid. See also Preamble of the Inter-American Commission on Human Rights, Resolution on Trial for International Crimes No.1/2003 (principle 5 states that territoriality prevails over nationality where the former state 'wishes to bring [accused] to justice' and ensure fair trial guarantees).

123 ibid 698.

124 ibid 696 (describing the complainant's interpretation of facts as impossible to be substituted for that of the judicial organ of the state itself).

125 ibid and 690 (Spain 'maintains normal diplomatic relations' with Guatemala and 'no mechanism or supranational court exists for either the positive or negative resolution of the eventual conflict').

126 ibid 697.

127 ibid 698.

128 ibid 701 (claimed that evidence in state practice of a requirement for a legitimizing link between offence and the prosecuting State, citing German decisions of *Tadic* and *Djajic* referred to in Chapter 4).

victim is the necessary legitimizing link seems arbitrarily chosen.[129] Attempting to avoid these challenges, the Court returned to its descending move to justify the concept on normative grounds and therefore, jurisdictional conflict would be averted by weighing the requisite interests in terms of reasonableness and good faith, albeit premised upon deference to the territorial jurisdiction. In its determination, the Supreme Court dismissed the appeal regarding the allegations of genocide and upheld the appeal on allegations of torture given certain victims were of Spanish nationality.[130] To a moralist position, this seems hopelessly political, sovereignly egoistical and incapable of avoiding accusation of apology.

Another formalist horizon was evident in the *Re Mofaz* case, which appeared to confirm an anxiety post-*Arrest Warrant* that its logic could be applied to other cabinet portfolios. The English Magistrates Court argued that the International Court of Justice's statement was non-exhaustive and equated an Israeli Defence Minister in terms of function with a Minister for Foreign Affairs. The Defence Ministry's mandate involves foreign travel of a similar status to the Minister for Foreign Affairs and consequently, personal immunity should apply to avoid interference in the effective performance of the Minister's mandate.[131]

4 A moralist counter-hegemony

This trend towards a formalist position was somewhat permeated by a moralist counter-point that pulled on *Re Sharon* and Joint Separate Opinion in an attempt to produce a moralist middle ground. Therefore, this combined the recognition of universal jurisdiction over crimes against international law (the *Eichmann* narrative) with a capacity to engage in a criminal investigation *in absentia* and in the form of a subsidiary basis of jurisdiction that prioritized the territorial jurisdiction.[132] Certain international lawyers embraced this alternative re-description of the *Eichmann* narrative.[133] Interestingly, the issue of immunity of state officials[134] was either ignored or acknowledged to apply without directly addressing whether there must be distinct rules between the different immunities.[135] Within the chaotic transformation from moralist to formalist

129 ibid 701.

130 ibid 699. See also Roht-Arriaza (n 31) 139 (decision of Spanish Government to refuse to issue formal extradition request in the Argentinian investigation in 2003 because Argentina was proceeding to investigate the accused, despite willingness of Argentinian Government to extradite).

131 *Re Mofaz* ILDC 97 (UK 2004) paras 14 and 15 (Defence and Foreign Affairs were equated in terms of overseas travel given role in 'maintaining troops overseas' and visiting UN missions).

132 *Guatemalan Generals Case* (2005) Judgment No. 237/2005 (26 September 2005) and Institute of International Law (n 105). See *Public Prosecutor v Scilingo* ILDC 136 (ES 2005) (proceeding to full trial and sentencing) and C Tomuschat 'Issues of Universal Jurisdiction in the Scilingo Case' (2005) 3 *Journal of International Criminal Justice* 1074.

133 Institute of International Law (n 105) Principle 3(b). See also C Kress 'Universal Jurisdiction over International Crimes and the *Institut de droit International*' (2006) 4 *Journal of International Criminal Justice* 561.

134 See the following discussion of Spanish cases and the Obligation to Prosecute or Extradite case in section 4.

135 Institute of International Law (n 105).

post-*Arrest Warrant*, Germany amended its Code of Criminal Procedure (*Strafprozessordnung*) to impose a duty on the Federal Prosecutor to investigate and prosecute crimes under the Rome Statute of the International Criminal Court.[136] Under article 1 of the Code of Crimes against International Law, the duty to investigate arose 'even when the offence was committed abroad and bears no relation to Germany',[137] which effectively abolished the 'legitimating link' that had been applied in the *Tadic* and *Djajic* cases.[138]

In other words, the discretion arises where the case involves an offence committed by a non-national against a non-national abroad where residency or anticipated residency does not arise and the offence is being prosecuted by other competent jurisdictions. Here, the Prosecutor can determine whether to exercise universal jurisdiction when 'the accused is not resident in Germany and not expected to so reside' (irrespective of 'sufficient factual indications' of the commission of an offence).[139] This discretion operates alongside other possibilities for dispensing with investigations into extraterritorial offences, including *ne bis in idem*.[140] In the midst of a Belgian retreat, an apparent contagion effect and its support within the literature, the timing of the German Code looked as if it misread the moment.

Even so, what appeared to be the first major rift from the dominant formalist position was the Spanish Constitutional Court's judgment in the *Guatemalan Generals* case. The Court returned the meaning of universal jurisdiction over genocide under article 23(4) to the outermost point of the *Eichmann* narrative, as set out in the *Pinochet* decision.[141] Yet this return was reshaped to move towards a moralist middle modelled on the Joint Separate Opinion and the Institute of

136 Article 3 (subject to section 152(2) of the German Code of Criminal Procedure where the prosecuting authorities 'must take action . . . provided there are sufficient factual indications'). See also C Wehle and F Jessberger 'International Criminal Justice is Coming Home: The New German Code of Crimes against International Law' (2002) 13 *Criminal Law Forum* 191, 213 (including English translation).

137 Section 1 of the Act to Introduce the Code of Crimes Against International Law of 26 June 2002 (Germany) (2003) 42 ILM 998. See H Satzger 'German Criminal Law and the Rome Statute: A Critical Analysis of the New German Code of Crimes Against International Law' (2002) 2 *International Criminal Law Review* 261, 280.

138 See Chapter 4, section 3.3.

139 See Code of Crimes against International Law (2003) 42 ILM 998, 1007–8.

140 Section 153(c)(2) of the German Code of Criminal Procedure. Section 153(f)(1) of the German Code of Criminal Procedure (regarding German nationals, the discretion to dismiss proceedings over extraterritorial offences only arises if an international court, the territorial jurisdiction, or the passive personality jurisdiction are prosecuting the crime, whereas regarding non-nationals, the discretion arises in the latter situations as well as situations where neither the suspect nor victim are German nationals and where no suspect is, or is expected to be, resident in Germany).

141 *Guatemalan Generals Case* (n 132) Part II, para 9 (jurisdiction based on the nature of the crimes, whose 'harmfulness . . . extends from one of the victims and reaches the international community as a whole' (translation of author)). See also Art 161(b) of the Spanish Constitution which permits individual petitions (*recursos de amparo*) against violation of the rights contained in section 53(2) of the Constitution and there is no appeal (art 164).

International Law's position.[142] The Court ruled that presence of the suspect was not a precondition for the exercise of jurisdiction and initiation of judicial processes, albeit it was required for trial.[143] Rather as the crimes 'affect the entire international community', extradition can be used to secure custody in order to bring the accused to trial under universal jurisdiction.[144]

The Constitutional Court then turned to the issue of subsidiarity and in principle, approved the dissenting minority opinion in the Supreme Court. The minority had considered that the only limitation on universal jurisdiction was *res judicata* (or final judgment in another jurisdiction) rather than non-intervention and a legitimizing link.[145] They reshaped the precondition for analysing whether the subsidiary basis of jurisdiction is triggered. Rather than inactivity, the precondition was the unwillingness to genuinely prosecute and therefore, a Spanish court must assess whether there is a 'necessity of judicial intervention' or the crime is effectively being prosecuted by the territorial jurisdiction.[146] Its assessment involves applying a test of reasonableness and simultaneously, a higher threshold of seriousness to determine if the state proceeded in an effective manner. This combination of two thresholds was to be applied 'without implying any pejorative judgement on the political, social or economic conditions' that led to 'a *de facto*' impunity.[147] A moralist position read this outcome as reflective of the underlying function in 'ending impunity' whereas to a formalist opponent, it could threaten stability and lead potentially to unwarranted interference. It would mean any state would be able to exercise jurisdiction unless there was a judgment in the territorial jurisdiction. Its test failed to resolve the Supreme Court's criticism of making 'pejorative' judgments on the national reconciliation processes in other states. From this formalist angle, the Constitutional Court's attempt to do so seems inadequate, grossly optimistic and has clear potential to lead to abuses of jurisdiction.

It follows then that the Constitutional Court dispensed with the difficult wording of the minority's dissent.[148] Rather, the Court considered that the principle of *non bis in idem* was the only express limitation without any further

142 ibid para 9 (approving the 2005 Resolution of the Institute of International Law). It is suggested that the *Constitutional Court*'s outcome implies that universal jurisdiction under Spanish law applied regardless of whether the state asserted universal jurisdiction over the offences at the time that they were committed because its outcome permitted Spanish courts to prosecute acts prior to 1985.

143 ibid para 8.

144 ibid para 9 (translation of author) (citing the 2003 German Code and the Institute's 2005 Resolution).

145 *Guatemalan Generals Case* (n 132) 704 (citing article 24(2)(c), which states 'the offender has not been acquitted, pardoned or sentenced in another country . . .').

146 ibid 705.

147 ibid.

148 *Guatemalan Generals Case* (n 132) para 3 (based on the documentary evidence, 'it is manifestly clear that many years have passed since the occurrence of these acts and for some reason or another, the courts in Guatemala have not been able to effectively exercise jurisdiction . . .').

elaboration[149] and argued that this principle introduced some rule of priority that was essential to avoid duplicity of proceedings.[150] The *Guatemalan Generals* case never advanced beyond the historic hearing of witnesses because the situation in Guatemala changed considerably when Rios Montt lost his parliamentary immunity in 2012.[151] As a result, he was joined as co-defendant in a trial regarding massacres, deportation, sexual violence and torture in the Quiche region. However, the trial was plagued by repeated suspensions, appeals and a constitutional review regarding the rights of fair trial.[152] His conviction in May 2013 was overturned by the Guatemalan Constitutional Court, which ordered a partial retrial that would involve a re-hearing of defence witness testimony and closing arguments.[153] Attempts at a retrial were frustrated and in the end, there was a decision that special procedures should be applied to Montt due to his unfitness to stand trial, including in camera hearings and the lack of sentencing if convicted.[154]

Another moralist's counter-hegemonic move was the *Habré* decision of the UN Committee against Torture, which addressed Senegal's failure to prosecute former Chadian leader Hissène Habré.[155] The Habré case arose from a criminal complaint brought by Chadian victims before a Senegalese investigating magistrate in 2000 and, in their complaint, they claimed that Habré had been complicit in the commission of torture during his regime in the 1980s. The magistrate indicted Habré, who had been living in Senegal since the fall of his regime, and placed him under house arrest. However, Habré's defence counsel challenged the magistrate's decision before the Senegalese appeals court based on claim that there was no extraterritorial jurisdiction over the crime of torture.[156] The court

149 ibid (referring to the minority opinion in the Supreme Court that found article 24(2)(c), prohibiting prosecution where an individual has been acquitted, pardoned, or convicted by another state, as the only limitation).

150 ibid para 4 (Guatemalan lower courts responded to extradition requests but extradition was halted when the Guatemalan Constitutional Court ruled that the state was not obliged to execute the extradition request). See also response of the Spanish investigating magistrate Judge Pedraz to the *Guatemalan Constitutional Court* decision of 12 December 2007 (16 January 2008) (unofficial translation), URL: www.ccrjustice.org).

151 Of note, the issue of whether Rios Montt and others were entitled to functional immunity was not addressed at any stage in the *Guatemalan Generals* case. This followed the earlier Spanish *Pinochet* case and as we noted in Chapter 4, it implied that Spanish courts deemed functional immunity inapplicable.

152 See *The Trial of Efrain Rios Montt*, URL: www.riosmontt-trial.org (timeline commentary of proceedings).

153 *The Guardian* 'Rios Montt Genocide Case Collapses' (21 May 2013).

154 Burt, JM 'Guatemalan Grave Crimes Cases Delayed' *International Justice Monitor* (13 July 2016), URL: http://www.ijmonitor.org/2016/07/guatemala-grave-crimes-cases-delayed/.

155 See *Guengueng v Senegal: Communication No. 181/2001* (Senegal 19/05/2006) CAT/C/36/D/181/2001. For case history, see SP Marks 'The Hisséne Habré Case: The Law and Politics of Universal Jurisdiction' in S Macedo (ed) *Universal Jurisdiction: National Courts and the Prosecution of Serious Crimes Under International Law* (University of Pennsylvania Press Philadelphia 2003).

156 Article 669 of the Senegalese Code of Criminal Procedure asserted extraterritorial jurisdiction over specific crimes such as counterfeiting currency, which did not include the Torture Convention.

agreed with Habré and it implicitly drew on the *Lotus* dissents that emphasized the territoriality of the criminal law ('the nature of the sanctioning criminal law tends to protect the interests of society').[157]

It then rejected the victims' counter-claim that the Convention against Torture could be a legal basis for jurisdiction without domestic implementation of article 5(2). The court made a distinction because of the Torture Convention's obligation to exercise jurisdiction under article 5(2). It in effect noted the lack of a similar explicit obligation under the Nuremberg model, yet this ignored how the Nuremberg Charter presupposed a validity of jurisdiction (rather than imposing a specific obligation) even though there were competing interpretations within the literature and subsequently, there was a challenge to jurisdiction by the defence counsel. Therefore, based on its distinction, the Senegalese appeals court defended its view that the nature of the crime could not justify extra-territorial jurisdiction and instead, an incorporation statute was required.[158] On appeal, the Court of Cassation agreed that a prior legislative enactment was needed to establish Senegalese jurisdiction. The Torture Convention obliged states to establish jurisdiction, implying the requirement to implement domestically, and consequently, the treaty obligation could not prevail over contrary national law.[159]

In their communication, Guengueng and other Senegalese victims argued that Senegal had violated articles 5(2) and 7 of the Torture Convention because they had refused to exercise jurisdiction and failed to act on a complaint of alleged torture against Habré. Although the crime of torture had been proscribed in Senegal's Penal Code, the Senegalese legislature had failed to amend its Code of Criminal Procedure to assert the various bases of extraterritorial jurisdiction, as required by article 5 of the Convention,[160] and failed to extradite in an instance where it did not submit the complaint to its prosecuting authorities.[161] In response, Senegal interpreted that the phrase 'subject to its jurisdiction' to mean only a violation of the Torture Convention within state territory or by state nationals, rather than acts committed extraterritorially by non-nationals.[162] It also argued that the treaty was silent on a time frame for states to comply with their obligations.[163] This pulled on the *Lotus* majority's presumption against limitations that underpins positions such as the need to interpret legal rules restrictively.[164]

157 *Ministre Public contre Habré* (2000) Dakar Court of Appeal Judgment No. 135 (4 July 2000), para 3.

158 ibid.

159 *Re Habré*, Appeal decision, Cassation No. 14, ILDC 164 (SN 2001), paras 37 and 38.

160 Article 5(2) obliges each state party to 'establish its jurisdiction . . . where the alleged offender is present in any territory under its jurisdiction and it does not extradite him . . . to any of the states in paragraph 1 [of article 5]'. Convention against Torture and Other Cruel, Inhuman or Degrading Treatment or Punishment (1984) 1465 UNTS 85.

161 Article 7(1) obliges that the state 'if does not extradite him, submit the case to its competent authorities. . . .' Torture Convention (n 142)

162 *Guengueng v Senegal* (n 155) para 4.

163 ibid para 7.13.

164 M Koskenniemi *From Apology to Utopia: The Structure of the International Legal Argument* (Cambridge University Press Cambridge 2005) 257.

Framing the situation in the ethos of the human rights regime, it is predictable that the Committee's conclusions privileged a moral naturalism and legal humanitarianism of the repression of the crime of torture and desirability of universal accountability (descending-ascending). Its interpretation of the Convention's provisions privileged the regime's ethos that centres on challenging the politics of the state. Therefore, the Committee rejected Senegal's interpretation of 'subject to its jurisdiction' and decided that 'the principle of universal jurisdiction in article 5(2) and 7 implies that the jurisdiction of States parties must extend to potential complainants in circumstances similar to the complainants.'[165] If Senegal's argument was accepted, it would restrict the parameters of the Torture Convention to reciprocal cooperation between states parties over alleged acts of torture committed on their territory or by their nationals. The Committee's interpretation meant that Senegal would be obliged to either prosecute or extradite allegations of torture committed outside of Senegal by non-nationals. The Committee concluded that the obligation to submit the case to prosecuting authorities does not depend upon a refusal of an offer to extradite and therefore, Senegal breached its obligations by failing to determine whether to extradite or prosecute given the Belgian extradition request in 2005.[166]

In this sense, it read article 5(2) in keeping with the *Eichmann* narrative and found that the only situation where extradition could act as a precondition (to the custodial state's determination) was when another state party sought extradition of the accused. The logical outcome of this position is that the state party is always under an obligation to investigate (and to prosecute if it so determines) rather than be dependent on an extradition request in order to exercise its discretion. If the Committee adopted Senegal's position, there would be a probable risk-of-impunity (or jurisdictional) gap as the custodial state could simply not proceed where no extradition request is forthcoming. Consequently, the custodial state party has the discretion to choose between the alternatives of either extraditing or submitting the case for prosecution.[167] When the Committee turned to the failure of Senegal to fully implement the Torture Convention, it turned to the notion of reasonableness as the treaty is silent on a requisite time frame. It argued that the obligations must be met within a reasonable period and on its analysis of the fact (through a moralist lens), Senegal exceeded this 'reasonable time frame'.[168] For a moralist position, the Committee's interpretation is self-explanatory and inevitable. It ensures that the political present is transformed from Senegal's sovereign egoism into an order of global justice where states parties secure 'universal' repression of torture.

Nevertheless, this appears too normative to a formalist position. Instead, the interpretation of the Convention is underpinned by privileging ideas of reciprocity in extradition treaties. This presupposes that the punishment scheme

165 *Guengueng v Senegal* (n 155) para 6.4.
166 ibid paras 8.12 and 9.9 and 9.11 respectively.
167 ibid para 9.7.
168 ibid para 9.5.

is designed to ensure a pool of jurisdiction that is supplemented by extended cooperation in extradition.[169] Harrington argues that the phrase 'if it does not extradite' must be interpreted as obliging extradition. Therefore, the obligation to submit the case to prosecuting authorities only arises if the state party does not extradite.[170] Juxtaposed against the Committee's outcome, this is an appeal to self-determination that reduces the Torture Convention to something more like a reciprocal cooperation agreement.

5 Securing of a formalist hegemony

Notwithstanding these discontinuities by a moralist's counter-hegemony, the continuing trend was a formalist position's hegemonic control.[171] The rallying cry of avoiding abuse seemed more appropriate in thwarting trials that were read as politically motivated and disruptive to relations between states. In this context, the moralist middle produced by the Spanish Constitutional Court continued to appear too normative and there was a move in the Spanish High Court to steer a further middle position between the Constitutional Court's 'moral naturalism' and the rallying cry of 'avoiding abuse' that underpinned the Supreme Court's judgment in the same case.[172] In the Spanish *Tibet* complaint, the outcome in the High Court seemed more concrete, less normative than the Constitutional Court's judgment. Although the only limitation was *res judicata*, the exercise of Spanish jurisdiction must be determined by balancing certain interests. Therefore, the Court argued that even if other jurisdictions are unwilling or unable and the International Criminal Court does not have jurisdiction, the Spanish courts should not exercise jurisdiction 'where there is seen to be an abuse of law'.[173] It read universal jurisdiction as the situation where the crime and perpetrator do not have a 'direct interest in or relationship' with the prosecuting state.[174] In this sense, it was more Harvard Research and less Hyde's close connection of the crime.

We noted the German Code of International Crimes (2003) that appeared at a moment when the triumphalism of the moralist position had waned. Within a few years, the Code's 'progressive' character seemed to be undermined by the

169 L Henkin, *International Law: Politics and Values* (Martinus Nijhoff Dordrecht 1995) 248.

170 J Harrington 'The Obligation to "Extradite or Prosecute" is not an Obligation to "Prosecute or Extradite" (EJIL:Talk! 23 February 2009), URL: http://www.ejiltalk.org/the-obligation-to-extradite-or-prosecute-is-not-an-obligation-to-prosecute-or-extradite/.

171 In the interests of brevity, the Canadian case law will not be addressed. It is referenced here as further examples of *Butare 4*-type cases, where there is a Security Council-approved post-conflict justice model and the cooperation of the territorial state. See *Mugesera v Canada (Minister of Citizenship and Immigration)* (2005) 2 SCR 100.

172 *Fundación Casa del Tibet and ors v Zemin and ors, Appeal Judgment on Admissibility* ILDC 1002 (ES 2006) (an appeal from the Central Court of Investigation decision to reject jurisdiction based on the Supreme Court's interpretation of universal jurisdiction law).

173 ibid para 10.

174 ibid.

actual practice of German prosecutors and German courts.[175] In the *Abu Ghraib* case, the Federal Prosecutor decided to dispense with the complaint against former Defence Secretary Rumsfeld and other senior US officials.[176] The Federal Prosecutor argued that the 'principle of universal jurisdiction does not automatically legitimize unlimited criminal prosecution'.[177] Rather the prevention of impunity 'must occur in the framework of non-interference in the affairs of foreign countries'.[178] Imitating the Spanish Supreme Court in the *Guatemalan Generals* case, the Federal Prosecutor argued that 'a third State cannot examine the legal practice of foreign states according to its own standards or correct or replace it in specific cases.'[179] Instead, the competence of 'uninvolved' third states is 'a subsidiary competence, which should prevent impunity, yet not inappropriately push aside the primary competent jurisdictions'.[180]

It follows that the territorial jurisdiction must have the freedom to decide 'in what order and with what means' it conducts an investigation.[181] Extraterritorial jurisdiction of German courts must only arise when the investigation by the territorial jurisdiction is 'being carried out only for the sake of appearances or without a serious intent to prosecute'.[182] According to the Federal Prosecutor, this priority has to be justified, given the 'special interest of the state of the perpetrator and victim', as well as 'greater proximity . . . to the evidence'.[183] Yet this deference to other jurisdictions compels a political choice because the meaning of genuine willingness to prosecute depends on context, that is, what is read as being just in the circumstances. In the end, the Federal Prosecutor analysed the facts through a formalist lens and deferred entirely to the United States authorities as 'the means and timeframe envisioned for the investigation of further possible suspects in connection with the violations . . . must be left to the judicial authorities of United States.'[184] A similar position was adopted with regard to the US nationals who were resident in a US Army barracks in Germany. Here, the United States

175 See C Ryngaert 'Universal Jurisdiction over Violations of International Humanitarian Law in Germany' (2008) 47 *Military Law and Law of War Review* 377, 392 (seventy complaints by mid-2007 yet only two complaints were admitted, namely allegations of torture in US military prison in Germany and allegations of human rights abuses in eastern Democratic Republic of Congo).

176 K Gallagher, 'Universal Jurisdiction in Practice: Efforts to Hold Donald Rumsfeld and Other High Level United States Officials Accountable for Torture' (2009) 7 *Journal of International Criminal Justice* 1087 and A Fischer-Lescano 'Torture in Abu Ghraib' (2005) 6(3) *German Law Journal* 689.

177 *Center for Constitutional Rights et al. v. Donald Rumsfeld et al.* (11 February 2005) (2006) 45 *International Legal Materials* 119, 120. See Gallagher (n 148) 1105 (decision allowed Rumsfeld to attend a Security Conference in Munich as planned).

178 ibid.

179 ibid (argued that universal jurisdiction is subsidiary to that of the territorial or national jurisdictions and only acts when the latter are unwilling or unable to prosecute).

180 ibid.

181 ibid 121.

182 ibid.

183 ibid 120.

184 ibid 121. Note s153(f)(2)(2) allows the Federal Prosecutor to dispense with proceedings where extradition is permissible and intended.

had 'unlimited access to a suspect' and therefore, a German request for extradition was unnecessary.[185] The complainants submitted a petition for judicial review that would have compelled the Federal Prosecutor to initiate an investigation. However, the petition was rejected by the Stuttgart Court of Appeal.[186]

The Federal Prosecutor's position remained unchanged towards subsequent complaints against Donald Rumsfeld regarding Guantánamo[187] and against the Uzbek Interior Minister regarding the 'Andijan Massacre' and other alleged acts of torture.[188] In the *Guantánamo* complaint, the Federal Prosecutor re-emphasized the necessity of a close connection with Germany in the interpretation of anticipated presence and in a sense, re-introduced the legitimizing link. In the end, the Prosecutor referred to a balancing test between individual criminal responsibility that militates in favour of prosecution and a need to prevent 'forum shopping' that forces investigating authorities into 'complicated but ultimately unsuccessful investigations'.[189] When striking this balance, he evidently considered the dismissal of the complaint as reasonable in the circumstances based on what he read as the difficulties in gaining legal assistance from the territorial state, the inability to execute enforcement measures on the territory of another state and the purpose of s153(f) in preventing 'overburdening through inexpedient investigations'.[190] From a moralist position, this sidestepped any assessment of the willingness of US authorities to investigate the complaint domestically.[191] This more concrete formalist's position was mirrored in France where prosecuting authorities adopted Fox and Gaeta's interpretation of the *Arrest Warrant*'s third scenario and dismissed a complaint against Rumsfeld because functional immunity must be applied irrespective of the nature of the crimes.[192]

Such outcomes were set against a context of the earlier Belgian Parliament's retreat in a situation of diplomatic embarrassment with powerful states and the contemporary vocal protests of the African Union against what was seen as Western hegemony and neo-imperialism. This seemed to create a perfect storm with a domino or contagion effect that led the two states at the centre of the triumphant *Pinochet III* proceedings to move into a retreat. In this sense, the formalist's hegemonic control seemed assured, yet to the moralist counter-hegemonic position, it looked like the triumph of politics over law. The Spanish and UK amendments law were prompted more directly by prosecuting authorities being compelled to execute arrest warrants over allegations pertaining to

185 ibid.

186 *AH Mahawis Derweesch et al. v Rumsfeld et al.*, Oberlandesgericht, 13 September 2005, para 2(b) (use of prosecutor's discretion is justified to avoid 'limitless . . . doubtful extension' of German jurisdiction).

187 *Re Rumsfeld et al.*, Prosecutor General, Federal Supreme Court (5 April 2007), Part B (2)(a) and (b).

188 See S Zappalà 'The German Federal Prosecutor's Decision not to Prosecute a Former Uzbek Minister: Missed Opportunity or Prosecutorial Wisdom?' (2005) 4 *Journal of International Criminal Justice* 602.

189 *Re Rumsfeld* (n 187) 2(a).

190 ibid.

191 Ryngaert (n 175) 395.

192 Gallagher (n 176) 1110 *et passim*.

the Rwandan and Israeli–Palestinian conflicts respectively. In 2008, the Spanish courts considered complaints against incumbent Rwandan President Kagame and other Rwandan government officials. They decided to dismiss the complaint against Kagame based on personal immunity, yet maintained their investigation of other officials, implicitly following the *Re Sharon* model.[193] This led to a formidable rebuke from the Rwandan government and the African Union.[194] In the UK, there were high-profile arrest warrants issued against Israeli Defence Forces Commander General Almog[195] and the former Israeli Minister for Foreign Affairs Tzipi Livni[196] that meant neither disembarked from their flight on landing in the United Kingdom and returned immediately to Israel. This led to a call within the British Parliament to address the situation and avoid visitors being prevented from entering the UK 'by some technical aberration'.[197]

In 2009, the Spanish Parliament passed an amendment to the Organic Law on Judicial Power that restricted extraterritorial jurisdiction over crimes against international law to passive personality jurisdiction or universal jurisdiction if the alleged perpetrators are present in Spain.[198] This meant that for any subsequent civil party complaints, the Constitutional Court's approval of investigation *in absentia* was overruled. However, the *Guatemalan Generals* case and the *Tibet* case continued irrespective of the lack of presence of the accused in Spain because the amendment law did not apply retrospectively to prior investigations.[199] The United Kingdom amended its laws on the capacity of a private citizen to commence a prosecution by applying to a magistrates' court for an arrest warrant.[200]

193 Commentator 'The Spanish Indictment of High-ranking Rwandan Officials' (2008) 6 *Journal of International Criminal Justice* 1003 and *Sala et al. v. Kabarebe and ors* ILDC 1198 (ES 2008), paras 4 and 5. Note also the opening of investigations into General Franco-era crimes, P Burbridge 'Waking the Dead of the Spanish Civil War: Judge Baltasar Garzon and the Spanish Law of Historical Memory' (2011) 9 *Journal of International Criminal Justice* 753, 760.

194 ibid. See also Allafrica 'President Kagame Blasts "arrogance" of Spanish Judge', Allafrica.com (2 April 2008): URL: http://allafrica.com/stories/200804030058.html and African Union 'Decision on the Report of the Commission on the Abuse of the Principle of Universal Jurisdiction', UN Doc. Assembly/AU/14 (XI) (19 October 2008).

195 *The Guardian* 'Israeli evades arrest' (12 September 2005).

196 *The Guardian* 'British Court issued Gaza arrest warrant for former Israeli Minister' (14 December 2009) and *The Guardian* 'Israeli Minister Moshe Ya'alon turned down UK visit', (14 December 2009).

197 *Hansard* 'Foreign Affairs and Defence' Vol 510 (26 May 2010) (M Rifkind).

198 Amended article 23(4) states that Spanish courts have cognizance over the offence where 'the alleged perpetrators are found in Spain or there are victims of Spanish nationality or there is an important connecting link with Spain' and that another jurisdiction or an international criminal court has not initiated investigative proceedings and effective prosecution of those offences. See *Boletín Oficial Del Estado*, No. 266 (4 November 2009).

199 Note that the Cavallo trial was annulled in 2008 after an extradition request from Argentina, combined with Mexican consent to Cavallo's re-extradition to a third state. See *Cavallo Case*, Supreme Court Criminal Division (18 July 2007). Note also Weill's discussion of the Gaza case, S Weill 'The Targeted Killing of Salah Shehadeh' (2009) 7 *International Criminal Justice* 617.

200 Article 6(1) of the Prosecution of Offences Act 1985 states 'any person' may institute 'any criminal proceedings or conducting any criminal proceedings to which the Director's duty to take over the conduct of proceedings does not apply'.

Section 153(1) of the Police Reform and Social Responsibility Act 2011 imposed a restriction on the power of a magistrate to issue arrest warrants, arising from private prosecutions, for certain qualifying offences unless the consent of the Director of Public Prosecutions is obtained.[201] This meant that the former Israeli Foreign Minister Tzipi Livni was able to disembark on her next trip in 2011.[202]

The formalist hegemonic control also appeared to influence incorporation acts of the Rome Statute of the International Criminal Court. In regards to instances where jurisdiction without any other legal nexus has been asserted; these incorporation acts generally only establish jurisdiction over a situation where the alleged offender is present on the state's territory.[203] It can also be seen in the African Union's decision to commission an examination of the 'abuse' of universal jurisdiction. The Report of the Commission issued a more concrete, less normative position, comparable to the *Pinochet III* dissent, that rejected the re-described *Eichmann* narrative and retreated from the idea of jurisdiction *in absentia* and non-application of immunities before foreign courts in circumstances of crimes against international law.[204]

The struggle between criminal accountability and diplomacy led to an attempt to reconcile the competing positions and come to some form of compromise. The AU-EU Report on Universal Jurisdiction sets out the competing positions of both organizations and tries to reconcile the competing margins. Yet the outcome seems uncomfortable. The AU stressed how European indictments give a perception of 'abuse' as they appear 'politically selective' while the EU stressed its advocacy for ending impunity yet simultaneously qualifying the practice of national courts as the exception rather than the rule.[205] The EU position was being forced to recognize the AU's counter-point and therefore, play down the extent of its practice to avoid the perception of merely being politically motivated. At the same time, the AU's position was compelled to acknowledge the EU's counter-point and recognize some measure of validity of universal jurisdiction practice, especially

201 Section 153(1) of the 2011 Act amended section 1(4) of the Magistrates' Courts Act 1980 (qualifying offences included piracy, grave breaches, torture and hostage-taking).

202 *The Guardian* 'Former Israeli Minister Tzipi Livni to visit UK after change in arrest law', (4 October 2011) and *The Guardian* 'Consent refused for Tzipi Livni UK arrest warrant' (6 October 2011). The British Foreign Office deemed both visits as special missions in order to invoke personal immunity. See Akande and Shah (n 7) 815.

203 Note assessment in A Zahar and G Sluiter, *International Criminal Law* (Oxford: Oxford University Press, 2008) 501. For example, see article 2(a) of the Netherlands International Crimes Act 2003 ('if the suspect is present in the Netherlands').

204 African Union 'Progress Report of Commission on Abuse of UJ', Doc. EX.CL/540(XVI) (January 2010) (not justified on the nature of the crime but on 'international rule-making', the distinction between universal jurisdiction and *aut dedere aut judicare* in treaty law, continued application of immunities of state officials based on *Arrest Warrant* and invalidity of jurisdiction *in absentia*). See also 'Decision', Doc. EX.CL/731(XXI) (July 2012). See M Kmak 'The Scope and Application of the Principle of Universal Jurisdiction' (*Erik Castrén Research Reports Helsinki* 2011) 71–4.

205 See Report of AU-EU Technical Ad-hoc Expert Group on the Principle of Universal Jurisdiction (15 April 2009), paras 34, 40 and Part V (Recommendations).

when it facilitates the surrender of suspects and, in some instances, trials such as *Butare 4*.[206] Similarly, in the UN Secretary General's Reports on Universal Jurisdiction and the General Assembly debates, states oscillated between moralist and formalist positions that we have observed in adjudication. There is an evident dominance of the 'avoiding abuse' concern, yet there also appears to be a dominant move towards presupposing universal jurisdiction applies to war crimes, crimes against humanity and genocide.[207]

6 Another *Pinochet III*?

In September 2005, a Belgian investigating magistrate issued an arrest warrant *in absentia* against Hissène Habré.[208] However, the Senegalese Appeals Court had ruled that the extradition request could not be acceded to because functional immunity applied.[209] The Appeal Court adopted the Fox-Gaeta interpretation of the *Arrest Warrant*'s *obiter* that was also subsequently adopted by the French courts in *Rumsfeld*. Senegal then turned to the African Union, which established a Committee of Eminent African Jurists that recommended in effect regional mechanisms, including prosecution by Senegal or an ad hoc solution.[210] The African Union decided that Senegal should prosecute Habré on behalf of Africa and in response, Senegal amended its law in 2007 to establish universal jurisdiction over war crimes, crimes against humanity and genocide.[211] However, there was no effort by prosecuting authorities to investigate the complaints against Habré and there continued to be repeated requests for extradition from a Belgian investigating magistrate. In turn, Habré petitioned the Court of Justice of the Economic Community of West African States that his right to fair trial would be violated by applying Senegalese law retroactively.

206 ibid (need for presence 'within their custody or territory' unless they decide to extradite, priority to the territorial/national jurisdictions based on the legal tests of willingness and ability and accord with all immunities). See also J Geneuss 'Fostering a Better Understanding of Universal Jurisdiction: A Comment on the AU-EU Report on the Principle of Universal Jurisdiction' (2009) 7 *Journal of International Criminal* Justice 945.

207 UN Secretary General Ban Ki-Moon, Reports on 'The scope and application of the principle of Universal Jurisdiction': UN Doc A/65/181(29 July 2010) and UN Doc. A/67/116 (28 June 2012). Agenda Item 84: 'The Scope and Application of the Principle of Universal Jurisdiction' (17 October 2012) UN Doc. A/C.6/67/SR.12 and (18 October 2012) UN Doc. A/C.6/67/SR.13. Note also the International Law Commission 'Second Report on Immunity of State Officials from Foreign Criminal Jurisdiction', UN Doc. A/CN.4/631 (10 June 2010) and International Law Commission 'Fourth Report on the Obligation to Extradite or Prosecute (*aut dedere aut judicare*)', UN Doc. A/CN.4/648 (31 May 2011).

208 *Questions Relating to the Obligation to Prosecute or Extradite (Belgium v Senegal)* (2012) ICJ Rep. 144, para 21.

209 ibid para 22.

210 African Union 'Report of the Committee of Eminent African Jurists on the Case of Hissène Habré', paras 27–33, URL: http://www.africa-union.org.

211 Decision on the Hissène Habré Case and the African Union, 2 August 2006, Assembly/AU/Dec.127(VII) and Article 2 of the *Loi No. 2007–05 du 12 Février 2007*, Journal Officiel de la Republique de Senegal 2384.

The Court agreed and interpreted the African Union decision as anticipating an ad hoc international tribunal rather than a trial before Senegalese domestic courts.[212] Given the inactivity by Senegalese authorities, Belgium applied to the International Court of Justice arguing that Senegal failed to fulfil its treaty obligations under the Torture Convention.

In its judgment, the Court adopted a moralist position (descending-ascending) on the issues of capacity to invoke responsibility and on the content of the obligation to prosecute or extradite (article 5(2)). Yet to avoid appearing too normative, it considered the state's responsibility as obligations *erga omnes partes* and turns to the principle of reasonableness rather than impose a time frame for submitting a case for prosecution. However, the Court adopted a formalist position (ascending-descending) on the issue of non-retroactivity despite its acceptance of torture as a crime against international law and the moral necessity of criminal accountability. Ultimately, the Court's middle position ends up seeming subjective and biased from both a moralist and formalist positions, as indicated by the dissenting opinions.

There are also silences or blind spots within the judgment. The Court focused on treaty law as opposed to addressing the claim of justification for universal jurisdiction over crimes against humanity under custom or whether there is a duty to prosecute or extradite under custom. This is despite Belgium's claim of a duty to prosecute or extradite.[213] Therefore, the Court sidestepped the contentious debates regarding multi-lateral treaty provisions which hinge on whether the treaty provisions are universal jurisdiction and whether they cumulatively give rise to an obligation *aut dedere aut judicare* under customary international law.[214] It is also noteworthy that the Court did not address the issue of functional immunity (albeit this was not requested by the parties). Instead, the Court merely acknowledged the letter of the Chadian government to the Belgian magistrate regarding Habré's immunity. It did not explore if this amounted to a waiver of immunity under international law by Chadian authorities[215] or whether functional immunity was extinguished by virtue of Habré's personal liability under international law, that is, to explore the 'true' meaning of its *Arrest Warrant obiter*. This silence privileges state liberty and deference to state policy, despite conflicting liberties of states which, in turn, ultimately negates law's normativity.

212 *Habré v. Senegal* (2000) Judgment No. ECW/CCJ/JUD/06/10 (18 November 2010).

213 *Obligation to Prosecute or Extradite* (n 208) para 54. Belgium's descending move is counter-attacked by Judge Abraham's ascending move, where he dismissed Belgium's evidence of state consent due to numerical insufficiency and the diversity of laws on the issue of custody. It noted that for certain offences, it was unclear whether states acted out of a sense of custom or on treaty obligations: *Obligation to Prosecute or Extradite* (n 197) (Judge Abraham) para 14.

214 Note division of opinion in MC Bassiouni and EM Wise, *Aut dedere Aut Judicare: The Duty to Extradite or Prosecute in International Law* (Martinus Nijhoff Dordrecht 1995). See also Fourth Report (n 207) paras 74–7.

215 See Gaeta (n 55) 187 (described the Chadian letter as 'puzzling' as the waiver relied on Chadian internal legislation that removed Habré's immunity before Chadian courts).

6.1 Locus standi

As would be expected, the Court unquestionably accepted the *jus cogens* status of the prohibition against torture under customary international law.[216] In support, the Court cites the international condemnation in the Former Yugoslav tribunal case law and the Human Rights Committee's General Comment 24. In this sense, the Court invokes the same 'unthinkability' that Koskenniemi refers to with regard to the crime of genocide; the acceptance of the criminalization *as it is*, without the need for technical argument.[217] Therefore, the Court approached its analysis of state behaviour through its privileging of the ethos of the human rights regime and the desirability of accountability for human rights abuses. It argued that the *jus cogens* norm was demonstrated in the domestic law of almost all states, which had prohibited acts of torture and in an acknowledged condemnation of the international community. This descending move was crucial for the Court's finding that Belgium had the capacity to invoke Senegal's responsibility. Senegal interpreted article 7 through the formalist position that privileged the reciprocity in extradition treaties and therefore, it interpreted the text of article 7 to mean that it can only involve extradition to another state party whose jurisdiction is provided for in article 5(1). This position would deprive Belgium of any *locus standi* if, as Senegal argued, Belgian jurisdiction was not justified on passive personality jurisdiction.[218]

In contrast, the Court emphasized normativity and stressed the significance of the references in the Convention's preamble to the shared values of the international community and the common interest in the repression of the crime of torture. Thus, the Court argued that any state party could invoke the responsibility of another state party because this common interest 'equates to a procedural right of one State party to invoke the responsibility of another. . . .'[219] Rather than the state's own interests, the repression of torture is in the international community's common interest, a position which appeals to a moral naturalism and conjures up the idea of agents acting on behalf of the community (or humanity). In this way, Belgium could invoke responsibility without necessarily having a special interest. This echoed a moralist's position justifying universal jurisdiction; the nature of the crime is the requisite close connection as it is a legal interest of the international community. However, the Court's outcome does not explain how it can bind Senegal by its consent when the latter argued in the opposite.

In her separate opinion, Judge Donoghue submitted that it was not a 'far-fetched' hypothetical as the Convention's obligations would be 'entirely hollow'

216 *Obligation to Prosecute or Extradite* (n 208) para 99.

217 M Koskenniemi 'Faith, Identity and the Killing of the Innocent: International Lawyers and Nuclear Weapons', reprinted in M Koskenniemi *The Politics of International Law* (Hart Publishing Oxford 2011) 213.

218 *Obligation to Prosecute or Extradite* (n 208) (Skotnikov) para 4 (complaint in Belgium involved a Belgian national of Chadian origin, who was not a Belgian national at the time that the offence was committed).

219 ibid para 69.

unless responsibility could be invoked *erga omnes*.[220] In other words, if only states with a 'special' interest could invoke responsibility, it suggests an arbitrary undermining of the normative object of the Convention, because the Convention would be immobilized in situations where a state party was unwilling to prosecute torture committed on its territory by and against its nationals and did not invoke the responsibility of the custodial state.[221] She justified this outcome on state consent and reciprocity. If all states (parties) are bound to prosecute or extradite, then the duty is owed to all. In the end, to avoid appearing too normative, the Court described these obligations as obligations *erga omnes partes* and therefore, every state party could invoke responsibility rather than being obligations owed by states to the whole of the international community.

The descending move was maintained in the Court's interpretation of the content of article 7(1). Here, it stressed that the purpose of these obligations of inquiry and submission to prosecuting authorities are to achieve the object of the Convention in avoiding impunity.[222] Through this lens, it interpreted the text of the provision as obliging states parties to submit the case for prosecution unless the state chooses to extradite.[223] It first considered that the obligation to prosecute is not dependent upon a prior request for extradition of the suspect. Rather if the state party receives a request for extradition, it can relieve itself of its obligation to prosecute by acceding to that request.[224] It then interpreted the state party's discretion to choose as somewhat qualified because it did not consider that the two alternatives are given the same weight.[225] Extradition is an option open to custodial state whereas the submission of the case for prosecution is an international obligation that is binding regardless of an extradition request.[226] This template of obligation to prosecute and an alternative option to extradite is more in keeping with Mikliszanksi's universal right to punish[227] and distinct from the subsidiary jurisdiction as embodied in the 1883 Resolution of Institute of International law.[228] Finally, the Court found that Senegal had breached its article 7(1) obligation because it delayed submitting the case against Habré while it awaited the outcome of the African Union referral and the judgment of Court of Justice of the Economic Community of West African States.[229] The International Court of Justice contended that these developments could not

220 ibid (Donoghue) para 9.

221 ibid para 11.

222 ibid (n 208) para 74.

223 ibid para 94.

224 ibid.

225 ibid para 95.

226 ibid.

227 K Mikliszanski, 'Le systéme de l'universalité du droit de punir et le droit penal subsidiare' (1936) *Revue de science criminelle et de droit pénal comparé*) 331, 338 (primary right of the custodial state and not subsidiary to the territorial jurisdiction, dependent on a prior refusal of an offer to extradite).

228 Institute of International Law (1883–85) 7 *Annuaire de l'Institut de droit international* (Munich Session 1883).

229 *Obligation to Prosecute or Extradite* (n 208) 109.

justify the delay in compliance. As Shah argues, the Court implied that 'primacy ought to be afforded to CAT obligations', which means the human rights regime is hegemonic vis-à-vis regional political engagement.[230]

Skotnikov and Xue produced a formalist counter-point, privileging stability and non-interference, and criticized the particular moral naturalism that was privileged in the Court's ruling on *locus standi* (ascending-descending). Attempting to be more concrete, Skotnikov drew an analogy to other human rights treaties and concluded that there is no precedent for the capacity of a state party to invoke responsibility *erga omnes* solely based on being a treaty party.[231] Instead, the Convention against Torture permitted state parties to deny jurisdiction to the International Court of Justice and Committee against Torture. In this way, the *erga omnes* element of the Convention was optional. He argued that if the state did have a right *erga omnes*, the Convention would not permit any discretion or exceptions to inter-state or International Court of Justice jurisdiction.[232] Therefore, there should be an express provision for invoking responsibility *erga omnes* and this should not be implied into the Convention through its object and purpose.[233] In his view, 'the Convention does not go as far as the Court suggests.'[234] This presupposed to know better what states parties have consented to and it failed to explain how to bind Belgium by consent when the latter argued in the opposite.

In another variant, Xue argued that the Court's interpretation has no precedent as the *Barcelona Traction* case did not indicate the parameters of an *erga omnes* obligation.[235] He made a distinction between the interest of every state in the compliance of treaty parties and the right to invoke responsibility for breach of the treaty in international dispute mechanisms.[236] Rather, if a state sought to invoke responsibility, it had to demonstrate an injury: 'Procedural rules don't diminish *jus cogens* and *jus cogens* do not automatically trump procedural rules.'[237] This rejected the idea of states suffering an injury through the breach of common interests and rather, presupposed the injured state to be the territorial jurisdiction only. On this basis, Xue read the Court's interpretation as going 'beyond the legal framework of the Convention'.[238]

230 S Shah 'Questions Relating to the Obligation to Prosecute or Extradite (*Belgium v Senegal*)' (2013) 13(1) *Human Rights Law Review* 351, 363.

231 *Obligation to Prosecute or Extradite* (n 208) (Skotnikov), para 20 (citing the inter-state petition under the European Convention on Human Rights and the failure of inter-state petitioning under human rights treaties in general).

232 ibid para 15. See also (Dissent of Judge Xue), paras 19–20.

233 ibid para 18.

234 ibid para 16.

235 ibid (Dissent of Judge Xue), para 11. *Barcelona Traction* only discussed the *locus standi* in regards to breach of a bilateral obligation and thus, Xue contended that the Court's judgment misused the *obiter* in *Barcelona Traction*. ibid.

236 ibid para 17.

237 ibid. For a comparable argument structure on immunities of state officials, see Chapter 3, section 2.2.

238 ibid para 39 (contended that the Court cannot pronounce on Senegal's compliance with its obligations if Senegal has decided to prosecute or is considering whether to accede to the extradition request).

6.2 Non-retroactivity

In its submissions, Belgium evoked the *Eichmann* narrative that read administrative atrocities as a singularity ('an extraordinary instance') and consequently, an exception to non-retroactivity was not excessive rather 'it enforces the dictates of elementary justice'.[239] Applying that approach to the Torture Convention, Belgium argued that the procedural obligations could apply to crimes committed before entry into force of the Convention, as the acts were criminal under customary international law at the time of their commission.[240] As we noted in Chapter 4, the majority in *Pinochet III* rejected this interpretation. Nevertheless, Senegal did not contest Belgium's argument[241] and therefore, as Trinidade noted, the Court was not 'formally asked to pronounce itself on this point'.[242] Rather the Court imposed a 'temporal limitation' that, in his view, is not explicitly provided for in the Convention.[243] This can be juxtaposed against the Court's decision not to address any question of Habré's functional immunity, which was an issue that was also not contested by the parties. From a either a moralist or a formalist position, this inconsistency could be accused of being completely arbitrary.

In addressing the issue of non-retroactivity, the Court privileged state consent, yet chose not to simply acknowledge that Belgium's position seemed to be unchallenged by both states. Merely acknowledging an apparent agreement of the parties would appear to negate law's normativity and therefore, the Court analysed the Torture Convention in terms of what is considered a fundamental (agreed) rule in the Law of Treaties.[244] The Court referred to article 28 of the Vienna Convention that precluded a state party from being bound by treaty obligations in relation to facts prior to the treaty's entry into force.[245] The Court assumed that article 28 reflected customary international law even though it did not tender any instances of state behaviour. Based on this ascending move (and the need to interpret treaty obligations restrictively), the Court interpreted the lack of any provision on non-retroactivity as evidence that the principle should continue to apply. Nothing in the Convention 'reveals an intention' to exercise jurisdiction over acts committed prior to the Convention's entry into force '*for that state*'.[246] In support, it

239 *AG v. Eichmann* (n 78) 12.

240 *Obligation to Prosecute or Extradite* (n 208) para 98. See also V Spiga 'Non-retroactivity of Criminal Law: A New Chapter in the Hissène Habré Saga' (2011) 9 *Journal of International Criminal Justice* 5.

241 *Obligation to Prosecute or Extradite* (n 208) para 98.

242 ibid (n 208) (Trinidade) para 160.

243 ibid.

244 ibid (Judgment) para 100.

245 Article 28 states that 'unless different intention, provisions don't bind a party in relation to act or fact which took place . . . before date of entry into force of that treaty with respect to that party.' See Vienna Convention on Law of Treaties (adopted 23 May 1969, entry into force 27 January 1980) 1155 UNTS 331.

246 ibid para 100, emphasis added.

referred to a 1988 Committee against Torture finding which concluded that 'torture for purposes of Convention can only mean torture that occurs subsequent to the entry into force of the Convention.'[247]

From a moralist position, this late 1980s approach seems too concrete and would be seen as ripe for reinterpretation. More problematically, this nod to earlier human rights jurisprudence is re-described further through a consensualism lens. Here, the Court narrowed the Committee's position and restricted the temporal scope of the Convention to the entry into force for each state. Through a formalist lens, this seems to be more in keeping with (probable) state consent. Yet the practical outcome of the Court's position was that proceedings either in Senegal or Belgium could only involve acts committed after 1987 or 1996 respectively. The latter outcome would be seriously problematic for the moralist position, as Habré was ousted from power in 1990 and therefore, extradition to Belgium would be completely futile. In fact, even the Senegalese proceedings would be quite limited.

When the Court addressed the time frame for the state implementing its obligations, the Court followed the Committee against Torture's interpretation in *Habré* and moved to apply a notion of reasonableness. The Court noted the absence of any express provision on a time frame in the Convention. However, rather than being left entirely at the state's discretion, the Court read the Convention's silence to mean that a time frame could be implicitly imposed (descending-ascending). This move privileges the normative project of accountability as conversely, the Court's position would seem to undermine state consent where a state party disagrees. To avoid a sense of arbitrariness, the Court applied an idea of reasonableness, that is, obligations must be performed within a 'reasonable time' in a manner compatible with object and purpose of Convention.[248]

Nevertheless it is possible to read the Court's approach towards non-retroactivity as mere apology. As Trinidade argued, the Court adopted 'voluntarist reasoning [that] focused on the will of states within the confines of the strict and static inter-State dimension'.[249] Trinidade premised his analysis explicitly on the idea that international law preceded the state[250] and argued that universal jurisdiction 'transcends inter-State dimension' because it secures the fundamental interests of the international community.[251] From this view,

247 See *OR, MM and MS v Argentina* (No. 1/1988, 2/1988 and 3/1988) CAT/C/WG/3/DR/1, 2 and 3/1988.

248 *Obligation to Prosecute or Extradite* (n 208) paras 113 and 115. The Court got around the problem of Belgium's ability to invoke the responsibility of Senegal for prosecution of acts prior to entry into force of Convention for Belgium in 1999. It concluded that the issue of non-compliance arose in 2000 when the Senegalese court decision was made, which was after Belgium became a state party.

249 *Obligation to Prosecute or Extradite* (n 208) (Trinidade) para 166 and (Judge Donoghue) para 19.

250 ibid para 177 ('international law itself precedes the inter-State dimension').

251 ibid.

he chastised the Court for ignoring approaches in international criminal law regarding the pleas of non-retroactivity. Here, non-retroactivity becomes a 'moot question' because the crimes are prohibited by customary international law 'at the time of their repeated or systematic commission'.[252] He referred to *jus cogens* as providing an ethical content to international law and evoking the margins of *Eichmann*, there could be 'no limits in time or space' for this 'universalist international law'.[253] As he noted, if the 'inter-State dimension had not been surmounted', the developments of the past few decades would not have taken place and therefore, based on this moral naturalism, Trinidade argued that the procedural obligations are 'not conditioned *ratione temporis* by the date of the alleged acts of torture'.[254]

The Court's move towards a formalist 'middle' looks like a 'return' yet it has pulled far more on its moralist counter-position, recognizing the latter's' 'validity'. This formalist middle ground has continued to be hegemonic in the United Nations Sixth Committee's debates, which elicits competing positions among states that appear incapable of being reconciled. This more dominant tendency towards a formalist position is combined with recognition among many state representatives that universal jurisdiction may be claimed over war crimes, crimes against humanity and genocide.[255] Within state practice, there have been numerous proceedings that follow the *Butare 4*-type model in that the allegations pertain to political conflicts under investigation by international criminal tribunals.[256] In the literature, there was a dominant tendency towards cautioning against the *Eichmann* narrative and reducing the idea of universal jurisdiction to a notion within treaty law or a subsidiary jurisdiction over limited offences.[257] The recent 2016 European Parliament's Report demonstrates this tendency.[258] Of course, there continues to be a

252 ibid paras 165–6.

253 ibid paras 182–3.

254 ibid paras 164–6 (Convention is 'focused on the victimized human beings who stand in need of protection . . . Human conscience stands above the will of States').

255 United Nations General Assembly 'The Scope and Application of the Principle of Universal Jurisdiction (Agenda 86)' URL: http://www.un.org/en/ga/sixth/70/universal_jurisdiction.shtml. See also International Law Commission Report of International Law Commission, UN Doc. A/70/10, 2015, Chapter X, para 243.

256 For instance, HL Trouille 'France, Universal Jurisdiction and Rwandan Génocidaires' (2016) 14(1) *Journal of International Criminal Justice* 195. See also cases involving refugees and migrants R Dicker and G Mattioli-Zeltner 'Syrian refugees help nab suspected war criminals', URL: http://www.politico.eu/article/syrian-refugees-help-nab-suspected-war-criminals/ and *The Guardian* 'Nepalese colonel faces torture trial in UK' (27 February 2015).

257 S Yee 'Universal Jurisdiction: Concept, Logic and Reality', (2011) 10 *Chinese Journal of International Law* 503 and L Reydams 'The Rise and Fall of Universal Jurisdiction' in WA Schabas and N Bernaz (eds) *Routledge Handbook of International Criminal Law* (Routledge New York 2011).

258 DG for External Policies Policy Department 'The Application of Universal Jurisdiction in the Fight Against Impunity' (European Parliament Sub-Committee on Human Rights, 14 March 2016) (that 'no safe haven' model has overtaken 'global enforcer' model).

moralist (middle) counter-point in national court jurisprudence[259] and in the literature,[260] including nostalgia for the *Pinochet III* moment's charisma.[261] The conviction of Habré by the Senegalese Extraordinary African Chambers under Senegal's universal jurisdiction feels to a moralist position like a celebratory return, albeit in a moralist's counter-hegemonic position and without the immediate sensational shock of the Pinochet arrest.[262]

Conclusion

The post-*Arrest Warrant* context pulled back towards the wary concern that feels somewhat familiar in that it repeats the position of some international lawyers who preferred to view the Eichmann Trial as an exceptional case and warned against its reasoning becoming a precedent.[263] It moved away from the feeling of other writers in the 1960s that *Eichmann* was a necessary and justified response to extraordinary circumstances.[264] However, international lawyers did not go so far as to ascribe to Arendt's position that saw the trial as necessary yet woefully inadequate. Rather the *Eichmann* narrative and moralist middle appeared too utopian and therefore, the architecture of accountability needed to be more concrete. Therefore, post-*Arrest Warrant* signalled what was read as a necessary retreat from this so-called 'court of humanity' and the hegemonic control of the moralist position. In this context, the *Butare-4* type cases were read as a reasonable (or uncontroversial) implementation of the international community's fundamental commitment to accountability because those cases in effect involved cooperation

259 For instance, MJ Ventura 'The Duty to Investigate Zimbabwe Crimes Against Humanity (Torture) Allegations' (2015) 13(4) *Journal of International Criminal Justice* 861, *Decision of Swiss Federal Criminal Court* (25 July 2012) para 5.3.5–6 (did not apply personal immunity to serving Defence Minister) and Fundación Internacional Baltasar Garzón 'Informe sobre el estado de la Jurisdicción Universal de España 2016' URL: http://fibgar.org/upload/publicaciones/27/es/informe-sobre-el-estado-de-la-jurisdiccion-universal-en-espana-2016-.pdf.

260 M Langer 'Universal Jurisdiction is not Disappearing: The Shift from "Global Enforcer" to "No Safe Haven" Universal Jurisdiction' (2015) 13 *Journal of International Criminal Justice* 245 and F Lafontaine 'Universal Jurisdiction – the Realistic Utopia' (2012) 10(5) *Journal of International Criminal Justice* 1277.

261 WA Schabas 'The Banality of International Justice' (2013) 11 *Journal of International Criminal Justice* 545.

262 Senegal concluded an agreement with the African Union to establish the 'Extraordinary African Chambers' to prosecute Habré for alleged crimes committed in Chad. In December 2012, Senegal passed the legislation to establish the EAC and proceedings began in February 2013. Under article 2 of the *Statut*, the EAC has a chamber within each level of the Senegalese court system with judges of Senegalese nationality. However, the Assize and Appellate Assize courts will be presided by judges from other African Union member states (article 11). See Shah (n 230) 364, *Statut des Chambres africaines extraordinaires*, URL: http://www.hrw.org/node/113271 and Human Rights Watch 'The Trial of Hissène Habré' URL: https://www.hrw.org/tag/hissene-habre (reporting Habré's conviction on 30 May 2016).

263 D Lasok 'The Eichmann Trial' (1962) 11 *International and Comparative Law Quarterly* 355, 373.

264 H Silving 'In re Eichmann: A Dilemma of Law and Morality' (1961) 55 *American Journal of International Law* 307.

in fulfilling the mandate of international criminal tribunals. Another reasonable notion were cases involving alleged perpetrators within refugee or migrant communities that were unlikely to provoke powerful political or economic threat from the state of nationality of the defendant. However, situations involving civilian and military leadership during past or ongoing conflicts where the state of nationality of the defendant objects to the trial of its nationals were read as entirely different. The *Eichmann* narrative seems to be constructing a threatening situation where 'frivolous' complaints could be investigated and 'show trials' could be conducted. Therefore, a return back towards Eichmann's defence counsel's position seems more preferable in the interests of stability and order between states.

It follows that the *Arrest Warrant* judgment's formalist position on personal immunity and Guillaume's on *in absentia* was an attempt to 'accommodate their moral intuitions with their professional competence'.[265] They sought to secure the normative purpose of immunity of state officials and political independence against the context of the appeal to end impunity (a move from oppressive homogeneity to self-determination). Van den Wyngaert's moralist position invoked the re-described *Eichmann* narrative in her attempt to accommodate moral intuitions, namely the normative purpose of individual criminal responsibility and universal accountability against the context of the appeal to respect the dignity of the state (a move from sovereign egoism to world unity). The Joint Separate Opinion was then the attempt to 'balance' the opposing positions yet privileged the moralist horizon and in this sense, sought to achieve a similar outcome to *Pinochet III*. These multiple interpretations were supported or rejected in the literature and later national court judgments. There was an evident dominant tendency towards a formalist position as in the context, van den Wyngaert's position appeared too utopian and an appeal to a moment that had since passed. Legislative amendments in the key sites of moralist hegemonic control from 2003 appeared to confirm this decline as well as feeling like a natural, inevitable dismantling of an imagined utopia that victims had 'mistakenly' put their faith in. Cases such as *Tibet* and *Rumsfeld* echoed this transformation. When the African Union loudly accused European states of abusing their jurisdiction to conduct another neo-colonialist project in Africa, universal jurisdiction seemed to pose another threat to the credibility of the field. The rhetoric of 'avoiding abuse', priority of territorial jurisdiction and strict interpretation of rights was more appealing.

This formalist hegemonic control has re-described the *Eichmann* narrative in order to privilege the territorial jurisdiction, conceiving universal jurisdiction as subsidiary that interweaves the piracy analogy with an idea of a subsidiary basis of jurisdiction. The latter precondition has been reshaped to describe the triggering situations in a manner similar to the Rome Statute's article 17 conditions of unwillingness and inability.[266] The formalist hegemony has invariably pulled on its counterpoint and moved towards a formalist middle. Increasingly, there is an

265 Koskenniemi (n 64) 159.

266 Although these conditions have some lineage in the debates on the subsidiary basis of jurisdiction as discussed in chapter 2, section 1.1.

unquestioned acceptance of universal jurisdiction over crimes against international law that has overruled the influence of *Javor* and the *Pinochet III* dissents. In the literature, the *Re Sharon* model of distinguishing the situation of personal and functional immunity has found favour and there is a tendency to invoke the idea of the first offer to the territorial jurisdiction to proceed. It also appears that *Pinochet III* returns in regards to treaty law provisions, as evident in the *Obligation to Prosecute or Extradite* case. Therefore, the formalist middle has reshaped the *Eichmann* narrative to involve a narrower set of possibilities, such as, *Butare-4* type cases, a broad concept of nationality or passive personality jurisdiction[267] and obligations arising from treaty law to exercise jurisdiction based on custody of the offender.[268]

References

African Union 'Decision on the Report of the Commission on the Abuse of the Principle of Universal Jurisdiction', UN Doc. Assembly/AU/14 (XI) (19 October 2008).

African Union 'Progress Report of Commission on Abuse of UJ', Doc. EX.CL/540(XVI) (January 2010)

African Union 'Report of the Committee of Eminent African Jurists on the Case of Hissène Habré', paras 27–33, URL: http://www.africa-union.org.

African Union 'Decision on the Abuse of the Principle of Universal Jurisdiction' Assembly/AU/Dec. 292(XV) (25–27 July 2010).

Agamben, G 'The Sovereign Police' in B Massumi (ed) *The Politics of Everyday Fear* (University of Minnesota Press Minneapolis 1993).

Akande, D 'Immunities and the International Criminal Court' (2004) 98 *American Journal of International Law* 407.

Akande, D and Shah, S 'Immunities of State Officials, International Crimes and Foreign Domestic Courts' (2010) 21(4) *European Journal of International Law* 815.

Allafrica 'President Kagame Blasts "arrogance" of Spanish Judge', Allafrica.com (2 April 2008): URL: http://allafrica.com/stories/200804030058.html.

Application to Institute Proceedings, *Case of the Arrest Warrant of 11 April 2000 (. Democratic Republic of Congo v Belgium)* (2002) ICJ Rep No. 121.

Ascensio, H 'Are Spanish Courts Backing Down on Universality? The Supreme Tribunal's Decision in Guatemalan Generals' (2003) 1 *Journal of International Criminal Justice* 690.

Bassiouni, MC 'Universal Jurisdiction for International Crimes: Historical Perspectives and Contemporary Practice' (2001) 42 *Virginia Journal of International Law* 81.

Bassiouni, MC and Wise, EM *Aut dedere Aut Judicare*: *The Duty to Extradite or Prosecute in International Law*, (Martinus Nijhoff Dordrecht 1995).

BBC News, 'Rwandan Genocide: Sweden jails Stanislas Mbanenande' (23 June 2013) URL: http://www.bbc.co.uk/news/world-africa-22992242

267 See *BBC News* 'Rwandan Genocide: Sweden jails Stanislas Mbanenande' (23 June 2013) URL: http://www.bbc.co.uk/news/world-africa-22992242 and FIDH 'Paul Barril indicated for complicity in Rwandan genocide', URL: http://www.fidh.org/paul-barril-indicted-for-complicity-in-rwandan-genocide-13567.

268 *Obligation to Prosecute or Extradite* (n 197). In August 2012, See also *BBC News* 'Nepalese army officer denies torture' (28 June 2013) URL: http://www.bbc.co.uk/news/uk-23103018. Note Spain's 2014 Amendment Law, see Boletín Oficial Del Estado No.157-1 (24 January 2014).

BBC News 'Nepalese army officer denies torture' (28 June 2013) URL: http://www.bbc.co.uk/news/uk-23103018.

Burbridge, P 'Waking the Dead of the Spanish Civil War: Judge Baltasar Garzon and the Spanish Law of Historical Memory' (2011) 9 *Journal of International Criminal Justice* 753.

Burt, JM 'Guatemalan Grave Crimes Cases Delayed' *International Justice Monitor* (13 July 2016), URL: http://www.ijmonitor.org/2016/07/guatemala-grave-crimes-cases-delayed.

Campbell, D 'Time is Broken: The Return of the Past in the Response to September 11' (2001) 5(4) *Theory and Event.*

Cassese, A 'When may Senior State Officials be Tried for International Crimes? Some Comments on the Congo v Belgium Case' (2002) *European Journal of International Law* 853.

Chinedu, O Okafor 'Globalism, Memory and 9/11: A Critical Third World Perspective' in F Johns et al *Events: The Force of International Law* (Routledge London 2011).

Commentator 'The Spanish Indictment of High-ranking Rwandan Officials' (2008) 6 *Journal of International Criminal Justice* 1003.

Counter-Memorial of Belgium, Case of the Arrest Warrant of 11 April 2000 (Democratic Republic of Congo v Belgium) (2002) ICJ Rep No. 121.

DG for External Policies Policy Department 'The Application of Universal Jurisdiction in the Fight Against Impunity' (European Parliament Sub-Committee on Human Rights, 14 March 2016).

Dicker, R and Mattioli-Zeltner, G 'Syrian refugees help nab suspected war criminals', URL: http://www.politico.eu/article/syrian-refugees-help-nab-suspected-war-criminals/.

EL Zeidy, M 'Universal Jurisdiction in Absentia: Is it a Legal Valid Option', (2003) 37 *International Lawyer* 835.

FIDH 'Paul Barril Indicted for Complicity in Rwandan Genocide', URL: http://www.fidh.org/paul-barril-indicted-for-complicity-in-rwandan-genocide-13567.

Fischer-Lescano, A 'Torture in Abu Ghraib' (2005) 6(3) *German Law Journal* 689.

Fox, H and Webb, P *The Law of State Immunity* (3rd edn Oxford University Press Oxford 2013).

Fundación Internacional Baltasar Garzón 'Informe sobre el estado de la Jurisdicción Universal de España 2016' URL: http://fibgar.org/upload/publicaciones/27/es/informe-sobre-el-estado-de-la-jurisdiccion-universal-en-espana-2016-.pdf

Gaeta, P 'Ratione Materiar Immunities of Former Heads of State and International Crimes: The Hissène Habre Case' (2003) 1 *Journal of International Criminal Justice* 186.

Gallagher, K 'Universal Jurisdiction in Practice: Efforts to Hold Donald Rumsfeld and Other High Level United States Officials Accountable for Torture' (2009) 7 *Journal of International Criminal Justice* 1087.

Geneuss, J 'Fostering a Better Understanding of Universal Jurisdiction: A Comment on the AU-EU Report on the Principle of Universal Jurisdiction' (2009) 7 *Journal of International Criminal Justice* 945.

Hansard 'Foreign Affairs and Defence' Vol 510 (26 May 2010) (M Rifkind).

Hardt, M and Negri, A *Empire* (Harvard University Press Cambridge 2000).

Harrington, J 'The Obligation to "Extradite or Prosecute" is not an Obligation to "Prosecute or Extradite" (EJIL:Talk! 23 February 2009), URL: http://www.ejiltalk.org/the-obligation-to-extradite-or-prosecute-is-not-an-obligation-to-prosecute-or-extradite/.

Henkin, L *International Law: Politics and Values* (M Nijhoff Dordrecht 1995).

Human Rights Watch 'The Trial of Hissène Habré' URL: https://www.hrw.org/tag/hissene-habre.

Institute of International Law (1883–85) 7 *Annuaire de l'Institut de droit international* (Munich Session 1883).

Institute of International Law 'Resolution on Universal Criminal Jurisdiction with Regard to the Crime of Genocide, Crimes against Humanity and War Crimes' (Krakow 2005).

International Law Commission 'Report of International Law Commission' UN Doc. A/70/10, 2015, Chapter X.

International Law Commission 'Second Report on Immunity of State Officials from Foreign Criminal Jurisdiction', UN Doc. A/CN.4/631 (10 June 2010).

International Law Commission 'Fourth Report on the Obligation to Extradite or Prosecute (*aut dedere aut judicare*)' UN Doc. A/CN.4/648 (31 May 2011).

Johns, F 'The Torture Memos' in F Johns, R Joyce and S Pahuja *Events: The Force of International Law* (Routledge London 2011).

Kendall, S 'Critical Orientations: A Critique of International Criminal Court Practice' in C Schwoebel (ed) *Critical Approaches to International Criminal Law: An Introduction* (Routledge London 2014).

Kiely, R *Empire in the Age of Globalisation: US Hegemony and Neoliberal Disorder* (Pluto Press London 2005).

Kmak, M 'The Scope and Application of the Principle of Universal Jurisdiction' (*Erik Castrén Research Reports Helsinki* 2011).

Koskenniemi, M *From Apology to Utopia: The Structure of the International Legal Argument* (Cambridge University Press Cambridge 2005).

Koskenniemi, M 'International Law and Hegemony: A Reconfiguration' (2004) 17 *Cambridge Review of International Affairs* 197.

Koskenniemi, M 'The Lady Doth Protest too Much: Kosovo and the Turn to Ethics in International Law' (2002) 65 *Modern Law Review* 159.

Koskenniemi, M 'Faith, Identity and the Killing of the Innocent: International Lawyers and Nuclear Weapons', reprinted in M Koskenniemi *The Politics of International Law* (Hart Publishing Oxford 2011) 213.

Koskenniemi, M 'International Justice: Between Impunity and Show Trial' (SOAS, University of London, 4 January 2013), URL: https://www.youtube.com/watch?v=2QTBdPyQtEw.

Kress, C 'Universal Jurisdiction over International Crimes and the *Institut de droit International*' (2006) 4 *Journal of International Criminal Justice* 561.

Krever, T 'Dispensing Global Justice' (2014) 85 *New Left Review* 67.

Lafontaine, F 'Universal Jurisdiction: The Realistic Utopia' (2012) 10(5) *Journal of International Criminal Justice* 1277.

Langer, M 'Universal Jurisdiction Is not Disappearing: The Shift from "Global Enforcer" to "No Safe Haven" Universal Jurisdiction' (2015) 13 *Journal of International Criminal Justice* 245.

Lasok D 'The Eichmann Trial' (1962) 11 *International and Comparative Law Quarterly* 355.

Macedo (ed) *Universal Jurisdiction: National Courts and the Prosecution of Serious Crimes Under International Law* (Pennsylvania University of Pennsylvania Press 2003).

Magliveras, KD and GJ Nald 'The International Criminal Court's Involvement with Africa: Evaluation of a Fractious Relationship' (2013) 82 *Nordic Journal of International Law* 417.

Marks, SP 'The Hisséne Habré Case: The Law and Politics of Universal Jurisdiction' in S Macedo (ed) *Universal Jurisdiction: National Courts and the Prosecution of Serious Crimes Under International Law* (University of Pennsylvania Press Philadelphia 2003).

Mikliszanski, K 'Le systéme de l'universalité du droit de punir et le droit penal subsidiare' (1936) *Revue de science criminelle et de droit pénal comparé*) 331.

Mueller, SD 'Kenya and the International Criminal Court (ICC): Politics, the Election and the Law' (2014) 8(1) *Journal of Eastern African Studies* 25.

O'Keefe, R 'Universal Jurisdiction: Clarifying the Basic Concept' (2004) 2 *Journal of International Criminal Justice* 735.

Orakhelashvili, A *Peremptory Norms in International Law* (Oxford University Press Oxford 2006).

Poels, A 'Universal Jurisdiction in Absentia', (2005) 23(1) *Netherlands Quarterly of Human Rights* 64.

Rabinovitch, R 'Universal Jurisdiction *in absentia*' (2004–05) 18 *Fordham International Law Journal* 500.

Randall, K 'Universal Jurisdiction in International Law' (1988) 66 *Texas Law Review* 785.

Ratner, SR 'Belgium's War Crimes Statute: A Post-mortem' (2003) 97 *American Journal of International Law* 888.

Reydams, L 'Belgium Reneges on Universality: The 5 August 2003 Act on Grave Breaches of International Humanitarian Law' (2003) 1 *Journal of International Criminal Justice* 679.

Reydams, L 'The Rise and Fall of Universal Jurisdiction' in WA Schabas and N Bernaz (eds) *Routledge Handbook of International Criminal Law* (Routledge New York 2011).

Roht-Arriaza *The Pinochet Effect: Transitional Justice in the Age of Human Rights* (University of Pennsylvania Press Philadelphia 2006).

Ryngaert, C 'Universal Jurisdiction over Violations of International Humanitarian Law in Germany' (2008) 47 *Military law and Law of War Review* 377.

Satzger, H 'German Criminal Law and the Rome Statute: A Critical Analysis of the New German Code of Crimes Against International Law' (2002) 2 *International Criminal Law Review* 261.

Schabas, WA 'Complementarity in Practice: Uncomplimentary Thoughts' (2008) *Criminal Law Forum* 19.

Schabas, WA 'The Banality of International Justice' (2013) 11 *Journal of International Criminal Justice* 545.

Schwoebel, C 'The Market and Marketing Culture of International Criminal Law' in C Schwoebel (ed) *Critical Approaches to International Criminal Law: An Introduction* (Routledge London 2014).

Shah, S 'Questions Relating to the Obligation to Prosecute or Extradite (*Belgium v Senegal*)' (2013) 13(1) *Human Rights Law Review* 351.

Shaw, MN *International Law* (6th edn Cambridge University Press Cambridge 2008).

Silving, H 'In re Eichmann: A Dilemma of Law and Morality' (1961) 55 *American Journal of International law* 307.

Simpson, G *Law, War and Crime* (Polity Press Cambridge 2007)

Slaughter, A 'Defining the Limits: Universal Jurisdiction and National Courts' in S Macedo (ed) *Universal Jurisdiction: National Courts and the Prosecution of Serious Crimes Under International Law* (University of Pennsylvania Press Philadelphia 2004).

Spiga, V 'Non-retroactivity of Criminal Law: a New Chapter in the Hissène Habré Saga' (2011) 9 *Journal of International Criminal Justice* 5.

Strawsom, J 'Provoking International Law: War and Regime Change in Iraq' in F Johns et al *Events: The Force of International Law* (Routledge, London: 2011).

Tallgren, I 'The Sense and Sensibility of International Criminal Law (2002) 13(3) *European Journal of International* Law 561.

The Guardian 'Israeli evades arrest' (12 September 2005).
The Guardian 'British Court issued Gaza arrest warrant for former Israeli Minister' (14 December 2009).
The Guardian 'Israeli Minister Moshe Ya'alon turned down UK visit' (14 December 2009).
The Guardian 'Former Israeli Minister Tzipi Livni to visit UK after change in arrest law' (4 October 2011).
The Guardian 'Consent refused for Tzipi Livni UK arrest warrant' (6 October 2011).
The Guardian 'Rios Montt genocide case collapses' (London May 21 2013).
The Guardian 'Nepalese colonel faces torture trial in UK' (27 February 2015).
Tomuschat, C 'Issues of Universal Jurisdiction in the Scilingo Case' (2005) 3 *Journal of International Criminal Justice* 1074.
Trouille, HL 'France, Universal Jurisdiction and Rwandan Génocidaires' (2016) 14(1) *Journal of International Criminal Justice* 195.
United Nations General Assembly 'The Scope and Application of the Principle of Universal Jurisdiction (Agenda 86)' URL: http://www.un.org/en/ga/sixth/70/universal_jurisdiction.shtml.
UN Secretary General Ban Ki-Moon, Reports on 'The Scope and Application of the Principle of Universal Jurisdiction': UN Doc A/65/181(29 July 2010) and UN Doc. A/67/116 (28 June 2012).
United Nations Sixth Committee 'Agenda Item 84: 'The Scope and Application of the Principle of Universal Jurisdiction' (17 October 2012) UN Doc. A/C.6/67/SR.12 (17 October 2012) and UN Doc. A/C.6/67/SR.13 (18 October 2012)
Van Alebeek, R *Immunity of States and their Officials in International Human Rights Law and International Criminal Law* (Oxford University Press Oxford 2008).
Ventura, MJ 'The Duty to Investigate Zimbabwe Crimes Against Humanity (Torture) Allegations' (2015) 13(4) *Journal of International Criminal Justice* 861.
Watts, A 'The Legal Position in International Law of Heads of States, Heads of Governments and Foreign Ministers' (1994-I) 247 *Recueil des Cours* 13.
Wehle, C and Jessberger, F 'International Criminal Justice is Coming Home: The New German Code of Crimes against International Law' (2002) 13 *Criminal Law Forum* 191.
Weill, S 'The Targeted Killing of Salah Shehadeh' (2009) 7 International Criminal Justice 617.
Winants, A 'The Yerodia Ruling of the International Court of Justice and the 1993/1999 Belgian Law on Universal Jurisdiction' (2003) 16 *Leiden Journal of International Law* 49.
Wouters, J and De Smet, L 'The ICJ's Judgment in the *Case Concerning the Arrest Warrant of 11 April 2000*: Some critical observations' (2003) 16(2) *Leiden Journal of International Law* 253.
Wright, Q 'War Criminals' (1945) 39 *American Journal of International Law* 257.
Yee, S 'Universal Jurisdiction: Concept, Logic and Reality', (2011) 10 *Chinese Journal of International Law* 503.
Zahar, A and Sluiter, G *International Criminal Law* (Oxford: Oxford University Press, 2008).
Zappalà, S 'The German Federal Prosecutor's Decision not to Prosecute a Former Uzbek Minister: Missed Opportunity or Prosecutorial Wisdom?' (2005) 4 *Journal of International Criminal Justice* 602.

Conclusion

In the debate surrounding the fight against impunity, the battle over the 'validity' of the *Eichmann* narrative brought the international law profession face to face with the full implication of constructing their utopia of global justice. In the 1990s, the *Eichmann* narrative fitted neatly within the field of international criminal law's move to supplant the dominant position of transitional justice in addressing post-conflict justice. Within this move, the *Eichmann* narrative was viewed as building an indispensable complement to international tribunals (from a moralist position). This, in effect, allowed international tribunals to self-identify as the 'real' sites of the field of international criminal justice yet simultaneously avoid any potential for their credibility being eroded, given their incapacity to prosecute all those accused or even secure their custody. When Pinochet was placed under arrest in 1998, it felt like a transformative moment and came to be seen as a powerful reaffirmation of a moralist horizon. This charisma and euphoria further galvanized a momentum that did not feel hampered by the counter-hegemonic positions within the dissents in *Pinochet III* and in some of the literature.

Yet there was already an evident wariness over the full implication of this moralist horizon among international lawyers adopting a more moralist position. At the end of the 1990s, the literature included references to 'avoiding abuse' and 'jurisdictional imperialism', alongside an acceptance of the validity of universal jurisdiction over crimes against international law.[1] Belgium and Spain then became the sites of struggle over the construction of an imagined utopia or court of humanity in which a court never adjourns from applying the laws of humanity. However, the complaints involved some of the most intractable political conflicts, past and present, and states, in particular, protested their outrage at the attempt to try senior civilian and military officials. From a formalist position, criminal investigations into political conflicts in foreign states looked more like politically motivated trials, particularly when they were prompted through a civil party complaint by victims and their representatives.

Among international lawyers, the 'bell tolling' for the moralist's horizon seemed a 'natural' and inevitable consequence of unfolding events. Yet this move

1 International Law Association 'Final Report on the Exercise of Universal Jurisdiction of Gross Human Rights Offences' (London 2000) 19–20.

in the debate was a turn away from the *Eichmann* narrative that was steeped in the moral naturalism of the field's project, which, for the Israeli courts, was considered deeply significant. This universal moral consensus involved an appeal to the idea that the crimes perpetrated against Jewish victims were crimes against 'humanity', not merely against the interests of a single state, and therefore, Israeli courts represented humanity in prosecuting Eichmann. Nevertheless, among international lawyers, this move was not seen as jeopardizing that utopian project so long as the project remained confined to international institutions, even if those institutions lacked global reach. As Simpson puts it, some international lawyers view the Eichmann trial as 'a hard case making bad law' and instead, the future lies with 'international criminal courts and the suppression of the provincialism of domestic courts'.[2] In this sense, the series of moves in the debate surrounding universal jurisdiction confirmed what everyone already believed; that the field should be removed from 'prejudices of national criminal justice systems' and instead, construct 'a unified system of transnational justice' embodied in international institutions.[3]

Given this wary suspicion of universal jurisdiction as being too political, the debate could not act as some sort of lessons learned for international institutions even though many of the national courts' investigations were a microcosm of what could happen if a criminal investigation pertained to foreign leadership that objected to the trial. It was, after all, simply a contentious form of localized justice and therefore, the diplomatic dilemmas were unique to this type of inter-state interaction. Nevertheless, moving towards a formalist hegemonic control in the *Arrest Warrant* judgment and its aftermath seemed to affirm a 'pattern of particularization' from the Nuremberg model, where the jurisdictional reach seemed beyond the Great Powers and the vast majority of states after the post-war 1940s trials of Nazi defendants. In this sense, personal liability (despite its supposed universal essence) 'was to remain, for some time, highly attenuated'.[4] We see this pattern in the move from the margins of the moralist horizon in the Belgian and Spanish *Pinochet* cases, to a moralist middle in *Pinochet III* and finally in a shift towards a formalist hegemonic control that is set against the context of indictments against powerful states, alongside the field's renewalist spirit and agony over international law in the post-9/11 environment.

Of course, this shift towards a formalist hegemonic control cannot avoid accusations of being mere politics. The formalist position is similarly compelled to recognize the 'validity' of the moralist counter-point. Therefore, as we observed, there has been a tendency to move towards a (formalist) middle in the post-*Arrest Warrant* practice. This formalist middle retains a sense that universal jurisdiction over crimes under customary international law is justified even though its justification pulled from moral naturalism of the nature of the crimes that the formalist

2 G Simpson *Law, War and Crime: War Crimes, Trials and the Reinvention of International Law* (Polity Press 2007) 34.

3 ibid 50–51.

4 ibid

position in other ways excludes. Its outcome seems self-contradictory to a moralist position in that individual criminal responsibility applies universally (laws of humanity) yet the ability to invoke such responsibility in national courts is believed to depend exclusively on consent of state of nationality of the defendant (no court of humanity). In this sense, the formalist middle cancels out that same political project (drawn from moral naturalism) through privileging a competing political project of stability and non-interference, which is also a normative position. We similarly observed how a moralist position (and its middle) appeared to be self-contradictory to a formalist position because criminal accountability trumped diplomacy yet apparently reflected state consent. The protests by various states against exercises of universal jurisdiction looked to a formalist position like confirmation of its suspicion that, rather than reflecting state consent, the practice was utopian and a particular politics masqueraded as law. To a moralist position, the protests looked more like an attempt to shield alleged perpetrators from facing justice.

Overall, the movement of positions within the debate reflects an oscillation in the minds of every international lawyer, an unavoidable internal split that means an endless swinging back and forth between moralist and formalist logics. It is a sensibility that the court of humanity is necessary because the 'demand for justice' cannot be 'ignored out of deference for considerations of temporality and retroactivity'.[5] It is also anguish that in the face of mass atrocities, an international rule of law could be always straitjacketed under state consent and could prove inadequate. It is the repetition of the Nuremberg model that 'resembles . . . its deference to sovereignty, and hegemony too'.[6] We desire the demand for justice (moralist) and simultaneously we believe the 'court of humanity' idea is impossible, even madness (formalist). This reflects what Koskenniemi describes as 'taking up Immanuel Kant's project for perpetual peace . . . and that the direction is towards some form of world unity beyond formal statehood'. Yet in practice, we use 'sovereignty to limit sovereignty'.[7]

In the end, the debate's transformation towards a formalist middle has closed certain avenues that results in a highly selective practice, which naturalizes and excludes 'from the political battle' some acts from jurisdiction of tribunals as opposed to others.[8] The current dominant position within legal practice is to read universal jurisdiction over crimes against international law as involving trials that complement the work of the international criminal tribunals and/or alleged perpetrators within refugee and asylum-seeker communities. This move to what some call a 'no safe haven' model obscures the structural forces (political and economic) that are in play in modern conflicts, including neoliberal policies and the

5 H Arendt *Eichmann in Jerusalem: Report on the Banality of Evil* (Penguin Books New York 2006) 254.

6 Simpson (n 2) 35.

7 M Koskenniemi 'What Use for Sovereignty Today? (2011) 1(1) *Asian Journal of International Law* 61, 62.

8 I Tallgren 'The Sense and Sensibility of International Criminal Law (2002) 13(3) *European Journal of International Law* 561, 594–5.

hegemony of global north.[9] This produces a tendency towards institutionalizing the '*de facto* impunity long enjoyed by the powerful' and reproducing 'one-sided narratives of complex conflicts'.[10] In this sense, 'every trial affirms and reaffirms a structure of power in this world' and therefore, this turn to legal expertise and technique allows us to look away from the structural injustices that are not addressed by those trials.[11]

Consequently, the tendency towards a middle ground with its hidden hegemonic position remains an ideological choice that invariably supports certain idiosyncratic interests more than others, rather than some neutral compromise. Any 'middle' ground also remains endlessly open to challenge as its hidden hegemonic position depends upon its supplement (and the counter-hegemonic point). Therefore, this debate, with its series of hegemonic and counter-hegemonic moves, reinforces Koskenniemi and Leino's observation that the struggle between criminal law and diplomacy tends towards 'either undermining diplomatic freedom of action – or turning criminal justice into show trials. Any middle ground is both narrow and slippery.'[12]

References

Arendt, A *Eichmann in Jerusalem: Report on the Banality of Evil* (Penguin Books New York 2006).

International Law Association 'Final Report on the Exercise of Universal Jurisdiction of Gross Human Rights Offences' (London 2000).

Koskenniemi, M 'What Use for Sovereignty Today? (2011) 1(1) *Asian Journal of International Law* 61.

Koskenniemi, M 'International Justice: Between Impunity and Show Trial' (SOAS, University of London 4 January 2013), URL: https://www.youtube.com/watch?v=2QTBdPyQtEw.

Koskenniemi, M and Leino, P 'Fragmentation of International Law? Postmodern Anxieties' (2002) 15 *Leiden Journal of International Law* 553.

Krever, T 'Dispensing Global Justice' (2014) 85 *New Left Review* 67.

Schwoebel, C 'The Market and Marketing Culture of International Criminal Law' in C Schwoebel *Critical Approaches to International Criminal Law: An Introduction* (Routledge London 2014).

Simpson, S *Law, War and Crime: War Crimes, Trials and the Reinvention of International Law* (Polity Press 2007).

Tallgren, I 'The Sense and Sensibility of International Criminal Law (2002) 13(3) *European Journal of International Law* 561.

9 C Schwoebel 'The Market and Marketing Culture of International Criminal Law' in C Schwoebel *Critical Approaches to International Criminal Law: An Introduction* (Routledge London 2014) 278.

10 T Krever 'Dispensing Global Justice' (2014) 85 *New Left Review* 67, 97.

11 M Koskenniemi 'International Justice: Between Impunity and Show Trial' (SOAS, University of London 4 January 2013), URL: https://www.youtube.com/watch?v=2QTBdPyQtEw.

12 M Koskenniemi and P Leino 'Fragmentation of International Law? Postmodern Anxieties' (2002) 15 *Leiden Journal of International Law* 553, 579.

Index

FSC
www.fsc.org
MIX
Papier | Fördert
gute Waldnutzung
FSC® C083411

Kolibri 360 GmbH
Ferdinand-Jühlke-Straße 7
99095 Erfurt, Deutschland
produktsicherheit@kolibri360.de